LIMNING THE PSYCHE

Limning the Psyche

EXPLORATIONS IN CHRISTIAN PSYCHOLOGY

Edited by

Robert C. Roberts

and

Mark R. Talbot

WILLIAM B. EERDMANS PUBLISHING COMPANY
GRAND RAPIDS, MICHIGAN / CAMBRIDGE, U.K.

© 1997 Wm. B. Eerdmans Publishing Co.

255 Jefferson Ave. S.E., Grand Rapids, Michigan 49503 /
P.O. Box 163, Cambridge CB3 9PU U.K.

Printed in the United States of America

02 01 00 99 98 97   7 6 5 4 3 2 1

Library of Congress Cataloging-in-Publication Data

Limning the psyche: explorations in Christian psychology /
edited by Robert C. Roberts and Mark R. Talbot
p.   cm.
ISBN 0-8028-4331-X (pbk.: alk. paper)
1. Christianity — Psychology. 2. Psychology and religion.
I. Roberts, Robert Campbell, 1942-   . II. Talbot, Mark R.
BR110.L56 1997
230'.01'9 — dc21   97-14456
                                                        CIP

The interdisciplinary seminar from which this book derives, and the publication
of the book, were supported with generous grants from the Pew Charitable
Trusts and Wheaton College.

Contents

Contributors

DIOGENES ALLEN is Stuart Professor of Philosophy, Princeton Theological Seminary. His interests include the philosophy of religion, spiritual theology, and theology and science. Among his fourteen books are *The Reasonableness of Faith, Philosophy for Understanding Theology, Three Outsiders*, and *The Traces of God*.

PAUL J. GRIFFITHS is Associate Professor of the Philosophy of Religions at the University of Chicago's Divinity School. He studies and writes, as a Christian, about Buddhist philosophy. His last book was *On Being Buddha: The Classical Doctrine of Buddhahood*, and he is now working on one called *Religious Reading*.

A. A. HOWSEPIAN, M.D., is a psychiatry resident at the University of California, San Francisco–Fresno, and a doctoral student at the University of Notre Dame. He is interested in the metaphysics of free will, the philosophy of religion, and the philosophy of medicine and psychiatry. He has published articles in *Religious Studies* and the *Review of Metaphysics*, including "Who and What Are We?" and "Philosophical Reflections on Coma."

ERIC L. JOHNSON is Associate Professor of Interdisciplinary Studies, Northwestern College. Interested in Christian psychology, early adult development, and the history and philosophy of psychology, he has published articles in the *Journal of Psychology and Theology* and the *Baker Encyclopedia of Psychology*, second edition.

STANTON L. JONES is Provost of Wheaton College and Professor of Psychology. In 1995-96 he was a Pew Evangelical Scholars Research Fellow.

He has written "A Constructive Relationship for Religion with the Science and Profession of Psychology" *(American Psychologist)* and a five-book series on sex education in the Christian family called *God's Design for Sex*, coauthored with his wife Brenna.

JEAN-MARC LAPORTE, S.J., is Professor of Systematic Theology at Regis College in Toronto and Director of the Toronto School of Theology, an ecumenical cluster of seven schools. His areas of interest include theological anthropology, christology, and medieval theology. He is the author of *Patience and Power: Grace for the First World*.

JAMES E. MARTIN is Associate Professor of Psychology at Pennsylvania State University. His current research includes empirical investigations of epistemological style and the structure of virtues. Recent articles include "The *Argumentum Ad Hominem* and Two Theses about Evolutionary Epistemology: Gödelian Reflections" *(Metaphilosophy)* and "An Investigation of the Structure of Epistemological Style" *(Personality and Individual Differences)*.

CYNTHIA JONES NEAL is Associate Professor and Chair of the Psychology Department, Wheaton College. Her research has focused on families involved in abuse and neglect. She has published articles in *Personality and Social Psychology Bulletin, Developmental Psychology, Merrill-Palmer Quarterly, Journal of Psychology and Theology*, and *Youth and Society*, and has contributed chapters to *Welfare in America, Nurture That Is Christian*, and *Vygotsky and Education*.

DENNIS L. OKHOLM is Associate Professor of Theology at Wheaton College. He is interested in monastic and medieval theology and spirituality and the theology of culture and is an Oblate of the Order of St. Benedict. Among his several books and articles is *Welcome to the Family: An Introduction to Evangelical Christianity* (co-authored with Timothy R. Phillips). In 1996-97 he was a Pew Evangelical Scholars Research Fellow.

CORNELIUS PLANTINGA, JR., is Dean of the Chapel at Calvin College and Professor of Systematic Theology at Calvin Theological Seminary. He is interested in theology as a spiritual discipline. He is co-editor of *A Chorus of Witnesses* and author of *Not the Way It's Supposed to Be: A Breviary of Sin*, a book written with a grant from the Pew Charitable Trusts. In 1956 Professor Plantinga was city runner-up in the Grand Rapids Recreation Department Fall Tennis Tournament, Peewee Division.

L. REBECCA PROPST is a psychotherapist in private practice and is in training as a psychoanalyst. She taught for five years at the University of Ohio and for fifteen at Lewis and Clark College. She is a member of a Mennonite congregation and is interested in the use of Christian concepts in psychotherapy. She has published articles in professional journals in psychology and in theology, and is the author of *Psychotherapy in a Religious Framework: Spirituality in the Emotional Healing Process.*

ROBERT C. ROBERTS is Professor of Philosophy and Psychology at Wheaton College. He is interested in issues surrounding the nature of persons and their flourishing and has published articles on the nature of emotions and virtues and vices. His last book was *Taking the Word to Heart: Self and Other in an Age of Therapies.* In 1992-95 he received a Pew Evangelical Scholars Program grant for work that includes the present book.

WALTER SUNDBERG, Professor of Church History at Luther Seminary, St. Paul, MN, studies the history of Christian thought, emphasizing America and modern Europe. He is a member of the Advisory Council of *Interpretation* and of the Editorial Board of *The Lutheran Quarterly,* and coauthor, with Roy A. Harrisville, of *The Bible in Modern Culture: Theology and Historical-Critical Method from Spinoza to Käsemann.*

MARK R. TALBOT is Associate Professor of Philosophy at Wheaton College. He is interested in philosophical and theological issues that verge on psychology and spirituality, as well as eighteenth-century British philosophy and theology. He has published articles in *Faith and Philosophy* and other journals, and has been an Andrew Mellon Fellow and a Thomas F. Staley Distinguished Christian Scholar.

PAUL C. VITZ, Professor of Psychology at New York University, specializes in the psychology of music. He is the author, with Arnold B. Glimcher, of *Modern Art and Modern Science.* In Christian circles he is well known for *Psychology as Religion: The Cult of Self-Worship* and *Sigmund Freud's Christian Unconscious.*

Introduction:
Christian Psychology?

Robert C. Roberts

Why *Christian* Psychology?

In the summer of 1994 a group of psychologists, philosophers, and theologians gathered on the campus of Wheaton College in Illinois, with support from the Pew Charitable Trusts and the administration of Wheaton College. We spent the better part of a week talking about the Christian understanding of what persons are, what makes us tick, how we develop, what fouls us up and how to get better, and also, how to go about this very process of thinking about our nature and our weal. We came in various flavors of Christianity — Mennonite, Baptist, Roman Catholic, Presbyterian, Lutheran, Christian Reformed, and Anglican, to mention some — but we shared the desire to think about persons in ways strongly guided by the Bible and the great classical tradition of orthodox Christianity. Despite some lively disagreements about how psychology is to be done and what Christianity implies for some aspects of psychology, our discussions were a testimony to the viability of ecumenism, to the existence of what C. S. Lewis calls a "mere Christianity" that runs through the whole church regardless of denominational peculiarities, insofar as it has not capitulated to the spirit of one age or another. Thus one of the frequently heard objections to the idea of a Christian psychology — "Who's going to decide whether it will be Baptist or Catholic or Presbyterian?" — seemed to be silently answered.

Many authors have noted that a distinguishing mark of *our* age's spirit is the dominance of psychology in our thinking about who we are, in our explanations of personal idiosyncrasies, in our aspirations, and consequently in our consciousness of ourselves and in our behavior (for

1

example, Rieff, 1966; Lasch, 1979; MacIntyre, 1981; Bellah, Madsen, Sullivan, Swidler, and Tipton, 1985; Sykes, 1992; Witten, 1993; Vitz, 1994). To an unprecedented extent, twentieth-century persons are preoccupied with their psyches and the damage sustained in childhood and the importance of making sure their own children are well adjusted and feel good about themselves. We are Psychological Man, Therapeutic Woman, Functional Child, Dysfunctional Family.

Talk about "the therapeutic" notwithstanding, there is no single set of psychological categories in terms of which twentieth-century North American souls tend to be shaped. "Psychology" is not the name of any body of mutually coherent beliefs and concepts. Instead, we are surrounded by vendors of psychic health and maturity, with different versions of our well-being and different accounts of why we are so messed up and how we can get fixed.

Some tell of a split between our collective unconscious and our conscious egos, that can be bridged by studying our dreams and tuning in to the mythologies of the world (Jung, 1968). Others refer to our dysfunctional families of origin and prescribe, variously, that we learn a proper _separation_ from those emotional entanglements (Bowen and Kerr, 1988), or that we recognize and cultivate our _ontological relatedness_ to our intergenerational families (Boszormenyi-Nagy and Krasner, 1986). Some psychologists find the root of our troubles in social standards that have hemmed us in and given us an artificial self-concept; and they attempt to get us "listening" more sensitively to our own individual needs (Rogers, 1961). Others describe our problems as mis-formations of the "self" that result from our early caretakers' failure to provide us with sufficient admiration, solicitude, and ideals to identify with (Kohut, 1977). Still others place the blame on bad training, and propose to cure our ills by retraining our behavior or our thinking or both (Beck, 1976; Ellis and Grieger, 1977). A popular view now in the very bloodstream of the American psyche, promoted by Oprah Winfrey, Robert Schuller, and other showbiz folk, is that our basic problem is thinking too poorly of ourselves; we need to be given pep talks and patted on the back a lot, by others and by ourselves (Schuller, 1982).

One might think that Christians, with their solid tradition of spiritual formation, would readily hack a straight path through this tangled jungle of options, picking up fruits and materials that are useful and consistent with Christian tradition, and letting the rest fall to the ground and rot. Unfortunately, the confusing array of possible soul-schemes has infected the churches, so that one hardly knows, in some congregations, where Jesus leaves off and Jung or Kohut begins. The vocabulary is (to some extent) that of Jesus and Paul, but the thoughts, diagnostic and prescriptive, are not. We see Jesus moving his mouth ventriloquistically, but hear the thoughts and voice of Abraham Maslow. The language of faith is so thoroughly imbued with issues of self-esteem and feeling good and psychic integration and individuation and being assertive and creative and taking risks and being kind to ourselves, that the spiritual food being offered has little of the old flavor and almost none of the old nutrition.

Diogenes Allen recalls a seminary course in pastoral counseling of which the effect (intended or not) was that pastors learned to look for psychological explanations of their parishioners' use of the primary language of faith, and thus developed an almost cynical distance from what is essential to the Christian understanding of persons and what they need.

> What we were told in pastoral theology often caused us to set aside the vocabulary of God the Word incarnate as our redeemer and to ignore the power of God the Holy Spirit to regenerate us. (Allen, this volume, pp. 314-15).

This subversion of the pastoral ministry, and thus of the people of God, would, I think, be far less likely to occur if Christian intellectuals explored the psychological resources within classic Christianity and formulated a robustly *Christian* account of personality that could interact, on equal or superior intellectual terms, with the secular theories and therapies of our day. The subtext of courses like the one Allen remembers is often a kind of intellectual capitulation and despair in which Christianity is viewed as a pre-scientific superstition, a psychology for primitive and simple people; but if you want the *real* scoop on the psyche, you go to the Freudians or some other school that is up-to-date.

This then is one reason we need Christian psychology. It is a matter of ecclesial self-defense against a subtle undermining of our spirituality, an unannounced degradation of that constitution of soul we call eternal life. The defense consists in becoming very clear what *we*, who stand in the tradition of Abraham and Isaiah, of Jesus and the Apostles, have to say about the nature of the psyche, about its proper development, about what can and does go wrong with it, and how it can be healed. If we know where we, as Christians, stand on the issues of "personality theory," we will be far less likely to be seduced into the alien forms of spirit that call with siren voices from the psychologies of our culture.

Not merely for defensive purposes must we develop a rigorous and deep-reaching understanding of the Christian psychology. The church's understanding of human nature, its vicissitudes, its character ideal and the ways of approaching that ideal, have traditionally been a mainstay of pastoral work. This understanding is at the center of pastoral wisdom.

Even if secular psychologies were not rushing in to fill the vacuum created by our derelict understanding, the church's health would require that somewhere in her bosom there be people who can supply their pastors with a rigorous account of the Christian psychology. We are, according to that psychology, verbivorous beings who feed on understandings of our God, our world, and ourselves (Roberts, this volume, a). It stands to reason that a rich and accurate account of our own nature is fundamental to the church's ministry.

Another reason for sifting out the Christian view of persons and becoming very clear about it is that we are called to love God with our minds. As the Intellect Division of Christ's church, we are the repository of this kind of understanding, and we must do it as well as we can, with all the integrity of mind we can muster. If we rest content merely to be competent and creative disciples of Bowlby and Vygotsky, of Nagy and Kohut and Bandura, we may be respected in the profession, but our profession as disciples of Jesus will be significantly underfulfilled. We should remember, though, as Mark Talbot's essay reminds us, that Christian wisdom is not merely a product of academic exercise, nor passed on primarily in classrooms and lecture halls. It is also a disposition of the heart, of the distinctively Christian *personality;* and it is passed on through those practices of church life that nurture the whole soul. It seems that the Christian understanding of persons depends rather heavily on our being Christian persons.

Psychology as Science

"But," I hear some friendly objector query, "you speak of psychology as though it's been around a long time, indeed at least as long as the Bible. But isn't psychology a science, and thus quite a recent thing — and indeed one of the youngest of all the sciences? Didn't it just turn 118? It seems to me I heard that it was born in Wilhelm Wundt's laboratory in 1879."

The question of the relation between psychology — especially the kind of large-scale account of human nature and well-being that is often called personality theory — and science is addressed by a number of the papers in this book. Paul Vitz suggests that there is a foundational stage in the process of devising a personality theory that is properly scientific, in the sense that its findings are not colored by philosophies of life, metaphysics, or religious (or anti-religious) commitments. This is the stage at which data are being collected, observations made about how humans behave under specified conditions. But you have to venture well beyond this stage, claims Vitz, to have anything as interesting as a personality theory, so personality theory will always have an inescapably unscientific character. To have a personality theory you have to commit yourself to the kind of philosophical, religious, or metaphysical propositions that are found in Christianity and other religions, or in the anti-religions to which psychologists often adhere. Paul Griffiths responds by claiming that even at the level of the simplest observations — assuming they are psychological observations — contestable metaphysical commitments control what is observed. He suggests that there is *no* difference in kind between the personality theories of our leading therapeutic systems and the psychological traditions of Christianity or Buddhism. If he is right — or even if Vitz is right — the Christian account of our psychic nature and its vicissitudes starts out on a level playing field with the contemporary theories. Though in a critical dialogue with them, Christianity might turn out to be more or less adequate or coherent than some of its psychological rivals.

(I should note that in the seminar where most of these papers were given, ten of them were assigned as responses, in some loose sense, to the preceding five. In successive drafts and under the guiding hands of the editors, however, these "responses" tended to acquire a more independent form. Some of the papers have entirely lost the character of responses; others, most notably Griffiths's and Jones's, have retained it. Jones's paper, originally a response to Plantinga's, now comes before Plantinga's because it better fits there in the book's sequence of ideas. The one paper that was not presented in the seminar was my "Parameters of a Christian Psychology," which was distributed beforehand to all the participants.)

Diogenes Allen proposes that one way the Christian psychological tradition might be brought into conversation with the scientific psychology of our time would be to test, by standard empirical methods, some of the law-like claims that members of the tradition have made. The desert fathers, for example, claim that certain emotional states tend to follow upon submitting to ascetic disciplines such as confinement to one's cell, fasting, and *lectio divina*, and that these disciplines, pursued over a fairly long period of time, can be expected to foster developments of personality such as purity of heart and serenity. These connectional claims seem to be of a sort that could be tested through careful observation and mathematical construction. In Dennis Okholm's paper on the Christian psychology of gluttony as found in some early ascetics, he comments briefly about the nature and limits of testing such psychology by scientific methods.

An effort to test Christian psychology scientifically might also be a test of whether Vitz or Griffiths is right about the relation between personality theory and metaphysics: Is there a level of observation, adequate for the pursuit of this scientific testing, at which scientists with widely varying metaphysical commitments (say, materialist metaphysics and

Christian theistic metaphysics) could agree about what was being observed? In other words, is there some level of psychological observation
at which what is specified and observed scientifically is like colors? Griffiths points out that the states observed by the desert fathers themselves
are not at that level: what *counts as* purity of heart or serenity will differ
from "theory" to "theory." Allen and Okholm seem to agree with Griffiths
when they point out that the apatheia of the desert fathers is quite a
different state of mind from the apatheia of the Stoics. Similarly Okholm
points out that fasting is a different activity from dieting, even if in a given
instance dieting and fasting involve identical food-abstaining behavior.

But Vitz might respond that Griffiths's use of the term "observe"
is ambiguous: Griffiths seems to mean by "observe" *notice and be committed
to the reality and importance of,* whereas all that is needed for work in social
science (e.g. anthropology) is the ability to identify something *as it is
conceptualized by some tradition.* Thus a materialist psychologist will not
believe in the God whom the desert fathers take to be honored in their
apatheia, and thus will not think that apatheia has the significance that
the desert fathers ascribe to it. But to study the correlations between
apatheia and the ascetic disciplines, she doesn't need to. She need only be
able to identify the mental state that the *desert fathers* call apatheia, and
she can do this by learning from the desert fathers what the criteria are
for that state. In other words, observations of personality-relevant phenomena may all be intrinsically laden with contestable theory. But scientific work, the results of which can be agreed to by practitioners committed
to widely varying metaphysics, does not depend on the observations'
being like observations of colors.

Stanton Jones points out that scientific studies of genetic and cultural
conditions for human behavior do not necessarily have the metaphysical
implications many scientists suppose them to have. In particular, the fact
that studies can establish that genetic conditions contribute causally to
alcoholism does not show that human behavior is determined (that is,
entirely caused) by factors beyond the agent's control, or that the agent is
not a free originator of his or her actions. Such studies certainly show that
the agent is not the *sole* causal ground of her actions, but scientific studies of
the causal conditions of human behavior leave open the possibility of a
libertarian interpretation of agency (that the agent contributes causally to
the action, beyond the contribution of factors such as physiological make-
up, training, immediate environmental stimuli, etc.). Jones (contrary to strict
Calvinists) regards Christian psychology as committed to a libertarian interpretation of agency. Thus he affirms, with Vitz, the looseness of connection
between the scientific study of human behavior and personality theory
constructs (such as the Christian commitment to free agency), and welcomes

Griffiths's even stronger claim that at no point is scientific work free from structuring by controversial metaphysical commitments. (Note that Griffiths holds that some metaphysical commitments are universal among humans; that is the point of his basic color terms example. However, terms relevant to our understanding of *personality* always presuppose one or another *contestable* metaphysics.)

My paper on attachment challenges the assumption, seemingly made by John Bowlby and very widespread among psychologists, that to be intellectually solid, psychological work must explain its subject matter ultimately in terms of very basic concepts from physics and biology, or at least with concepts very much like those of the physical sciences. For example, Bowlby agrees with the Christian tradition that our proneness to get "attached" to other persons is a fundamental structural feature of the psyche. He then goes on to explain this psychological feature by using Darwin's idea that an organism has the properties it has because those properties were passed on to it by ancestors that would not have survived without those properties. Thus biological survival explains our proneness to attachment. I point out that even within Bowlby's own thought, attachment has a character and significance in human life that is not commodiously explained in such biological terms. If we think of attachment psychologically — that is, in terms of its meaning in the life of the attached person, its importance to one's happiness — then a theological explanation is a more fitting kind of explanation than the biological. "Science" and "scientific" are honorific terms meaning *knowledge* and *leading to truth*. If we ascribe "science" this basic sense, then better explanations are more scientific than poorer ones, and if a theological explanation is better, for a certain phenomenon, than a biological one, then it is also more "scientific." I would thus join Griffiths and Jones in suggesting that the line between science and metaphysics (in this case theology) is by no means a sharp divider.

In our seminar (but not in the revised version of his paper) Mark Talbot identified a controversial metaphysical commitment that many scientists and believers in science have had since the seventeenth century, and which undermines a Christian understanding of self and world. It is the view that values reside in the mind and only in the mind — that they are "secondary" or even "tertiary" qualities, not properties of the objective world. Using an argument derived from Charles Taylor, Talbot argued that this metaphysic so radically undermines our concept of personhood that we must, in effect, choose between believing in the existence of persons and believing that values are mere figments of our minds. Since, as persons, we cannot stop believing in persons, we must conclude that the reductivist metaphysics so often associated with science is in fact not essential to science construed as the careful and systematic pursuit of knowledge about our world and ourselves. The ironic implication of the Talbot-Taylor argument is that much of what has passed for *scientific* psychology is, because of its naturalistic metaphysics, blind to its primary subject-matter: *persons*. A Christian psychology, not being blind to persons in this way, is to that extent more "scientific" than much that has been touted as such.

Eric Johnson chronicles a gradual improvement in the scientific eyesight of psychologists in the twentieth century. Under pressure from the natural science paradigm, early behaviorists reduced human agency to a more or less mechanical response to environmental stimuli. But agency per se has distinctively human mental features, such as its connection with beliefs and desires, deliberation, intention, and self-criticism of motivation, all of which bear on choice and responsibility. "Scientific" reductionism has not been able to hold out in the face of these observable facts about human agency, and so the trend of twentieth-century psychology has been to approach closer and closer to the Christian understanding of agency, without, however, travelling all the way.

The Pertinence of Theology

Such considerations about the nature of science, and especially of psychology as a science, tend to support the members of this seminar in a style of thinking that subverts what is normally regarded as "professional." We are unabashed about bringing theology right into the heart of psychological reflection and research, not as an afterthought, to be "integrated," but as a basic guiding commitment; and not merely as supplying "control beliefs" that set limits to what we can accept from twentieth-century psychology, but as contributing substantively to our conceptualization of the human person. Paul Vitz suggests, in quite Augustinian fashion, that we model our basic view of the human psyche on the trinitarian God who is revealed in the history of the incarnation and in Pentecost. We derive from a Reality that is ontologically social and are said to be created in his image; furthermore, the most fundamental command, the one that is meant to guide our behavior, attitudes, desires, and character, is that we should *love* him with our whole heart and our neighbors as ourselves. This is a clue to our nature, a clue that should guide us in our research and our thinking, in our diagnosis and our therapy; a clue that seems to cut against the individualism ("contractual" sociality) and narcissistic reflexivity (preoccupation with one's own psychological needs and development) that much of modern psychology assumes and encourages.

Similarly, Rebecca Propst finds in the theology of the Trinity a model of personhood in which individuals are distinct from one another, having their own viewpoint but at the same time related to other persons in such a way that their personal identity is ontologically affected by the relationship(s). She finds that this trinitarian ontology of persons is supported by a contemporary school of therapeutic conflict resolution, and that the Christian ontology in turn provides a needed theoretical basis for the theory and practice of that school.

James Martin argues that the Bible has a robust and substantive conception of human nature that controls the behavioral injunctions of its writers and provides a starting point for a biblically oriented account of personhood. In particular, Jesus' and Paul's pronouncements about proper and improper sexual behavior and gender-specific behavior are not arbitrary decrees of God, but flow, according to Martin, from the centrality of the family in the biblical conception of human nature. We should note, however, that several of the contributors to this volume are uncomfortable with Martin's claim that the biblical texts directing women to be submissive to their husbands and not to speak in church derive from the basic biblical view of human nature.

In a similarly bold expression of commitment to the psychology of the Bible, Cynthia Neal orients her reflections on healthy parenting with biblical reflections about what it is to be a mature agent and how the mature person relates to the teaching received from those who went before. Jean-Marc Laporte reflects on Christ's relinquishing of his divine prerogatives in the incarnation, and his disciples' analogous self-denial, as basic to our understanding of the nature of the human psyche and its well-being. This is especially provocative in the context of contemporary psychology, which is far more focused on filling the self than emptying it. Walter Sundberg alerts us to a basic psychological idea that comes from the Bible and from the Reformation and Counter-Reformation of the sixteenth century — the idea that personality can be deepened and strengthened through adversity and its right use in penitence. This fact has connections with the Christian claim that our dysfunction as persons is most profoundly understood as sin or the result of sin. The idea that personal adversity should not be escaped from, but rather used for our own benefit and for God's glory, is a concept of "therapy" quite foreign to the age we live in. In my paper on attachment, I develop first the biblical account of it, putting the Christian tradition in the conceptual driver's seat while weighing the views of Bowlby. A. A. Howsepian encourages us to rethink psychosis in theological terms: psychosis is not just a matter of distorted beliefs, but of distorted passions (concerns, loves, commitments). And it is not a relatively rare phenomenon; rather we are all psychotics in that

we commonly experience as most real what is not real, and often fail to
notice what is most important in life. This is quite a different style of
thinking "integratively" than we have seen in recent years, where Christian psychologists have tended to start with a basic commitment to some
non-Christian psychological theory, and then to consider ways in which
the biblical revelation reinforces it or is continuous with it or parallel to
it, or might inspire some tinkering with it.

What then is the relation between psychology and theology? Insofar
as theology makes statements about human nature and its fulfillment,
about proper and improper human motivation, about ways in which the
human spirit can develop properly and improperly, then a part of theology
seems to *be* a kind of psychology, and one formally similar to "personality
theory." Insofar as psychology indulges in broad and fundamental claims
about the structure of the psyche, its needs, development, and the shape
of its fulfillment, then, while it is not theology proper unless its sets these
claims in a context of statements about God, still it is very much the same
kind of intellectual product as that part of theology that bears on human
nature. The difference between the two disciplines seems to be primarily
a difference of sources.

In Christian theology the source is preeminently the Bible, and then
the reflections of wise persons across the Christian ages whose experience
and thought have been shaped by the Bible. Several of the contributors to
this book make direct use of the Bible; Diogenes Allen and Dennis Okholm
mine the second-century hermits of the Egyptian desert, Vitz appeals to
the church councils, Laporte refers to the developmental reflections of St.
Ignatius Loyola, and Sundberg draws on the psychology of Luther, Calvin,
and Loyola. Mark Talbot explains how, as Christian psychologists, we can
rest confidently in the agency-framework of the Bible while acknowledging that its claims are contestable, in the sense that all evidence for
them can be resisted by people who are, in some wide sense, rational. In
psychology, by contrast, the sources for personality theory are to some
extent the highly disciplined observations of human behavior reported in
mathematicized discourse, but in large part the reflections of the "sages"
of one psychological tradition or another — Freud and his many disciples
or anti-disciples, Rogers and Maslow, Aaron Beck, and the many gurus of
family systems thought. To do Christian *psychology*, as contrasted with
ascetic theology or theological anthropology, is to be acquainted with and
to use those data-collecting and reporting methods characteristic of the
academic psychological establishment, and to be in conversation with the
great psychologists of the twentieth century. This conversation, which on
the Christian side stands firmly on the "theological anthropology" of the
Bible and the Christian tradition, is particularly evident in the papers of

Vitz, Roberts, Johnson, Propst, Howsepian, Jones, and Neal. This is the required endeavor, in my view, and the one to which the present book is a contribution. But I should note that not all contributors to the book agree that Christian psychology should be pursued in conversation with the mainstream psychology of the twentieth century. Griffiths holds that a healthier and less confusing policy for Christians is simply to mine the rich psychological traditions of Christianity, and ignore the Freuds and Maslows, the Becks and Adlers and Bowlbys.

A corollary of seeing theology and psychology as two quite separate disciplines is a distinction which the contributors to this book tend *not* to make. One often hears, in Christian circles, a distinction between emotional problems and spiritual problems, and this may go with the claim that we humans are both psychological *and* spiritual beings with psychological *and* spiritual needs. The pastor, it is said, deals with the spiritual side of our nature, and the counselor or therapist deals with our psychological needs and distortions. But if the dominant tenor of the essays offered here is correct, then such a clean distinction is a dangerous confusion. For it obscures the fact that the psychotherapies of the twentieth century, the personality theories behind them, and the various popular person-constructs with which they seed our culture and offer to reshape our souls are *alternatives* to Christian spirituality. The converse is also true: that the psychic hunger being met so poorly by the psychologies might be met by Christian spirituality, if only the church had the confidence, the resolve, and the skill to offer its own distinctive psychology, rather than be held captive by the alien ideologies of personhood floating around on the breezes of our culture.

What are some of the parameters of a Christian psychology? Many are touched on in the course of these essays, but three in particular seem to pervade the discussions: the sociality of the psyche, the Christian concept of agency, and the centrality of sin as a psychological concept.

The Sociality of the Psyche

Secular personality psychologies have tended to be individualistic, in the sense that they stress emotional separation from other persons as a condition of maturity and mental health. Psychologists tend to regard emotional dependency on friends, family members, and God as a chief source of much psychological dysfunction, and thus make personal maturity a matter of individuation (Carl Jung), getting in touch with oneself (Carl Rogers), differentiation of self (Murray Bowen), learning to love oneself (the co-dependency movement), the ability to calculate and achieve one's self-interest (rational emotive therapy, assertiveness training), and the like. We may live together, and find help and incidental enjoyment in one another's company, but our most fundamental personal identity or emotional makeup should be characterized by independence. These psychologists explain much psychological dysfunction by reference to such concepts as dependency, enmeshment, and accepting other people's values; and therapy consists to a large extent in psychologically dislodging people from their social connections and dependencies. This tendency has not been universal; John Bowlby, L. S. Vygotsky, and Ivan Boszormenyi-Nagy are notable exceptions. Christian personality psychology stands much closer to the exceptions, holding that mental health is to be found, not in being emotionally separated from other persons, but in being emotionally *bound* to them in certain specially prescribed ways. Paul Vitz comments,

> Personality is fulfilled in love and not in isolation: in love of God and ultimate union with God, and in love of other humans, leading ideally to a union of wills. (this volume, p. 27)

Vitz even goes so far as to contrast persons with individuals. Individuals — these emotionally isolated, self-sufficient, independent, personally unrelated autonomous paragons of contemporary psychological virtue — are not really persons. Rebecca Propst, following closely the model of the Holy Trinity as *one* God in three *distinct* persons, would not use the word "individual" in the rather pejorative way Vitz does, since she has a high regard for individuality. But her concept of the person is deeply social nevertheless. As Dennis Okholm points out, the Christian tradition has regarded gluttony as a sin — as a source and form of personal dysfunction — in part because it is a blindness to one's neighbor; it makes egoists of us. The same point could no doubt be fruitfully explored with respect to some of the other "deadly sins," such as greed and lust.

Why is a socially enmeshed life, with its unavoidable painful emotions, healthier than a life of emotional independence? The main business of my second paper is to explore the biblical personality concept of attachment, in conversation with John Bowlby. He claims that attachment is a structural feature of the human psyche, to be properly developed rather than suppressed or outgrown. In the Christian view some attachments are unhealthy (for example, all but the mildest attachment to material goods, and inordinate attachments to fellow human beings), and others are proper, above all an ultimate attachment to God, and also a proper attachment to fellow human beings. Attachment is to a large extent a matter of the emotions, and so the advocacy of attachments is also advocacy of a properly formed emotional life (character). This aspect of the Christian view of personality stands in stark contrast to the neo-Stoic view of such psychologists as the cognitive therapist Albert Ellis and the family therapist Murray Bowen.

James Martin argues that the Bible grounds the prohibition of perverse sexual practices not in the arbitrary decrees of a commanding God, but in the human nature of the beings to whom the commands are directed. We are so structured as to flourish in the setting of a family arrangement with certain definite features — two parents bound together by their sexual union, and the children that proceed from that union. Sex is not just a source of pleasure, to be used in any way that yields the pleasure. Nor, even, is it a principle of bonding with other persons, whoever the persons may be; our created social nature is more determinate than that. This theme of our sociality continues in the papers by Eric Johnson and Cynthia Jones Neal on the nature and development of human agency.

Agency and How We Get It

Johnson shows how most of the major schools of psychology in the twentieth century, for all their preoccupation with "behavior," have had little to say, or misleading things to say, about a central fact of human nature: that we are performers of *actions*. Machines behave (that is, their parts move in response to stimulus from some energy source), sunflowers turn their "faces" to the sun, clams "clam up" when they are touched, and everything in the animal kingdom "behaves" in response to stimuli in the physical environment. Humans behave as well, but the Christian tradition (and, we think, human common sense) holds that we do more than this: we act on principle, we lay plans, we decide which of our desires to follow and judge both the actions we might perform and the desires from which they might spring to be appropriate or inappropriate, noble or ignoble, worthy of beings like ourselves or not worthy. Mark Talbot shows that mature human "behavior" is shaped by large-scale normative understandings of who we are and how the universe is constituted. Any adequate personality theory must give a rich account of human agency in its various dimensions, and a specifically Christian account will set our actions in the context of our faithfulness or unfaithfulness to God, our corruption by sin, and our potential for a regenerate co-agency with God and our neighbors.

Neal is particularly concerned to discredit a style of parenting that is based on a disregard of the biblical conception of mature agency. On this mistaken view, parents (and alas many of these are serious Christians) aim, in training their children, to get them to internalize the rules of good behavior (say, the Ten Commandments), and follow these rules on their own. But such internalization is at best a *stage* in the development of proper agency, argues Neal. It is, of course, better for the children to have internalized the rules than for them to need constant supervision by father and mother. But they become true *agents* only when they develop discernment (wisdom) that allows them to make their *own* decisions on the basis of the tradition in which they have been brought up. If they have only internalized rules of right and wrong, they are still what Neal calls "heteronomous agents," agents following somebody else's rules simply because these are the rules, rather than "intelligent agents" who have *understood* the import of the rules, taken on the tradition as lending significance to *their* lives, and thus made those rules their own. Indeed, we might hesitate to speak of *rules* in connection with this kind of wise agency, and speak instead of understanding a way of life. The specifically Christian form of this kind of agency involves the indwelling of the Holy Spirit, or having the mind of Christ. Neal proposes a certain style of parenting, even a nurturant character trait, that she calls "scaffolding" which is designed to encourage intelligent agency in our children. (Stan Jones's ruminations about the interaction of causal factors and free agency should quiet our worries that the effectiveness of scaffolding might itself undermine the freedom of our children's agency.)

Thus Talbot's insight about the human agent's need for a moral/metaphysical framework is elaborated in Johnson's discussion of the inadequacy of twentieth-century psychological models of agency, and the two are further supplemented by Neal's exploration of what it is for that framework to be assimilated into the character of the agent. What Neal calls "intelligent agency" resembles what an Enlightenment thinker like Immanuel Kant might call "autonomy," or an existentialist might call "authenticity." The three conceptions have in common their opposition to heteronomous agency, an unthinking following of some authority's rules. Existentialists like Jean-Paul Sartre go so far as to say there are no pre-established rules for the conduct of human life, that each of us must *make up* our own moral framework, the meaning of our own life. Kant says the autonomous person is his or her own lawmaker, but he is not an existentialist because he believes in the pre-existence of rules that each of us must follow to live a good life, rules of practical reason that we find written into our nature as agents. Neal's intelligent agency differs from both existentialist authenticity and Enlightenment autonomy because it allows for an external source for the shape of one's agency, such as a tradition. The Christian, having a Lord, is attuned to and guided by an authority different from the agent himself or herself. The "autonomy" of the Christian is characterized by what the Apostle Paul calls "the obedience of faith" (Romans 16:26).

Thus the other side of agency, in the Christian construal of it, is that the agent at his most mature is, in Eric Johnson's phrase, a co-agent. He does not act entirely on his own, but his agency itself has a social nature. The Christian is fundamentally a steward, one whose actions are not ultimately his own, but those of his Lord; to be fully mature is to be a "slave of righteousness" (Romans 6:18). The Son, says Jesus, "can do nothing of his own accord, but only what he sees the Father doing" (John 5:19). Similarly, the Apostle Paul remarks, "I have been crucified with Christ; it is no longer I who live, but Christ who lives in me" (Galatians 2:20). If the so-called "autonomy" of Christian agency is the stress of Neal's paper, its bi-polarity is the stress of Johnson's. These are, of course, two sides of a single distinctive concept that is central to the Christian idea of personality. Both sides — the transcendence of heteronomy and the forfeiture of autonomy — are products of *development*, rather than naturally given features of the personality, though the development in question is one for which we are fitted by our nature. Laporte's paper on *kenosis* (self-emptying) is especially relevant to that side of the development of our agency that involves forfeiting autonomy, and Neal's paper on scaffolding is about fostering the transcendence of heteronomy. Johnson's paper ends with an overview of factors that foster and enhance the development of agency as it is modeled in the Christian tradition.

Sin and What Ails Us

Every psychotherapy or personality theory includes ways of identifying and explaining psychological ailments. A third distinctive of the Christian psychology, that emerges especially in the papers of Plantinga, Howsepian, Allen, and Okholm, is the idea of sin as a way of understanding and explaining deviant behavior and distorted personality. The sociality and agency of the psyche, in the Christian view, are prominent also in the concept of sin. To be in sin is not merely, or even most fundamentally, to be in a state of intrapsychic collapse; it is to be fouled *in relationship* to personal beings external to oneself, and most fundamentally in relationship to God. When we think in terms of sin, comments Plantinga,

> we think of the defrauding of one's business client, for instance, not merely as an instance of lawlessness, but also of faithlessness; and we think of the fraud as faithless not only to the client, but also to God. (p. 246)

As Plantinga goes on to exploit the continuities between addiction and sin, it becomes clear that addiction too, at least in the Christian understanding of it, is a relational matter (addictions are tellingly described as "dependencies"), a treating as God of something that is not God and in many cases is not even a person. (Indeed, even when what one is addicted to has a distinctly personal dimension, as in the case of sex, the personhood of the persons involved has become obscure.) Thus to make the concept of sin fundamental to Christian psychological diagnosis distinguishes Christian psychology starkly from its secular counterparts, most of which, as we have seen, are individualistic, and none of which makes a disrelationship with God basic to human dysfunction.

To diagnose psychic dysfunction in terms of sin is not only to construe it as originating in and having the character of bad relationships with other persons; it is also to place it squarely in the arena of our agency. Sin is not something that just happens to us, like being born with a certain genetic makeup, or having had a horrendous childhood. It may get such a grip on us that it becomes second nature, and what our parents and culture and physical nature contribute may predispose us to it, but our own contribution as agents is always essential. As Plantinga remarks, "moral and spiritual evil are agential evil" (p. 247). Behind Jones's effort to protect the human agent from becoming merely a factor or complex of factors in a setting that is, metaphysically, exhaustively event-causal, is the concern (among others) to guard the possibility of a diagnosis of our pathologies in terms of sin. The centrality of the concept of sin as a diagnostic category derives from the fact that the repair of our nature through the incarnation, death, and resurrection of the Son of God, and the indwelling of the Holy Spirit, is repair from the ravages of sin.

Partly because of locating sin in the arena of our agency, the Christian tradition has resisted the Socratic proposal that sin is ignorance. Sin affects our minds, darkens our understanding, confuses our thought, but it is located at least as primitively, and perhaps more so, in our will and in our desires. This theme comes out in A. A. Howsepian's proposal that, contrary to the *Diagnostic and Statistical Manual* of the American Psychiatric Association, psychosis should be thought of less as a form of disordered belief and more as a form of disordered appetite. That is, it should be thought of as analogous to addiction. The stress on appetite is also essential to the Christian psychological tradition about which Dennis Okholm and Diogenes Allen write, for the "seven deadly sins" of the desert hermits (lust, gluttony, greed, pride, envy, anger, and sloth) are all, broadly speaking, appetitive disorders.

But the desert fathers do not neglect the connection of spiritual dysfunction with thought. Not only do disordered appetites distort and confuse our thoughts; they seem also to originate in disordered thoughts. Evagrius Ponticus, the early formulator of the teachings of the hermits, speaks not of the seven deadly sins, but of the eight deadly thoughts. And it does seem that human desire (say, anger's desire to get revenge, lust's desire for an illicit sex object, or greed's desire for larger and more valuable acquisitions) always involves one or another way of *thinking* about what is desired. The glutton's inapt behavior interacts with a distorted *conception* of food (he may, of course, be able to switch into a coherent way of talking about it); the lecher has a distorted *view* of (way of thinking about) the desired persons. Thus an important part of Christian therapy for sin has always been to reorient the mind to reality, to try to get the agent to see the world aright, to notice God's hand in it, and thus to understand himself aright as well. Plantinga comments:

> Healthy people enjoy the freedom that is born of contentment (a "freedom from want"), which in turn is owed to a sturdy and persistent discipline of desire. Healthy people deliberately note, for instance, how many material goods they can do without, and then take extra pleasure in the simple and enduring ones they possess. They make it their goal, most of the time, to eat and drink only enough to relieve hunger and thirst, not to sate themselves. They integrate their sexual desire into a committed relationship, bonded by vows and trust. (p. 260)

Persons with such well-formed psyches have found desires that do not delude, and ways of understanding themselves and their world that beget order in their desires.

How to Do Christian Psychology

I have argued that guardianship and promotion of such healthy understanding is in our day the province not just of theologians and pastors, but of Christian psychologists as well. Our age is psychological; people hunger and thirst for understandings of themselves and healing of the miseries of their souls. It is an opportunity for a quiet sort of osmotic evangelism, both inside and outside the churches. But success depends on our having, ourselves, an understanding of Christian psychology, and this will involve a great deal of hard intellectual work, for here we seem to be largely in the dark. Without an understanding of *Christian* psychology, we may promote something quite different from that understanding of the human psyche (and the shape of character that goes with it) that has come down to us from the Apostles. How is this understanding to be achieved? Several things are suggested by the chapters in this book, and even by its general character.

Rebecca Propst expresses disappointment with the grand theorizing about "the Christian view of persons" often found in books on Christian psychology. Such presentations, while sometimes not wrong, are so outlinish as to provide insufficient traction where the wheel is supposed to contact the road. She proposes that, instead of writing more outlines, we try out Christian psychological thinking in very particular contexts, such as clinical conflict resolution, and see what we can learn. This seems to me a wise and challenging proposal. If our psychological thinking is to have integrity and interest and is to command the respect of psychologists who work in careful detail, this integrity will be found in the outworkings of clinical practice, in empirical studies, and in the detailed proposals of theory. On a scholarly plane, we see this pattern of thinking psychologically close to the ground in Okholm's paper on gluttony, Plantinga's on addiction, and Neal's on scaffolding. Such work demands far more time, creativity, and commitment than writing outlines. Studies like these need to be done by Christian theologians, philosophers, and psychologists in every concrete corner of psychology.

But it seems that keeping the big picture firmly in mind will be necessary for protection against the seductions of the alien psychological systems that so many Christians have succumbed to. It is possible to get so focused on particulars that we fail to see the larger presuppositions and models that guide our thinking and research. This big thinking operates to good protective effect in the sweeping contrasts of the first half of Paul Vitz's paper. It is also present in my programmatic essay on the parameters of a Christian psychology.

I should note that two of our authors are uncomfortable with the notion of a Christian psychology. Paul Griffiths thinks that the Christian tradition is already so rich in understanding of the nature of persons that it has no need of modern psychology, and that modern psychology is so fundamentally indebted to notions that are inconsistent with Christian belief, that interaction with it can have only the negative value of poisoning our minds. So poisonous is modern psychology, in his view, that it is better to avoid even the term "psychology" in reference to the Christian understanding of persons. Diogenes Allen also expresses discomfort with the idea of a Christian psychology, but not for Griffiths's reason. He thinks of psychology as a scientific method that can be used to test psychological claims that Christians like the desert fathers make about the dynamics of spiritual life, and he sees this method as essentially neutral, neither Christian nor non-Christian. The rest of our authors agree, with varying slants, that the articulation of a Christian psychology for our day is an important task.

This book is interdisciplinary, drawing on the resources of psychology, theology, and philosophy; and I think this is a feature of the task we face. Our job is largely one of *retrieval* — of making accessible to ourselves and our contemporaries the psychological parameters of Scripture and the insights of great Christian psychological thinkers such as the desert fathers, Augustine, Thomas Aquinas, Saint John of the Cross, Saint Teresa of Avila, Luther, Pascal, Kierkegaard, and Dostoievski. For much of this we will depend on the theologians in our midst. It is obvious we must have psychologists in the conversation, as psychology is the matter we're attempting to work out. Philosophers too, as specialists in conceptual clarity and precision, as ambiguity hounds and distinction framers, will be useful to the discussion, however painful it may be to have to deal with them. A good deal of metaphysics *is* psychology; the great philosophers had views of their own on such issues as the nature of the self, the character of motivation, the relation of mind and body, the nature of emotions and virtues and proper psychic functioning. Some of these views will be continuous, and some discontinuous, with the Christian psychology, and we will need scholars in this field to instruct and warn us and to teach us critical thinking. It seems clear, then, that the Christian psychology must be framed through the kind of interdisciplinary conversation that characterizes the present book.

A Christian Theory of Personality

Paul C. Vitz

A FIRST REACTION TO the proposal of a Christian theory of personality is apt to be: "Isn't that impossible? After all, personality theory is part of modern psychology, and psychology is a science, isn't it? How can something Christian also be scientific?" The simplest answer to such an objection is that the psychology of personality is not scientific, except in a very limited sense. Thus, Sigmund Freud's theory of personality is, as a general rule, not considered part of science. Such central Freudian concepts as the Oedipus complex, the id, the super-ego, penis envy, and the death instinct are hardly the stuff of science. Likewise, Carl Jung's theories of personality may have a few modest scientific components, e.g., measures of introversion and extraversion, but the establishment of any scientific basis for his archetypes seems remote. The same is true of basic ideas drawn from humanistic psychology, such as self-actualization. Both Jung and humanistic psychologists explicitly propose self-actualization as the purpose of life — and the purpose of life has never been recognized as belonging to science.

To distinguish the scientific from the non-scientific aspects of personality theories, it useful to see that such theories have three different conceptual levels. The first level is made up of terms and categories that are closely tied to observation in the clinical setting. These terms are scientific in the sense that different psychologists can reliably identify them from clinical observation. Examples of such categories can be found in the American Psychiatric Association's *Diagnostic and Statistical Manual IV* (1994), where they are used as diagnostic categories for mental pathologies. For example, the section on borderline personality disorder notes eight observable patterns, any five of which constitute a basis for diagnosing a person as having

Some of the ideas in this paper first appeared in Vitz (1984, 1987a, b).

borderline personality disorder, e.g., "a pattern of unstable and intense relationships" characterized by alternating extremes between overidealization and devaluation; "affective instability that is due to a marked reactivity of mood" (pp. 649-50); etc. These categories are primarily descriptive and usually contain relatively little theoretical bias. Indeed, the widespread utility of the *DSM* derives to a substantial degree from its descriptive efficacy. Other Level One categories that can be identified reliably and have implications for a theory of personality include extraversion and introversion (as developed by Jung), and separation anxiety (as developed by Bowlby) shown by a three-year old-child when its mother leaves it at school. Slightly less reliably identifiable categories would be Freud's notion of transference, and the evidence we have for certain defense mechanisms, such as projection, reaction formation, etc.

The second level consists of conceptual and theoretical concepts distinctive to a given theory. These involve interpreting a complex pattern of observations. This level involves concepts like the Oedipus complex, Jungian archetypes (such as the persona, the shadow, the animus/anima), and so forth. In most cases, a theory's notion of the self belongs here. In general, there is little reliable scientific evidence for any Level Two concept. One major difficulty with these concepts is that support for them is typically derived from the psychotherapeutic session. Such sessions are usually private and therefore the evidence obtained in them to support a concept often cannot be publicly verified. Even more problematic is the fact that the interaction between the therapist and patient is subjectively guided by the therapist and so cannot be independently replicated. Thus, Jungians find evidence for their interpretations, while Freudians find evidence for theirs, and so forth. To date, all such "evidence" fails basic tests for scientific objectivity (see Grünbaum, 1984).

The third level contains the general presuppositions which underlie or control the personality theory in question. These presuppositions are often of a metaphysical or ethical nature. This level has been cogently treated by Browning (1987), who notes that psychological theories are deeply embedded in "implicit principles of obligation" (p. ix). At this level, where such things as the purpose and meaning of life come in, no theory should be called "scientific."

Because of the great importance of the second and third levels for most personality theories, such theories are best regarded not as results of scientific investigation, but as applied philosophies of life. To the limited extent that their applications involve reliable clinical observation on the first level and concepts tied to these observations, they are indeed scientific. A Christian theory of personality can be scientific in this same way.

Part One: Presuppositions

For the present our concern is with the non-scientific, essentially philosophical, assumptions that condition and structure modern personality theory — i.e., with Level Three assumptions. Analysis of these assumptions should demonstrate that personality theories are fundamentally non-scientific. These foundational assumptions are rarely acknowledged or understood, but they pre-determine how human nature is seen.

My concern here is with the fifteen or so personality theories commonly covered in college textbooks: Freud's, Jung's, Adler's, Erikson's, Object Relations, Horney's, Fromm's, Rogers's, Maslow's, Allport's, Existential Psychology (e.g., Rollo May), Kelly's, Murray's, Cattell's, and Skinner's. Occasionally reference is made to Bandura, and sometimes to cognitive theorists, or to the cognitive behavioral approach, of (e.g.) Albert Ellis or Aaron Beck. Some textbooks also include a chapter on biological and hereditary approaches. The dominant theorists almost all made their mark before 1970. These dominant approaches can be described as "modern," as distinguished from a small number of very recent contributions we might call "postmodern" personality theories. "Modernist" approaches usually emphasize or assume atheism, determinism, reductionism, moral relativity, autonomy, subjectivity, and so forth. I discuss these assumptions below.

Postmodern theories include the contextual family theory of Boszormenyi-Nagy (1987; see discussion by Roberts, 1993); McAdams's narrative approach (1990); de Rivera's (1989) emphasis on the mutualist self focused on love; and perhaps Buddhist personality theories (see Engler, 1991). Buddhism itself is hardly postmodern, but a Buddhist theory of personality is. Explicitly Christian theories of psychology or of personality are also postmodern. (For examples, see Roberts, 1993; this volume a, b; Vitz, 1987.)

Prior to the modern period, sophisticated philosophies of human nature (for example, Aristotle, 1985; Thomas Aquinas, 1948; see also Nussbaum, 1994) offered accounts of human motivation, personality development, normal and abnormal personality traits, and normal and abnormal patterns of human interaction, and proposed methods of therapy for disorders of the psyche; but they did not develop the idea of the unconscious as deeply as modern thinkers have done, nor was their understanding of abnormal personality as detailed as the modern.

Recent constructivist approaches to psychotherapy and personality theory are partly modern and partly postmodern. For example, Meichenbaum (1993) proposes the therapist as a "co-constructivist" who collaborates with the client to transform the narrative of his or her life. (See

Guidano, 1991; Hermans, Kempen, and van Loon, 1992; and Mahoney, 1988.) Meichenbaum is postmodern because he rejects reductionism and the idea of an isolated or autonomous self. But he also assumes relativist values and ignores the existence of God; and so he remains halfway between the two mentalities.

The difference between modern secular personality theories and postmodern Christian ones can perhaps best be brought out by noting six pairs of contrasting assumptions.

1. Atheism versus Theism

A. All the widely considered modern secular theories of personality and counseling assume, either explicitly or implicitly, that God does not exist. Many psychologists, such as Freud, have been outspoken in their rejection of God and religious belief. But all of these theories, regardless of the personal positions of their founders, are atheistic in the sense that God is omitted from the theory, and religious motivation, when it does come up, is usually ignored or treated as pathological. The rejection or omission of God, and the omission of religious life, is crucial for any personality theory. Since the Gallup Poll began asking the question in the 1940s, over 90% of Americans have consistently said they believe in God. Many have a religious life that is important to them. Even adult unbelievers were often reared religiously, and this has often affected their personalities. The revival of traditional religions, as well as New Age spirituality in the last twenty or thirty years, continues to demonstrate the extraordinary power and persuasiveness of religious life.

Whether psychologists accept the existence of God and the metaphysical validity of religion, they should at least address the psychological importance of religious life for their clients. After all, religion is at least *psychologically* real, and it constitutes the Level Three understanding of life for many people. To ignore this obviously important psychological reality is an egregious example of bad clinical practice. It would be like doing a physical examination on someone by testing only functions that exist above the neck and below the waist. Humanistic psychology, and especially Maslow's concept of "peak experience," may seem to be an exception but is not. Maslow believed that in the past this natural experience had been *misinterpreted* as an experience of God. Cultural factors such as religious beliefs gave rise to the diverse religious interpretations of mystical or peak experience (Maslow, 1970, p. 164).

Jung's theory of personality at least accepts the psychological validity of religion, and this makes Jung's theory unique among modern personality theories. But even Jung's psychology of religion fails to deal with the variety of childhood religious experiences. He has no way to distinguish, for example, between the psychological impact of being reared by devout Christian Scientists or Orthodox Jews or Pentecostals. Within a Jungian framework, religious experiences are seen as fundamentally psychological: we all have an archetype of God, and the experience of God involves nothing more than the activation of the God archetype. Within Jung's religious psychology, the object of worship is nothing but an aspect of the psyche; the religious world is just the world of the archetypes, and especially the archetype of the Self. For Jung, as Roberts comments, "the Self and God are really not distinguishable" (1993, p. 119). We are reminded of New-Ager Shirley MacLaine's statement: "When I pray, I pray to myself." The reality of God's existence — as distinct from the reality of our psychological structures — is not found in Jung. Jung claimed that the issue of the existence of God was not properly a psychological issue, and refused to deal with it.

Recent object-relations theories also interpret God psychologically. That is, God is understood to be an introjected object, or person, in the same way that other people we have experienced are treated as fundamentally psychic realities. Here again, God is conceived as an internal psychological structure, with religious experience being the result of its activation. Mothers and fathers are regarded as external objects on which the corresponding introjects are modeled, but God is not regarded as an external object at all. Instead, the internal representation of God is derived from other internal psychic representations. (For a valuable religious critique of the object-relations approach to religion, see Spero, 1992.)

But even these psychological interpretations of God are rarely noted in the general approach to personality found in university textbooks and courses today. In the typical undergraduate or graduate course on personality, God, religion, and Christianity do not come up as topics; they are presumed to be irrelevant to understanding personality. For examples, see Hall and Lindsey (1985), Maddi (1980), and Ryckman (1993).

B. A Christian theory of personality begins by assuming that God exists and that he is a person with whom one has a relationship. This relationship has psychological consequences, to which we shall return. The assumption of theism is no less scientific than the assumption of atheism. After all, atheists haven't proved that God does not exist. One psychological advantage of accepting the existence of God and the validity of most religious life is that the psychologist can then treat a religious client more honestly. If the therapist is an atheist or a skeptic, the religious life of the client is taken to be an illusion, an error; indeed, from such a perspective, religion is dubious at best, and, at worst, a psychological pathology. If such a therapist decides to steer clear of the client's religious life, and thus to focus on the client only as a secular individual, this cuts out much that is psychologically important in the client's life, and the therapist's attitude toward the client is often more negative.

2. Reductionism versus Constructionism

A. Modern secular personality theory commonly assumes that so-called "higher" things, especially religious experience and related ideals, are to be understood as caused by underlying lower phenomena. For example, love is reduced to sexual desire; sexual desire to physiology (as in Masters and Johnson, 1966, 1975); spiritual life or artistic ideals are reduced to sublimated sexual impulses (as in Freud); and much of consciousness is assumed to be caused by unconscious forces (as again in Freud or in Jung).

Freud did not, to be sure, assume that all consciousness could be reduced to unconscious forces. But in practice he regularly reduced "higher" ideas to "lower" ones. In particular, he reduced religious experience and much love to unconscious forces. For instance, in his interpretation of a conversion to Christianity as it was described to him in a short autobiographical letter from a medical student, he said that the student's new-found belief in God was based on a displaced Oedipal impulse, which created "an hallucinating psychosis" (Freud, 1950, pp. 245-46). This presumes that the student's motivation is unconscious, but in fact the student appears to have been perfectly normal — except for his "psychotic" conversion. Freud interpreted Christian ideals, bourgeois morality, romantic love, etc., as in fact motivated by, or as disguised expressions of, the id. Such reductionism, with its debunking of "higher" things, was also practiced by Marx. It has been a major modern ploy, as is now widely recognized.

B. A Christian theory is constructionist; it emphasizes the higher aspects of personality as containing, and either causing or transforming, the lower aspects, and sometimes as being in conflict with them. Thus, my conscious thought causes me to seek out education, to search for someone to love, to choose to respond hatefully or charitably to an injury. The conscious mind, then, can become the master and guide of one's lower nature, rather than its slave or victim.

Constructionist thinking is synthetic, bringing things together in an integrated pattern of coherence, while reductionist thought is analytic — breaking whatever is being studied into parts. This integration is often hierarchical, whereas the modern mentality is generally anti-hierarchical.

(For a historical example of constructionist thought, see Lovejoy's 1936 classic, *The Great Chain of Being*.) One of the few modern constructionist personality theorists is Viktor Frankl (1960, 1963), with his emphasis on the search for meaning. Unfortunately, his work has remained outside the mainstream of modern personality theory.

3. *Determinism versus Freedom*

A. Many modern secular theories of personality — e.g., those advanced by Freud and Skinner — explicitly reject human free will; others do so implicitly. Determinism is usually part of a materialist philosophy; but it need not be, since some believe that the mind, though different from body, is nevertheless strictly determined. Although such theories interpret, and consider important, such cognitive and emotional mental states as perceptions, thoughts, memories, and feelings, they generally ignore the will. But psychologists, and especially psychotherapists, beginning with Freud, have not been consistent determinists. After all, psychotherapy assumes that the client will freely choose psychotherapy and will, as a consequence of it, become less controlled or less bound by unconscious or other psychological forces. Freud inconsistently said that a purpose of psychoanalysis was that "where id was, ego will be." Psychotherapy that does not assume common sense understandings of free will can hardly function. Perhaps only B. F. Skinner, among modern psychologists, attempted to be a really consistent determinist.

Nevertheless, secular theories of personality and their applications in therapy have been massively deterministic. In our culture, criminal and other kinds of destructive behavior are routinely excused as the products of irresistible psychological forces created by childhood or adolescent traumas. The idea that persons are responsible for their actions has greatly diminished over the past century — and modern psychology is a major contributor to this change.

B. A Christian theory, in marked contrast, accentuates both human freedom and the will expressing and embodying it. The emphasis on voluntary agency entails a corresponding emphasis on positive character traits — virtues — that support the will as it chooses a response. Some secular theories, such as those of Carl Rogers and the Existential theorists, affirm human freedom. In doing this, they made an important early anti-modernist statement. But they too largely ignore the role of the will in the exercise of freedom, and reject the traditional virtues as traits that support the will. (For much more on free agency, see Johnson, this volume; Jones, this volume; and Neal, this volume.)

4. Individualism versus Interdependence

A. Secular personality theory tends to assume that the personality, at least when it is mature and healthy, is an isolated autonomous self. These psychologies focus on how the individual becomes independent — how the individual separates from its mother, father, community, religion, and everything else upon which it was previously dependent. Individuation is seen as fundamental to human maturity. If individuation is incomplete, then pathological fixations, neuroses, and regressions result. The great fear is that one will remain attached to, or dependent on, or controlled by, someone else.

B. Since Christianity does not assume that the goal of life is independence, and even sees a dark side of independence in the common pathologies of alienation and loneliness, a Christian personality theory takes a very different approach. It postulates interdependence, and mutual but freely chosen caring for the other. Personality is fulfilled in love and not in isolation: in love of God and ultimate union with God, and in love of other humans, leading ideally to a union of wills.

Interdependence is neither dependency nor independence. It is not dependency, which is an inappropriate sense of need for the other, since the relationship is freely chosen. Nor is it independence, since the persons choose to relate to another, and to give themselves to each other. As conceived by secular psychologies, the notion of independence ignores the importance of relationships in bringing the truly adult self into existence. (I refer the reader to the interesting work of de Rivera, 1989, on "mutualism" as opposed to individualism and collectivism.)

5. Self-Centered Morality versus Morality Centered on God and Others

A. Modern secular psychology assumes that all values are relative to the individual. Wallach and Wallach (1983) have shown that every prominent modern psychology, from Freud and Jung to cognitive dissonance theory, assumes that the only good is what is good for the individual self. This view can take a variety of forms, ranging from the moral philosophy of ethical egoism to individual relativism of a radical kind to the simple assumption that the only thing we ever choose is what we think is in our own best interest. The semi-compatibility of these views is rarely acknowledged, and still more rarely defended. Taken together, these moral views have helped greatly to undermine traditional religious teachings. They have also helped to bring about the "individualistic morality" so prevalent today and so frequently bemoaned by social critics (e.g., Bellah et al., 1985).

It is worth noting that most relativistic systems of morality are absolutist about something — typically about moral relativity itself, and about those psychological processes that support moral relativism. Thus, for example, "getting in touch with your feelings" is an absolute value in the thinking of Carl Rogers because it supports the development of a self that will choose its own values. The point is that the absolutism of such systems is at the service of relativism.

B. The existence of absolute moral principles, revealed by God, is fundamental to Christianity and to Christian personality theory. The two great commandments summarize this: Love God and love others. Love is an absolute value, and absolutely superior to hate. It is taken for granted that there are certain actions we must do, and others we must not do. Christianity also assumes the moral truth and psychological validity of the Ten Commandments. Finally, it is understood that at least some of a person's mental pathologies can arise from violating the moral law, which comes from God, and that psychological well-being develops from keeping the moral law.

Here again, some deeply relativistic systems have (paradoxically perhaps) "absolute" implications. For example, Rogers assumes that psychological pathologies can arise from disobeying the absolute principle that individuals should create their own values and rules. There is, then, a similarity between a Rogerian and a Christian theory. The difference — and it is major — is that the latter believes that the law comes from God, not from the self.

6. Subjectivism versus Realism

A. Most secular theory, especially humanistic psychology, is based on the assumption that all we can really know is the various states of our own minds. Sometimes these theories also accept the kind of knowledge found in the physical sciences, although that kind of knowledge is normally irrelevant to psychology. Since Kant, even knowledge of physical reality has been assumed to be knowledge only of mental states and not real knowledge of things existing independently of our perceptions. Although some philosophers today are realists, contemporary theories of personality commonly assume that knowledge, like morality, is non-objective and dependent on each individual's interpretation.

Closely related to the subjectivistic assumption is the notion that the important thing is to express, understand, and communicate one's own thoughts and feelings, whatever they are; to affirm them, whatever they are; and to be open to the same thing in others. "Truth" is therefore fundamentally psychological, and there are as many "truths" as there are individual psychologies. We must know our "real" feelings; we must know what happened to us when we were young; we must know our past traumas in order to find psychological peace; we must get in touch with ourselves. Our subjective world is the only real one, and the final court of appeal for something's validity is what we think — or rather, how we feel — about it. The view that feelings can be transitory, that they can be illusory or even false, is not found in such theories, nor do they acknowledge that many feelings are, rather like clothes, meant to be changed or discarded.

B. The objective nature of God as external to us, and of the external world created by him, is assumed by a Christian personality theory. Although our own particular thoughts and feelings are of legitimate importance, they do not define reality and cannot be given highest priority. Moreover, we must submit not only to God but to the lawful and beautiful world that God has created. As I noted above, this realism is at odds with the dominant modern philosophies. It is, however, in profound sympathy with the general assumption of realism found throughout science since its origin. It is also at home with the common-sense philosophy of ordinary people since the beginning of time, including even subjectivistic philosophers and psychologists when they are on the ski slope or at the dinner table. Exactly what kind of philosophic realism is intrinsic to Christianity is an interesting and unresolved issue. For a valuable discussion of this topic, see Martin (1987), who concludes, in line with this author, that persons and love are central to any realistic epistemology. The temptation to narcissism obviously found in secular subjectivism is also something that a Christian personality theory quite consciously resists.

These six pairs of contrasting principles clarify two things: many fundamental assumptions of modern personality theory have nothing to do with empirical science and are at cross-purposes with any Christian theory.

Part Two: The Model

Personality and the Trinity

As many psychologists know, the word "person" comes from the Latin word *persona*, which means "mask," as worn in the Roman theater, and also from the theatrical role that went with the mask. The Latin term translated the Greek word *prosopon*, which had the same meaning and was first used in this sense.

But this etymology of the word "person" is not, in fact, very important or revealing. It is more important that the concept of a person rose to prominence, as a major philosophical and theological issue, in early Christian thought. Müller and Halder (1969) have gone so far as to claim that the concept of a person was "unknown to ancient pagan philosophy, and first appears as a technical term in early Christian theology" (p. 404). We do not need to agree with this extreme assertion to recognize that Christianity has a special place in the development of the concept of the person, and the Christian origins of the concept may help us to understand what today's Christian psychologist will want to emphasize about the nature of persons.

The concept of a person was developed to help formulate the doctrine of the Trinity — God as three persons. This early theological use placed a strong emphasis on dialogue — it was largely through dialogue within the Trinity, as found in Scripture, that the plurality of persons in God was recognized. Because we are made in the image of a trinitarian — and thus interpersonal — God, we ourselves are interpersonal by nature and intention. Human beings are called to loving, committed relationships with God and with others, and we find our full personhood in these relationships.

According to T. F. Torrance (1983, 1985), the essential feature of the Christian conception of the world, in contrast to the Hellenic, is that it regards the person, and the relations of persons to one another, as the essence of reality, whereas ancient Greek thought conceived of personality, however spiritual, as a restrictive characteristic of the finite — a transitory product of a life which as a whole is impersonal (Torrance, 1985, p. 172). Torrance has done much to illuminate the interpersonal implications of the trinitarian concept of God. He identifies two basic understandings of God as a person. The first view, which has dominated Western philosophy, comes from Boethius, who defines a person as "an individual substance of a rational nature," thus emphasizing what differentiates one such substance from another. The second understanding derives primarily from the patristic, primarily Greek, period of the church, and also from the twelfth-century French philosopher and theologian, Richard of St. Victor. The Fathers and Richard of St. Victor derive their concept of the person from the idea of the Holy Trinity. Richard defines a person "not in terms of its own independence as self-subsistence, but in terms of its ontic relations to other persons, i.e. by a transcendental relation to what is other than it, and in terms of its own unique incommunicable existence" (1985, p. 176). So, "a person is what he is only through relations with other persons" (1985, p. 176). The Latin West's use of Boethius is a highly influential continuation of pre-Christian Hellenic tradition, which apparently failed to accept personal relations as part of the structure of reality itself. The early Fathers' view that makes relationship essential to personality is found also in Augustine, but it was largely displaced in the Latin West by the Boethian stress on the individual and did not receive further development until Richard of St. Victor, whose influence on subsequent Christian philosophy was far from dominant.

The contemporary Catholic theologian Joseph Ratzinger (1970, 1990) takes a position strikingly similar to that of Torrance, although the two writers are apparently unaware of each other's thought. Ratzinger (1970, p. 132) writes,

> Christian thought discovered the kernel of the concept of person, which describes something other and infinitely more than the mere idea of the "individual." Let us listen once more to St. Augustine: "In God there are no accidents, only substance and relation." Therein lies concealed a revolution in man's view of the world: the relation is discovered as an equally valid primordial mode of reality. It becomes possible to surmount what we call today "objectifying thought"; a new plane of being comes into view.

Ratzinger (1990, p. 442) states that

> person must be understood as relation. . . . [T]he three persons that exist in God . . . are in their nature relations. They are, therefore, not substances that stand next to each other, but they are real existing relationships. . . . Relation[ship] . . . is not something added to the person, but it is the person itself. In its nature, the person exists only as relation.

The notion of person as relation has implications beyond the theological:

> the phenomenon of complete [relatedness], which is, of course, in its entirety only in the one who is God . . . indicates the direction of all personal being. The point is thus reached [where] . . . there is a transition from the doctrine of God into . . . anthropology. (1990, p. 445)

Ratzinger's "anthropology" is equivalent to "psychology." Ratzinger may seem to imply that a person is only relation, and by implication that substance is not a necessary component of personality. Elsewhere, he (1970, p. 132) corrects this impression by writing that relation and substance are equally valid primordial modes of reality, and this view is also evident in the quotation from Augustine above. In the model that I wish to propose, substance and relationship are each jointly necessary, but not individually sufficient, determinants of personality. In our own historical context, however, special emphasis needs to be laid on the place of relationship in personality. Like Torrance, Ratzinger points out that Boethius's definition of "person" as an "individual substance of a rational nature" had unfortunate consequences for Western thought. If substance dominates our thinking about persons, we may lose the earlier Christian insight that personality essentially involves relationship.

We have psychological evidence of the importance of relationship in the formation of the person. Relationships are necessary for normal human existence and development. A newborn child who lacks a mothering relationship with another human will die, even if its physical needs are met. A person learns to speak through relationships that begin in the first weeks of life, when the infant first listens to its mother's voice. Language-learning requires relationships, and without language we are hardly human. Developmental psychology has provided evidence that the individual's sense of "I think" and of his own individual thought processes derives developmentally from a more primitive "we think." As Vygotsky (1978, p. 57) says, "an interpersonal process is transformed into an intrapersonal process."

Additional Psychological and Theological Characteristics

In light of these considerations, it is clear that from the Christian perspective Carl Rogers's title *On Becoming a Person* (1961) is false advertising. His book is about becoming, not a person, but an individual, and in particular an autonomous, self-actualizing, independent individual. An individual, in the present sense of the word, is created by separating from others, by concentrating psychological thought, energy, and emotion on the self instead of on God and other people. The founders of modern psychology clearly knew this. The first expression of the ideas that Rogers made more widely known can be found earlier in the writings of Alfred Adler and Carl Jung. Adler called his psychology "Individual Psychology"; Jung called the central developmental process "individuation."

Philosophy has long distinguished the individual from the person. Jacques Maritain (1947) does not focus on "relationships" for understanding the person, but he emphasizes the spiritual dimension of the person, which allows for the transcendence of individuality (the secular self). In important respects a person is the opposite of an individual, for a person comes into existence by connecting with others, not by separating from them. So much of modern psychology, especially humanistic self-psychology, is the anti-psychology or anti-structure of a Christian psychology.

Consider the following opposition between Christian and secular psychology. Christians are challenged to love and to forgive, while much of secular psychology calls on people to trust and to forget. Does it make sense to make trust in others (or in oneself) the fundamental virtue? Clearly not. Jesus never asked us to do it. He was too much of a Jewish realist for that! He certainly never "trusted" others; and if he did not trust the apostles, it was for good reason: one would betray him, another deny him, and almost all the others abandon him. But he did love them! A mother may not always trust her child (she knows he can be naughty); a husband may not trust an alcoholic wife; but both can love. After being betrayed once, much less "seventy times seven," it is foolish to trust the other person, but it is still possible to forgive. Secular psychology is being completely foolish, then, to ask people first to trust and then to forget. It is impossible, and frequently unwise, actually to forget that another has hurt you. By contrast, to love and, when hurt, to forgive are, though difficult, realistic and possible.

A Christian theory of personality is, then, psychologically realistic. But it is not realistic in a merely psychological sense; it is based on reality, on what exists outside the self. To be a person is to respect external realities. By making the individual self the center of personality, all modern theories of personality remove people from reality, from the external world created by God and filled with real others. For example, Carl Rogers's (1980) theory is based in a thoroughgoing subjectivism: "there are as many realities as there are persons"; we must prepare for a world of "no solid basis, a world of process and change . . . in which the mind . . . creates, the new reality" (p. 352). The tendency of much personality theory to merge with Eastern religion, with subjective drug states, and with many kinds of occult world views that claim reality is the creation of each self, is more evidence of its subjectivism.

Becoming an individual — that is, separating and distancing yourself from others — has a logical progression. First, you break the "chains" that linked you to your parents, and then to others, and then to society and culture. Finally, you reject the self itself; that is, you separate consciousness from the illusion of the self. You reject the self and all its desires — and thus the process of separation culminates in an experience of a state of nothingness. Radical autonomy ultimately means separation from everything; it means total or ultra-autonomy, where even the self is gone.

The development of a person is, in many respects, the "anti-process" of the development of the autonomous individual. The person is created for union with God and others. Love brings about this union, this enlargement. This is seen in the words of Jesus, "I and the Father are one," and in his desire that his followers be one. The person knows not the "peace of nothingness," but instead the joy of union in love.

To summarize:

A Person is created by God in the image of God.
An Individual is created by the self in the image of self.

A Person loves and trusts God, and loves others as self; persons forgive those who have hurt them.
An Individual loves and trusts the self, trusts others, and rejects or ignores God; individuals forget hurts, and those who have hurt them.

A Person has the goal of committed relationships with others, and a state of union with God.
An Individual has the goal of separating from others, and, in the extreme logic of individualism, of separating even from his or her self.

For a Person, true freedom is choosing complete dependence on God, who is completely free.
For an Individual, true autonomy is choosing complete dependence on the self.

A Person accepts the reality of God, other people, and the physical world.
An Individual rejects everything outside of the self as subjective and a non-reality.

Putting the Individual in Perspective

These contrasts overstate the case in the sense that no individual is apt to take these modern principles to such an extreme. Reality doesn't let us; and most of us have enough common sense to protect us from taking our theories too seriously. My image of a person is also idealized. We are all aware how poorly even the best of Christians live up to such ideals. In the everyday world, it can be hard to distinguish who is operating from which of these two theoretically very different models.

Secular emphasis on independence and individuation can be good. Independence from the unexamined views of others is an important virtue, not just for the secular world but in the Christian world as well. Christian theology emphasizes free will or free choice. God gives us freedom to choose him or not. Throughout Scripture, this is a central theme. The emphasis on freedom found in the secular world of the last few centuries can be understood as the immanentizing of a basic Christian principle; it is the theological concept of freedom translated into the social and political world.

To display this more clearly, it will be useful to describe the three different models of the self developed by de Rivera (1989). A "collectivist" derives the self from his place in the social order, and especially in the family. In this environment, the self complies with others to secure their support and to supply his own to them. Obligation to family or to one's social role is the basis of morality, and the self's purpose is to maintain group harmony. This kind of self is part of a whole, and it values connections with others and the good of community. It emphasizes manners, social traditions, and caring and feeling for others. The political system of such a society (de Rivera identifies Japan and China and premodern Europe as "collectivist societies") aims to secure the collective good. In the present context, this kind of society is close to the natural society found in mother-and-child relationships, and in a child's relationships with family during the early years. In this developmental stage and in this kind of society the "we" precedes the "I."

De Rivera contrasts the collectivist self with the "modern individualist" self. This is the self I have been criticizing (i.e. the modern secular self). In the kind of society that develops and supports the individualist self, which de Rivera equates with the contemporary West, and especially with the U.S., the individual's strategy is to look out for himself. The society is ego-centric and contractual, not socio-centric and organic. Morality is based on abstract principles and the goal is self-integrity. This self values autonomy and individual rights, secured by justice, reason, and law. The goal of the modern political system is above all to protect individual rights.

De Rivera believes both of these models are gravely flawed. The first presents a self that has relationships but no freedom, and the second a self with freedom but no true relationships. He argues for what he calls a "mutualist" self, based on care for the other, love for others, the transformation of fear into love, an emphasis on freedom in community, a deep concern for justice, and action that transforms real circumstances into more ideal conditions. De Rivera writes as a social psychologist who is implicitly but not explicitly Christian. Here I speak from an explicitly Christian and more narrowly psychological or interpersonal point of view. The Christian self, or "person," must combine both relationships and freedom in the manner of de Rivera's "mutualist" self.

The Actual Process of Becoming a Person: "Personagenesis"

But what is the process of becoming a person within such a Christian theory of personality? What is "personagenesis," as Connor calls it (1992, p. 47), within such a "mutualist" model?

First, a Christian theory does not reject the claim that a person is a substance, but gives equal or greater emphasis to the person as relation. In the language of Karol Wojtyla (now, of course, Pope John Paul II), a person is constructed on the "metaphysical site" of substance, but the process of construction involves the dynamics of relationships (Connor, 1992).

According to Wojtyla, the first step in personagenesis "seems to be passivity, receptivity of love from another" (Connor, 1992, p. 45). In the natural world, this is usually the love a newborn receives from its mother. In the spiritual realm, which is at the core of personality, it is listening to the call and love of God. Once initiated, the process of becoming a person continues as a "vertical transcendence" in which the person gives "the self to another" (Connor, 1992, p. 47). The process of lovingly giving the self to another both transcends and determines the self in its act of performing service. The giving of the self to another is how the individual self is transcended; it is also how one comes to know both the other and, from the perspective of the other, to know oneself much more "objectively" than one ever can from inside an autonomous self. Thus one becomes a person. Wojtyla (1979) notes that free will is at the center of a person's self-gift to another, for while man freely determines his action, he is "at the same time fully aware" that his actions "in turn determine him; moreover they continue to determine him even when they have passed" (Connor, 1992, p. 48).

When the other person receives one's gift of love and gives himself or herself in return, the highest form of intimacy results. Such intimacy has been lucidly described by the Christian philosopher Kenneth Schmitz (1986):

> Metaphysically speaking, intimacy is not grounded in the recognition of this or that characteristic a person *has,* but rather in the simple unqualified presence the person *is.* . . . Indeed, it seems to me that the presence in which intimacy is rooted is nothing short of the unique act of existing of each person. Presence is but another name for the being

of something insofar as it is actual, and in intimacy we come upon and are received into the very act of existing of another. We are, then, at the heart, not only of another person, but at the heart of the texture of being itself. No doubt it is true that the person is incommunicable in objective terms insofar as he or she is existentially unique. But in intimacy, as we approach the very act of self-disclosure, we approach the center of all communicability. It is this "secret" that we share with the other person. It is the sense of being with another at the foundation not only of our personal existence, but of being with each other in the most fundamental texture of being itself. Put in the most general terms — though we must not forget that each intimacy is through and through singular — the "secret" that we discover through intimacy is this: *"that reality is not indifferent to the presence of persons."* (p. 45; emphasis in original)

Although Schmitz is describing the metaphysical nature of intimacy, the same understanding is at the core of psychological intimacy. Intimacy — with God and with others — thus becomes a major characteristic of a person. This intimacy is not cognitive knowledge based on abstraction, but knowledge based on experience, on union with the other.

Psychological Applications

One of the important tasks of any personality theory is to bring new or overlooked psychological aspects of personality into focus. Christian theorists are doing this. Some of their more important and distinctive contributions are summarized here.

The Traditional Virtues

The traditional virtues — for example, faith, love, patience, humility, hope, compassion, self-control, forgivingness, forbearance, steadfastness, chastity, justice, courage, temperance, and wisdom — have long been a concern of Christian thinkers. Taken together, these virtues constitute a Christian maturity ideal for personality, a standard of psychological well-being.

In a sense, each modern psychological theory has its own set of "modern" virtues, for these theories have a strong moral or prescriptive character. The fact that psychologists seldom use the word "virtue" does not prevent them from talking about virtues! Thus, a Rogerian set of virtues would include unconditional positive self-regard, self-actualization, congruence of actual self and ideal self concept, being in touch with one's feelings, etc. Jungian virtues would involve the quest for a balance between animus and anima and a balanced expression of the four major mental activities (thought, sensation, intuition, and emotion). The greatest Jungian virtue, as we have seen, is individuation. Even Freud might be said to prescribe virtues, including among others a general stoicism and self-knowledge that leads to the removal of repression and illusion. It would be interesting to compare these secular virtues with the traditional Christian virtues, for then we would see that the secular virtues are over-whelmingly the virtues of what I have called the "individual," while the Christian virtues are traits of a psychologically well-developed "person." Traditional Christian thought has always been concerned with such vir-tues because they are understood as psychological habits developed over time by the agency of the will that fit the person for the relationships to God and neighbor that we have been stressing in these pages. The Chris-tian tradition not only affirms the value of these traits, but also contains much reflection and advice (in that body of literature known as ascetical theology) on how these traits are acquired. Thus there is in the Christian tradition a native and ancient "psychotherapy." When we consider that many of the psychological problems for which people go to therapists — problems like depression, anxiety, family strife, addictions, criminal be-havior, a sense of meaninglessness, low self-confidence, and so forth — are much less likely to occur, or are simply ruled out, in people who have the Christian virtues, the "psychological" value of these traits should be obvious not only to Christians, but to virtually everybody.

Examples of Christian psychological theorists who have con-tributed in this area are Kirk Kilpatrick (1992), Thomas Lickona (1991), and Robert Roberts (1984b, 1992a, 1993, 1995).

Forgiveness

Probably the single most important clinical phenomenon that Christian therapists have emphasized is forgiveness. Forgiveness is certainly a major therapeutic process, probably the most beneficial one that can take place between two people. Secular therapy and theories of personality have largely ignored it, but in recent years many Christian psychologists have begun to analyze it and introduce it into psychotherapy. These include: Augsburger (1970, 1981), Benson (1992), Brandsma (1982), Bonar (1989), Cunningham (1985), DiBlasio (1992), Enright and Zell (1989), Fitzgibbons (1986), Gartner (1988), Linn and Linn (1988), Pattison (1965, 1989), Pingle-ton (1989), Roberts (1995), Smedes (1984), Strong (1976, 1977), Veenstra (1992, 1993), Wapnick (1985), and Worthington and DiBlasio (1990).

Relationships (Interdependence)

Let us look at a hypothetical family situation: a widowed mother and son. In our first scenario, the son is dependent on the mother, lives at home even as an adult, and obviously has a neurotic dependency on his mother. The mother needs a "child," someone who needs her, while the son has become fearful of the outside world in which he has never functioned; and he needs to maintain the warm support of his mother. But neither has freely chosen to love the other. They are controlled by psychological forces they unknowingly chose many years ago, without understanding the consequences or the strength of the habit that would develop. One of this pair must choose to break this cycle of dependency, which contains only small amounts of genuine love. But it is not uncommon for people to make such choices — witness the choice of many alcoholics in breaking their addiction. In this scenario the mother and son have a relationship, but without true freedom.

Another scenario could involve a mother/son pair in which the son, fearful of dependency and of being controlled by his mother, chooses to reject her, to leave home and move far away, so that he can remain at a considerable psychological and physical distance. Neurotic dependency has thus been avoided. But the son remains afraid of being close to his mother. He suffers from what might be called "neurotic independency." The mother, of course, is likely to feel hurt and rejected, but may continue to harbor the controlling needs that the son fears, which are based on her own fears of being unneeded and unloved. In any case, the price of the son's independence is the loss of any serious relationship with his mother. In this scenario, the mother and son have freedom of a sort, but no relationship.

A third, more satisfactory possibility is for the mother and son to have strong, loving relationships with God. This frees them from vulnerability to a neurotic need for love from one another. They are free to help and love each other, while avoiding pathological emotional involvements. This situation contains no basis for neurotic dependency or fearful independency. Both mother and son have relationship and freedom. Each freely chooses to give self to the other.

Many psychologists might say: "Fine, you have avoided dependent relationships with other people, but at the price of a neurotic dependency on God — who may not even exist, and who is just a fantasy composite of early parent introjects." As to God's existence: this is a matter of faith, just as the affirmation of God's non-existence is a matter of faith. The fear of faith in God is, in many psychologists, itself a neurotic fear: it is the fear of being "duped"; the fear of losing one's personal autonomy; the fear of intimacy; the fear of giving oneself in love to anyone or anything; the fear of losing one's pathological defenses. As in the second scenario, this fear of faith can be a kind of neurotic independency.

To return to the issue of "neurotic dependency on God": the very term of course implies something harmful to the person. But do the people we know to be close to God strike us as unhappy, maladjusted, and in general pathological? Perhaps some people who claim to be close to God do communicate these traits, including religious fanatics. But fanatics contradict their own religious ideals in that they do not love others and are filled with hatred. For the Christian, the love of God brings peace, tranquillity, and an obvious love of others. True Christians, like Mother Teresa of Calcutta, attract all kinds of people because of this love and their other positive qualities.

In conclusion, the core of a Christian theory of personality has a clear and distinctive rationale and a set of distinctive psychological emphases. This paper only touches on the task of developing such a theory; some important issues have not even been addressed here. In the future, the various aspects of a Christian theory of personality will need to be addressed systematically by the Christian psychological community. For a stimulating discussion of many issues relevant to a Christian theory of personality, see Van Leeuwen (1987).

Metaphysics and Personality Theory

PAUL J. GRIFFITHS

W HAT I HAVE to say in this essay is prompted by Paul Vitz's paper, "A Christian Theory of Personality." I begin by summarizing what I take to be Vitz's argument. I then suggest that developing a properly Christian theory of personality requires more radical criticisms of modernity than Vitz's, and that Vitz has moved only part of the way toward the kind of critique he really needs. My criticisms should be understood within a broad context of appreciation for Vitz's constructive comments about what ought to belong to a Christian theory of personality; what he says about that is, I think, largely correct. The weaknesses of its theoretical frame, though, are illuminating because they (or their logical kin) are found in much work by Christians on the relations between Christian commitments and the methods and goals of non-Christian psychology. So discussion of them ought to be of interest to all Christians thinking about what it means to develop a Christian theory of the person. I argue, in brief, that a properly Christian theory of personality should no longer be constructed principally out of discussion with (and thereby partial capitulation to) the categories of modernity, of which the discipline we call "psychology" is a creature, but instead principally out of conversation with its own past.

Vitz's Argument

Vitz begins by distinguishing three levels according to which the conceptual contents of any theory of personality may be ordered. First-level

---

This paper has been made much better than it would otherwise have been by the discussion it received at the Wheaton Interdisciplinary Seminar on Persons in June 1994. I am also indebted to the useful comments made on an earlier version by Laurie L. Patton.

41

concepts are those closely tied to observation in the clinical setting; these are supposed to be widely recognizable, to contain relatively little theoretical bias, and to be objectively observable. Examples include concepts used to pick out and label patterns of behavior, and affective conditions of various kinds. Second-level concepts are those distinctive to a given theory; they involve a higher-level interpretation of the phenomena picked out by first-level concepts, and include concepts such as the Oedipus complex or the kind of thing a self is. Third-level concepts, finally, are those whose content is metaphysical. They underlie or control the theory of personality in question, and cannot be called scientific. It appears from these distinctions that, for Vitz, a personality theory is scientific to the extent that its "applications involve reliable clinical observation on the first level and concepts tied to these observations" (Vitz, this volume, p. 21). A Christian theory of personality, then, can be scientific according to these criteria, though it will tend to differ from other (equally scientific) personality theories in its second- and third-level concepts.

I note in passing here an assumption I will return to later: that the property *being scientific*, defined in the way just mentioned, is good. Theories that possess it are better, other things being equal, than theories that don't. To say that a Christian personality theory can be scientific is therefore, for Vitz, to say that it is good.

Vitz proceeds to distinguish among premodern, modern, and postmodern personality theories. Modern theories are distinguished from their predecessors and successors chiefly in terms of their third-level concepts, such as atheism, subjectivism, and so forth. Most of the first part of Vitz's paper is devoted to a detailed analysis and critique of these concepts. Modern personality theories differ from premodern ones, for Vitz, chiefly in that the latter typically do not thematize or make explicit their third-level commitments and concepts, while the former do. Modern personality theories are, apparently, systematic and explicit at the third level, while premodern ones are not. Postmodern personality theories aren't given a detailed or precise definition by Vitz. About all he says about them is that they tend to be constructivist and mutualist in ways that premodern and modern ones are not.

I will come back to Vitz's way of distinguishing among these three kinds of personality theory to argue that his way of setting up the distinctions suggests that he is in thrall to modernism in ways deeply inappropriate for a Christian. Now I want only to notice that Vitz's identification of premodern personality theories as lacking systematicity and explicitness about their third-level concepts is problematic. This implies that the theories as to the nature of persons developed and elaborated by Christians from, say, the fourth century to the sixteenth are neither explicit nor systematic. But theological anthropology as understood and prosecuted by, e.g., Aquinas or Calvin was, so far as I can tell, hardly lacking in these properties. Such enterprises were deeply self-conscious and explicit about their metaphysical assumptions, their second-level theoretical concepts, and even the practical and behavioral implications of their theories. The tradition of Christian ascetical theology from Evagrius Ponticus (349-399) to John of the Cross (1542-1591) is hardly lacking in precision, systematicity, and explicitness at any level. The same is true of Buddhist theories of personality. These too, in the hands of such thinkers as Buddhaghosa (fifth century), Vasubandhu (fourth-fifth century), Śāntarakṣita (d. ca. 788), and Tsong Kha Pa (1357-1419), are detailed, precise, and explicit at all levels. These individuals, like their Christian counterparts, developed a complex and subtle battery of technical terms to denote (what we might now call) psychological states and their behavioral concomitants. If anything, the personality theories developed by these premodern thinkers are *more* systematic, subtle, and precise than those of modern clinical or theoretical psychology.

But to return to Vitz's argument. Much of his paper is devoted to an exploration and critique of six third-level concepts he takes to be important elements in most modern personality theories: atheism, reductionism, determinism, individualism, self-centered morality, and subjectivism. His analysis of these concepts leads him to the perfectly proper conclusion that "many fundamental assumptions of modern personality theory have nothing to do with empirical science, and are at cross-purposes with any Christian theory" (Vitz, this volume, p. 29). Notice here once again that "empirical science" is taken to be good; it would be problematic for Vitz's argument if the six third-level modernist assumptions he analyzes could reasonably be claimed to have some positive relation to empirical science. He wants to reject the former but not the latter.

The second part of Vitz's paper contains his constructive proposal. The argument here, in brief, is that a Christian personality theory should depend on trinitarian theology; that good trinitarian theology emphasizes the constitutive import of relationality for God's identity; and that good Christian personality theory should therefore do the same for the identity of persons. Vitz apparently does not wish to give an exclusively relational account of persons; some room is to be kept for thinking of persons as enduring substances. But the emphasis nonetheless is on mutuality, and in this respect Vitz prefers postmodern theories to modern ones. An account of the person in these terms should also, Vitz thinks, be placed in the context of an emphasis upon freedom. If this is done, a practical and therapeutic recovery of traditional Christian emphases upon such things as the virtues can occur. Vitz does not explain clearly just how this recovery of a trinitarian mutuality will affect the first-level concepts deployed by a renewed Christian theory of the personality. The impression is that the first-level concepts will remain largely the same just because they are largely independent of the second- and third-level concepts.

Science, Modernity, and the Place of Theory

However modernity is characterized, it is clear that it must be connected, *inter alia*, with the following three phenomena: first, the rise of experimental science and the spread of its technological products; second, the critique of metaphysics that effectively began with Kant and that has become one of the dominant trends in modern philosophy; and third, the separation of fact from value that is exemplified in the ideal of the detached, neutral, impartial research scientist of both the *geisteswissenschaftlich* (human science) and *naturwissenschaftlich* (natural science) kind. There were, of course, other developments in the establishment of the modernist view of the world and of modern nation states; but these three are central, conceptually speaking, and discussion of them is unavoidable in the context of a project such as Vitz's. It seems clear that none of these developments is especially easy to reconcile with Christianity. This is perhaps most obvious of the Kantian and post-Kantian critique of metaphysics. If it is really the case that the scope of metaphysical thinking is limited in the way Kant thought it was, then it follows fairly directly that the historic creedal affirmations made by Christians can no longer be made. It also follows, though less directly, that views as to the nature of human persons antithetical to those required by Christianity will be strongly supported and more and more widely held. Vitz's discussion of the third-level concepts implied by modernist personality theories shows this with much more clarity and detail than I can hope to do.

But the rise of empirical science and the spread of its associated technologies is also hard to reconcile with Christianity, and since Vitz is much more positive in his attitude to these developments than he is toward the metaphysics (or anti-metaphysics) of modernity, it is worth showing this. The argument that Christianity (or at least a certain kind of theism) was among the necessary conditions for the development of science and technology has often been made — most systematically perhaps by Stanley Jaki (1978). It is not, in the end, a convincing argument, though it is beyond both my scope here, and my competence, to begin to show why. What I can do, I think, is to show that, and why, the version of scientific practice Vitz feels so positive about is only dubiously compatible with the version of Christian personality theory he wants to defend. In doing this, I can also show how the insights and arguments of at least some versions of postmodernism can be used in the service of a properly Christian critique of modernity — a critique that I think Vitz has moved only part way toward.

Finally, the enlightenment ideal of the detached, value-neutral scientist, whether research physicist or practitioner of the human sciences, is also not easy to reconcile with Christianity. There are strong currents of thought, evident already in the New Testament and dominant among most Christian systematic thinkers after Augustine, that sit very uneasily with the ideal of neutrality or objectivity in the cognitive sphere. I have in mind especially the claim that the capacity to make right judgments, whether in metaphysics, morals, or science, is strongly connected with a cultivation of the virtues; and that such cultivation is in turn dependent on a rightly ordered ethical and religious life. This was the view of Augustine and Aquinas, of Calvin and Luther; it was also, arguably, the view of Paul. If faith is a virtue, as the Christian tradition generally affirms and as Robert Adams (1987) has cogently argued, then it is hard to see how to avoid the conclusion that a great deal of the cognitive life of human persons (I do not say all, as will become apparent in a moment) is also dependent for its proper functioning upon the presence of virtues. But whatever the depth of the roots of this view in Christian tradition, there are also arguments against its contradiction that do not depend upon appeal to this tradition, and I would like to begin with those.

First, let us consider Vitz's assumption (if I rightly attribute it to him) that first-level concepts in clinical psychology are largely independent of properly metaphysical third-level concepts and even of the relatively ramified second-level theoretical concepts within whose ambit the first-level concepts move. Let us consider with it the closely related assumption that the phenomena that can be observed and studied by clinical practice are, as Vitz puts it, "scientific in the sense that different psychologists can reliably identify them from clinical observation" (Vitz, this volume, p. 20). Vitz gives a few brief examples of such concepts and such phenomena from the fourth edition of the American Psychiatric Association's *Diagnostic and Statistical Manual* (DSM IV). The Association certainly seems to think that the concepts it uses in this manual to identify and categorize the behavioral and psychological phenomena used by clinicians in diagnosis are scientific in the way Vitz intends. It says of its own method:

> [In this manual], each of the mental disorders is conceptualized as a clinically significant behavioral or psychological syndrome or pattern

> that occurs in an individual and that is associated with present distress
> (e.g., a painful symptom) or disability (i.e., impairment in one or more
> important areas of functioning) or with significantly increased risk of
> suffering, death, pain, [and] disability. (DSM IV, p. xxi)

A "clinically significant behavioral or psychological syndrome," apparently, is one that can be identified by an appropriately trained clinician or diagnostician in a clinical setting. Here, for example, is the Association's definition of the clinical features of a major depressive episode (this is a fuller example than any given by Vitz; I need an instance of this length for later comparative purposes):

> The essential feature of a Major Depressive Episode is a period of at
> least 2 weeks during which there is either depressed mood or the loss
> of interest or pleasure in nearly all activities. . . . The individual must
> also experience at least four additional symptoms drawn from a list
> that includes changes in appetite or weight, sleep, and psychomotor
> activity; decreased energy; feelings of worthlessness or guilt; difficulty
> thinking, concentrating, or making decisions; or recurrent thoughts of
> death. (DSM IV, p. 320)

About examples of this kind Vitz, astonishingly, says that they are primarily descriptive and contain relatively little theoretical bias. I will return to the Association's (and Vitz's) understanding of its own diagnostic categories in a moment, but before I do I would like to juxtapose to this passage one from a Buddhist work and one from a Christian work, each purporting to be, in a sense roughly analogous to the Association's descriptions, descriptive of a psychological state. First, consider the following passage from Vasubandhu's *Abhidharmakośabhāṣya*, a Buddhist work written in Sanskrit in India in the fourth or fifth century A.D.:

> Intense affection, moreover, is of two kinds, defiled and undefiled.
> Defiled intense affection is emotional thirst that has as its object things
> like wives and sons. Undefiled intense affection is confidence, which
> has things like the good qualities of one's teacher or master as its object.
> One can have confidence without having intense affection; this occurs
> when one has confidence in the Four Truths. Likewise, one can have
> intense affection without having confidence; this occurs when affection
> is defiled. (Shastri, 1981, p. 203 [ad ii.32c])

Then the following passage, from an early twentieth-century Christian manual of ascetical theology by Adolph Tanquerey, a work widely used by Roman Catholics in the United States until the effects of the Second Vatican Council began to be felt:

> Envy is at once a passion and one of the capital sins. As a passion it consists in a sort of deep sadness experienced in the sensitive part of our nature because of the good we see in others. This sensitive impression is accompanied by a contraction of the heart, slowing the activity of this organ and producing a feeling of anguish. (Tanquerey, n.d., p. 404)

These three passages bear significant formal similarities among which four seem to me especially revealing. Each passage is concerned, first, to identify, descriptively, a broadly affective psychological state. Second, each evinces commitment to certain values in its descriptive identification. Third, each uses a precise technical vocabulary to fulfil its descriptive purposes. And fourth, each specifies the affective state it wants to describe in part by indicating its object.

The first of these shared properties is, I take it, unproblematic and uncontroversial. The second, though — evincing commitment to certain values — requires more comment. In the American Psychiatric Association's description of the clinical symptoms of a major depressive episode there are clear commitments to an axiology that includes, at least, the views that recurrent thoughts of death and feelings of guilt are undesirable. The very fact that such symptoms are included in a work whose goal, as expressed in its title, is to help clinicians to diagnose mental disorders indicates, I think, not just that the symptoms in question are unpleasant to their subjects, but that they are in some broader sense undesirable; mental disorders include states that are evidence of either distress or disability, and therefore to be removed. The judgment that the symptoms of a major depressive episode are indeed symptoms of disorder, then, cannot be separated from implicit judgments as to what constitutes order; and these latter are necessarily axiological in character. Value-commitments of a similar kind are equally evident in the Buddhist and Christian examples given. Our Buddhist example uses terms like "defiled" and "undefiled" in order to place the emotions identified on a continuum of value; and our Christian example categorizes the passion it identifies as one of the capital sins. Are such judgments about value, then, necessary concomitants of the process of specifying and descriptively identifying emotions? I will return to this question in a moment.

The third property shared by each of these passages — that of using a precise technical vocabulary — is equally evident. It is probable that rather few native speakers of English could read the three brief extracts set out above without feeling unsure about the meaning of at least some of the vocabulary used therein. What does "psychomotor" mean? What are the "Four Truths"? What can it mean for "intense affection" to be "defiled"? And how can the claim that envy is one of the "capital sins" be construed? Two of the passages, of course, are translations, but the same points are true of their originals: a native user of Latin would not, in virtue of being such, be able to understand Adolph Tanquerey's technical vocabulary, just as a native user of Sanskrit would not automatically be able to understand Vasubandhu. And this is not a trivial point. The presence of such vocabulary always indicates at least two things: first, that the capacity to understand and use such terms is, and is meant to be, restricted to an élite group; and second, that the élite group in question is constituted by special intellectual training, training that essentially — not just accidentally — includes not just the internalization of some value-laden and technical vocabulary, but also the appropriation of a complex metaphysic, a theory of value, and the mores of a particular community. All these things were intrinsic to the training of a Buddhist monk in medieval India or a Christian one in twentieth-century Europe (as the detailed and fascinating account given by the Oxford philosopher Anthony Kenny [1986] of his own training as a Roman Catholic priest during the 1950s shows for our own time), just as they also are to the gaining of a doctorate in psychology or an M.D. with a specialization in psychiatry.

The fourth and final property shared by all three passages is that they specify the emotional states they want to describe in part by indicating the intentional object of those states, and in some cases also by indicating their etiology. In the case of the American Psychiatric Association, claims as to etiology are generally eschewed since such claims are taken by the Association to involve theory; but no attempt is made to avoid specifying the objects of such states (in the description of a major depressive episode quoted above the objects are, variously, the subjects' activities or their sense of identity), nor to avoid attributing value to them. Tanquerey specifies the object of envy as "the good we see in others"; and Vasubandhu specifies that of defiled intense affection as "wives and sons." The inclusion of reference to the intentional object of an affective state in its descriptive identification also seems, on the face of it, to carry with it extensive theoretical commitments as to the kinds of objects there are in the world, and, returning to value-commitments, as to what are and are not *proper* objects of emotional states, as well as to what are and are not proper objects of mental states in general.

This analysis, sketched rather lightly as it has had to be, is intended to call into question Vitz's judgment that the first-level concepts of a personality theory are relatively free from theoretical commitments and that this is what differentiates them from second- and third-level concepts. The difference between first-level concepts and second- or third-level ones has not to do with the extent of their theoretical commitments and implications, but rather with their place on a continuum from specificity to abstraction. Third-level concepts, as Vitz analyzes them, are the most abstract; second-level concepts hold an intermediate place; and first-level concepts are the most specific. But they are all equally, though rather differently, implicated with theoretical commitments. This is true for all of the human sciences: the *wissenschaftlich mythos* is historically integral to them, but it lingers only as a ghost, an unwelcome relic of positivism; it should be abandoned. Gananath Obeyesekere has made similar points about anthropology (1981, pp. 8-9); his elegant argument can be applied also to psychology.

Let me recapitulate the argument. I am trying to show that Vitz's view of the nature of the first-level concepts belonging to the personality theories connected with contemporary clinical psychology is unduly and uncritically influenced by one part of the modernist myth — that part which asserts the possibility and desirability of a detached, impartial observation of phenomena, a kind of observation that issues in description that reflects the observed phenomena without extensive theoretical commitments and so also without distortion of the phenomena by such commitments. The point of arguing that no one should have such a view of the descriptive and diagnostic procedures of clinical psychology is to suggest that it is perfectly defensible — indeed, epistemically desirable — for a Christian not to have such a view, and in so doing to provide the groundwork for suggesting that a properly Christian personality theory need not meet Vitz's desideratum of being "scientific." There are two broadly divergent views of what is involved in specifying — descriptively identifying — an emotional state. They are connected, inevitably, with two different views as to what emotions are, for what you think about the latter issue will affect what you think about the former. In what follows I shall focus on the former question, for answering this clearly will help us see that Christians need not, *pace* Vitz, identify their emotional states according to APA categories.

The first view suggests that one can specify an emotion only by appeal to some broadly conceptual facts: facts, that is, of one or more of the following kinds: (i) what the subject of the emotional state in question takes its object to be; (ii) what she takes the etiology of her emotional state to be; (iii) what she takes the value of her emotional state to be. Wayne Proudfoot states this view clearly when discussing Aristotle's views on emotion:

> Each of Aristotle's examples suggests that emotions assume and are in part constituted by concepts and judgments. To say that a concept is

constitutive of an emotion is to say that the emotion cannot be specified without reference to that concept. An emotion, like an action, must be identified under a description. The emotions described by Aristotle would also be unavailable in a state of nature. They presuppose concepts, rules, and institutions. Consequently, it seems likely that there are whole classes of emotions that are accessible only within particular cultures. (1985, p. 87)

To put the point slightly differently, the descriptive identification of any emotion inevitably involves appeal to highly ramified and precise concepts: neither the description nor the occurrence of any emotional state is separable from properly theoretical commitments of the kinds already discussed. Criticisms of Proudfoot's work on emotions have been offered, most recently by G. William Barnard (1992); Proudfoot's response (1993) shows, I think, that this central point need not be altered, even if some elements of his formulation will need adjustment.

There is another view, however, expressed most clearly in modern times by David Hume, according to which emotions are simple mental events, uncontaminated and unstructured by conceptual or theoretical commitments. Hume's analysis of the passions in the second book of the *Treatise of Human Nature* makes them a species of impression rather than a species of idea, and as a result much more like simple perceptual events (the perception of a patch of blue, say), than like complex events whose specification requires reference to concepts. This view is implicit in what the American Psychiatric Association says of emotions. Hume, for example, divides the passions into direct and indirect; the paradigm cases of the former, which for him are desire and aversion, are produced by an original instinct of the human mind (1960, p. 438 [II.ix]), and are therefore universal, capable of being specified without highly ramified concepts. If Hume is right and Aristotle wrong, then emotions can be specified without appeal to the kinds of conceptual commitments mentioned. Emotional states, on Hume's model, would be more like states of measurable physiological arousal than like highly structured cognitive events; and if they were like this, it would seem likely that the classificatory systems used to describe them would be relatively invariant across cultures. This view strongly suggests that the most authoritative source for a descriptive analysis of a particular emotional state is its subject. Introspection, on this view, guarantees accuracy.

It should be evident that I take the first view to be correct. Providing a full-dress argument for this would involve engaging some extremely delicate philosophical issues, including (at least) whether Wittgenstein's argument against the possibility of a private language is correct, whether there are natural kinds, and what kinds of mental states (if any) can properly be said to fall into such kinds. I want to proceed, instead, by suggesting, first, that a particular conditional statement is true; secondly, that its conclusion is empirically known to be false; and, thirdly, that therefore we should take its antecedent to be false as well. The conditional is this: *if emotional states could be specified in a (relatively) atheoretical and value-free way, then one would expect descriptions and classifications of such states to be relatively invariant across cultures.*

The intuition behind this claim is that the extent and complexity of the theoretical ramification of any discourse or conceptual system is likely to be inversely proportional to the extent to which it occurs across cultures. That is: if some discourse is theoretically complex and has undergone a long process of development and application in culturally-specific institutions, it will be extremely surprising to find it duplicated elsewhere. The theoretical commitments of the American Psychiatric Association's DSM IV, I have already suggested, are highly ramified in just this sense. It is therefore not surprising that its category system came into being, after much work, in a single cultural location. To take a rather different kind of example, the theoretical commitments implicit in the system of musical notation developed in Europe from the sixteenth century to the present to represent sound graphically are also highly ramified; this practice, too, is culturally unique: one doesn't find it scattered widely abroad, either, and for just the same reasons. The connection between degree of theoretical ramification and specificity of cultural location need not, of course, be a tight one. It might be that some theoretically highly-ramified discursive practice is found in all or almost all cultural settings, and that this is explicable by the fact that all (or almost all) cultures share, for some reason, the theory in question. But it is hard to think of good examples, and so with this proviso I shall stay with the conditional as given above.

Working with this conditional means that we need a contrastive case: are there any kinds of discourse or categorical systems that do not exhibit a high degree of theoretical ramification, and that are, partly as a result, found to occur independently in a wide variety of cultures? If there are not, then the intuition grounding the conditional is thereby less plausible. But, fortunately, there are.

Consider the case of the relatively simple categorical and linguistic system found in every natural language for the specification of primary colors. This is not a highly ramified system. Its theoretical commitments are very modest, since all it does is develop a list of nouns to refer to colors. It approximates in this modesty what Vitz and the American Psychiatric Association think is the degree of theoretical commitment evident in that Association's use of diagnostic categories. And, or so it seems, the categorical system found in every natural language for the purpose of color-classification is essentially invariant. This, at least, was the conclusion of Brent Berlin and Paul Kay on the basis of their study of color terms in 98 natural languages; among other things, they showed that "there exist universally for humans eleven basic perceptual color categories, which serve as the psychophysical referents of the eleven or fewer basic color terms in any language" (1969, p. 104). The experimental evidence amassed by Berlin and Kay strongly supports their thesis that all human languages categorize colored objects in essentially the same way. More precisely, when faced with the artificial situation of being asked to classify a large number of small, colored two-dimensional items into color-kinds, subjects who speak different natural languages produce classifications that overlap to a degree far beyond that predictable by chance. Berlin and Kay's work has received considerable discussion by anthropologists and ethnolinguists, some positive and some negative: Sahlins (1976) is broadly positive, as also is Hickerson (1975); Durbin (1972) and Saunders (1992) are more negative, but on an ideological basis rather than on the basis of a challenge to the reliability of Berlin and Kay's results. None of this discussion, however, calls into question the significance of the experimental results, though some relatively minor modifications in Berlin and Kay's interpretation of them may be called for. For our purposes, it is sufficient to note that Berlin and Kay's work does provide an example of just the kind of relatively atheoretical unramified category system needed, a system which is relatively invariant across cultures.

The conditional for which I'm arguing has thus received some preliminary support. What about the empirical question intrinsic to it? Are classifications and specifications of emotional states relatively invariant across cultures? Emphatically not. The three passages already cited and discussed should be enough to suggest this. It is sufficiently well known that categorizations of emotional states (and even the deployment of the category of emotion) are very culture- and tradition-specific. There is no easy translation between, say, the classification of emotions given in medieval Buddhist scholastic works and that given by the American Psychiatric Association. A splendidly rich example of a culturally-specific categorization of emotions may be found in Catherine Lutz's (1988) work on the Ifaluk, a Micronesian people. It is in almost every important respect incompatible with the American Psychiatric Association's categorization. This strongly suggests that terms for emotions do not pick out natural kinds in anything like the same way that terms for color-kinds do. And this in turn strongly suggests that the antecedent of my conditional — that emotional states can be specified in a (relatively) atheoretical and value-free way — ought not be affirmed. Which means in turn that Aristotle is, broadly speaking, right about what is required to specify an emotional state, and Hume is wrong.

Translatability across systems of categorization for emotional states is not easy. It is rather like attempting to transpose a Bach Passion into music that can be played by an Indonesian Gamelan orchestra. It is not that there is incommensurability of a strictly theoretical kind; it is rather that the practical difficulties are enormous, and they are enormous just because the theoretical commitments implicit in Gamelan music are so different from those implicit in European choral music.

Attempts to categorize psychological states in a value-free way, so characteristic of modern thinkers from David Hume to the theorists of the American Psychiatric Association, are necessarily every bit as committed to second- and third-order theories as are their premodern counterparts. That such thinkers deny this, and in so doing claim for themselves a procedurally hegemonic status, is the intellectual error typical of modernity. That they are still sometimes allowed to get away with it is, among other things, a result of the intellectual self-doubt of faithful religious people. Metaphysics is unavoidable for us all; explicit confession of this, and of the contestability of all metaphysical claims, is a consummation devoutly to be wished.

How to Construct a Properly Christian Theory of Personality

What does all this mean for Vitz's enterprise, and for the broader enterprise of constructing a Christian theory of personality? First, it seems fair to assume that specifying psychological (including emotional) states is, as Vitz suggests, a vital part of any such theory. Second, if the arguments just given are good, we should also assume that such specification is already and necessarily a heavily theory-laden enterprise. And third, if (following Vitz) we identify theory with third-level concepts that are broadly metaphysical in scope, then decisions as to these third-level concepts have a logical (and often also a practical) priority over decisions as to how to specify emotional or other psychological states.

Vitz seems at times almost to realize this. His plea in the second part of his paper for the recovery of a personality theory based on Christian doctrines — specifically, those of humans as *imago dei*, and of God as essentially relational, as expressed in the doctrine of the Trinity — moves a good way toward it. But his own vocabulary and choice of interlocutors belie much of what he says there. If a Christian personality theory ought to be explicitly and self-consciously based upon a Christian metaphysic, and if this metaphysic is largely incompatible with that implicit in the practice of modern clinical psychology, why bother with modern clinical psychology?

To put this still more forcibly: Christianity already has a highly ramified personality theory of its own, complete with precise and specific first-level concepts, increasingly abstract second- and third-level concepts, and diagnostic and therapeutic/salvific procedures. One of the traditional names for this is theological anthropology; it is closely connected with ascetical theology, the former providing the theoretical frame within which the diagnostic and therapeutic procedures of the latter are practiced. The papers by several of the other contributors to this volume (Laporte, Okholm, Plantinga, Roberts, and especially Allen) show the importance, for Christians, of using this tradition of reasoning and practice to frame and give sense to the findings of psychology, rather than the other way around. Christian theological anthropology, together with its concomitant practices, is sufficiently complex that it has taken two millennia to develop, and has required the theoretical and practical efforts of many practitioners over many centuries. Why then abandon it as a resource in favor of conversation with modern clinical psychology — which is, after all, a recent, short-lived, relatively unsophisticated, and theoretically anemic discipline?

I can think of only one reason: that the discourse of "scientific" clinical psychology is privileged over that of Christian theological anthropology (and that of its Buddhist counterpart), just because of its cultural and institutional status as "scientific." But giving such privilege to the *wissenschaftlich* discourse of modernity is surely something that no reasonably self-aware and thoughtful theorist in any discipline can or should any longer do. The default position should rather be the rejection of prima facie privilege for any discourse, which entails the possibility, both within and without the academy, of appropriating, standing within, and using any discourse you like, and as a result of so doing allowing it to enter, freely and fully, into debate with others.

There are theoretical, or perhaps better metatheoretical, arguments in philosophy that give sense and persuasive power to the position gestured at in the preceding paragraph. Prominent among them is the claim, now very widely accepted, that classical foundationalism is incoherent, and that its kissing cousin, evidentialism, is therefore also untenable. By "classical foundationalism" I mean the view that a properly ordered system of beliefs ought to be ordered hierarchically, with beliefs that are self-evidently true or evident to the senses at the base (or foundation), and all other beliefs derived from this basis by clear and demonstrable patterns of argument. "Evidentialism," most clearly and classically expressed by

John Locke in the *Essay Concerning Human Understanding* (1975, pp. 687-88 [IV.xvii.24]), is a view about epistemic duty. This view, most simply put, is that one has fulfilled one's epistemic duties if and only if one's non-foundational beliefs are held with due regard to the amount and kind of evidence for them — which means that one's nonfoundational beliefs ought to be related properly to one's foundational beliefs. Both these views are intrinsic to the epistemology of modernity; they are most clearly seen in Descartes and Locke, but they were also part and parcel, until relatively recently, of the assumptions of many practitioners of experimental science. Criticisms of classical foundationalism and evidentialism have been de-veloped by very diverse thinkers. Some have been overtly Christian. I think of the recent work of Alvin Plantinga (1993a, 1993b), William Alston (1989a, 1989b), and Alasdair MacIntyre (1988, 1990). Diverse though this work is in many respects, it shares a common rejection of the epistemo-logical hegemony of modernity, and some of the same arguments against it recur among these diverse authors. Other thinkers have been, in some broad and undefined sense, postmodernists, such as Richard Rorty (1989, 1991) and Jacques Derrida (1982, 1988). But whatever their provenance, criticisms as to the internal coherence of the epistemological paradigm of modernity are now widely accepted, and are, I think, entirely correct.

The upshot of such criticisms is an epistemological levelling. Chris-tians should welcome much that flows from this; it means that the ascetical theology of a Bonaventure or an Augustine can be deployed in the con-struction of a personality theory with every bit as much confidence, intel-lectually speaking, as can the diagnostic categories of the American Psy-chiatric Association. The playing field is level, in that everyone's theoretical or metaphysical commitments are equally subject to critique and challenge; there is no overarching or hegemonic metaphysic to which all must submit. This fact — and I take it to be a fact, understood as a descriptive claim about the intellectual state of English-speaking culture at the end of the twentieth century — frees Christians to be Christian in the intellectual resources they choose to draw upon; it frees them also to choose with whom they talk in developing their views about the nature of human persons — or about anything else.

The epistemological levelling I'm referring to should not be con-fused with a relativism according to which the metaphysic you choose and the interlocutors you choose to discuss it with are nothing more than matters of contingent preference. If classical foundationalism and eviden-tialism are not defensible as epistemological positions, it does not follow from this that truth is unavailable; nor that all modes of forming beliefs are equally likely to produce true beliefs; nor that we cannot decide be-tween rival and incompatible metaphysical systems. What does follow, to repeat, is that no particular doxastic practice, no particular mode of form-ing beliefs, should be given a position of procedural privilege over any other. Some doxastic practices ought, of course, to be abandoned just because they produce largely false beliefs, and can be shown to do so. There are many ways in which this can be done: perhaps the beliefs so produced are incoherent one with another; perhaps the practice that pro-duces them cannot fulfill its own declared desiderata; perhaps the beliefs produced by the practice cannot be held together with beliefs produced by other doxastic practices that seem unavoidable, and so forth. For in-stance, someone who forms beliefs about the near future by consulting the entrails of sacrificed goats is likely to end up with beliefs that do not meet the desiderata of the practice that produced them: that is, one's success at prediction is likely to be extremely modest (though probably no more modest than the success of economic theory at predicting events within its sphere of relevance). But if a particular doxastic practice is to be abandoned for such reasons, this will have to be shown case by case. It cannot be assumed as a procedural rule that a doxastic practice of any one kind should have hegemonic status; and it follows from this that the doxastic practice of clinical psychology cannot be assumed to have such status vis-à-vis that of Christianity.

What, then, would a properly Christian theory of personality look like? What would be its modes of procedure and its points of reference? Here I can do no more than offer a sketch. Such a theory would begin, inevitably, with the sacred texts of the tradition: the Old and New Testa-ments. It would read and reread these texts in an attempt to discern the theological anthropology implied by them. It would then take extremely seriously the long traditions of interpreting these texts, both theoretically and in terms of the application of the theory through the penitential and ascetical practice of the church. A properly Christian personality theory would thus be self-conscious in choosing as its principal interlocutor the intellectual, diagnostic, and therapeutic/salvific practices of its own past. It would be odd for it to spend energy on discussions with those engaged in doxastic practices whose theoretical assumptions are, at every level (as Vitz shows so splendidly for the third-level concepts of contemporary clinical psychology), dramatically at odds with its own. Doing so would very likely be a waste of energy.

Exactly what a personality theory constructed in the way I've sug-gested would look like I'm not sure. It would, no doubt, contain many of the elements suggested by Vitz: it would be in profound ways related to trinitarian theology; it would emphasize the virtues, since these are the main theoretical concepts developed by Christians for the analysis of what properly oriented human persons should be like; and it would place all of this in a context of practice whose lineaments would be given by the ascetical and penitential practices of the members of the body of Christ. It would also, I think, be very unlikely to call itself a theory of *personality*, since that term, so far as I can tell, is itself a creature of psychology and carries with it implications largely unacceptable to Christians.

Therapeutic Conflict Resolution and the Holy Trinity

L. Rebecca Propst

THE CHRISTIAN TEACHING that God is a trinity of divine persons has implications for our understanding of human persons and their proper functioning. It suggests that while persons are distinct from one another, deep features of their identity are determined by their relationships to one another. This concept of persons coheres nicely with a contemporary understanding of the mental health implications of interpersonal conflict and the process of resolving such conflicts. The main work of this paper is to expound a clinical view of conflict resolution against the background of trinitarian theology. My thesis is that our understanding of the Trinity not only enriches what we know about decision making and conflict resolution, but provides an ontological basis for therapy and a motivational tool in work with some clients. Before I get to the main task, I will explain why I have chosen the interpersonal conflict resolution process itself as an occasion for reflecting on the nature of personhood. Then I will examine three components of the conflict resolution process.

Some Personal Notes

My choice of the interpersonal conflict resolution process to shed light on the more general notion of personhood derives from my approach to the integration of psychology and theology. Rather than develop an overarching theoretical view, I start by trying to understand what a particular therapeutic technique would look like were it to draw on both psychological and theological understandings of the person. The particularistic approach enjoys advocates in both contemporary psychology and contemporary theology. For example, Goldfried, Castonguay, and Safran (1992) suggest that one way the current rapprochement among the schools of psychotherapy could be furthered is by focusing on specific clinical problems, mechanisms of change, and interventions. In a similar vein, speaking of biblical exegesis, Goldengay (1977) states:

> We can in fact only rightly hear the Bible's message as we . . . bridge the gap between its world and ours. Appreciating its meaning in its own day, even "objectively," cannot be a cool, academic (in the pejorative sense) exercise. We may only be able to do so in the act of working out and preaching the equivalent (which may well not mean the identical) message [for a specific circumstance] today. Thus exegesis and exposition are interwoven after all. . . . In exposition as with most other human activities . . . *practice precedes theory.* (p. 352)

In my approach, integrative models derive from practice rather than precede it. The paradox of integration is that to be comprehensive we need to be very specific. The more we know about a given problem, the more we realize the complexity of issues that need to be addressed. In keeping with the tenor of the field of psychotherapy and counseling, I believe that large comprehensive theories will have little or no impact, at least for the foreseeable future. However, specific integrative approaches detailing specific interventions for specific problems may have an impact on theory if the interventions show themselves to be robust.

At least four divergent influences have motivated me to choose the interpersonal conflict resolution process as a case for analysis and reflection. First, I am influenced by the convergence of trends in contemporary psychotherapies (cf. Norcross & Goldfried, 1992, pp. 595ff.). The two most important trends have been the recognition of the central role of cognitive processes in human functioning and the shift toward an interpersonal perspective. Regarding the first trend, most schools of thought have shifted toward a social-constructivist epistemology. Thus psychoanalysts have come to recognize that the analyst does not always uncover historical truths, but often works with the client to construct coherent or plausible narratives (cf. I. Z. Hoffman, 1991). Some of my past work has already focused on the individual's present conscious thoughts and assumptions and the commonality of these themes across psychotherapies (cf. Propst, 1988, 1992). I turn my attention in this paper to the second major theme in current psychotherapy scholarship — the shift towards an interpersonal perspective. The move toward a relational perspective has been the major trend in psychoanalytic theory, in cognitive-behavioral therapy, and even in experiential therapy such as Gestalt (cf. Wheeler, 1991). Cognitive theorists, for example, are becoming more interested in using the therapeutic relationship and other relationships of the client as a fundamental motivational principle to challenge dysfunctional assumptions.

The second influence on my choice of the interpersonal conflict resolution process is my own clinical experience. I treat a large number of women with clinical depression, many of them Christians. Almost all these women are very passive in their relationships, marital or otherwise. Typically, they overfunction in their marriage by being the family "emotional caretaker," achieving "peace" in the relationship by accommodating totally to the other's viewpoint. These women assume it would be disastrous if someone were angry at them; at the first sign of conflict, they acquiesce. Typically they carry resentment at being in this role. Most of them, however, especially the Christian women, also experience guilt when they make any of their own desires known. They feel that to insist on personal wants is "selfish and unacceptable for a Christian woman." But the quietude often brings feelings of helplessness, resignation, and depression.

The clinical literature suggests a strong correlation between marital dysfunction and clinical depression in women. Beach, Sandeen, & O'Leary (1990) found that over 50% of couples presenting for marital therapy had at least one spouse who was clinically depressed. Furthermore, even though significantly more women than men are depressed, the association between marital discord and depression is equivalent between the sexes. Weissman (1987) reports that the risk of having a major depressive episode is approximately 25 times higher for both males and females if they are in a discordant marital relationship than if they are in a non-discordant one. (Retrospective research suggests that the negative marital events often precede the onset of depressive symptoms.) Recent evidence links the presence of marital discord and perceived criticism by the spouse with relapse following successful somatic treatment for depression (e.g., Hooley and Teasdale, 1989). Clearly, conflict, including marital conflict, is at the root of many emotional ills.

The third reason for my interest in the conflict resolution process comes from my observation of work places and churches today. In the work place, because of recent cutbacks and uncertain economics, tension is high and conflict ubiquitous. Unfortunately most of the conflict is not well handled. In the work place (e.g., industry and academic institutions) upper-level management or administrators encourage or even demand that conflict be kept under the rug to avoid publicity. Often, bosses or administrators who themselves do not know how to work cooperatively make arbitrary decisions that aggravate or disempower their subordinates. In many cases, these administrators do not believe in a cooperative work style. Churches are not immune from conflict. Perhaps because of a greater pluralism of ideas today, church members find themselves differing and not knowing how to deal with differences, which often become covert issues in a congregation because it is feared that open conflict will either "split the church" or "not bear positively on the name of Christ in the community." After a while, members with a minority position leave.

The final influence on my choice of the conflict resolution process as a subject for integrative reflection on the nature of persons is Scripture, as interpreted through my own religious affiliation, Mennonite. The prophet Isaiah reminds us that the kingdom of God means that "nation shall not lift up sword against nation, neither shall they learn war any more" (Isaiah 2:4). In other words, one of the marked differences in the kingdom of God is our approach to conflict. We shall not practice a "war" approach to relationships.

Conflict Resolution in Light of Christian Theology

Conflict is dealt with in many ways. Perhaps the most common approach in our society is avoidance. Conflict is avoided by not expressing an opposing opinion, or leaving the presence of a person who is expressing such an opinion. For example, one spouse suggests a vacation trip to the Grand Canyon, and the other finds the idea unattractive but is afraid of a conflict. The second spouse either leaves the room or avoids the discussion, hoping that somehow the issue can be avoided. A variation on this theme is the dominance theme. One spouse may demand a certain type of vacation. The other will say, "That's fine," or "Whatever you want, dear." In this pattern one party always gets his or her way. The other has some fear, either conscious or unconscious, of disagreeing.

A third approach, which perhaps receives more publicity but is actually less common than the first two, is confrontation. The hearer directly states a disagreement with the first person, in a way that clearly draws the lines between the positions. For example, spouses may both be desperately fighting to be heard in the relationship or for a sense of personal space. Both may feel that to give up any wishes to the other means losing. She says, "I would like you to pick up Susan after school tomorrow." He says, "I picked her up yesterday, I won't pick her up tomorrow. You pick her up." She says, "I always pick her up, I always do the work around here." He says, "I am not going to pick Susan up tomorrow." They are at a stand-off. Typically, such couples or groups have stand-offs, not just about some issues, but about most issues.

A fourth approach to conflict is suggested by Christian theology. The Harvard negotiation project (e.g., Fisher and Ury, 1991; Ury, 1993) and Heitler (1990) describe it as *building relationships as you negotiate.* In this approach, differences are regarded as healthy and necessary, and are welcomed as opportunities to deepen relationships.

Some may assume that a Christian position on community and conflict means that there will be no opposites, and typically one view will simply prevail. But some prominent Christian thinkers have not held this view, but thought that some kind of "opposition" of persons is necessary for real community. Indeed, for them, fullest personhood exists only when there is genuine differentiation of viewpoint within the community. In the relational ontology of Dietrich Bonhoeffer (1960) the individual fully exists only through the other. It is in coming together with the other that the individual again and again develops personhood through the other. One could not have self-consciousness without a consciousness of the other. In Bonhoeffer's view, however, the other becomes a thou for me not simply because of myself but through the presence of God (pp. 32ff.). Bonhoeffer parallels the thought of Martin Buber in *I and Thou* (1937), which states that all real living is meeting. But if community is constituted by reciprocal wills, community requires that its members have distinct identities. Community and individuality thus rest upon each other (Bonhoeffer, 1960, pp. 54ff.). Two wills coming together result in a social structure in which Christ exists and within which each is affirmed as unique.

Bonhoeffer also viewed opposition as a natural implication of interpersonal relations. He contended that self-consciousness arises only in opposites, and thus it is in actual confrontation of wills that genuine life arises. Opposition as such is not a consequence of the fall. In fact, Bonhoeffer believed that unless individuals are differentiated and particularized in a group via differences of opinion, it is difficult to have a community (pp. 54ff.). It is in the differences-from-the-other that each individual gains a sense of self. It is in the experience of different wills pressing against one another that a person becomes aware of his or her own personal power, and thereby gains a personal identity. Karl Barth (1960) also argued that one is a person through interactions with another. For Barth, the individual is fully an individual only after the I-thou encounter. Therefore, the minimum definition of humanity is being in encounter (pp. 243ff.). "I am as I am in a relation" (p. 246).

In the traditional Christian doctrine of God, the Father, Son, and Spirit are distinct persons who are nevertheless defined in their personal essence (deep identity) by their relations to one another. The Spirit is not just any Spirit, but the Spirit *of the Father and the Son*; the Father is the Father *of the Son* and the Son is the Son *of the Father*. Thus they are distinct persons but inseparable as one Godhead. We can infer that for human beings to be created in the image of God (Genesis 1:26) is for them also to be at the same time distinct individuals and yet not to have their person-hood independently of one another and God. I am an individual, but not in the classical liberal definition of the individual autonomously defining her or his own individual essence. I am an essentially communal being, but not in the social-behaviorist definition of persons as nothing more than a set of relations to a social environment (Lacugna, 1991).

This concept of persons as in the image of the triune God is the one on which I shall base my recommendations about conflict resolution. Something like this concept of persons is found in the Harvard negotiation project to which I have referred, and in the thinking of some family systems theorists. Thus, Salvador Minuchin, one of the founders of the family therapy movement, often uses a technique he calls complementarity (Minuchin and Fishman, 1981). He assumes that each family member's behaviors are initiated and maintained by other family members, with each person, including the most passive, making his or her effectual contribution to the behavior in the family system. Minuchin repeatedly documents that behavioral change in any one individual has behavioral repercussions in all other members of the family. Thus he often asks a stone-silent husband who complains about an overtalkative wife, "How do you keep your wife talking so much?" Or he may ask the exuberant wife, who complains about a silent husband, "How do you keep your husband so quiet?" Of course both spouses will deny that they are re-sponsible for defining the existence of the other in the relationship. They tend not to think in terms of this deep interconnectedness. In this model, however, the whole is more than the sum of the parts, just as the trinitarian God is more than the three distinct persons of the Trinity. The relationship defines them.

Despite the similarities between these secular psychologies and the concept of a person that derives from trinitarian theology, these psychologies apparently lack an advantage that the Christian one has. The Christian concept of a person is solidly based in an ontology — that is, an account of the most fundamental character of being in the universe, the very nature of God. By contrast, the other psychologies are either ontologically unbased systems of pragmatics, or, if they are ontologically based (as some of the family systems thinking is), the ontology is specu-lative and not grounded in a long and tested tradition like that of Chris-tian theology (see MacIntyre, 1990). In the absence of an ontological tradition that assures us that we only gain status as real persons as we exist in real working relationship with those we differ from, the building of relationships and community as we negotiate conflict may be too difficult to persist in. I turn now to the conflict resolution process that is suggested by trinitarian theology.

Conflict Resolution in a Trinitarian Style

In trinitarian psychology individual differences are regarded as healthy and necessary for good relationships. Persons grow (and thus change) as their relationships develop, but they remain individuals; they retain their distinctness as *different persons.* Likewise, mutually relating self-definition and other forms of dependency, unity with one another, even some of what some psychologists might reject as unhealthy "enmeshment," may also be acceptable and healthy within a trinitarian psychology (1 Corinthians 12). This follows from our concept of persons as created in the image of God. But as clinicians we are painfully aware of the many distortions that are possible both in individuation and in relationship, distortions of that image, distortions that for us come under the general theological rubric of "sin." It is the partial healing of this sin, the partial correction of distortion of the image, that the Christian therapist undertakes to effect in helping clients to resolve their interpersonal conflicts.

Three principles of conflict resolution stand out as implications of a trinitarian perspective, and I will devote the rest of my paper to exploring their clinical application and their derivation from the concept of the Trinity. They are: (1) state clearly your own position; (2) understand where the other is coming from; (3) adopt a generous mode with the other.

1. State Your Position

George and Beth are a good example of the detouring effects of depression and silence on conflict resolution. Beth originally consulted me for severe depression. She said she wanted to be more confident in talking to her husband. She felt that her husband was aggressive. She reported that there had been times of abuse in the past, but not in the last five years. Disagreements with him used to escalate into violence, so she now avoided conflict.

As I watched the couple interact in my office, I observed the following behaviors. For the most part, they did not overtly disagree. Beth did not look at her husband during the interaction, and he usually got his way. She would start out stating her position strongly, and then back down. Her body posture was usually bent, putting her in a lower vertical position than her husband. Typically her backing down was to avoid conflict.

George undermined her positions, often by laughing at them. He also brought in outside issues, including the difficulties in her family. She said, "I listen to George, and I start to back down. That is what I always do." Beth finally decided she wanted to withdraw from the relationship.

"I see no reason to try to talk or even state my opinion. I am scared and angry. Should I leave the relationship?"

George was confused: "What am I doing wrong?"

My approach with Beth was to encourage and train her to state her opinions clearly and forthrightly. In some dyads, the illusion prevails that to state one's own position firmly is to be insensitive or disrespectful toward the other's position. This mistaken idea is a barrier to communication and the therapist must make it clear that two people who respect each other *can* disagree and be firmly committed to their own views. Often the most dysfunctional relationships are maintained by those who refuse to state their own opinions and feelings, or even lie about them. If, as trinitarian psychology implies, our very being as persons depends on our relationship with those others by whom our identity is partly determined, it stands to reason that we do damage both to ourselves and to our partners in life if we minimize or distort how we differ from them. The combination of seemingly opposite responses — acknowledging your counterpart's views and firmly expressing your own — is the communicational ideal, and either one of these taken by itself spells potential trouble. Changing the couple's assumptions about individuality-in-relationship can be a difficult but very important therapeutic goal. It is nothing less than teaching the rudiments of a concept of personality.

The conflict resolution literature suggests that not stating one's position or one's difference from another does not tend to resolve conflict, but that each party's clearly stating his or her position does. The Harvard negotiation project concludes that we do not improve a relationship by merely making concessions (cf. Ury, 1993). Carnevale and Pruitt (1992) hold that neither high demands-low concession nor low demands-high concession best resolves conflicts; the most effective method is a combination of concession making, contending (forcing the other one to change), and problem-solving — finding a way for both parties to be satisfied.

Conciliating in a manner that does not lead to mutual satisfaction not only inhibits the ultimate resolution of the conflict, but may lead to various types of emotional pathology. Beach, Sandeen, and O'Leary (1990) found that depression, especially in women, was likely to be maintained by discordant marriages. The main characteristic of these "depressed marriages" was that in addition to severe spousal denigration, there was criticism, disregard of opinions, and blame by the non-depressed spouse. The depressed spouse responded by avoidance, decreased problem-solving comments, passivity, and concessions. By teaching spouses to be direct and to focus on problem-solving, both marital discord and depression were alleviated (pp. 65ff.). Interestingly, while this pattern was identical for depressed women and men, the incidence was twice as high for women (pp. 43ff.). Beach, Sandeen, and O'Leary cite evidence that suggests that the differential sex ratio is not due to hormonal effects; instead, the women appeared to respond differently than men, by taking a more passive and less problem-solving approach in general. These women benefited immensely, however, from appropriate assertiveness training.

Similarly, Heitler (1990) contends that the clinical syndrome of depression is characterized by an approach to interpersonal conflict in which the depressed individual gives up on trying to get what she or he wants, with the accompanying feelings of resignation and negativity towards self, others, and the future. In marriages or group situations, one partner dominates and the other denies her or his own preferences to keep the other from being critical. The submissive partner may feel virtuous, martyred, resentful, or depressed.

I have suggested that for Christian psychologists, the Holy Trinity with its perfect balance between the distinct divine persons and the one "ousia" of God provides an ontological grounding for the style of conflict resolution that the Harvard negotiation project and other secular psychologists have recently been commending. We glimpse the social dynamics of the Trinity in Jesus' conversation with the Father on the Mount of Olives before his arrest and crucifixion: "Father, if you are willing, remove this cup from me" (Luke 22:39-44). Jesus clearly states his feelings about the matter of his crucifixion, even when it differs from what the first person of the Trinity has resolved upon. Some in the Christian tradition may maintain that Jesus' resistance arises from his humanity drawing back from physical agony; but it is equally plausible that this is the divine Jesus recoiling from the burden of sin he will bear on the cross. Indeed, if Jesus did not express his difference as the divine Son at this point, we might wonder whether the persons in the Trinity are really distinct. If that difference was ever to come out, it would appear here, and it does.

Christians may be encouraged to the self-communication I have been recommending by considering the divine nature as we know it in Jesus Christ. Not only does God combine individuation and community in God's nature as a trinity of persons; God is also a self-communicator in relation to us. In traditional trinitarian doctrine, God's nature as Father, Son, and Spirit is not merely a way that God appears *to us;* God is not faking for our sake, but is, *in se,* a loving community of persons, and as such reaches out to us to establish our selves in community with God. God's communication is honest and realistic. When we express ourselves honestly with the human others that our personal identity and fulfillment as persons is tied up with, we are, in yet another way, expressing our nature as created in God's image. If not, we are dysfunctional, expressing a distortion of that image.

As Beth became more able to tell George about her opinions and her feelings, their relationship improved and Beth's depression lifted. Simultaneously, I helped George to understand that only if Beth could safely disagree with him without fear of reprisal, would they have a truly healthy marriage. I also pointed out how Beth's depression, resulting from her inability to communicate directly with him, resulted in his "walking on eggshells" around her depression. Thus, he was as much a loser as she. Because they are Christians, I also suggested that they needed to allow for distinct differences just as there are distinct persons in the Trinity. This was a new idea for them, and proved to be motivating.

2. Understand the Other

On the trinitarian model of personhood we are in the fullest sense functioning as persons when we are in communication (communion, fellowship) with one or more distinct other persons. So far we have discussed the importance, for this communion, of making oneself understood by the other. It is equally important to understand the other, not only because no amount of self-expression will result in communication unless the other person understands what you are saying about your opinions and feelings, and you must understand where the other is coming from in order to make yourself understood by him or her, but also because the communion will not be complete if the communication flows in only one direction. Sensitive, empathic "hearing" of the other is thus, in the trinitarian model, essential to mature personality. For this reason a goal of conflict resolution therapy will be to dispose the clients to become more sensitive to, and respectful of, one another's opinions and feelings. Let me again illustrate with a clinical example.

Mike and Mary, who had married later in life (mid-40's), sought marital counseling because of constant conflict. When asked about the issues that divided them, they produced a long laundry list. It soon became apparent that they were both afraid of losing the self-identity each had developed in the long years of singleness (this was the first marriage for both of them). This fear came out whenever either one felt disagreed with. Both somehow felt that if their own opinion did not win the day, they had lost freedom and status. Both, as it turns out, grew up in families where disagreements were not tolerated, and perhaps their slowness to marry stemmed from fear of being in the same type of relationship again.

I aimed to get Mike and Mary to feel comfortable with disagreeing. We reframed differences as good, and pointed out that a disagreement is not a disaffirmation of the other person. This couple responded well to a discussion of the "I" and the "thou." "Mike," I said, "do you realize that if you learn to tolerate Mary's different ideas and figure out ways to accommodate to them that encompass both your ideas and hers, you will also gain yourself, because your 'I' is completed by her as 'thou'? In a sense, Mary is doing you a favor in making you define yourself in relationship to her." Such is the individualism of our culture, that this was a totally new idea for both Mike and Mary. It was not enough, however, merely to tell them that differences were OK. Because of their family backgrounds, each had an immediate knee-jerk reaction to being disagreed with. It was necessary to demonstrate in their *experience* that they would not lose themselves in the conflict. I required Mary and Mike to summarize the content of each other's statements to the other's satisfaction before they proceeded with their own point of view. This prevented the conflict in the discussion from escalating.

Recently, in situations in which a couple is Christian, I have tried linking the experiential exercise of hearing the other as a distinct person and clearly stating one's opinion with the notion of the Trinity as having three distinct persons. This allows some couples to let down their defenses somewhat. Indeed, the impact of this theological lesson is increased when the individuals involved actually experience a human parallel. While a rational structure is necessary for the counseling process, it is not sufficient for change. Experience is also necessary.

Mary and Mike were to deal with a disagreement and I would coach them. Mike chose their conflict process. Notice in the following actual excerpt from a counseling dialogue the following components: (1) Each individual must state clearly what he or she wants and acknowledge that it is his or her idea by using "I" or "Me." This reinforces that individuals are distinct personages in their relationships and that it is legitimate for each to have a distinct viewpoint. (2) Each individual must hear and acknowledge the other's point of view in the conversation. This reinforces that each is not radically autonomous, but must take the other seriously.

Mike starts with an edge in his voice. "I want to be able to come back and discuss an issue at another time, not necessarily right when it happens."

Mary: "You want to come back at another time and talk about the issue."

Mike: "That's not quite right — I want to have the choice to come back later."

Mary summarizes and then says, "It's hard for me. We don't get back to it. We have so much going on. It is not time-efficient for us to do that."

Mike: "You feel we do not come back to it."

Mary: "That's part of it. The other part is that we are both so busy,

I would rather learn how to take care of a problem when it is a problem rather than later. It seems like a waste of time."

Mike: "You are too busy to do it then."

Mary: "It is not that I am too busy; it is a waste of time." (The therapist asked her to say, "I *perceive* it as a waste of time.")

Mike: "I feel it is not possible to deal with it at the time." (The therapist asked him to add, "for me.")

Mary: "You can't deal with it at the time."

Mike: "No! (angrily) I won't be able to deal with it at the time, not that I can't. 'Can't' implies I can never deal with it at the time." (Notice that Mike is angry because he feels he is not being clearly heard and Mary is assuming he is saying something he is not saying.)

At this point I ask each of them to define their words more clearly and understand that the same words might mean different things to each of them.

Mary then repeats and clarifies her summary: "You are saying, at times I choose not to deal with it."

Mike: "That's close enough." (Being heard defuses his anger.)

Mary (upset): "It's like right now, I can say right now I am a little bit agitated, and I am a little bit upset and I don't feel like doing this, but I am doing this."

The therapist reminds Mary to stay with the structure, and also asks her, "Mary, it sounds like you are feeling put off, and saving things for later means some very negative things for you." (Mary is having difficulty clearly stating who she is and what she wants right now.)

Mary: "Yes (tears), when I was growing up, people always attacked each other, and it was as if it was never done. No one ever came back and apologized for it. We never talked about it. This feels like the same thing." Relationships which depart from the balance of the Trinity either disregard the individual person (as in this case) or the group (as with narcissistic individuals). While the temptation is for the therapist and the spouse to give in to her tears, it is important to continue with the process and allow each to express what he or she wants using the summarizing process. Mike is then able to share some of his own early family pain, "When I was growing up, I constantly felt not listened to, and forced to do things I didn't want to do. No one considered my opinion. This feels like the same thing." (Mike's family also did not have a balance between the individual and the group.)

Eventually, but only with both individuals expressing their "I" while respecting the other's "I," the couple was able to arrive at a solution in which the person who broke off the conflict was to come back to the issue within a certain time frame. Both felt good, and both felt they had input into the discussion. Two distinct persons were one in relationship.

Neither was absorbed in the other, but the identity of each included the relationship to the other.

For the Christian psychologist, the ultimate justification for valuing differences among persons and clearly expressing them in the context of a larger unity (community) of persons is again the mutual relationships in the Trinity. We see in Jesus' prayer on the Mount of Olives before the crucifixion not only his clear statement of his own will, but also his honest listening to the will of the Father ("yet not my will but yours be done," Luke 22:42). Jesus, the divine Son who is equal to the Father and not less in status, also chooses to listen, to empty himself and do the will of another, not because of less power, not because of a lower position on a status hierarchy, not because he was less God (though various heresies throughout the ages have asserted these things), but because he was a person in a relationship essential to his identity and was responding in true mutuality. Applying trinitarian psychology (ethics) on the human level, the Apostle enjoins, "Be subject to one another out of reverence for Christ" (Ephesians 5:21; see Laporte, this volume).

3. Adopt a Generous Mode with the Other

Much of the contemporary conflict resolution literature suggests that generosity will also be a useful asset in negotiating conflict. Generosity is expressed in at least three types of behavior. First, it is the willingness to frame all issues positively and inclusively. For example, if a couple disagree over something, rather than say, "We always disagree, and can never get along," it is more useful to say, "Both of us are trying to figure out the best way to arrive at a solution." In other words, always assume that at some level the other person is really trying to get along. This will be true 99% of the time (cf. Heitler, 1990). Second, in the face of strong disagreement from another, generosity means not initially disagreeing with him or her. That will only set up a strong opposition between the two persons. Instead, it is most useful to empathize with the other and summarize his or her position (see previous subsection) before giving one's own position. Third, generosity means to compliment the other on his or her attempt to resolve the conflict. If someone says in a hostile manner, "This is not working, and it's not a very good idea to talk to everyone before making a decision," say something like, "You think having everyone involved in the process will only complicate matters. Your comment shows you are really trying to make this process work. I am glad you feel free to disagree with me. But I feel we would benefit from getting everyone's point of view before continuing, so that everyone will be involved." If the speaker had just said the last sentence, and not the previous ones, the other would be much less likely to listen to the last sentence.

Step to the other's side. Listen to what she has to say, acknowledge her point, feelings, competence, and status, and agree with her whenever possible. Blend the conflict into problem solving. Rather than immediately express disagreement, acknowledge how the other feels; compliment her on bringing up the issue, and then ask her how you can resolve this problem to the satisfaction of both of you. This approach may change a potential standoff into a partnership in problem solving.

The above are of course generous *behaviors* rather than the true spontaneous virtue of generosity. But if practiced as a behavioral structure under a therapist's direction, the behavioral skill will transform, in the context of a growing relationship, into true spiritual generosity. Joyful satisfaction in the relationship and in one's own generous behavior will reinforce the behavior and make it natural. This joy is a psychological power from which generosity comes. Power has traditionally been defined as the ability to influence another (Pfeffer, 1981). However, for process thinkers such as Bernard Loomer (1976), relational power is the ability both to influence and to be influenced by others; it is a characteristic of activity in mutuality. In healthy relationships, individuals both give to each other and receive from each other, and they do so naturally and gladly. Each is enriched and/or partially constituted by the other (cf. also Livezey, 1989), and they are more or less aware of this fact about their relation. I turn now to a final clinical example.

Judy had been sexually abused as a child. Recently an incident of sexual abuse of a young parishioner by one of the pastors of her church came to light, and apparently was covered up by the church authorities. Judy was furious and wanted to leave the church immediately. Jim, however, was puzzled at the intensity of her reaction and saw no need to leave the congregation. Judy was enraged by Jim's refusal to leave the church. Jim said in confusion, "I am not the one who abused you." The marriage festered for a number of months, and at the time I first saw them, Judy had already engaged a divorce lawyer and was ready to leave. Jim had withdrawn into hurt, anger, and confusion, and refused to speak. They saw me only at the urging of Christian friends.

This situation was full of misunderstanding and lack of communication. Neither individual knew the distinctive feelings or concerns of the other. The disregard for distinct persons in the congregation (supposedly for the good of the community) had translated into a disregard for distinct persons at the couple level. There had to be a first step. Judy, with the divorce lawyer in tow, held many of the cards and much of the "power," so she was in a position to take a first step.

My response to Judy was to acknowledge her pain, her anger, and even her right to leave as she felt she had been disregarded and unacknowledged as a distinct hurting person. When I judged that she felt safe enough, I made a suggestion. Below is a shortened version of my comments.

> Judy, you are fully in your rights to leave. I can see where attempting to help someone you see as insensitive as your husband see your point of view, is very painful for you. In fact, I think given the pain of your past abuse, it would be like a cross for you to remain in this situation any longer. I want to suggest that that is exactly where Jesus was in the Garden. He did not want to go to the cross. He was fully within his rights as a distinct person within the Godhead. He could have chosen not to, but for purposes of reconciliation, he chose the cross. This was a choice for him. In fact he, as equal to God, said, "No one takes my life from me, I lay it down myself."
>
> I do not know whether you, as the Christ figure in this situation, as an equal person, equal in authority, would be willing to try the "cross" for the purposes of attempting reconciliation. I think if there is to be any type of reconciliation of interpersonal conflict, there must be a "cross" for all involved. The "cross" for reconciling relationships is the courage to continue stating your own opinion, to hear the other, and to give and take.

After more discussion, Judy was at least willing to try a few more sessions of counseling. Note that her willingness to take the "cross" is not a metaphor for the subordination to which some traditionalists consign women in the marriage relationship. Rather, it is the image of an equal who *chooses* the "cross" as an instrument of reconciliation. Such subordination is inconsistent with the trinitarian psychology that I am advocating, and would have backfired for Judy. Judy needed to be affirmed as an equal in the relationship, one whose choice to bear suffering for the relationship would have the character of *generosity*.

It is important also to realize that for Judy to take the "cross" does not mean acquiescence and quietness. That may also be too easy and will not solve the problem. To take the "cross" means to continue to struggle with the relationship, to listen to the other, and to hold onto herself by making herself heard, saying who she is and what she feels. She had been quiet much too often.

The author of the letter to the Hebrews calls Jesus "the pioneer and perfecter of our faith, who for the joy that was set before him endured the cross, despising the shame . . ." (12:2). The object of his joy is presumably the reconciliation of the world to God. Being God himself, Jesus performs this act of generosity as a *participant*, as one of the parties to the reconciliation. This is not disinterested altruism, but passionate outgoing love. He wants to be reconciled to sinners, and chooses this act as being in his own interest, as well as theirs. Jesus' ontology, which is the background for all true generosity, is that of the *individual who belongs in relationship*. Generosity is giving to the other, and you can do that only as an individual who is in a position to choose and act; but it is an interested giving in which the giver identifies with the recipient. In the cross Jesus gives gifts — to God the Father and to a sinful world — and thus shows himself, in his joy, to "belong" spiritually (though in different ways) to both God and the world.

My therapy with Judy was based on this ontology and aimed at the kind of generosity that we see in God. I was, in effect, trying to facilitate Judy's becoming an imitator of God (Matthew 5:48; 1 Corinthians 11:1). When couples, families, churches, or groups resist this approach of acting generously by listening to the other and suffering for the sake of reconciliation, but instead prefer to remain in a defensive, individualistic stance, I ask them to consider what their alternatives are if they should fail to reach an agreement, and develop the ability to work together. In Jim and Judy's case, it was the realization that failure meant divorce, and the possibility that their little boy would have to experience the pain and damage of their separation. This may seem to some like therapeutic bullying, but from the point of view of trinitarian psychology it has the character of an ontological reminder — this is the kind of beings we are: individuals in relationship. Sitting tight and insisting on our own way has consequences for the quality of our life. For human beings in such cases — and indeed in all cases — failure to give is a failure to be.

Summary

I have presented a way of dealing with conflict based on a conception of personhood that takes its cue from the persons of the Holy Trinity. Just as the persons of the Godhead are distinct persons and yet have their identity in virtue of their relations to the other members of the Godhead, so we as persons are both distinct individuals and beings whose character, personality, and identity are consequences of our relationships with others. This "relational ontology" serves as the basis for an effective conflict resolution process in which the protagonists make themselves clearly heard as individuals, listen carefully to the individuality of others, and generously choose to allow themselves to be defined somewhat in terms of the others for the sake of the others and the relationship.

Parameters of a Christian Psychology

ROBERT C. ROBERTS

And he said to me, "Son of man, eat what is offered to you; eat this scroll, and go, speak to the house of Israel." So I opened my mouth, and he gave me the scroll to eat. And he said to me, "Son of man, eat this scroll that I give you and fill your stomach with it." Then I ate it; and it was in my mouth as sweet as honey.

Ezekiel 3:1-3

Introduction

Psychology's influence on people differs from that of medical technology, which is plenty influential in its own way. Medical treatments of heart disease have given many a new lease on life; we no longer think of heart disease as marking the end of hope. But psychology's impact comes not only from its offer to free us from "problems," to "heal" us, but above all in its promise to edify us, to induct us more deeply into our humanity, by directing us to a richer and more mature life. By-pass surgery may deeply affect our opportunities, but we don't think it makes us different persons, unless we take the experience of surgery to have helped us psychologically. (Perhaps it sobered us about our all-out commitment to money-making, and occasioned a renewed enthusiasm for family and friends.) We may get specific help from our therapist, but we often come away with more than that, something deeper and more exciting. We come away feeling that we have a better grasp of our personal lives.

We have learned from Kierkegaard, with hermeneutical help from Wittgenstein, that the concept of edification is not univocal. An indefinitely large number of outlooks on what it is to be a person and to flourish as a person are possible, each with its own way of diagnosing our troubles, and its own prescriptions for cure. Applying this insight to psychology, we see that there is no such simple thing as *"human* edification," but only Rogerian edification, Jungian edification, Rational-Emotive edification, neo-Freudian edification, varieties of Family-Systems edification — and Christian edification. These edifications bear structural similarities to one another, but they also display, to careful attention, discontinuities and mutual inconsistencies. With Kierkegaard, the Christian thinker will have to say, in answer to each of these psychologies, "either/or."

A psychology edifies by articulating a view of personhood that tells us what makes us tick, by providing encouragement and an "upward call" to a better personality, and by sketching some methods for travelling the distance from where we are as persons to that better state. It gives us a vocabulary, with a distinct conceptual grammar, by which to make sense of ourselves, to see the goal of fulfilled personality, and to prosecute the tasks of our personal quest. These, it seems to me, are features found in any psychology. In the particular grammars of the various psychologies, further similarities and contrasts are also found, and especially differences in the individual and communal personalities that will be "built up" through sustained feeding on the vocabularies in question.

I have examined the grammars of a number of psychotherapies and personality theories and displayed some of their continuities and discontinuities with Christianity (Roberts, 1993). Such clarification is important for the life of the church, insofar as its business is to mold *Christian* personality in people, and thus to avoid forming distinctively Rogerian, Jungian, neo-Freudian, etc., personalities. But the critical task is only one aspect of the work of a Christian psychologist. If the church is to speak to the hunger for edification that the contemporary interest in psychology evidences, inside and outside the church, it must have something more to offer than a critique of current psychologies. It must articulate its own distinctive psychology. Here I shall sketch a Christian psychology, using just biblical materials and without much reference to non-Christian theories. Of course I will have the latter in mind as I develop the biblical ideas, since it is the biblical counterpart of those psychologies that I am trying to develop. But I shall try to pull a psychology straight out of the Christian tradition, rather than "integrate" insights from outside the tradition into Christian thought and practice. It should go without saying that the present paper can only be a sketch, meant to be suggestive for further research and reflection.

Elements of a Psychology

A psychology is a systematically integrated body of thought and practice that includes the following five elements:

1. An account of *basic human nature* answers two kinds of questions. First, What is the teleology of human nature? What are the basic directions or needs of human persons? What are we made for, what would our most fundamental yearnings and interests be if they were fully wise and self-conscious, fully in accord with our essential nature as persons? What is the good which, if we find it, will fulfill or complete us, or at least allow us best to cope with life? These questions will normally be answered only by taking into consideration the kind of world we live in. For example, God's existence must be taken into account, inasmuch as our relation to God is part of our fulfillment. Second, How are human persons structured, most basically? What about us must function properly if our needs are to be met and our inbuilt teleology actualized? Alternatively, how do we break down and fail to realize our good? (I am indebted to Maddi, 1980, for stimulation and insights concerning these two kinds of questions.)

2. A psychology will sketch, or at a minimum imply, a set of *personality traits that characterize a fully functioning, mature person.* In the psychologies of the ancient philosophers, as well as in the Christian tradition, these traits are called "virtues." Modern psychologies imply their own virtues, even when they are not very articulate about them (see Roberts, 1993, Part One). The grammar of these personality ideals is determined by the view of human nature the psychology espouses. Analysis of the grammar of a psychology's virtues reveals, in principle, the structure of the entire psychology. It is especially important for Christian psychologists to notice that psychologies are virtues-systems, since this makes explicit their structural similarity with Christianity, and thus encourages us to articulate a Christian psychology. A detailed exploration of the grammar of the Christian virtues would be a large part of a Christian personality psychology. It would be the kind of richly detailed, and thus compelling, account of personhood that the church needs today.

3. A psychology will describe the *successful development* of personality. How, given the basic structures of human nature and its basic theology and the environment to which it must adapt, does one develop the traits of a mature person? Although simple physical maturation has much to do with it, no psychology I know of thinks this is all there is to it; the account is always "psychological," and this includes interpersonal interaction and its qualities. Human nature is constituted by the structural features of human personality, such as verbivorousness and agency; see below.

4. The obverse of elements two and three is a psychology's *diagnostic scheme*. Corresponding to its list of virtues is a list of vices — neuroses, psychoses, patterns of internal conflict or maladaptation to the environment, dysfunctional traits. And corresponding to its account of correct development is a set of developmental explanations for these vices.

5. A psychology need not actually include a *psychotherapy* — a set of interventions that aim to correct or prevent unhealthy patterns of interaction and traits of personality — but the development of one is natural, and psychologies that arise out of the practices of life can be expected to have at least a rudimentary therapy. Therapeutic interventions do not just come out of the blue, but are implied by, and imply, some account of human nature, some conception of the shape of healthy personality, and an account of development, both healthy and pathological. (Of course in practice the implication may seem to run the other way: one discovers a technique that "works" and then follows out its implications concerning human nature, proper development, etc. But we must ask, Where did the idea of what "works" come from, if not from some at least implicit view of what is proper to human nature?)

Let us turn now to the Bible to sketch the psychology implicit there. We will find information fitting each of the five elements of a psychology; we must interpret these in terms of each other so as to outline a systematic structure regarding the nature, ideals, development, corruption, and repair of personality.

Basic Human Nature

Basic Teleology

The Bible emphasizes three basic directions of human nature: the need to honor, serve, and depend on God as Father; the need to stand in a relationship of mutual dependency and harmony with other human beings; and the need to take care of the creation. Thus human nature is basically "relational," our well-being depending on relationships with God, our human fellows, and the natural world that befit the nature of each of these. The Bible does not put these points in terms of "needs" — that is psychological lingo. Rather, it represents God as commanding us to love him with all our heart, and our neighbor as ourselves, and to be faithful stewards of the creation. But it certainly does depict us as created for these kinds of relationships, and as not flourishing in the highest sense when we violate these commands. Thinking psychologically, we

would say that the symptoms of dysfunction that follow a disregard for
God, or hatred or indifference to one's fellow human beings, or a failure
of proper stewardship of nature, come from being at odds with our very
nature as persons. These are not just affronts to God, humanity, and
nature, but an assault on ourselves, a denial of our true selves and our
deepest needs.

Love of God

The need for God is evidenced in the near ubiquity of religious worship
among human beings. The Apostle Paul interprets the Athenians' motive
for making an altar to an unknown god as a sort of groping after the
true God, and he quotes a pagan poet approvingly as having seen
(through a glass darkly, no doubt) that in God we live and move and
have our being (Acts 17). The Christian will see evidence of the need
for God in the "archaic" demand, that Heinz Kohut notes, for a perfect
ideal self object, and in the claims of people like Anselm and Descartes
that we are equipped with an innate idea of a perfect being. William
James comments:

> the emotion that beckons me on is indubitably the pursuit of an ideal
> social self, of a self that is at least *worthy* of approving recognition by
> the highest *possible* judging companion, if such companion there be.
> This self is the true, the intimate, the ultimate, the permanent Me that
> I seek. This judge is God, the Absolute Mind, the "Great Companion."
> . . . The impulse to pray is a necessary consequence of the fact that
> whilst the innermost of the empirical selves of a man is a Self of the
> *social* sort, it yet can find its only adequate *Socius* in an ideal world.
> (James, 1950, pp. 315-16)

Carl Jung is famous for exploring universal themes, which he takes to
have broadly religious significance, in the mythologies, symbols, and
dreams of culturally diverse peoples. The psychotherapeutic power of
religious experiences, noted by some psychologists, is also evidence.
Augustine's "our hearts find no peace until they rest in you" (1961, Book
I, Chapter 1) is the classic statement, and again we have Jung:

> During the past thirty years, people from all the civilized countries of
> the earth have consulted me. . . . Among all my patients in the second
> half of life — that is to say, over thirty-five — there has not been one
> whose problem in the last resort was not that of finding a religious
> outlook on life. It is safe to say that every one of them fell ill because

he had lost that which the living religions of every age have given to their followers, and none of them has been really healed who did not regain his religious outlook. (Jung, 1933, p. 264)

Never mind that all these evidences can be interpreted otherwise than as supporting a God libido in the human psyche. Never mind that Jung takes his observations, not as evidence of our need for God as Christianity conceives him, but as indicating another "God" that sometimes seems identical with the larger human Self. In underdetermining the conclusion, and requiring a certain framework for its evidential force, this evidence is not so different from other evidence in the social and natural sciences. Christians, at any rate, will see these facts and similar ones as evidence of our need for the Father of Jesus Christ.

Love of Fellows

Some need for human fellowship is widely acknowledged even by the most individualist psychologies. Rarer is assent to a need for the *kind* of fellowship that Christianity calls for — one in which we deeply identify with others, weeping with those who weep and rejoicing with those who rejoice, dying to self in humility for one another's sake, bearing one another's burdens and laboring in harmony, yoked together in the service of one greater than we. Non-Christian psychologists are likely to see "enmeshment" and an immature lack of "individuation" in the social relations that, in the Christian view, the human psyche needs. (For an exception to this generalization, see Boszormenyi-Nagy & Krasner, 1986.) This disagreement reflects, of course, a different vision of what human beings basically are and need, a vision likely to intimidate Christians if we are not very clear about our own psychology. Is there any evidence for the Christian view? We do fairly often see an approximation to the kind of mutual identification that the Bible calls "love" operating in families, and I think it is pretty clear that a sort of fulfillment exists here, in this belonging and self-giving service, that is lacking in more instrumental relationships (see Martin, this volume). We might also point to the therapeutic power of a biblically faithful congregational fellowship, which often is a powerful kind of psychotherapy.

Nurture of Nature

Christians will see evidence of the stewardship tendency in the familiar circumstance of people taking unpretentious and unacquisitive joy in tending their gardens, growing livestock, and keeping pets. In its most immediate form this stewardship involves hands in the dirt and on the plants and animals. Stewardship can and must take the form of management, but it seems to me that psychologically such management must be based, in the individual memory, on immediate nurturance of natural things. In the Christian psychology people find fulfillment in this respectful, responsible use of nature because they themselves are natural beings, but are also "little less than God" (Ps. 8:5), quasi-creators themselves, appointed to this responsibility by the Creator. The stewardship need finds fulfillment neither in the worship of nature nor in the heedless rape of it. Romantics who find in nature a vital spiritual force and a source for their own personal vitality are not wrong, though they may recognize less clearly than they ought that the wonder of nature derives from the beauty of God. The capitalist idea that we own our pieces of nature and can do with them whatever we please is a perversion of stewardship. This is dominion, all right, but a falsely absolute lordship.

We will no doubt want to explore other basic tendencies of human nature that are posited or suggested by the biblical witness. The fact that human beings are made in the "image" of God the Creator suggests exploring, in biblical terms, the human tendency to acts of creation — especially artistic and technological inventions. Paul Vitz emphasizes (see Vitz, 1987a) the human fulfillment that comes from pursuing parenthood, biological and otherwise, suggesting that we also image God's status as Parent. And Rebecca Propst (this volume) explores the way that a dialectic between individuality and sociality reflects the relatedness within the Holy Trinity.

Basic Structures

As I have read the Bible looking for psychology, six basic structural characteristics of human personality have stood out. These are (1) that human beings are verbivorous, (2) that we are agents with limited freedom, (3) that we have an "inward" dimension highly important for personality, (4) that our selfhood is determined by what we love, (5) that persons are permeable by other persons, and (6) that we associate or dissociate ourselves from parts of ourselves. These structures of the psyche will serve to explain how people's personalities develop — that is, how they come, as adults, to actualize their basic teleology or, on the other hand, to fail to actualize it, developing instead perversions of this in-built good.

Verbivorousness

In Deuteronomy 8 Moses tells the people that human beings do not live by bread alone, but by every word that proceeds from the mouth of the Lord. Whoever feeds on the word of God lives; whoever does not take this word into himself, ruminate upon it, swallow it and digest it into his very psyche, starves himself as truly as he would if he quit eating physical food. Moses seems to have God's commandments especially in mind, but it is clear from other parts of Deuteronomy that stories — especially the one about the deliverance from Egypt — are food on which the people of God nourish themselves, come to know who they are, take on the character of God's people, and come to love the Lord with all their hearts and their Hebrew neighbors as themselves. And of course in the Old Testament the commandments and the stories are intertwined with many other forms of discourse: expressive exclamations concerning God's attributes, attitudes, and deeds in the Psalms and elsewhere; prayers, prophetic warnings and promises; proverbs, instructions for specific actions, explanations of people's behavior, allegories, parables, and much more. These are inseparable from what the postbiblical church calls "theology" — more or less didactic comments about God's nature and his relation to the human and nonhuman creation. In the New Testament the emphasis on the formative power of the word of God is just as strong, but now the word is the gospel, the word about Jesus Christ — which again has many of the forms just identified.

In being verbivorous, humans are unique among the earth's creatures. We have a different kind of life than nonverbal animals, a kind of life that we can call generically "spiritual." Since we become what we are by virtue of the stories, the categories, the metaphors and explanations in terms of which we construe ourselves, we can become spiritual Marxians by thinking of ourselves in Marxian terms, spiritual Jungians if we construe ourselves in Jungian terms, and so forth. It is because we are verbivores that the psychologies have the "edifying" effect on us that I noted at the beginning of this paper: They provide diagnostic schemata, metaphors, ideals for us to feed upon in our hearts, in terms of which our personalities may be shaped into one kind of maturity or another.

Our nature as word digesters suggests a partial explanation of our nature as God-needers. In distress about the very nature of the world, Solomon cries "Vanity of vanities," and offers a diagnosis: He wouldn't feel this way were it not for his *wisdom*. And wisdom, in the book of Ecclesiastes, is the ability to take the world in whole, to see that a generation goes and a generation comes, that what has been is what will be, that there is nothing new under the sun, that all achievement succumbs to oblivion, that everything is swallowed up in death. (That is why his prescription is to imitate the animals: Eat and drink; enjoy your work and your spouse; you won't much remember the days of your life because God will distract you with simple joys. The prescription, however, does not seem wholly successful.) Solomon's yearning for immortality is not the Christian thirsting for eternal life; it is too crass for that, looking more for retention of property and achievements than for the "righteousness" of enjoying God and God's human creatures. There is an incompleteness here. We can see in Solomon's desire a perverse or immature expression of the need for God and his kingdom, whose mature and true counterpart is the hungering and thirsting for righteousness that Jesus refers to. But neither of these desires is possible for a being who cannot grasp its life as a whole, in conception or imagination; and this ability seems to depend on the ability to assimilate words in the construction of the self.

Agency

On the biblical view of persons, we are self-determining agents, but our psychologically real options are bounded by the inertia of character (good or bad) and by facts (in particular, the structures of creation and the acts of God and other people). It is assumed that we are responsible for such "passions" as lust, anger, and covetous desire, on the one side, and love, compassion, and gratitude, on the other. Our actions not only express our character, but also form it, so that we contribute to the inertia of character by our own undertakings. We are thus responsible for what we are as well as for what we do. Our verbivorousness is a ground of our freedom, because possibilities of being and action otherwise inaccessible to us are presented in our speech and in our ruminations and digestions of it. Speech presents objects of love and hate, and reasons for both, and so makes real potentialities of our hearts that would remain mere remote potentialities without it. The word of God enables us to see possibilities, without the seeing of which we would lack the real options needed for our freedom. We are liberated from our bondage to sin by a word of grace that declares we have been made righteous in Christ. And thereby actions become open to us that would otherwise have remained in the dark night of pure potentiality.

The narrative of a life, in the Pauline psychology, is a story of "slaveries" (Rom. 6). Progress, or personal growth, is a movement from one slavery to another: from being slaves of sin to being slaves of righteousness. In between is something like the "free will" so highly regarded by our contemporaries, the power of *basic* self-determination. (I stress "basic" because Paul does not hold that very good or very bad people are *generally* slaves in their agency; both the saint and the reprobate have many options, but they do not have the option of choosing to be good or evil.) In Paul's view moral free will is a transition, helped along by a kind of action that he calls "yielding" (παριστάναι), from having unholy "passions" to having holy ones. Having been struck to the heart by the gospel, yet without having been fully sanctified, I am neither a complete slave to sin nor a complete slave to righteousness. My affections are indeterminate enough that I can "go either way" — sin still has its attractions, but so does the life of the kingdom. Thus I have free will with respect to good and evil (though even the good that I choose may be tinged with evil desires). Having one foot in each world, I am in a position to yield to the one *or* the other, in a way that the reprobate, whose mind is totally darkened by sin, cannot, and the saint, who can no longer see any attraction in the life of sin, cannot either.

This demotion of the freedom of moral choice to the status of an interim condition far short of the ideal contrasts with a prominent ideology in our culture, which makes the individual, in the ideal case, one who at every moment freely chooses his own destiny and his own self. In the interest of such freedom Sartre (1956) is willing to make us a "nothingness," Rorty (1989) revels in the "contingency" of the constitution of our selves, and Frankfurt (1988) makes freedom of the will a matter of *our* choosing whatever will is to be our own. By contrast, in the Christian psychology we are always a "somethingness" because we are always in love with something, either for good or for evil — to be a person at all is to be formed, to have character, inertia, and dispositions. Our true nature is not contingent, but established in the order of creation and the nature of our God; and perfect freedom is so to love God and his kingdom as to be slaves who "can do no other."

Marital chastity is one way of being a slave of righteousness. The chaste married Christian (as contrasted with the merely self-controlled person) does not choose chastity anew each day, does not decide whether or not she will be faithful to her spouse. Instead, she has been so "gripped" by the vision of life in God's kingdom, she so loves righteousness, the life that God has called her to, that she finds the prospect of marital infidelity positively repugnant. If she finds it repugnant not just occasionally and depending on circumstances, but steadily and regularly and independently of circumstance, then chastity is a Christian virtue in her. It is part of the constitution of her self, and it means that in this respect, at least, her will is not free: she cannot (psychologically) choose unrighteousness, for she is a slave of righteousness.

The radical behaviorists, in contrast with the radical libertarians, deny that we are agents at all: we are just conditioned responders to the stimuli that impinge on us from our environment. This psychology seems to depend on systematically ignoring that as verbivorous we are seers of options, transcenders of our environment with their stimuli, beings who can "play" with the stimuli, investing them with indefinitely many different meanings.

Inwardness

In addition to an "outward," publicly observable dimension — our body, with its "behaviors" — we have a less publicly observable dimension, the character of which we can often hide, at least in part, from our fellow human beings. In this inward dimension, which the Bible calls the "heart" or "mind," are found our wishes, cares, intentions, plans, motives, emotions, thoughts, attitudes, and imaginings. Jesus is critical of people who put on an outward show of virtue, but whose inwardness is corrupt (Matt. 15:1-9), and he commends behaviors that minimize the temptation to do for public display and human praise what should be done out of honor and obedience to God (Matt. 6:2-6, 16-18). God discerns the states of our hearts and rejoices in our pure thoughts and proper motives (1 Pet. 3:3-4). God's word (Rom. 10:8), as well as Christ himself (Gal. 2:20), can be "in" a person's inwardness (more on this below). Proper personhood as actualized in the Christian virtues, by consequence, is not merely a set of dispositions to behave properly, but above all a rightly qualified inwardness — patterns of thought, wish, concern, emotion, and intention shaped by the Christian story and the truths about God, ourselves, and the world, that follow from that story.

Our second basic structural feature of human nature was the fact that we are agents, beings who undertake actions and do so with a degree of freedom and responsibility. Most of the "mental events" that I have mentioned as constituting our inwardness might seem classifiable as passions rather than as actions. But I think the biblical psychology doesn't distinguish strictly here. When Jesus says that it's what proceeds from a person, rather than what enters him, that corrupts (Mark 7:14-23), he seems to suggest that at least some of the evil thoughts, coveting, licentiousness, envy, pride, etc., are states we produce voluntarily. In most cases it would be going too far to say that emotions and wishes are actions, but still, they often result from our actions, and we can intentionally foster or curb them. (Perhaps Paul refers to this when he speaks of "yielding.") Some of these actions will be purely "inward" — not at all behavioral. For example, if I find myself lusting after a woman, and intentionally dispel this urge by reflecting on my marriage vows and remembering some wonderful thing about my wife, or by attending to God's presence within me, my action may have no behavioral element at all. On the other hand, if my children (or I) are short on that inward reverence for nature that forms part of the Christian virtue of stewardliness, I may foster it by getting us out into the dirt in the springtime, nurturing a little plot of nature and watching it grow. Here inwardness is served by outward behavior.

The Bible doesn't speak thematically about unconscious mental states, though we might take some encouragement from the fact that dreams play a significant role in a number of biblical narratives. If a chief mark of our inwardness is its potential to be hidden, then unconscious mental states have a double claim to this status — they are likely to be hidden not only from others but also from ourselves (see Jer. 17:9). A Christian psychology will countenance unconscious mental states because they are so useful in explaining things: emotional phenomena, the effectiveness of self-examination, the unacknowledged drive to worship God, and the phenomena of self-deception that are so important to a psychology of sin, to mention just a few things.

Attachment

The Bible emphasizes that personality is determined by the character of what one loves. This point is most succinctly summed up in Jesus' comment, "Where your treasure is, there will your heart be also" (Matt. 6:21). Your heart is your inward self, your personality, the actual "you"; and what you treasure — what is important to you, what you love, what you are centrally attached to — determines what that self is like. This seems to suggest that a self is not "self-contained," on the Christian psychology, but is essentially oriented to things "outside" itself, whether these be healthy or unhealthy objects of its absorption. If we conjoin this structural feature with the first two basic directions of human nature — the needs to live in harmonious fellowship with God and our fellow human beings — we can see that the double commandment that you shall love the Lord with all your heart and your neighbor as yourself is not just an "ethical" command, but a prescription for psychic health, for fulfillment of our psychological nature. Since the most worthy object of praise is God, it stands to reason that the fully developed self will be oriented to God by a love commensurate with its object; God is the one who ought to orient a person's *whole* life, and is thus the one who must be loved with *all* your heart. "A second [commandment] is like it": You shall also be oriented by the goodness that is in your neighbor. The neighbor is of course not good in the way God is; his goodness derives from God's. But each of us seems to have a native disposition to see goodness in himself, and the commandment is saying: See that same goodness in your neighbors; care about them in the way you care about yourself, and in this too you will find yourself.

We can see how central, absorbing attachments have ramifications throughout the personality if we think of personality as dispositions of what I earlier called "inwardness." Emotions are construals of the world in various kinds of terms (depending on the grammar of the emotion in question) *as they impinge on some care or love of the subject* (see Roberts, 1988b; for analysis of how some emotional dispositions enter into the constitution of virtues, see Roberts, 1992a). Desires, urges, and wishes, insofar as they are characteristic of a person, also reflect underlying commitments and directed concerns. Our loves also direct our plans, our thoughts, our imaginings. (For more analysis of the concept of attachment, see my article on attachment, this volume.)

Self-association and Self-dissociation, and Permeability

I shall treat the fifth and sixth basic structures together, since they are so closely interwoven. One striking feature of the New Testament psychology is the willingness to multiply selves, to speak of the new self and the old self, the "inmost self" and the "flesh," etc. Another, related feature is that one person can permeate or be "in" another: Christ can be "in" the believer, the believer can be "in" Christ, Christ is "in" the Father, the Father is "in" Christ, the Holy Spirit dwells "in" the believer. At one point, Paul talks almost as though Christ's self replaces his own as he becomes more sanctified: "I have been crucified with Christ; it is no longer I who live, but Christ who lives in me" (Gal. 2:20). But in the sequel he makes it clear that he has not really disappeared, ceding his body to a reincarnated Christ: "And the life I now live in the flesh I live by faith in the Son of God, who loved me and gave himself for me." So it is Paul who lives after all, but it is a different Paul, who associates himself with Christ who is now "in" him. The Paul who lived independently of Christ has died (though as we will see in a moment, he is still present, dissociated from Paul).

Heinz Kohut's concept of a self object (Kohut & Wolf, 1978) gives us a model for understanding how one person can dwell in another. In interacting with our parents, we take them into our self, into our "heart," to use Paul's word. As potential selves, we are hungry for a sense of our own worth, and in their approval, their empathy, their enthusiasm for us, we see our worth "mirrored." We are also hungry for orientation in "moral space" (the term is borrowed from Taylor, 1989), for a sense of the direction of our life, a sense of what we are to be and do. By identifying ourselves with our parents, we get a free ride on their ideals (see Talbot, this volume). In these ways, we "incorporate" our parents into our psyches. In Jesus Christ God presents himself to us as accepting, merciful, forgiving, nurturing, respectful, empathic — as a "mirroring self object." We come to see our value reflected in God's love. Thus we become a self in a quite different way than we would be apart from the gospel; our self is *constituted* of God's regard for us. At least, this is one of our selves, on the Pauline psychology, indeed the truest one, the one with which we ought to associate ourselves. And the bestowal of this self does not just satisfy a generalized need to be loved but the specific need to be loved by God. As God thus dwells in our hearts, we become spiritually his children. In being addressed with God's love and thus identified as God's children, we are also called to do his work, to live a certain life, to pursue certain goals. ". . . and if children, then heirs, heirs of God and fellow heirs with Christ, *provided we suffer with him* . . ." (Rom. 8:17). In this too we identify ourselves, and thus are formed as selves, in his terms. God our Abba becomes to us an ideal-bearing self object as well. We take on God's goals as our own, and thus find in ourselves divine value and divine orientation, a self that was not there before. It is clear that the self object — human or divine — "dwells in" us in this sense through the power of association, because we associate ourselves, identify with, the divine or human parent. As Christians we grow by associating ourselves with the new self that has been created by God's loving address.

We see the phenomenon of self-association at work in marriages as well. A young husband will find that he has two selves, an old bachelor self that is uncommitted, unattached; and a married self that belongs to this particular woman. Each self has its own behavioral- and emotional-response repertoire, its own sense of identity. The young husband may find himself, at certain moments, confused about which set of dispositions to associate himself with and may have to "yield" to the one or the other. This yielding may be by default, or he may quite intentionally choose *not* to "go with the flow" and choose instead to associate himself with his wife and his married self. As the marriage matures, and he matures as a husband, his unmarried self will die or at least fade to a mere ghostly presence. A negative example of the phenomenon is the son who keeps seeing, to his dismay, traits of his father in his demeanor and affect, and consciously dissociates himself from them, saying to himself, as it were, "that's not me, not the *real* me." Part of my point is that this need not be "denial" in the sense of dishonesty; it may, instead, be a creative or constitutive denial, an act that brings about a psychological reality: that these dispositions inherited from the father gradually cease to be part of the individual's real self.

I think that Kohut's neo-Freudian psychology can help us understand one person's indwelling another, but the biblical concept also differs significantly from his. The Gospel of John talks volubly about the Father being in the Son and the Son in the Father, and the Father and the Son being in the disciples, and the disciples in the Father and the Son. But the one relationship that is not described in terms of indwelling is that between ordinary human beings; in the NT, indwelling always involves at least one divine person. We do not hear of Paul being "in" Barnabas, or anybody's mother or father being "in" him, etc., though of course Christians are "members one of another," and this comes close to some idea of being "in" one another. I think we have to admit that the parent does not *really* indwell the child; it is rather the child's *impression* of the parent, in the form of impressions of memory, that is carried off by the child, and with which the child may or may not associate himself. This impression is a disposition of construal, disposing the child to construe himself, as well as both his actual parent and other "parent figures," in certain ways. When Jesus (John) and Paul speak of Christ dwelling in us, or us dwelling in Christ, or Christ dwelling in the Father or the Father in Christ, the expression is not metaphorical. It is Christ who is in the Father, and the Father himself who is in Christ, and it is Christ himself who dwells in us. This is possible because Christ is God, and God can be literally and always present to or in anyone; while human beings, when they are absent from one another, can only be "present" to one another in some metaphorical sense. Thus the indwelling of Christ or the Holy Spirit is a kind of fellowship, a real present relationship between God and the believer.

Indwelling, then, seems to have the following characteristics: (1) it is a positive relationship between two or more distinct individuals; (2) in Pauline and Johannine usage, at least one of the individuals must be divine, though we can imagine a metaphorical extension of the concept to relationships between mere human beings; (3) the identity of each individual is profoundly and centrally affected by the indwelling (or "indwelling") of the other(s); (4) somewhat more speculatively, the indwelling is conditioned on the indwelt person's associating himself or herself (voluntarily or involuntarily, consciously or unconsciously) with the indwelling person.

Thus Christ indwells people who associate themselves with him, and thus with the new self that loves Christ and regards itself as loved by him. But when Paul speaks of sin dwelling in him (Rom. 7:7-25), he *dis*sociates himself from it. Two Pauls coexist here, one that delights in the law of God and wants to do the good, and another that is in servitude to sin and lacks respect for the law. The one Paul is a "body of death" to the other. But there is no doubt which one is the real Paul: "I myself serve the law of God." He even goes so far as to suggest that he himself is not sinful, but is derailed by an alien power: "Now if I do what I do not want, it is no longer I that do it, but sin which dwells within me" (v. 20). Most of us do not experience sin as such an alien principle, because we do not dissociate ourselves so radically from our sin as Paul does. We "dwell in" it, uneasily perhaps, or with only one foot; but we identify with it to some extent. And the reason for this, I think, is that we do not associate ourselves as strongly with Christ as Paul does. It is Paul's passionate seriousness about Christ, and the strong sense he has of belonging to Christ, of being "in" Christ, that gives him the impression that sin does not belong to him — that is, not to the real Paul, not to Paul's "inmost self." And this is not just Paul's "impression," but a true perception of Paul's situation, a perception of it from God's point of view.

These six features — verbivorousness, agency, inwardness, attachment, association/dissociation, and permeability — are among the central "structures" of personality as it is conceived in the Bible and especially in the New Testament. These are the "mechanisms" by which personality is formed, for better or for worse.

Maturity

In addition to an account of basic human nature, any personality theory will have, or at least imply, a description of the ideally well-formed personality. Since a personality is made up of traits, this description will in essence be a list of ideal personality characteristics, traditionally known as virtues, along with an account of the particular "grammar" of each of these traits. In the Christian psychology, these traits are faith, hope, love, joy, peace, gratitude, compassion, contrition, tenderheartedness, patience, meekness, truthfulness, forgivingness, forbearance, contentment, kindness, gentleness, self-control, humility, confidence, obedience, holiness, hospitality, wisdom, stewardliness, perseverance, generosity, peaceableness, and others. Since these virtues fit a person to live a proper human life, and since that life must always be lived in some context or other — in a "world" which presents particular problems of living — the traits will be at once actualizations of basic human nature, and modes of adaptation to the setting in which one's life is lived out. For example, if one of the basic psychological needs of human nature is loving communion with God, a number of the traits of mature personality will involve and facilitate this love relationship. But equally, if the world in which we are to live out this communion is frequently characterized by dangers, temptations, offenses, and irritations, then the mature person must be equipped with courage, self-control, forgivingness, and forbearance, as modes of adaptation to these features of the world. The Christian virtues adapt us for life in two contexts: the kingdom of God, and this present imperfect world. Hope, for example, is a partial realization of our need for divine and human love; but it also has central features making it quite specific to the conditions of *this* world, which is *not* the kingdom of God.

I believe this brief summary of the basic needs and structures that Christianity ascribes to human nature begins to indicate the distinctiveness of the Christian psychology. This distinctiveness, though, may be obscured by the fact that most of the words for the Christian virtues are shared by other psychologies. Contentment and peace are also virtues in both Stoicism and its twentieth-century update — Rational-Emotive Therapy. Courage is a virtue much touted by existentialist psychology, self-control is a frequent aim of behavior therapy, Jungian individuation can be read as a form of humility (see Roberts, 1993, chapter 6), and so forth. These facts might lead us to think these psychologies are promoting the same personality traits that the church attempts to nurture, and it seems that much of the Christian clergy has uncritically adopted the theories and methods of the psychologists. I have argued (Roberts, 1993) that a psychology's personality ideal is conceptually tied to its other precepts — especially to its view of basic human nature, which after all is what gets actualized in the virtues, but also to its diagnostic constructs, its theory of development, and its practices of therapy.

The virtues projected by a psychology possess a "grammar" — a structure or logic; and we will not know very precisely what kind of hearts and souls are promoted by a psychology, and how these compare with Christian personality, unless we represent that grammar perspicuously. (On the idea of the grammar of a virtue, see Roberts, 1991.) Christian psychology has a special interest in articulating the structure of its personality ideal, because it is more aware than most psychologies of human verbivorousness and the "edifying" function of psychologies; and of all the dimensions of a psychology, it is perhaps the personality ideal that functions most powerfully in edification. The more articulate we can become about the grammar of the Christian virtues, the less easily will we fall captive to other personality ideals.

How do the Christian virtues reflect, or partake of, the basic needs and structures that Christianity ascribes to the human psyche? What follows is far from a detailed grammar of the Christian virtues, which would need to take the virtues more or less one at a time and would elaborate on more connections. (I have attempted grammatical accounts of a number of Christian virtues in Roberts, 1983, 1984a, and 1993.) I make just a few remarks about a couple of virtues, suggesting a few of the many connections that would have to be elaborated in a well-developed Christian psychology.

Stewardliness is the fulfillment of the human need to nurture nature, but in its fullest expression it is a consciousness of doing this for God, in obedience to him and in appreciation of his goodness. In this way it is also a fulfillment of the need to love and be approved by God, to be allied to God, to identify with God by joining him in his projects. A psychotherapy that prescribes gardening or animal husbandry as "occupational therapy" would not inculcate the *Christian* virtue of stewardliness, even if it managed completely to dispel the client's depression by getting him enthusiastically involved with the rabbits, if it did not also manage to get him to see this work as an obedient alliance with God's purposes.

Humility is a disposition to perceive oneself as basically equal with any other human being, even if the other is conspicuously superior or inferior to oneself in looks, intelligence, skill, or social status. Since we are inclined to stress our superiorities to others and take pleasure in them, and to experience emotional pain at "not measuring up," the development of humility may be a painful process of dying to self. But if it is a basic need of our nature to love and be loved by some fellow humans in frank, open, joyful, non-instrumental fellowship, then humility is a formula for fulfillment. A psychology with an individualistic or egoistic conception of basic human nature — such as we have from Albert Ellis or Sigmund Freud — will either have no place for humility in its personality ideal, or the humility that it does commend will have a different grammar from Christian humility.

As to our verbivorousness, it is clear that none of the Christian virtues is possible, in its fullness, apart from the self-understanding and understanding of the social and natural world that is generated by Christian discourse — the stories, the commandments, the theology of our tradition. All of the Christian virtues derive their grammar from the gospel and its Old Testament antecedents; their distinctiveness is largely a matter of their "cognitive content"; they are "theological"; they involve taking the word to heart. It is part of the grammar of all the Christian virtues that individuals (at least "normal" ones) can be morally praised for possessing them and blamed for lacking them; they are, or have been, broadly, within the purview of our agency and responsibility. Yet they are all inertial, too — they are dispositions, powers, that have a now irreversible history; the states of our inwardness that exemplify them are initially passions rather than actions. In all of our virtues — as well as our vices — we are that paradoxical mixture of agent and slave. In con-

nection with our verbivorousness I have noted that virtues all involve
an understanding of ourselves and our world; they are not just dispositions to behave in certain ways — say, hoeing the garden, burping forth
true propositions, taking in guests — but to do these things and much
else for certain reasons, with certain attitudes. What I have called our
inwardness is thus absolutely crucial to our personalities' having a grammar at all. The Bible suggests that the character of our selfhood is a
function of our attachments — the goal of life, insofar as it is to become
a proper person, is to get attached to the right things in the right way.
This supposition lies behind the double commandment: If you wish to
become what you were created to be, you must be passionately, wholeheartedly attached to God, and you must be concerned about your neighbor and involved in his life and well-being in much the way that you
are concerned about your own well-being. Again, virtually all of the
Christian virtues either are, or presuppose, the attachment to God and
neighbor; this is a pervasive feature of their grammar, and one that
distinguishes them from the virtues projected by individualistic psychologies, which tend to emphasize *de*tachment from things and persons
as an avenue of freedom and thus fulfillment. And lastly, the Christian
personality ideal differs, in its structure, even from that of psychologies
that emphasize attachment, in this mysterious feature of the mature
personality's being a constant inward fellowship with God, with Christ,
with the Holy Spirit. The Christian virtues are forms of that presence to
God which the New Testament expresses with the little word "in" —
they are Christ in you and you in him.

Development

Any psychology must have a story to tell about how personality is grown
into, and this will be a story of how the child's — and also the adult's —
social environment interacts with the basic structural and teleological
features of his psyche to produce, or fail to produce, the virtues projected
by that psychology.

Human verbivorousness implies that our psyches will in fact feed
on narratives and outlooks and theories and metaphors that are particularly insistent, salient, or otherwise fetching. Accordingly, the Christian
psychologist will be especially alert to the developmental significance of
stories and philosophies of life with which the child in a pluralistic culture
is bound to be bombarded. The Bible as a whole forms a sort of supernarrative, composed of other narratives as its parts. The supernarrative might
be outlined thus:

We the human race were created with certain potentials and fell away from these into alienation from God and one another; yet God has nursed us along through these millennia, forming for himself a representative people in the children of Israel and abiding with them through spiritual and political vicissitudes. In the person of the Son, God became incarnate as a human son of this appointed people and more generally of the human race. The Son identified with us even to the point of "becoming sin" for our sake and dying the death of a criminal, so that we might be made righteous before God in him, whom God raised from the dead. Insofar as we are "in" him and he is "in" us, we are accounted as sinless before God, and look forward to the consummation of our perfection in the world to come.

The narrative thus sketched is the most basic form of that "word" in terms of which Christians understand themselves as persons, and which, consequently, forms them as persons. If a person's formation is to be psychologically correct, the teaching needs to be kept "original," not deformed by various kinds of psychological, philosophical, and religious reinterpretations.

It is part of the grammar of the Christian word that it is itself a personal communication, the voicing of God's own love to the hearer. The Christian stories and forms of teaching should be so presented that they speak to the "heart" of the child, to evoke a response of love and contrition. The faith has a rhetoric as well as a grammar. The word of God should be presented "psychologically," so it becomes clear to the child how this word applies to his own heart. This means that the parents or guardians should reflect in their own demeanor towards the child the nurturing love ascribed to God, and expressed by God in the word, and their demeanor should reflect also the orientation by God's word and devotion to him that is implied by his being God. The parents, speaking to the child's need for loving fellowship with God and humanity, are in fact "priests" to the child. In nursing the infant, in changing her diapers, in holding her and reading stories to her, in manifesting joy at her successes and growth, the Christian parents understand themselves as reflecting the nature of God to the child, and they verbalize this as the child gains understanding. Thus, through the word, the child's world is larger than the family, or the society, or indeed, than the physical universe. This word also provides important parameters for the child's self-articulation in a narrower, more psychological sense. Part of the Christian word is itself a personality theory; it is the teaching that we need God, that we are made for fellowship with him and our human brothers and sisters, that we develop through listening to God's word, and so on. The word readies the child to see these features of himself in his own behavior and feelings and thus to be built up in characteristically Christian ways. Since the Christian virtues are in large measure a matter of inwardness, it will be a chief function of Christian discourse to articulate, and thus to shape, the individual's awareness of his own attitudes, emotions, and motivations, both proper and sinful. The child will be encouraged to get in touch with his feelings, his unconscious yearnings, his needs for God, human fellowship, and stewardly activities, as well as his anger, his disobedience, his cruelty, his pride and envy, his competitiveness. He will be encouraged to set his mind on the things of the Spirit, to associate himself with Christ and dissociate himself from sin. He will be taught awareness of Christ's presence with and in him; and also awareness of sin's presence in him, yet also its alienness from his inmost self.

In accordance with our nature as agents, we develop as persons by doing things "on our own," by being given responsibility and left to undertake actions ourselves, as well as by being trained in how to act, and being encouraged (largely through modeling) in the loves and emotions that function as motives to our actions. Since we are not only socially embedded, dependent creatures of "habit" and "passion," but also responsible agents, the proper development of a child requires the parent to respect the child's growing autonomy and initiative, and to "back off" and let the child have some responsibility. The parent who does too much for the child, or who sets too strict a limit on the child's choice-making, will stifle the child's agency and leave him fundamentally frustrated, just as readily as the parent who loads him with responsibilities he is not yet ready for. Guided freedom, measured to the child's stage of maturity, is the formula for what is needed (see Neal, this volume). In guiding the child toward actions that exemplify the Christian virtues, the Christian parent will be oriented by the grammar of those virtues and thus by the three basic targets of human nature, to love God and neighbor and responsibly shape the nonpersonal created world.

Diagnostic

Perhaps you have felt uneasy with the Christian psychology I've been sketching, because I have made so little reference to sin, a concept quite central to the biblical picture of human persons. My reason is that the scheme of exposition has been to start with basic human nature and to derive a Bible-spirited account of maturity, development, diagnosis, and therapy from that. Sin is not a part of basic human nature. Furthermore, we are not really in a position to understand what sin is unless we know

what that nature is of which sin is a perversion, what the proper completion of that nature would look like, and how a proper development of
personality would go. The concept of sin belongs in the diagnostic aspect
of a Christian psychology of personality. It is in part a *summary concept* for
a variety of perversions of human nature, traits of personality failure
(enmity, strife, cruelty, and hatred instead of love, forgiveness, gentleness,
and peaceableness; anxiety and distrust instead of faith and peace; pride
and envy instead of humility and proper joy and confidence; etc.). In part
the concept of sin is a set of *explanations* of those perversions, an account
of how they come about (sinning begets sin). The diagnostic part of a
Christian psychology will be a conceptual-psychological exploration of
the structure or dynamic of these vices, and will develop, out of the
resources provided by the Christian account of human nature, an explanation (as far as explanation is possible) of these pathologies.

Given Christianity's relational view of human nature as harmonious interaction with God, fellow persons, and nature, the basic paradigm
of personality corruption will be that of alienation from God, fellow persons, and nature. Persons are dysfunctional to the extent that they refuse
to submit to God and acknowledge him as Lord and wish to occupy his
place in the scheme of things (disobedience, unfaith, anxiety, ingratitude,
pride, envy); and to the extent that they fail to love and live in harmony
with their human brothers and sisters (cruelty, indifference to suffering,
injustice, grudge-bearing, pride, self-centeredness, stinginess, arrogance,
envy); to the extent that they lack due regard for, appreciation of, and care
for the natural world (greed, a sense of ultimate ownership, insensitivity).
Of course, much of this corruption is not just behavioral, but motivational
and emotional — a corruption of our inwardness.

We can generate explanations of sin out of the various structural
features of human nature. In light of our nature as agents, we explain sin
by saying that we chose it, we did it, and thus corrupted ourselves by our
own actions. We are responsible for our own dysfunction. C. Plantinga
includes both the relational dimension of sin that I mentioned in the last
paragraph, and the reference to agency, in his definition of sin as culpable
shalom breaking (this volume; and more extensively, Plantinga, 1994). But
the "we" is not just the individual "I"; we are led into corruption and
dysfunction and sin by others' sin. We are modeled in it, taught its doctrines, and provoked to it by other agents. Not only is sin grounded in
agency; but our agency is affected, from the first, by sin. In light of our
verbivorousness, we can say that sin is caused by feeding on "words" that
are other than, and contrary to, the word of God — person-corrupting
words, words lacking truth about our nature and the nature of our world,
words that encourage pride and envy and a sense of despair about the

state of the world, words that deny our responsibility for our condition or our dependency on one another and on God, words that encourage us to be selfish, and words that obscure the fact that we are brothers and sisters. All this can be quite subtle and hard to recognize, and psychologies are sometimes as much infused with these perverting words as the advertising and journalism and family myths that naturally come to mind when we think of this sort of thing. Since our character is determined by what we love, it stands to reason that vicious states of personality are caused by false loves — inordinate loves, loving the creature as though it were God, making into "hypergoods" (see Taylor, 1989) things that are not fit to be such. Our sin comes from "setting our minds on the things of the flesh." Again, this is something we can be held responsible for, and yet there is inertia here. We get into the habit of setting our minds on the things of the flesh, we come to love them as familiar friends, and so we lose our perspective, become insensitive, and our minds are darkened.

I have suggested that the guardians of a child's infancy are first and foundational in the meeting of her need to be loved and to love, and that they are also her priests, mediating to her, in a preconceptual way, an impression of the character of God. We have in this an important source of personality perversion. In extreme cases the personality may be so damaged at this early stage that the individual lacks the motivational/perceptual resources for significant moral agency, and thus cannot be held morally responsible for contributions to her own personality defects. She thus has *only* inherited sin. But in most of us the deficiencies of our earliest interpersonal experiences only set us back or exacerbate our problems, making it more *likely* that we will choose perversely, but without depriving us of our freedom (see Jones, this volume).

Sin is promoted and sustained through self-deception concerning the states of our inwardness. A developed account of the Christian psychology would delve into the nature of the various mental states that make up our inwardness, examine their interactions with each other and with our behavior, and use these insights to explain psychological development, degeneration, repair, and fulfillment. I cannot do that in the present sketch, but I would like to say just a bit about self-deception. The Bible touches on self-deception only occasionally (e.g., James 1:26); its careful study in a Christian psychology would be warranted by the ubiquity of the phenomenon and its relevance to the psychology of sin. One of the chief justifications for the metaphor of inwardness for our mental life is that we can, to a fairly large extent, hide our sin from others and from ourselves. The main motive for such hiding, according to the Bible, is the desire to appear righteous when we aren't. This motive is probably a corrupt version of the first basic goal of human nature that we discerned earlier — the need for a harmonious love relationship with God. The main motive for deceiving ourselves is the same — the desire to appear righteous to ourselves when we know (in some sense) we aren't. Our power to deceive ourselves, which seems a pretty odd ability on first consideration, is based on our ver-bivorousness and our agency. We have options as to how we construe ourselves because we can talk, and this gives us an almost virtuosic poten-tial for inventing little stories about our inward and outward life. When these stories are untrue they are called rationalizations. They don't need to be *told*, even in sub-oral speech, to operate in our self-understanding. As agents, we are not on steel tracks as regards our feelings and thoughts and wishes, but are capable of choosing among them, as I have noted. So if we are motivated to choose untrue stories about ourselves, and not to notice too saliently that they are untrue, it should not surprise us that we some-times tell them. Self-deceptive experiences come in varying depths of deceptiveness (convincingness), ranging from cases in which we are hardly deceived, really, to cases in which the deception is so complete that it ceases to be *self*-deception except in the sense that my inability to perceive myself as I am is *traceable* to some earlier self-deceptive acts in which I really chose between options of self-construal.

Therapy

Psychotherapy is guided remedial personality development. It consists in interventions that aim to reorient the personality in the prescribed basic directions or further its development in those directions — in the Christian case they are aimed toward the Christian virtues; and the nature of these interventions correlates with the posited basic personality structures.

The central and chief intervention in the Christian psychology is God's own incarnation, sacrificial death, and resurrection in the person of God the Son. In this act God aims to set persons back on the track of acknowledging, honoring, and obeying him as God; of harmonious fel-lowship with their human fellows; and of responsible nurturing and use of nature. As we will expect from the basically relational account of human nature, virtue, and personality defect given by Christianity, this interven-tion is a reconciliation. The atonement is an act of forgiveness and resto-ration to a proper state of son- and daughtership. In accordance with our verbivorousness, this atonement is mediated to us through a "word," which then becomes a chief device of Christian psychotherapy, a concep-tual background regulating what is said and establishing the grammar of what is done and aimed at. In accordance with our nature as agents, the

Christian combats sin and promotes virtue in himself by undertaking actions that are contrary to his "sin nature" or dysfunctional personality: especially actions of service and praise of God, love to his human fellows, and stewardship of the creation. In accordance with our inwardness, Christian psychotherapy encourages articulation of our mental states, conscious and unconscious, that express our dysfunctional personalities (the confessional, and conversation with a spiritual director are perhaps the chief examples of this) and prescribes cognitive/behavioral exercises such as contemplating one's enemies in the terms of the gospel, asking for and receiving forgiveness, setting one's mind on the things of the Spirit, performing acts of charity and patience and self-denial (on this last, see Okholm, this volume). The exploration of the patient's inwardness may also serve to unearth features of a self that is healthier but dissociated; the exploration may even uncover the presence of Jesus Christ in the patient. Therapy would then consist in strategies for encouraging the patient to associate himself with this better self and dissociate himself from what is dysfunctional in him. In accordance with the Christian principle that selfhood is a function of what one loves and regards oneself as loved by, the Christian therapist, like the Christian parent, will regard herself as a sort of priest to the client, a mediator and representative of God's love. And so the kind of empathic communication and personal presence that is so strongly stressed in some secular therapies will also characterize the Christian — with the difference that the secular therapist does not see herself as modeling and mediating the love of God to the client. All of this will aim to encourage the client to associate himself with Christ and to dissociate himself from his sin, yet without becoming oblivious to its existence or unwilling to take some responsibility for it. ("Associate" here has both the social-interactive sense and the psychological sense of "identify with.")

Conclusion

This paper is not a Christian psychology, but only a sketch of one, an effort to make it seem plausible that one might be worked out, and an encouragement to do so. The development of a biblical psychology is strategically important in the church today, if we are to speak to the hunger for personal development and self-understanding evidenced in the widespread enthusiasm for the psychologies, and yet to do so in a way that preserves the integrity of Christian personality. But our purpose is not defensive only. A compelling Christian psychology would not only liberate us from our Babylonian captors; it would also hold the potential for deepening our wisdom and increasing the church's ability to form true disciples of Jesus Christ.

Postscript

At the conference where this paper was first presented, Nicholas Wolterstorff questioned my easy identification of Christian psychology with biblical psychology, and Eleonore Stump and Paul Griffiths asked whether what I expound in this paper should even be called a psychology. I would not, Wolterstorff suggested, want to identify a Christian cosmology — one that late twentieth-century Christians could espouse — with the cosmology of the early chapters of Genesis; only with quite heavy-handed reinterpretation might the Genesis material contribute to a "Christian cosmology." How, then, can I think that a Christian psychology can be read more or less directly out of the Bible? My answer is that the truths of psychology, in the sense in which I use the word in this paper, are not learned by esoteric techniques, mathematical computation, and special equipment such as are required to learn the truths of the physical sciences. These techniques have made available to modern cosmologists information and theoretical constructs utterly inaccessible to the biblical writers. By contrast, the vast majority of psychological claims that Aristotle makes in his *Nicomachean Ethics* are espoused by many twentieth-century thinkers. The reason is that the psychology of the *Nicomachean Ethics* is a practical one — what we in our day would call a personality theory or clinical psychology or psychotherapy — one whose primary business it is to discern what motivates people, how they think about what they do, what it is to perform actions and experience emotions, what a mature personality and human flourishing are like, what a person has to go through to develop a mature personality, and what kind of actions, if any, can be taken to correct defective personalities. These are questions to which any reflective culture will have more or less successful answers.

I do not deny that some advances have been made in 2400 years, but I am saying that the most basic method of answering these questions — long-term careful observation of human beings in more or less natural life settings and in interactions with other human beings (including, importantly, situations of stress) by wise observers — has not changed very much. In neuroscience, an area that is sometimes allied to psychology, Aristotle has nothing to say, because he did not possess the theoretical background, the techniques, and the equipment needed to make observations here. If the Bible said anything about brain functions, it is unlikely that its claims would be taken up in a modern Christian psychology. What the biblical writers have to say about psychology is said out of a wisdom matured in reflective practical interaction with God — in worship of him, in struggles with and against and in favor of him and his revealed will. It is a psychology hammered out in the corridors of nonacademic, non-scientific life by reflective people whom God specially chose to perpetuate the traditions concerning himself. Since the parameters of the moral and spiritual life in the twentieth century do not differ fundamentally from those of the first, or of the third century B.C., it should not surprise us that the New Testament psychological concepts, like those of the *Nicomachean Ethics*, present the parameters of a psychology viable in its own terms, not in need of radical revision to bring it into the twentieth century. This is not to say, however, that the biblical psychology is not different from the personality theories and psychotherapies of the present century. (The New Testament psychology is also different, in fundamental ways, from that of the *Nicomachean Ethics*, just as the psychology of Carl Jung differs from that of Aaron Beck, and that of orthodox Freudians differs from those of the various family-systems theorists.)

Griffiths and Stump wondered whether I wasn't "re-inventing the wheel." Stump said that much of what I say here can be found in Aquinas, and Griffiths suggested that what I present is not psychology, but "ascetical theology," again something that I certainly did not invent. I do not claim to be inventing anything in this paper, but only to be expounding the biblical psychology, and comparing it, in a modest and *ad hoc* way, with some of the claims of the modern psychologies. If what I have found in the Bible is similar to what Aquinas found there and in the earlier Christian tradition, this seems to me an encouragement that I'm on the right track. As to saying that it is not psychology, but ascetical theology, why not say that it is both? I call it psychology here because that is what it is called in the twentieth century, and our contemporaries are hungry for this sort of thing, more or less under this label. I predict that their spirits will salivate less if they are served the same thing under the name of ascetical theology. And not only the name of ascetical theology will put people off, but probably a fair amount of its working vocabulary. If we are careful, we can perhaps bridge between the Bible and the twentieth-century psychologies by carefully employing some of the vocabulary of the latter (see my use of Kohut's "self object" above) in the interest of distinctively Christian psychological concepts. I do not do that very much in the present paper, but I believe that a full version of the Christian psychology for the twenty-first century would adapt contemporary psychological vocabulary and offer reinterpretations of it.

One fundamental way to begin the project of articulating a Christian psychology for the twenty-first century is to take all of the nine biblical parameters and to explore them in interaction with the best of psychological research and thinking on cognate topics. My paper on attachment (this volume) illustrates one way in which this might be done. In a full-scale articulation of this psychology, the connections among each of the parameters and others would also be carefully explored, with a working out of the implications for character ideal, development, diagnostic, and therapy.

Starting from Scripture

Mark R. Talbot

> How . . . can they call on the one they have not believed in? And
> how can they believe in the one of whom they have not heard?
> And how can they hear without someone preaching to them? . . .
> Consequently, faith comes by hearing the message, and the mes-
> sage is heard through the word of Christ.
>
> Romans 10:14, 17

FROM THE START, Christianity has been recognized to be a religion of
revelation. God acted in Christ not only to redeem us and to put us
on the path to future glory, but also to reveal to us life's most fundamentally important truths (see Heb. 1:1-3; Mark 9:7; John 18:37; Gal. 1:11f.;
2 Tim. 1:8-11; Pelikan, 1971, p. 152f.; Kelly, 1978, p. 29; and Gilson, 1936,
chapters 1 and 2). Being a Christian certainly means much more than just
accepting these truths and trying to live according to them, but it also
never means less (see John 3:16-21; Gal. 3:1-14; Justin, 1948, p. 51; and
Kelly, 1978, p. 40). For Christian faith starts in hearing and accepting the
word of Christ (see also Eph. 1:13). Christians center their lives in the
truths most fully and most perfectly disclosed in the life, death, and
resurrection of the eternal and incarnate Word of the Father.

The good news of the gospel was foreshadowed in the Jewish Law
and Prophets, proclaimed openly by Jesus Christ, echoed faithfully by his
apostles, and finally enshrined in Scripture. As all the church Fathers agreed,
Scripture is "the foundation and pillar of our faith" (Irenaeus in Richardson,
1953, p. 370; and see Kelly, 1978, pp. 37-39). Centering our lives in Christianity's revealed truths means centering our lives in the truth of Scripture.
For Scripture gives us God's most explicit and complete "word" on things.

This includes God's "word" on matters psychological. Of course, the Bible is not a work of psychology; and even committed Christians can wonder how the claims about human personality found in such an ancient text can be relevant to such a distinctively modern discipline (see Wolterstorff's worries as reported by Roberts, this volume a). Yet psychology allures us by promising to help us understand ourselves — to understand what it means to be human, where our fulfillment lies and how to achieve it, and why things go wrong with us as well as how to fix them. Because Scripture obviously addresses the same issues, Christian psychologists should start from what Scripture says about these things. Its principles ought to govern and guide all their thinking about human beings.

But are Christian psychologists really warranted in starting from Scripture? A Christian's appeals to Scripture can all too easily appear as *ad hoc* threats to psychology's integrity. In this paper I shall argue that *any* school of psychology — even one attempting to understand human beings wholly naturalistically — grounds itself in a "word" like Scripture's "word," a "word" about what human beings are and the kind of world they live in. (For more on the Christian "word," see Roberts, this volume, a.)

Vitz (this volume), Griffiths (this volume), and Roberts (this volume a) point out that diverse "words" form the bases for different personality theories and their related psychotherapies. Roberts (1993) has shown in detail how six contemporary psychotherapy models diverge from one another and from Christianity in their basic conceptions of human nature, in their diagnostic categories of mental unhealthiness, and in their therapeutic prescriptions. Much of the disagreement among these models really boils down to disagreements about who has the correct "word" on human life. In arguing that some "word" underlies any psychology, I shall also argue that some of these "words" are more adequate to human life than others, and that the Christian "word" is as adequate as any.

Any adequate "word" will acknowledge that we approach relatively mature human beings differently than we do almost anything else. Societies aim at making human beings into full-fledged *persons*. Persons are *agents* who perform *actions* that are not reducible to mere bodily behaviors or even to the goal-directed behaviors of the higher animals. Actions are understood by agents to have some *significance*. A properly human agency, I shall argue, is always exercised within some framework of values that is held in place by an agent's hearing and accepting some "word" on life and reality that gives his acts their specific significance.

Some of the values underwriting human agency are practically non-controversial. Virtually everyone everywhere agrees, for instance, that each of us should respect the needs and interests of others (see Wong, 1993, pp. 446f., and Lewis, 1947, pp. 95ff.). Of course, we may disagree about some of the details. For example, most but not all of us believe that it is not only wrong to steal or to attack someone for no good reason or to deceive someone for gain, but also to discriminate against someone on the grounds of, say, race or gender or ethnic origins.

In America, various public rights and duties make up virtually the whole of what we call "morality." In some societies, "morality" also addresses what people do privately. But no matter how widely or narrowly "morality" is defined, in everyday situations virtually everyone assumes that human beings ought to act morally. Given the normal development of some basic human capacities, we expect each other to do what is right and to avoid what is wrong. Those doing right merit our praise, while those doing wrong are subject to blame. Some accounts of human behavior exclude or radically reinterpret these features of human agency (see Johnson, this volume, and Jones, this volume), but no one can avoid assuming them in everyday life. The most rigorous behaviorist will blame her children for irresponsibly disturbing her train of thought — and not just because she believes (as a good behaviorist should) that her doing so will condition her children not to disturb her again, but also because she actually perceives (as a good behaviorist shouldn't) their behavior as irresponsible, and hence as truly worthy of blame (see Strawson, 1974, pp. 1-25). In my first section, I focus on the kinds of cognitive and volitional capacities we assume people to have when we consider them to be responsible moral agents. I then argue that our discovery of various "determinants" of human behavior can modify how we think about these capacities but cannot reasonably challenge our belief in them.

Full human agency, however, requires more than responsibility and minimal morality. We need a wider evaluative framework that supplies us with ideals that focus our lives and make them seem worth living. In my second section I argue that our cognitive and volitional capacities make it absolutely essential for us to have such a framework; and I show how we get one.

Yet there are rival frameworks, based on different "words" about the world and human life. Effective and confident personhood, however, develops only within a stable framework, and our awareness of the rival possibilities can destabilize our sense of agency by making our framework seem to be just a product of imagination. For instance, Richard Rorty (1989) thinks we construct these frameworks not merely in the sense in which any human theory is constructed — as a product of our thinking that may or may not be adequate to the reality it purports to explain — but in the sense that constructing these frameworks actually invents the human reality they are about. (It is somewhat like living in a world of "make-believe.") Therefore, Rorty argues, each of us ought to be tolerant of everyone else's value system. But, in fact, this pluralistic posture is one that neither Rorty nor anyone else can sustain. Rorty himself mercilessly attacks the "word" underlying the Christian evaluative framework. And, as I show in my third section, we all inevitably take at least parts of our wider evaluative frameworks to be based in more than mere preference. We cannot help believing that it really would be better if everyone adopted at least some of our non-"moral" ideals and led their lives accordingly.

But if none of us can avoid acting from some particular framework grounded in some particular "word," and if the various secular schools of psychology and psychotherapy are allowed to ground their particular frameworks in their distinctive "words," then Christian psychologists ought to be allowed to ground their framework in their "word." Starting from Scripture is not in principle any different than starting from any of these other "words." Consequently, it alone cannot keep Christian psychologists from doing genuine, academically respectable psychology. For Christian psychology, as for every other kind, the proof is in the pudding: Does starting from this "word" lead to new psychological insights, to new academic and clinical advances in psychology?

Yet resistance to Christians doing psychology as Christians remains very high. So in my fourth section I shall say a bit more about why we should not be too troubled by continued and vehement opposition to our project of developing a thoroughly Christian psychology.

Responsible Agency

Psychology attempts to understand actual human behavior rather than some burlesque of it. Yet avoiding these burlesques is more difficult than it would seem. Let's start, then, with a case of typical human irresponsibility, of the kind we might encounter on any given day.

Suppose I borrow $10 from you. And suppose that every time I have another $10, I fritter it away. Sooner or later, you will be inclined to blame me for ignoring my obligation to repay you. For you will think that I *ought* to have given the task of repaying you higher priority.

Your thinking so depends on your having a certain view of human agency. You are assuming that I possess certain *cognitive capacities.* You think that I possess the capacity to know — and in fact do know, probably by having been told — that borrowed money ought to be repaid pretty quickly. And you are assuming that I remember — or at least ought to remember — that I borrowed $10 from you. If I somehow lack these capacities, you won't blame me for not repaying you. If, for instance, you discover I have Alzheimer's, and you're a reasonable person, you won't

blame me, because you'll realize that I probably don't remember having
borrowed the money from you.

Blaming me also assumes I possess enough *volitional capacities* to
have some control over what I do. More specifically, it assumes that I could
have chosen not to frivol away my money. This depends on my being able
to stand back and take stock of my various desires and drives, deciding
which among them I should satisfy or fulfill, and when. Not to do this,
when I possess the capacity to do so, is what elicits blame. Suppose I know
I won't have another spare $10 until well beyond the time when I should
have repaid you, and then Roberts points to a couple of beautiful Mac-
unudos in a tobacconist's window and suggests that we find a park bench
and smoke the $10 away in the cool spring twilight while discussing the
psychology of responsibility. I now must choose between the desire
evoked by this diabolical proposal and fulfilling my obligation to you. If
I succumb to the devil's blandishments, then so long as you think I knew
what I should do and could have done it if I wished, you will blame me
for not repaying you.

Whether we possess all the cognitive and volitional capacities we
need is not completely up to us; early upbringing and environment loom
large in their development (see Neal, this volume; Johnson, this volume;
and my later reference to the British documentary *28UP*). If you think I
lack the capacity not to frivol $10 bills away because my extremely pe-
nurious childhood has made me a pathological spendthrift, then you
won't blame me for not repaying you. If you discover that I have grown
up in some odd subculture where borrowed money is not quickly repaid,
you may judge me less capable of discerning exactly what I owe you and
thus be less inclined to blame me for not promptly repaying you. There
are no doubt many gradations of volitional and cognitive incapacity here,
and thus many degrees of responsibility.

We can, of course, wonder whether we really do possess all these
capacities. In fact, one problem with our culture's increasing tendency to
look at human beings psychologically is that, as various determinants of
our behavior are identified by psychology and the other social sciences,
doubts arise about our capacity to act responsibly (see Jones, this volume).
Doesn't the discovery of such determinants warrant the belief (or at least
the expectation) that finally all responsible human behavior may be explained away?

No, it does not, for some aspects of distinctively human behavior
cannot in principle be explained deterministically. Sometime ago in Saint
Louis, after a bus carrying five passengers had been hit by a car, fourteen
bystanders boarded the bus before the police arrived and began complain-
ing of back injuries (see Braybrooke, 1987, chapter 1). When we hear this,

we assign to the bystanders' behavior a specific kind of significance. In our society, people are entitled to sue for financial remuneration of damages incurred while riding in a vehicle involved in an accident; the bystanders saw an opportunity to become party to such suits by claiming to have been physically injured in the bus accident; and so with that intention they boarded the bus and began to complain. A correct understanding of the bystanders' behavior requires knowing that they, by making certain sounds, meant to be making particular claims, and that those claims, in that context, had a particular meaning. (For an argument that speaking itself requires recognition of and conformity to norms, see Wolterstorff, 1987.) Understanding the behavior requires understanding our society's rules about who stands responsible for what in circumstances like these.

So understanding and accounting for specific kinds of human behavior requires grasping how the human beings involved interpret it. What is the framework of meaning within which, for this agent, this act, in being done in these circumstances, takes on a specific significance? The same behavior, in other circumstances or other societies, can mean something quite different. Wearing certain colors in an inner-city American neighborhood may get you killed, while wearing the same colors in Kenya means nothing, because the gangs there don't "read" those colors as meaning certain things. In social-science jargon, knowingly to don a certain-colored jacket in the American neighborhood is to perform a specific *act*. That act has a kind of significance undiscoverable if we approach it solely by methods adequate to understand the movements of electrons or even the somewhat more purposeful behavior of rats. It involves a more or less deliberate response to the norms articulated by those gangs about human life. Understanding it requires awareness of that normative framework. We need to see an agent's activities from "inside" his framework of significance, if we are to understand what he is doing.

Only behavior not completely set by the kinds of determinants sought in the more naturalistic social sciences has fully human significance. Acts, by their very nature, *signify* something; and while wholly determined behavior tells us something about the lets and hindrances placed on someone's agency, it is only the behavior shaped by this agent that can signify how this particular person is approaching things.

It is part and parcel of human society to take human beings to be agents who act in significant ways. Indeed, the "socialization process" we put children through aims at developing the cognitive and volitional capacities that will allow them to think and then act in socially significant ways. The existence of enduring and cooperating social groups depends on their members' knowing that they should control themselves in various ways as well as on their being more or less capable of behaving as they know they should. (Even moral relativists concede this; see Wong, 1993, pp. 446f.) If a normal child has not learned how to control herself to the degree we expect of someone her age, *someone* is going to be blamed — either the child herself or those responsible for her training.

Moreover, much psychology — and especially much applied psychology — takes it for granted that human beings are, or are supposed to be, agents capable of acting meaningfully. Of course, many popular therapies say we must free ourselves from norms that have confined us in unhealthy ways (see Roberts, 1993, on Albert Ellis's "musturbation" and Carl Rogers's "introjection"). Yet this only shows they think we are capable of living within normative frameworks, for ill as well as for good. Again, when psychoanalysis aims to free its patients "from the tyranny of [their] inner compulsions" and give them "a power to choose that is not otherwise [theirs]" (Rieff, 1966, p. 93), it is assuming, at this most crucial point, our everyday view of human agency.

Psychoanalytic terminology — those under the "tyranny" of compulsions that limit their choices are "patients" in need of psychoanalytic "cures" — emphasizes that we take normal human beings to possess capacities allowing us to address each other in distinctively personal ways. We often judge human behavior by how it affects human life. Insofar as we take those involved to be responsible for the good or ill they produce, we regard them as worthy of praise or blame. Our gratitude or resentment, our forgiveness or anger — the *"reactive* attitudes and feelings"* (Strawson, 1974, p. 6) we experience toward each other every day — are just part of our "commitment to participation in ordinary inter-personal relationships" (p. 11). Respecting other human beings, regarding them as persons, approaching them as something more than merely objects "to be managed or handled or cured or trained" (p. 9), means taking them to possess the capacities that make them proper objects of such feelings and attitudes, and thus proper recipients of praise or blame. It means taking them to be *addressable* in distinctively personal ways. Persons, we assume, possess the capacities needed to judge for themselves the significance of specific sorts of acts and then to decide whether or not to act in those ways. As such, they can be asked to consider the significance — the value or disvalue — of doing various kinds of things. In addressing other persons — in saying things like "Please don't do that!" or "Will you consider this?" or "You shouldn't have done that!" or in simply saying "Thank you" for a job well done — we pay them the compliment of assuming they possess the capacities needed to shape their lives responsibly.

Normally, we want to be addressed this way. For we recognize that our value lies in our decisions counting for something, in our being originative sources of value and disvalue and not just hapless flotsam in the scheme of things (see Nozick, 1981, pp. 291ff.). Indeed, we become more convinced of this the more the "socialization process" succeeds, for it trains us to think of ourselves as exercising some control over our lives — as being able to respond to life's exigencies in various ways (see Nozick, 1981, pp. 304, 307). Successful socialization encourages us to think that if someone is regarded as no more than a nexus of external determinants, then that person is being devalued and disrespected in the most fundamental of ways. Sometimes, of course, this is unavoidable (see Strawson, 1974, pp. 6-13); and Christians, of all people, should recognize that responsible human agency can be undercut in any number of ways. (See Jones's survey of acceptable and unacceptable theological positions on human freedom in this volume.) But when our agency is undercut, things are "not the way they are supposed to be" (see Plantinga, 1994).

Of course, some social scientists have claimed that we no longer can afford to think of ourselves as addressable beings; to gain control of human behavior before it is too late, we must abandon our belief in responsible agency (see especially B. F. Skinner, 1971). They hold that science has already shown us to be wholly the products of various genetic or environmental determinants, but that we resist acknowledging this because we still like to think of ourselves as free. Strawson would counter that our commitment to interpersonal relationships is just "too thorough-going and deeply rooted" for us to take such suggestions seriously (p. 11); it is impossible for *any* theory to overturn our belief in responsible human agency; and even if we did have a choice not to continue addressing each other in the common ways, we could choose "rationally" whether or not to do so "only in the light of an assessment of the gains and losses to human life, [the] enrichment or impoverishment" that would result (p. 13). Adopting a wholly deterministic attitude toward each other's behavior would, Strawson argues, be immensely impoverishing to our life together because we would no longer be justified in feeling resentment, gratitude, forgiveness, anger, or even a distinctively human love toward each other. A moment's thought about the cases where we do view some particular human being's behavior as completely or even just largely the product of various determinants should make it clear how bleak our lives would be if we were to start viewing *all* humans this way. The logical end of denying responsible agency is the sort of devastation a determinist ought to feel if he could keep his convictions in mind as he took the love of his life into his arms.

Orientation in Evaluative "Space"

Morally significant actions especially prompt our praise or blame. But in
our pluralistic culture we really have two bases for praise and blame, two
frameworks for evaluation. There is what we call "morality," which we
take to consist in respecting the rights of others, and which we take to be
objective at least in the sense that a tolerable social order cannot exist
unless most of us are willing, for whatever reasons, to observe its dictates.
But "morality" in this narrow sense does not supply the kind of value-
orientation needed for full-fledged personhood. Mature persons have an
evaluative framework enabling them to make general sense of their lives.
Such a framework supplies them with ideals that help them to chart
meaningful courses through life. So, in addition to "morality," there are
"values." Each of us needs such a framework if we are to lead a full and
satisfying life, but because widespread acceptance of any particular framework seems unlikely, we declare these values to be matters of mere personal preference. I shall now focus on what it is about us that requires
these richer frameworks for the full flowering of our agency and on how
we get them. In the next section, I argue that these richer frameworks
cannot and should not be thought of as matters of mere preference.

        Consider, once again, our cognitive and volitional capacities.
Human beings, unlike even the higher animals, are spiritual creatures in
this sense at least: our "psychology" is not nailed down to our physiology.
We are much more than the sum of our physiological drives, as the failure
of various research programs in psychology has made clear (see Johnson,
this volume). We can, and as we mature we inevitably do, consider more
than our immediate wants and needs: I may feel rested, well-fed, and
satisfied right now, but I worry about what will happen to me in five years.
You may be plagued by your past, even though to your acquaintances you
appear to be a picture of success. We are capable of living — and indeed
encourage each other to live — within a "world" that stretches back into
a now-but-remembered-or-related past and anticipates a not-yet-experi-
enced future. Mommy tells Bobby that Christmas is coming and that Santa
is likely to bring him the bike he wants, especially if he is good; Sarah
considers her family's illustrious history at Wheaton College, and finds
herself moved to work hard while she is there so that she too may do well.
Such is the stuff of human life — stuff that depends on our distinctive
cognitive and volitional capacities. Once the cat is fed, she doesn't have a
care in the world; we don't encourage our dogs to behave better by
promising them Milk-bones for Christmas; and a great ape is not motivated to make something of himself by remembering who his great-grand-
father was. Our cognitive and volitional capacities give us a freedom from

the immediate present that forces a certain range of questions on us —
questions about how we shall approach life — questions that require us
to get ourselves oriented within some more than merely "moral" evaluative space. (My talk about evaluative "space" adapts Charles Taylor's talk
about moral "space" in 1989, chapter 2.)

Psychology itself witnesses to the fact that we flourish only within
richly articulated evaluative spaces. As Christopher Lasch has observed,
"[e]very age develops its own peculiar forms of pathology" (1979, pp.
41f.). Our era's character disorders involve a sense of deep futility or a
numbing emptiness or a crippling loss of self-esteem. These disorders
have increased with our century's growing "disenchantment" — with its
dissipation of any commonly accepted perspective within which the
world might be seen as possessing some significant meaning. Disenchantment destroys the evaluative spaces within which people live (see Taylor,
1989, pp. 17, 19). Clinical depression, now alarmingly prevalent in the
industrialized, disenchanted West, can almost be defined as the loss of a
sense of purpose or meaningful agency (see the DSM IV, pp. 320ff.). Its
onset often involves an individual's failure either to find something that
makes life worth living (as happens particularly in children's depression)
or to retain a sense of life's meaningfulness as the years bring their changes
(as when the loss of a child or a spouse makes life seem no longer worth
living).

Psychology's popularity corroborates our need to get oriented
within such a space, since it presents itself as the science of human flourishing. We turn to it for guidance about how we should live our lives
because it promises to enlighten and enrich us in scientifically respectable
ways. It offers us "a normative order of life, with character ideals, images
of the good life, and methods of attaining it" (Bellah, Madsen, Sullivan,
Swidler, and Tipton, 1985, p. 47). It promises to help us flourish by supplying us with the non-"moral" coordinates by which we should live.

So how do we get such coordinates? Initially, it is not a matter of
individual choice, since we first borrow our identities from others. Persons are called forth by interaction with the more developed persons
around them (see Johnson, this volume; Neal, this volume; and Roberts,
this volume b): very young infants start the journey toward developed
personhood through making and enjoying visual contact with their
mothers' eyes; their slightly older siblings learn to speak by playing
games with their parents that identify objects and isolate gestures and
tones in ways that make language acquisition possible (see Bruner, 1983);
and, once linguistically equipped, we get our biggest boost towards fully
oriented personhood through hearing those closest to us talk about —
and then watching them pursue — whatever it is that gives purpose and

meaning to their own lives. We first get a fix on life by riding piggyback on those around us who already have a clear sense of where they are going in evaluative space. (See Roberts, 1993, pp. 133ff., on Kohut's theory of the development of a self; and Taylor, 1989, p. 35.)

If all goes well, we come to know who we are as individuals by finding our place within some well-defined social space. Already, in watching babies squeal with delight as they peer around obstacles to find their mothers' laughing eyes, it is apparent that individual satisfaction comes primarily from fitting within a social space. Judicious use of blame — "You shouldn't be so concerned about getting that toy!" — and praise — "That's a good girl! You've eaten your beans!" — helps us to chart our courses by encouraging us to internalize some "word" about how our lives ought to be led. Children who have been inadequately socialized, who have not been taken in hand and helped to internalize some "word," show by their unsettled behavior that they just don't know where they fit.

Internalizing a livable "word" also involves getting some scale of goods that helps us to avoid just frittering life away. Rich evaluative frameworks proscribe certain ways of living, even though those ways are not immoral in the narrow sense. You may be scrupulous about paying your debts promptly, but willing to waste hours in front of a T.V. Even if wasting time doesn't involve a "moral" breach, many of us would hold that there is something wrong with doing too much of it. For our frameworks lead us to believe that, if everything else is equal, it is objectively better to have something to show for one's time than not. Thus most of us admire someone who has used her leisure hours to write children's stories or to sew quilts. Again, most of us would agree that possessing some degree of ambition and stick-to-itiveness is good. Yet, as the British film *28UP* documents (see Schoeman, 1987, p. 10, n. 7), the development of these traits is very largely dependent on the kind of social environment we spend our early years in. Whether I will stick with a project once it becomes difficult is usually connected with the value-scales I did or didn't internalize — and the corresponding volitional capacities I did or didn't develop — in my first few years.

So we come to know who we are, not so much by knowing our names and genealogies, as by understanding "what is of crucial importance to us. To know who I am," as Charles Taylor says,

> is a species of knowing where I stand. My identity is defined by the commitments and identifications that provide the frame or horizon within which I can try to determine from case to case what is good, or valuable, or what ought to be done, or what I endorse or oppose. (1989, p. 27)

Getting one's bearings within such a space is even intimately connected with getting and keeping our bearings in physical space. We can get a perceptual fix on our physical environment only when we (or at least *parts* of us — our *eyes,* especially) are moving (see the studies cited in Hodges, 1986, pp. 60-64, and especially Gibson, 1979). But we move primarily to seek various kinds of satisfactions, and so only agents on the hunt for goods make clear sense out of physical space. (My new granddaughter, Rebekah, likes splashing the water in the toilet bowl, and her valuing that experience has led her to identify where the bathroom is so that she can get at that bowl whenever her parents have left the bathroom door un-latched.) Indeed, extreme cases of the "narcissistic personality disorders" — all of which involve radical uncertainty about oneself and what one values — can result in a loss of spatial orientation (see Kohut, 1977, pp. 153-56).

Our Inevitable Realism about Our Evaluative Space

The last sentence alludes to another feature of the evaluative frameworks required for full-fledged personhood. Effective and confident human agency can be exercised only within some *settled and stable* evaluative space. If I am sufficiently unsure I have the right framework, then it does not matter how richly articulated it is. For then I am unsure that what it identifies as worthwhile really is, and that takes me to the borders of psychopathology.

What holds our evaluative frameworks firmly in place? Different parts are held in place at different times in different ways. Initially, as I have already said, we just swallow a framework more or less whole as we are inducted into a family. But once we are old enough to reflect on what we have previously accepted more or less unquestioningly, we may con-clude that parts of it are matters of preference or taste. For instance, it would be foolish for you to insist that my family should enjoy camping just because yours does, since liking to "rough it" is pretty clearly not grounded in anything essential to human beings.

By contrast, there is an implicit "must" in the blame we attach to moral violations — a "must" attesting to our conviction that we should not harm others or infringe on their rights. This "must" is always grounded in an appeal to some aspect of reality and the place of human beings within it. Particular appeals vary widely and often conflict, but some appeal to reality is needed to ground the moral "must" (see Taylor, 1989, chapter 1).

We also need to be confident about the objectivity of our non-

"moral" evaluative frameworks. Suppose I am debating whether to get on my Schwinn Air-Dyne or to spend the hour lounging in my easy chair. If I choose to exercise, it will be because I think the reality of ill-health is likely to catch up with me if I don't do some hard aerobic exercise at least four times a week. We are realists about the core non-"moral" coordinates of our evaluative space partly because we recognize that reality forces itself upon us in various ways. Anticipating a decline in my life's quality if I don't do something now to avoid clogged arteries in twenty years, I look to medicine for objective standards of healthy living.

Yet the conviction that our core ideals are grounded in reality is what cultural pluralists deny (see Rorty, 1989, chapters 1-3). They insist that there are no objective non-"moral" standards; they celebrate the freedom they say we have to chart whatever course we want through evaluative space. They defend their position by pointing out that the core coordinates of any rich evaluative space are always anchored in a contestable metaphysics or ontology; and they conclude it is irrational and immoral for anyone to think that his non-"moral" coordinates possess objectivity.

But the landmark sociological study, *Habits of the Heart: Individualism and Commitment in American Life,* corroborates that no one can live in such an ontologically unanchored evaluative space. It opens by recounting how four Americans have made sense of their lives. The values of each differ remarkably from those of the others, and each gives careful lip-service to the live-and-let-live language of American cultural pluralism, even as each obviously takes his or her own way of life to be based on real insight into the way a human life ought to be lived. Brian Palmer, a top-level manager in a large California corporation, has become more of a family man, and more interested in thinking, reading, and classical music, after a divorce. He avoids calling his earlier single-minded pursuit of material success wrong, because his social and business environments encourage him to describe his new allegiances as changes in personal preference (see Bellah et al., 1985, p. 6). Yet his real feelings come out when he says, "I don't think I would pontificate and say that I'm in a position to establish values for humanity in general, *although I'm sufficiently conceited to say that if the rest of the world would live by my value system it would be a better place*" (p. 7; my emphasis).

Obviously, there is an implicit "should" here, even if Palmer himself feels bound to deny it. He knows, moreover, that such "shoulds" need to be backed up by reasons. And so he is distressed when he cannot explain why personal integrity is good and lying is bad. He speculates that such standards are grounded in the Judeo-Christian heritage, but he retreats from citing that heritage as a reason why everyone should subscribe to them. (He may suspect that to tag what ought or ought not to be done to a specific tradition would require him to defend why we should follow that heritage by making some claims about that tradition's truth, which would involve invoking an eminently contestable view of reality.) In the end, he abandons the task of explaining why dishonesty should be universally proscribed: "Why is integrity important and lying bad? I don't know. It just is. It's just so basic. I don't want to be bothered with challenging that. It's part of me. I don't know where it came from, but it's very important" (p. 7).

As the authors of *Habits of the Heart* observe, "to hear [Brian] talk, even his deepest impulses of attachment to others are without any more solid foundation than his momentary desires," and so his "justification for his life . . . rests on a fragile foundation" (p. 8). A public commitment to cultural pluralism can thus force us to "live out a fuller sense of purpose in life than [we] can justify in rational terms" (p. 6). When this private, fuller sense of purpose conflicts directly with our public commitment to the nonobjectivity of almost all of our values, the cognitive dissonance between what we actually believe and what we think we should believe becomes harshly evident.

Psychology can appear to give us a way around this difficulty by presenting itself as the value-neutral "science" of human flourishing. Psychologists sometimes offer to supply us with rich and stable evaluative environments merely by investigating "the facts" about human beings. Therapists can think that all we need to discover is what each of us *really* desires, in the most distinctively individual parts of our beings, and that then the knowledge of those desires will automatically orient us in a personally stable and richly articulated evaluative space. Such therapists pride themselves on not being "judgmental" by helping us to seek the most effective ways of satisfying our deep desires, *whatever* they may be. Thus we get "the triumph of the therapeutic" (see Rieff, 1966), where questions about what is *truly* good, and about how human beings *should* live — in short, questions about the *proper ends* of human life — are taken to be rationally unresolvable. Non-"moral" values then become matters of preference and taste. Individual wants and needs become primary, unchecked by any generally accepted societal standards about what desires, drives, urges, wishes, projects, and so forth, are *worth* satisfying. Each of us becomes autonomous, having the right "to discover fulfillment independent of the restraints of precedent and community" (Lundin, 1993, p. 41). Only acts that infringe on the rights of others to pursue and enjoy whatever they wish are then recognized as really wrong. And so *blaming* someone for her non-"moral" choices becomes almost unforgivable.

Initially, shrinking the sphere of objective valuation would seem to give us new opportunities for unfettered personal growth, but in fact nearly the opposite is true. For our "spiritual" nature, with its inevitable hopes and fears, always seeks the reassurance that can only come from grounding our basic values in some account of the nature of things.

This is true even for the psychotherapist Margaret Oldham, another interviewee in *Habits of the Heart*. Oldham has definite standards by which she herself lives; "she feels," e.g., "that one of the most important things she learned from her parents was the value of hard work — 'not just work, but taking pride in your work and being responsible for your work and doing it as well as you possibly can and doing a lot of it'" (Bellah et al., 1985, p. 14). At the same time, she values tolerance very highly, so she regularly lets her clients' ideas challenge her own. She believes everyone aims at individual fulfillment, and so the fact that different individuals value different things means that her therapeutic role is just to help her clients understand themselves better "so that they may deal more realistically, and perhaps more fruitfully, with life and realize their personal preferences" (p. 15).

Of course, Oldham has some idea of what realistic and fruitful living consists in. She thinks "the happiness of a fulfilling life cannot be won without a realistic willingness to make the effort and pay the costs required" (p. 15), and that "[i]n the end, you're really alone and you really have to answer [just] to yourself" (p. 15). But many of her clients, she thinks, are unwilling to recognize these truths and then do what is necessary to achieve their own happiness. So in spite of her explicit commitment to respect her clients' values and experiences, her therapeutic practices are not in fact value-free. A client expecting her to solve his problems for him is acting "childishly" (p. 16). "People want to be made happy, instead of making themselves happy" (p. 15). Taking responsibility for our own lives is, in fact, one non-"moral" value she finds rooted in reality: "What I think the universe wants from me is to take my values, whatever they might happen to be, and live up to them as much as I can. If I'm the best person I know how to be according to my lights, then something good will happen. I think in a lot of ways living that kind of life is its own reward in and of itself" (pp. 14f.).

As unsophisticated as this is (what does it mean to say that *the universe* requires something of someone, and why believe that good things will happen to responsible people?), this is the "word" about human life and reality that underlies the core coordinates in Oldham's own evaluative space. And even her self-conscious pluralism does not stop her from judging the courses of others' lives according to it.

Even Richard Rorty, as a much more sophisticated proponent of tolerance and cultural pluralism, has a definite "word" behind the core coordinates of his own evaluative space, although he maintains he does not. Rorty's "liberal ironist" believes that "an ideal . . . society is one which has no purpose except freedom" (1989, p. 60); he desires above all else that all suffering and cruelty will cease (see p. xv). And yet he faces up to the contingency of even these, his own most central beliefs and desires, because he is "sufficiently historicist and nominalist to have abandoned the idea that [his] central beliefs and desires refer back to something beyond the reach of time and chance" (p. xv). Rorty does not deny that we need to be able to adhere "unflinchingly" to our core convictions (see pp. 44ff.). He acknowledges that each of us has a "final vocabulary" — "a set of words which [we] employ to justify [our] actions, [our] beliefs, and [our] lives" — "words in which we formulate praise of our friends and contempt for our enemies, our long-term projects, our deepest self-doubts, our highest hopes[,] . . . words in which we tell, sometimes prospectively and sometimes retrospectively, the story of our lives" (p. 73). Yet he thinks that if we are to be as free as we can be, and if our intolerance and inhumanity to each other is to cease, then we must resolutely reject the idea that any "final vocabulary" is grounded in reality. We must learn to live committed lives without having to believe that our "word" gives us some once-and-for-all truth about the world and human beings. Then and only then are we likely to stop persecuting others for valuing things differently.

If we could learn to live like this, then the world would be "de-divinized" (see p. 21). We would be at that liberating point where we would "no longer worship *anything*, . . . where we [would] treat *everything* — our language, our conscience, our community — as [just] a product of time and chance" (p. 22). And living this way, Rorty maintains, would not involve making any illicit assumptions about reality. For it would not involve a claim that its own "final vocabulary" is any closer to reality than any other (see p. 73). Indeed, Rorty knows that the one thing he must avoid is even hinting that his proposal "gets something right, that my sort of philosophy corresponds to the way things really are" (p. 8). For that would drag the whole idea of a vocabulary fitting reality back in. Yet Rorty's brand of cultural pluralism does rest on an eminently contestable view of reality. It is a view that believes there is no truth about the way things are, because, since God does not exist, human beings may say whatever they want about the world (see Rorty's whole first chapter). But surely this idea — that we are the final arbiters and creators of truth — is a highly contestable view of reality, and an arguably *untrue* one at that!

So Rorty's own evaluative framework stands or falls with his assertion that our world is *not* "the creation of a being who had a language of his own" (p. 5). His standards are credible only if he is *right* that our world is not God's project. If he is wrong about that, then even he will have to admit the folly of his ways. So even a really sophisticated version of cultural pluralism rests on a contestable "word" about the kind of world we live in.

Confidence in the Christian Framework

In "Trotsky and the Wild Orchids," Rorty recounts how he got to his brand of cultural pluralism after starting from a Trotskyite childhood and youth. One phase in his development stands out: as a University of Chicago undergraduate, he tried "to get religion" because of T. S. Eliot's suggestion "that only committed Christians (and perhaps only Anglo-Catholics) could overcome their unhealthy preoccupation with their private obsessions, and so serve their fellow humans with proper humility" (1992, p. 144). But he couldn't stomach reciting the Episcopal General Confession, with its rich language about the depths of our wickedness and sin. So he soon quit trying to make sense of his life on Christianity's terms and fell back on "absolutist philosophy" (p. 144), initially by turning to Plato and his ilk.

Rorty's self-described "prideful inability" (p. 144) to believe what he was saying when he recited the General Confession highlights one more fact about our evaluative frameworks and the "words" underlying them: the traffic between our beliefs and our values doesn't go just from believing to valuing. Rorty is attracted by a radical freedom and creativity, and so comes to believe that no god is the author of things. Indeed, as Rorty's values became "more and more raucously secularist," he found even nontheistic attempts "to hold reality and justice in a single vision" to be beyond belief (p. 147).

We can remain more confident about the Christian "word" if we keep this in mind. For remembering that what someone treasures in his heart of hearts affects what he believes can keep us from being too troubled by continued and vehement opposition to our project of developing a thoroughly Christian psychology.

It is important to see that the Christian "word" meets all the requirements for an adequate "word" mentioned so far. It acknowledges that we approach relatively mature human beings differently than we do almost everything else. It encourages us to address each other as responsible moral agents. It supplies us with a set of ideals so we can make general sense of our lives. And it grounds all this in a detailed view of reality.

It is also important to realize that the "words" underlying many of the psychologies and psychotherapies are less than adequate to the lives we actually live. For instance, some of the more deterministic and be-havioristic schools of psychology ignore the more distinctive elements of human agency. Enamored by the successes of natural science, they try to understand human beings entirely "from the outside" without recogniz-ing our need for conscious significance. So they try to understand all human behavior on a model that would serve better to understand the movement of electrons or the behavior of rats and chimpanzees. Again, some of the applied psychologies — such as Carl Rogers's "nondirective counseling" and Albert Ellis's "Rational Emotive Therapy" — downplay the importance of moral standards in our lives; and some therapists mis-takenly claim as well that they can practice therapy in a way that is "value-free." Moreover, sometimes, as we have seen, the more tolerant and pluralistic among us even falsely maintain that their own values presume no particular "word" about reality.

With much of this, the Christian psychologist can afford to be tolerant, for her "word" on human life is broad enough to acknowledge that there is something in each of these approaches. Her "word" doesn't require her to deny that some aspects of human behavior are best under-stood naturalistically. She can acknowledge that the proper functioning of our distinctively human capacities is tied to the proper functioning of our bodies as natural systems. And she may also believe that sin makes human behavior unnaturally subject to — and thus explicable by — the lower creation's laws. It may constrict our options and thus make our behavior more open to analysis in terms of this or that "determinant" (see Lewis, 1940, chapter 5, following Hooker, 1865). Again, her "word" does not prohibit her from admitting that a lot of damage can be done by those (like the New Testament Pharisees) who approach life too "moralistically." And, again, if she has thought her theology through, she will realize that while the Scriptures encourage her to recommend her values and her faith in the appropriate settings, she should do so without insisting that others see things her way. For she knows that we embrace the core coordinates of our evaluative frameworks with our whole selves, and that such whole-hearted acceptance neither should nor can be forced. Sometimes the best she can do for a non-Christian is just to help him clarify exactly what he desires and believes.

Nevertheless, Christian psychologists will believe and maintain that, while each of these approaches can cast some light on human life, none of them should be taken as the final "word" about human beings. For none of them can furnish us with a fully livable evaluative space. Each, when taken as the whole story, burlesques human life as it is actually lived.

In maintaining this, Christian psychologists have not even gotten to articulating their specifically Christian "word" on human life and reality. Yet they will already face strong opposition, for human beings can have many reasons for wanting to deny that persons can flourish only within some stable and highly articulated evaluative space. For instance, psychological naturalism can be attractive to any of us in certain situations for the ways it can let us off the hook by diminishing or dismissing our responsibility. Again, Carl Rogers's "client-centered therapy" can allure us with its promise that no matter what we believe or feel we shall be accepted nonjudgmentally and empathetically — that we need not be inhibited by being forced to "introject" anyone else's "conditions of worth" (see Roberts, 1993, chapter 2).

Yet the greatest opposition to Christians doing psychology as Christians is undoubtedly tied to claims intrinsic to the Christian evaluative framework and its underlying "word."

It would take another paper to specify adequately what it is about the gospel that is likely to rub non-Christians the wrong way. John Stuart Mill and Stanley Fish, as well as Rorty, are classic liberals who elevate above almost any other value the individual's right to choose how he wants to live. All three object very strongly to the Christian ideal of godly obedience (see Mill, 1912, *On Liberty*, chapter 3; Fish, 1996; and Rorty, 1989, chapter 2). Rorty adds that "moderns" like himself consider the Christian doctrine of sin — which involves the notion that "there is a Being before whom we humans should humble ourselves" — to be "a really terrible idea" (Rorty, 1996). Of course, opposition like this to Christian values and beliefs is exactly what Scripture itself tells us to expect. The apostle Paul declares that "the message of the cross is foolishness to those who are perishing" (1 Cor. 1:18); and he adds elsewhere that the gospel's messengers have "the smell of death" to those who will not believe (2 Cor. 2:16). The Christian "word" is often utterly incredible to those who value things differently. And if what we value affects what we believe, what else should we expect? Christians and non-Christians often value remarkably different things, and if someone is indifferent or hostile to Christian values, she may very well ignore or oppose or even be unable to consider the Christian "word" about reality and human beings.

Moreover, Scripture does not see the failure of non-Christians to believe the Christian "word" to be prompted by their just valuing things differently than Christians do; it declares them to be valuing the *wrong* things or to be valuing some of the right things *inordinately*. It also implies that when we misvalue things, we somehow know that we are repudiating what we were made for, that we have at least a dim awareness that in forsaking the proper standards we are forsaking the very basis of proper personhood (see Baillie, 1942, chapter 6; and Talbot, 1996b). And it takes such misvaluing to be endemic to the human race (see, e.g., Rom. 3:9-20).

A central claim of Scripture is that each of us has at least some awareness that God exists and that he wants us to live in specific ways (see Talbot, 1989). Christians and Jews and Muslims all believe that we become aware of our responsibilities not simply because other people address us but because God himself is addressing us, through nature and our consciences as well as through the words of other human beings (see especially Rom. 1:18–2:16; and Wolterstorff, 1996). They believe that our becoming fully fledged persons depends on God's addressing us, on God's calling us into being as persons by speaking to us in these ways (see Talbot, 1996a). They also believe that each of us knows that if we do not do what God says, then we sin and become liable to his punishment (see especially Rom. 1:18-32).

If our values manifest themselves in our desires and feelings, and if both our desires and feelings affect our beliefs (see de Sousa, 1987; and Damasio, 1994), then we ought to expect, as Rorty's case corroborates, that persistent misvaluing may very well lead to progressive unbelief. For it is with our hearts we believe (see Rom. 10:10). In Scripture, the *heart* is the whole person — a person's inner life or character, the center of his or her personality (see Prov. 27:19 and many other passages, including Gen. 6:5; Exod. 25:2; Deut. 4:9, 29; 13:3; Ps. 14:1; 20:4; 51:10; 86:11; 139:23; Matt. 5:8 and 6:21). While it includes many of the rational powers we usually attribute to a person's mind or "head," it is the seat and source of *all* our powers — rational, volitional, emotional, and spiritual — and as such it ultimately determines what we believe, feel, do, and say (see Sorg, 1976).

Consequently, change of heart is singled out throughout the Scriptures as the central and decisive factor in genuine acceptance of the Christian "word" on reality and human beings (see Ps. 119:32; Acts 16:13-15; and Eph. 1:18). It involves changes in our desires and feelings (see Gal. 5:16-24) that enable us to recognize truths about ourselves and our world that we otherwise do not clearly see or that we have deliberately avoided acknowledging (see Eph. 2:1-3). Ultimately, Scripture declares, our ability to believe the gospel is God's gift (see Eph. 2:8-10): God plants faith in us by giving us new hearts (see Ezek. 36:26f.; 11:19f.; and Jer. 24:7). The proclamation of his "word" is the instrument God uses to effect this change: God's Spirit, running along the pathway that the proclamation of his "word" creates, changes our hearts in a way that makes that "word" believable and allows us to desire and hope for the goods it proclaims (see Rom. 10:14-17 and 1 Pet. 1:3-6).

So Christian psychologists should not be shocked or shaken or dismayed when they find continued and vehement opposition to their project of developing a thoroughly Christian psychology by starting from Scripture. Indeed, practicing psychologists and psychotherapists, both

secular and Christian, should be the last of all people to succumb to the
blandishments of "Whig psychology," with its bogus belief that psychology is the sort of value-free discipline that, if properly pursued, will make
slow but steady progress toward an unchallengeable body of truths (see
Van Leeuwen, 1985, pp. 5-7; and Rudner, 1953). For they see, almost every
day, just how radically our desires and feelings can affect our beliefs.
Occasionally, Christian psychologists may even be justified in claiming —
in a way closely akin to some psychotherapeutic claims — to see exactly
how someone's desires and feelings have gone so wrong as to have made
him *epistemically blind* to such truths as God's existence and his own
wrongdoing (see Talbot, 1984, 1985, 1989; Schlesinger, 1984; and Basinger,
1988). Yet in doing so, we must not say or imply that he is a worse sinner
than ourselves. For it is part of deep Christian experience to confess that
we too were once blind even if now, by God's grace, we can see some
things (see John 9:25).

Recognizing the inevitable influence of our values on our beliefs,
we can also recognize that non-Christian psychologists will inevitably
disagree with many of our claims. But if we work out those claims with
intellectual rigor and empirical honesty, we have no reason not to bring
them to psychology's table. Indeed, many psychological staples began
their life in the Christian tradition. The Puritans pioneered the study of
self-deception (see Martin, 1986, pp. 32f.), and even Freudian theory has
some Christian underpinnings (see Vitz, 1988). As the history of intellectual development has shown (see, e.g., Gilson, 1936 and 1941; Cochrane,
1940; Pelikan, 1965; Foster, 1935 and 1936; Taylor, 1989; and MacIntyre,
1981, 1988, and 1990), and as this volume itself should corroborate, Christians, by starting from Scripture, often bring to the academic feast delicacies that no one else can find.

Human Nature vs.
the Hermeneutics of Love

JAMES E. MARTIN

Nearly all the wisdom we possess, that is to say true and sound wisdom, consists of two parts: The knowledge of God and of ourselves. But while joined with many bonds, which one brings forth and precedes the other is not easy to discern.

Jean Calvin, Institutes, Book I, Chapter 1

Man's central, his — I might say — metaphysical problem is no longer the existence of God and his own existence in terms of that sacred mystery. The problem is now the conflict between [absolute technological] rationality and what has hitherto constituted his person. That is the pivot of all present day reflection, and, for a long time, it will remain the only philosophical issue.

Jacques Ellul, The Technological System, p. 74

THIS ESSAY PRESENTS an examination of the conception of human nature found in Scripture. From a biblical perspective the issue of human nature is crucial for understanding human personhood. Our view of human personhood, its responsibilities and privileges, will therefore de-

I wish to thank Gordon Keddie, Duncan Lowe, Curtis Martin, Robert Roberts, Phil Ross, and Garry Sutley for many helpful conversations, suggestions, and criticisms at various stages of this project. Throughout this paper I have used the inclusive masculine pronouns and inclusive masculine terms (e.g., mankind) for theological reasons internal to the argument of the paper. Genesis 1:27 teaches that Man (Adam) includes both male and female. For reasons that will be evident, I view the rejection of the inclusive masculine terms to be a rejection of human nature and human community as created by God.

pend on our notion of human nature. If we go wrong here, in our theory
of human nature, then we will err in everything else, not only in our
psychology and anthropology, but, as Calvin implies, in our understanding of God and Scripture as well.

Jacques Ellul (1980) argues that the question of human nature is the
fundamental issue of the modern age. Ellul is characteristically lucid in
recognizing the importance of the clash between the absolute rationality
of technology, with its concern for efficiency, and what has traditionally
constituted human personhood (e.g., human nature). At the end of the
twentieth century the rationality that constrains the world toward maximal efficiency of means has created an apparently irresistible drive toward
the integration of every aspect of human existence into a totalizing technological system. To the extent that a specific human nature is not
completely adaptable to the demands of technological rationality, it ob-
structs that integration. The clash between a specific human nature (one
incompatible with the demands of technological rationality) and that absolute rationality creates an ever increasing problem for those being
assimilated by the technological system. Moreover, in its final stages, the
clash will be seen less as "the difficulty of technological rationality" and
more as "the difficulty of human nature." We are now in those final stages.
Those who have accepted the absolute rationality of this age will inevitably see a specific human nature as the enemy of progress — economic,
social, and ecclesiastical. From my point of view, Ellul has hit the mark
on all these points.

Nevertheless, it appears to me that Ellul is mistaken in saying that
the clash in question has replaced the problem of the existence of God and
our own existence in terms of that sacred mystery. To the contrary, from
a biblical perspective, the existence of God and our own existence in light
of that sacred mystery is a precondition for the clash between technological
rationality and human nature. It is precisely our status as beings created
by God for his own purposes that gives specific, concrete form to our
human nature and thus structures our calling. Further, it is the specificity
of those purposes and the calling they imply that clash with the rationality
of efficiency. Accordingly, the two problems Ellul refers to are not antithetical, but mutually reinforcing. The issue for us, as for Calvin, is the problem
of God's existence and our own in relation to God's. In the present age,
however, the issue is perhaps most manifest in the clash between technological rationality and human nature.

In view of the above, this essay offers a discussion of human nature
in light of Scripture. This may seem an odd starting point for a psychologist. To begin, however, by inquiring about human nature in the mode
of the empirical social and biological sciences would be seriously prema-

ture and possibly misleading in a number of ways. First of all, any empirically derived evidence concerning human nature would have to be interpreted in light of the biblical doctrines of the creation and fall. This leads to significant difficulties. On the one hand, as created, human nature involves a normative dimension. In part, human nature is defined in terms of an ideal whose realization is not immediate or automatic. On the other hand, the doctrine of the fall implies that the normative element of human nature will be, at best, imperfectly realized in empirical descriptions of human activity. Accordingly, any attempt to identify human nature directly and uncritically from the data of the empirical sciences alone would be, as Calvin put it, like "seeking in a ruin for a building" (*Institutes*, Book I, Chapter XV). Important as the results of the empirical sciences undoubtedly are, what they signify for a biblically informed account of human nature will depend upon what the Scriptures say about human nature (both pre- and post-fall) as well as an argument relating Scripture to the empirical findings. Such an argument would take us beyond the limits of this essay.

The Scriptural Argument

My first thesis is that Scripture portrays our human nature as structuring to a significant degree the basic relationships that define our existence as created beings called to live in families and in communities comprised of families and extended families. Those particular relationships (husband/wife, parent/child, brother/sister, for example), with their associated differential roles, privileges, and responsibilities, are fundamental to the definition of specifically *human* personhood; and this is because those relations, privileges, and responsibilities are to a large extent grounded in the specific character of human nature. Second, I will argue that Scripture not only teaches a specific conception of human nature, but that the same view of human nature is an important part of the assumed context of the scriptural commandment structure. In support of this second thesis, I will show that a hermeneutic that assumes this view of human nature integrates and illuminates a number of important biblical texts. In contrast, a hermeneutic that presupposes a less structured view of human nature — a view more amenable to the demands of technological rationality — *dis*integrates those texts and contradicts the commandments they clearly express. Insofar as I am able to show this, the importance of the proposed conception of human nature for the interpretation of Scripture is thus corroborated, as is, by implication, my prior thesis that the Scripture teaches such a conception.

Minimalist Human Nature and the Hermeneutics of Love

As Ellul suggests, because of the technological transformation of Western (and now global) society, biblical conceptions of human nature have been increasingly rejected in favor of a more abstract view. In the latter, the rich structure of natural relations specified in creation has been gradually replaced by a pattern of more abstract relationships that are amenable, because of the flexibility abstraction makes possible, to the demands of a technological society — to the requirement that persons be maximally adaptable to the ever changing organizational patterns that promote optimal effectiveness and efficiency. The result has been to obscure what the Bible rather directly designates as a normative natural order — an order that reflects God's purposes in creation. The biblical order is seen as merely conventional, or perhaps as natural for a pre-technological age, but not as a calling, normative for all cultures at all times. The consequence, I will show, has been a decreasing ability to read Scripture, resulting in an ever increasing deformation of the New Covenant community, as well as the larger human community the church was intended to preserve. In the course of explicating these claims it will be necessary to sketch some of the outlines of what I take to be a biblical notion of human nature and the hermeneutic compatible with it.

Let me begin by contrasting the view that human nature is richly structured with what I will call the minimalist position on human nature — the position that human nature is limited to a relatively few, highly general cognitive capacities that enable humans to reflect and create cultures subject only to environmental constraints. Within these broad limits, the variations we observe in human activity from culture to culture are said to be entirely learned, and none is to be preferred as more natural or normative than any other. Any distinctions between "natural" and "unnatural" activities may be thought of as local cultural conventions, themselves learned in the context of cultures that represent nothing more than the learning to survive adaptations of minimal human nature.

For the reasons given above, the minimalist conception of human nature has become increasingly popular in secular culture and, consequently, in most Christian circles. Unfortunately, it leads to a particularly striking exegetical error. This error is, I believe, that of reading Jesus, Paul, and James through the spectacles of what I call the hermeneutics of love. The New Testament is often read as introducing a general principle of love which, because it is associated with a minimalist view of human nature, is conceived as applying across the boundaries of cultural context in a way that relativizes the specific commandment structure of Scripture.

In the context of the assumption that human nature has little if any natural structure, the commandment to love God and to love one's neighbor as oneself is seen as providing not only necessary, but also sufficient guidance for the believer. I will attempt to show that this view is mistaken. It is, among other things, the result of ignoring a rich and specific context of human nature. The consequence has been an interpretation of the biblical texts, New Testament as well as Old, that relativizes their content and thus renders them incoherent as sources of guidance and destroys their integrity as documents purporting to be the Word of God.

How does this happen? Consider, for example, a common exegesis of Jesus' debates with the Pharisees. In these controversies, Jesus is seen as presenting a kind of universal moral code — "Love God, and love your neighbor as yourself" — as contrasted with the particularism of the Pharisees' concern for the sabbath, the distinction between the clean and the unclean, and the various hedge laws. Likewise Paul, and even James, is taken as supporting the move away from particularistic legalism toward the invocation of an abstract "faith that works through love" (Galatians 5:6) and "the royal law . . . Thou shalt love thy neighbor as thyself" (James 2:8). Accordingly, growing as a Christian is understood to involve growing in love, and love is a universal principle by which we can rightly assess, apply, or even desist from applying, more concrete commandments.

Paul's recommendations about eating meat offered to idols (1 Corinthians 8 and 10) or honoring one day above another (Romans 14) are sometimes taken as models for understanding all particularistic injunctions. If one is too devoted to what we may call a particularism, then that will be taken as a sign of spiritual immaturity — an immaturity to which we might (depending on the situation) condescend in terms of our behavior, but which we must not allow to bind our consciences (1 Corinthians 10:23-33). On this view, the truly mature will know that all that really matters is that they act from the principle of love alone.

So the problem of eating meat offered to idols can appear to provide a strategy for dealing with what, in light of our current cultural situation, may be seen as idiosyncrasies in the commandment structure of the Scriptures. The result is a kind of situation ethics. Some evangelicals, for example, have denied that extramarital sexual relations — including homosexual relations — are sinful if they are executed in the context of committed (i.e., non-promiscuous), non-exploitative (e.g., non-pederastic) love (see, for example, *Christianity Today*, November 22, 1993, pp. 38, 39). In the absence of a distinction between what is natural and unnatural for human beings, the principle of love alone has been taken as sufficient for deciding the right thing to do.

Admittedly, arguments in favor of Christian extramarital sex do not always explicitly invoke the hermeneutics of love. But it should be borne in mind that an argument may sometimes appear plausible because its conclusion is supported by assumptions that lie beyond what is explicitly stated in the argument itself. So although an argument for homosexual behavior or extramarital heterosexual behavior may make no explicit reference to the minimalist vision of human nature or the hermeneutics of love, the judgment that its conclusions are plausible — that such behaviors may be the will of God — arguably presupposes the hermeneutics of love. In the absence of a principled argument against the hermeneutics of love, a continuing move toward the relativism of situation ethics seems not only likely, but unavoidable.

Beyond Minimalism and the Hermeneutics of Love

Are there principles that would show how the particular commandment structure of Scripture was summarized but not overridden by the commandment to love? I argue that one such principle is the biblical doctrine of human nature. The injunction to love (the thesis that love is the fulfilling of the law) was given in the context of a rich (i.e., non-minimalist) set of assumptions about human nature, themselves derived (explicitly or implicitly) from Scripture — especially Genesis 1–3. It is only because Jesus could assume that his hearers shared with him a set of presuppositions about human nature that he could summarize the law and the prophets in terms of the two great commandments to love. Accordingly, by recognizing the existence of a biblical doctrine of human nature we can provide a principled argument against the hermeneutics of love and the kind of situation ethics described above.

I am not arguing that every biblical commandment is grounded solely in human nature, nor that every question of practice that obedient Christians might ask is answerable without reference to local cultural conditions. According to 1 Corinthians 10, the question of eating meat offered to idols must be answered relative to the consciences of those involved and their neighbors. How one ought to behave with respect to this question is, to a degree, culturally determined. Nor yet am I arguing that the principle of love is irrelevant to the problem of deciding the right thing to do. I am, however, claiming that the Scriptures both teach and presuppose a doctrine of universal human nature that must be consulted if one is to discover God's will in many practical situations.

To support this claim, I will present a necessarily brief examination of the notion of human nature found in Scripture, focusing primarily on the letters of Paul, and principally 1 Corinthians. In this context, I will argue first for the existence of a specific human nature, and secondly that human nature is intimately linked to the created structure of the human family. Since the hermeneutics of love derives primary justification from a peculiar view of human nature, a more biblical notion of human nature will, I believe, result in a more adequate and revealing hermeneutic. The integration of the biblical texts achieved by that hermeneutic will then be offered as evidence for the biblical status of the proposed conception of human nature.

Paul's first letter to the Corinthians provides an obvious point of departure for a discussion of human nature in light of Scripture. The differing roles for men and women prescribed in chapters 11 and 14 are explicitly justified by the apostle in an argument from creation: "But I want you to know that the head of every man is Christ, the head of the woman is the man and the head of Christ is God." "For a man indeed ought not to cover his head, forasmuch as he is the image and glory of God: but the woman is the glory of the man. For the man is not of the woman; but the woman is of the man. Neither was the man created for the woman; but the woman for the man. For this cause ought the woman to have (a symbol of) authority on her head because of the angels" (1 Corinthians 11:3, 7-10). In chapter 14 Paul enjoins the women to silence in the assembly on the basis of "the law" — "Let the women keep silent in the churches; for they are not permitted to speak, but let them subject themselves, just as the law also says. And if they desire to learn anything, let them ask their own husbands at home; for it is improper for a woman to speak in the church" (1 Corinthians 14:34, 35).

The reference to the law in verse 34 is probably pointing to the already cited creation account. That this is what Paul has in mind appears especially likely in view of striking parallels between 1 Corinthians 14:34, 35 and 1 Timothy 2 — "Let a woman quietly receive instruction with entire submissiveness. But I do not allow a woman to teach or to exercise authority over a man, but to remain quiet. For it was Adam who was first created, and then Eve. And it was not Adam who was deceived, but the woman being quite deceived, fell into the transgression" (1Timothy 2:11-14). In the latter text, explicit reference is made to the creation account as a justification for women's silence and submission to the authority of men in the church.

For some time I had held that these injunctions were grounded in Paul's views of the differing purposes of God in creating men and women. By implication, I supposed that those differing purposes were accompanied by the provision of somewhat different capacities, or aspects of human nature. That is, I supposed that Paul was teaching that the role differences he was prescribing for the church were in some sense "natural." However, it had not occurred to me that the notion of human nature would be important for the exegesis of material beyond what appeared to me to be two isolated texts. When I recently began to reread the letter, I did not expect the doctrine of human nature to emerge as foundational to most of 1 Corinthians, and certainly not to the Scriptures as a whole. Nevertheless, to my considerable surprise this is what happened. I now hold that the character of human nature, as presented in Scripture, is crucial not only for an understanding of apostolic prescriptions concerning gender roles, but also for sound exegesis of Scripture as a whole. The apostle's arguments surrounding gender roles are then simply examples of a more general category of scriptural arguments.

I will demonstrate the foregoing thesis by showing that an adequate exegesis of 1 Corinthians and a number of related texts requires a rich view of human nature — a view dependent upon the Old Testament Scriptures and elaborated by Paul and others elsewhere in the New Testament. 1 Corinthians is deeply concerned with the contingencies and peculiarities of human nature throughout. In no other New Testament letter do we find such a close confrontation of the consequences and responsibilities attendant upon the unique interdependence between sexuality and family life that is so central to human nature. Chapters 5 through 7 are devoted largely to difficulties that arise from the centrality of that interconnection. Incest, adultery, fornication, conjugal rights, divorce, separation, celibacy — these all pertain to problems deriving from the familial character of human nature. Paul's arguments clearly depend upon a rich set of assumptions about the character of human nature, including its strengths and weaknesses with regard to the difficulties associated with family life, derived from the Scriptures as a whole and common human experience interpreted in light of Scripture. In support of this claim, I will show that Paul held three positions that are consistent with a rich and specific view of human nature and incompatible with the minimalist view: First, human nature is the ground of a distinction between natural and unnatural activities; second, human nature has normative implications, defined in terms of specific purposes of God in creation; third, as a principle by which God orders and governs the world, human nature and its associated claims have continuing validity in the era of the New Covenant.

First, consider Paul's position that human nature grounds the distinction between natural and unnatural activities. He initiates the fifth chapter of 1 Corinthians by confronting the issue of the man who is living incestuously with his father's wife. It is significant here that he does not treat this as an ordinary act of fornication. Rather, he expresses shock because this is a sin that even the Gentiles would regard as unnatural. No doubt his own sense of the unnaturalness of the act was not grounded in the judgment of Gentile consciences — consciences he probably viewed as relatively insensitive. Instead, he must certainly have had in mind the fact that to have sexual intercourse with one's father's wife is one of the abominations listed in Leviticus 18. Moses pronounced such practices not only unnatural, but unnatural in a way that is not relative to the cultural context — "Do not defile yourselves by any of these things; for by all these the nations which I am casting out before you have become defiled. For the land has become defiled, therefore I have visited its punishment upon it, so the land has spewed out its inhabitants" (Leviticus 18:24, 25). The implied reference to the passage in Leviticus points to the existence of an assumed natural order — an inherently moral order whose claims transcend the claims of local culture. After all, it is the land (i.e., nature itself) that has vomited out its inhabitants.

The unnaturalness of the activities proscribed in Leviticus 18 is distinctly noted by Paul in his comments about homosexuality in the first chapter of Romans — a passage which also appears to be informed by Leviticus 18. In Romans 1, Paul refers to those who engage in homosexual perversions as departing from the "natural use" of their own, and their partners', bodies. Homosexuality is said to be wrong because it is unnatural — even if it is culturally acceptable. It violates the purposes of God in the creation which, as Genesis 1–3 tells us, include that mankind is created male and female to the end that they should be fruitful and multiply in the context of families. In contrast to the activities discussed in Leviticus 18, families are natural in the strong sense that they are the direct result of God's creative act. Humans have been created to live in families. In the Genesis account of creation, even marriage is presented as a part of the creative act of God. Man is created male and female. In Christ's discussion of divorce in Matthew 19, he affirms the status of marriage as ordained by God at the time of creation. Each family is something like a distinct natural kind. Man is not to undo God's creation by engaging in divorce, nor is he to pollute it through adultery. Families are natural and sexual practices are natural or unnatural as they are consistent or inconsistent with the natural family structure. The perversions proscribed in Leviticus — incest, homosexuality, bestiality — are unnatural because their practice is incompatible with the natural family structure. That structure, which grounds the distinction between natural and unnatural activities, is incompatible with the minimalist view of human nature.

Let us proceed to the second point. We have seen that Paul's notion of human nature is sufficiently rich to ground a distinction between natural and unnatural activities. However, the examples given above also show that the distinction between natural and unnatural activities is not merely descriptive. It is normative as well. For Paul, human nature is defined in terms of God's purposes in creation and the calling those purposes imply. So, fornication is proscribed because "The body is not for fornication, but for the Lord" (1 Corinthians 6:13). As with the just mentioned passage in Romans 1, we see here that Paul's ethics depends on a rich conception of the purposes of God in creation. Not only must we be concerned about the intended use of the body with respect to sexual partners, but also about the uses that God has for the body as his temple. Although the issue of love is central to the message of 1 Corinthians, no reference to a general principle of love is found in the discussion of fornication. Instead, the dominant question is quite concrete: "What is the body for? What calling does it imply?"

For Paul, these questions point to the fact that the created structure of human nature, with its normative dimension, is a means through which God intends to order and govern the world. It is an aspect of his kingdom. This is brought out more fully in connection with the doctrine of husband headship (1 Corinthians 11; Ephesians 5). The natural order of the human family, including the headship of the husband, is said to depend on God's different purposes for men and women. Thus, one legitimation for husband headship is that the man was not created "for the woman, but the woman is for the man" (1 Corinthians 11:9 [presumably, to be "an help fit for him" — Genesis 2:18]).

The structure of the headship metaphor is clear: as the head is over the body so the husband is head "over" the wife. In general, when the term *head* is used metaphorically to designate a person, some dimension of superior authority, leadership, or prominence is in view. In Scripture, this is a common figure of speech. Consider Exodus 18:25: "And Moses chose able men out of all Israel, and made them heads over the people, rulers of thousands, rulers of hundreds, rulers of fifties, and rulers of tens" (see also Judges 11:11; 1 Samuel 15:17; 2 Samuel 22:44; 1 Kings 8:1; 2 Kings 2:3; 1 Chronicles 5:24; 2 Chronicles 5:2; Psalm 110:6; Isaiah 7:8, 9). In the absence of any good reason for supposing that Paul was departing from this precedent, I conclude that the husband is called the head of the wife because he has authority to lead his wife. The headship metaphor implies that the husband has been given the authority and responsibility to rule in the family. It is through responsible acknowledgment of the complementary differences in nature and calling between husbands and their wives that God rules in families.

Support for the foregoing interpretation of headship is found in Ephesians 5:22-25. There the apostle explicitly argues that headship entails asymmetric responsibilities with respect to leadership. So, "(22) Wives, submit yourselves unto your own husbands as unto the Lord. (23) *Because* the husband is the head of the wife as Christ is the head of the church;

and he is the savior of the body. (24) *But,* as the church is subject to Christ, so let the wives be subject to their own husbands in everything. (25) Husbands, love your wives, even as Christ loved the church and gave himself for it" (italics added). The implications of verse 23 are bi-directional: In 23, *because* points back to 22 stating that the reason for the submission of wives is husband headship. In 24, *but* brings the focus back to the implications of the headship relation between husbands and their wives (from which it had been temporarily diverted at the end of 23). In this context, 24 states the manner and degree of submission required of wives in light of their own husbands' headship. In 25, Paul goes on to spell out the responsibilities of husbands in light of their own calling to headship. Their love for their wives is to be modeled after Christ's re-demptive love of the church. Again, it is through the acknowledgment and practice of the natural and complementary differences between husbands and wives, differences and complementarities that are invisible from the perspective of minimalism, that the kingdom of God comes to a family.

Of course, all this may seem unbearably sexist and unjust to those who presuppose a minimalist view of human nature (a view incompatible with such asymmetries). Differing views of human nature can result in quite different judgments about what is just. However, it is important to keep in mind what is at stake in focusing on the asymmetrical aspects of the husband/wife relationship. I am not arguing that all aspects of the husband/wife relationship are asymmetrical. Still, the husband/wife asymmetries emphasized here are important because they represent clear counterexamples to the minimalist conception of human nature and thus refute the hermeneutics of love.

Third, in view of the fact that human nature is one of the avenues through which God governs the world, Paul affirms the enduring validity of the claims of human nature relative to other claims of the kingdom of God manifest in the church and the gospel. Even the limitations placed upon the rights associated with human nature (e.g., temporary abridgment of conjugal rights and the legitimation of celibacy as a to-be-preferred gift) are enunciated in a way that supports the validity of human nature as God's creation. Although it is only human nature, other claims that arise in connection with the kingdom of God — for example, prayer and un-distracted devotion to the Lord — are to be qualified and limited in light of the claims of human nature.

Similarly, the already discussed passage in 1 Corinthians 11 teaches that the created order is not to be obliterated or ignored in light of the New Covenant. The fact that the Holy Spirit has been distributed to all flesh (both sexes) does not justify ignoring the husband/wife headship asymmetry grounded in God's purposes in creation. Paul appears to be saying that the husband's natural leadership of the family is not altered by the fact that both men and women receive the Holy Spirit, and this is to be underscored in the manner in which the gifts of the Spirit are expressed. Again, the claims of human nature are real and valid. Again, other aspects of the kingdom of God are harmonized with the concerns of human nature.

Further, recall in this connection that an attack on God's purposes for creation in the name of spirituality was an aspect of the heresy Paul warned of in his prophecy (1 Timothy 4:3) that in the latter times, some would depart from the faith, "forbidding to marry, and commanding to abstain from meats which God hath created to be received with thanksgiving." Again, observe that the apostle honors God's specific purposes in creating human nature over against the claims of a false spirituality that does not see the created order as an important means through which God's will for the world is achieved. Even in the era of the New Covenant, failure to appreciate the just claims of human nature and creation can be a symptom of apostasy.

Finally, so far from being set aside in light of the New Covenant, the enduring value of the created family and its just claims is radically affirmed by the apostle in that it is made an analogy of God's government and redemption of the world. As we have seen, 1 Corinthians 11 and Ephesians 5 present husband headship as analogous to Christ's governmental and redemptive relation to the church. These analogies are instructive on two levels. First, they tell us something important about the nature of God and his relation to us, as well as informing us about our own human nature and the responsibilities that accompany it. Second, the value of the created order is deeply affirmed. Its inner structure provides categories through which the character of God's own being, as well as his governmental and redemptive activities toward us, are revealed in Scripture. In this respect, biblical revelation is intelligible because it is given to us in terms of categories that are natural to human beings. On the other hand, if the natural structure of humanity (the vehicle of the analogy) is obscured and devalued, as it is in the minimalist theory of human nature, the biblical revelation of God and his ways with us (the tenor of the analogy) will be obscured and devalued as well. Of course, this has already begun to happen.

To summarize, I have offered three lines of argument supporting the conclusion that Paul held a rich conception of human nature, one incompatible with the minimalist view. First, human nature is sufficiently rich that it grounds a distinction between natural and unnatural human activities that may be applied across cultural boundaries. Second, human nature is defined in terms of God's specific and differential purposes in creation, purposes that structure our calling and provide a basis for God's government of the world. Third, since human nature is a fundamental ingredient of the kingdom of God, it is not set aside with the advent of the New Covenant. To the contrary, the categories of human nature are taken as an analogy through which the New Covenant is communicated in Scripture. To invalidate those categories, as the minimalist view does, would render the biblical revelation unintelligible. Taken together, these considerations constitute a strong argument against minimalism and the hermeneutics of love which depends upon it.

Another Look at the Hermeneutics of Love

The hermeneutics of love depends on a particular reading of a number of New Testament passages. But we have seen that there are many other passages which, because they point to a much richer conception of human nature than that presupposed in the hermeneutics of love, suggest another hermeneutic. With this new set of hermeneutical spectacles in place, let us return to some of those passages that provided the primary motivation for the hermeneutics of love, and see if they can be read differently.

Consider, first of all, the debates between Christ and the Pharisees concerning the sabbath. Just what did Jesus argue against the Pharisees? Did he condemn the concrete particularism of the Pharisees while advocating a more abstract ethic of love? Not at all. He referred instead to the creative purposes of God in making man and instituting the sabbath. He held that "the sabbath was made for man, and not man for the sabbath" (Mark 2:27). The sabbath was a time for rest and release from the ordinary burdens of life. Keeping sabbath was not intended by God to be a burden but a joy. Even the oxen, not to mention slaves and servants, were released from their burdens on the sabbath. It is even more appropriate, then, to release the children of Abraham from the bondage of disease and satanic oppression on the sabbath (Luke 13:16). The Pharisees were not wrong because they were too concrete, but because they failed to understand what the sabbath and men were for.

A second line of argument in favor of the hermeneutics of love lies in those passages (1 Corinthians 10 and Romans 14) that speak of the role of differing consciences in determining what to do. However, the fact that Scripture addresses this question in a way that explicitly recognizes cultural differences provides important support for the argument developed here. In the first place, the passages in question refute the caricature that the authors of Scripture were not sufficiently sophisticated to recognize the importance of cultural differences. The first-century Mediterranean world of the Apostle Paul was certainly more culturally diverse than that of middle-class North America. As a non-Palestinian Jew, Paul was far from naive about the role of cultural differences in determining appropriate behavior. In the second place, the fact that Paul explicitly recognized the constraining role of cultural differences strengthens, by way of contrast, the force of those injunctions he grounds in considerations that transcend the differences among cultures — considerations involving claims about created human nature. Thus, the distinction between constraints that may or may not be obligatory in a given culture and those that constitute obligations on all cultures is already found in Scripture. Even as he recognizes the importance of cultural differences, Paul asserts that there are questions that can and must be answered in ways that are relatively independent of local culture; and that the overarching context for these issues has been determined by God in his creative act recorded in Genesis 1–3 — an act which, as the above evidence shows, Paul believed to include the constitution of universal obligatory conditions on human culture. On such questions, exclusive attention to local context can be seriously misleading.

Conclusion

I wish to conclude with a reflection on the significance of the clash to which Ellul has directed our attention. As already indicated, distortions of the biblical view of human nature imply distortions of the biblical view of God and of the fundamental practice of Scripture. On the other hand, from the perspective of the modern, technological rationality, human nature as characterized in Scripture is at best a nuisance to be tolerated, and at worst an evil whose eradication is the price of progress. It is no longer to be respected and lovingly cared for as the creation of God, or nurtured as an aspect of God's calling. Ellul is undoubtedly correct in seeing the clash between human nature and technological rationality as decisive. No self-deception should be permitted here. If human nature is suppressed and knowledge of it rejected and as much as possible eradicated, then that will also mean the rejection and eradication of the knowledge of God and of the life he wills for us. Scripture will in large measure be closed to us.

It is important to understand that the difficulty we face is not only theoretical, but a matter of practice as well. It derives from the increasingly pervasive domination of the human world by what Ellul called the technological system, a system organized around the imperative to be effective and efficient in achieving our technically specified goals. The various economic, social, and ecclesiastic forces arrayed against human nature today are, in large part, the differing faces of the technological system and its imperative. The disintegration of human life produced by the technological system has, of course, led to a diminished sense of what is natural for us. In this context, it has become increasingly difficult to recognize in Scripture a theme that was relatively obvious to another age.

From the perspective of Scripture, human nature is constituted in relation to certain ends that give structure to our existence and inform our calling. These ends have very little to do with promoting efficiency and very much to do with the glory of God and the blessing of mankind in its specific humanity. Contrary to modernity, Scripture does not place a high priority on efficiency. The sabbath, for example, actually impedes economic efficiency. The sabbath has special significance in light of the theme of this paper since it recalls the creation of the natural order and blesses man in his specific human nature (i.e., the sabbath is for man as he actually is, not as he might, theoretically, have been). Of course it is clear that almost no one takes the sabbath seriously anymore. The created order it recalls and the specific human nature it blesses are no longer occasions for rejoicing, but conditions of resistance to the technological system. In the modern age, when there is a clash between the demands of the technological system and the created order, technology wins out. The conditions for man's meaningful existence are being progressively eliminated; and for many, the time may come (for some it is already here) when there will not seem to be much reason left for living.

In summary, we have seen, from a biblical perspective, that for humans some of the most fundamental person-defining relationships are those that constitute persons as members of families. Scripture regards the husband/wife, parent/child, and sibling relations as the basic familial configurations. These configurations carry with them patterns of relationships within which the personhood, rights, and responsibilities of those involved come to be realized. But those patterns of relationships are not deducible from a minimalist view of human nature, which originates in the demand for technological efficiency. Instead, they derive from a certain contingency, or even peculiarity, of creation and calling. Of the many conceivable patterns that might have been chosen, only one was chosen — one that would, among other things, reveal to us something essential about the nature of God and our relation to him, and in so doing, nurture us toward expressing his image. A biblically oriented account of human personhood should begin with this sort of consideration in mind.

Human Agency and Its Social Formation

ERIC L. JOHNSON

IF WE DEFINE an "agent" as something that contributes causally to bring about some state of affairs, then tornadoes and people are both agents. For example, a tornado comes along and clears away a chicken coop, clean as a whistle. Or the farmer may do the same thing. But the word "do" has very different surroundings and implications in the two cases. Of the farmer you can ask, Why did you do that? and he will have reasons: The coop was about to fall down anyway, and he wanted to plant cabbages on the spot. This answer is pregnant with psychology. The farmer had a *desire* (to plant cabbages on the spot) and a *belief* (that the chicken coop was in the way, and wasn't doing anybody any good anyway), and in consequence of *deliberating* the pros and cons, he formed an *intention* to take down the coop, which he *attentively executed* by various applications of crowbar and pickup truck. The farmer's action has a background in many other beliefs and desires, for example, the belief that the well-manured soil under the chicken coop would be good for growing cabbages. Furthermore, if the action turns out to be strikingly good or bad, we are likely to attribute *responsibility* to the farmer for his action. For example, if he inadvertently takes down the neighbor's shiny new chicken coop instead of his ramshackle one, we will blame him and possibly hold him liable. But in fact he got the right one, and feels as though the action came from *him* in a way that, say, his hiccups and heartbeat did not. The hiccups merely *happened to* him, but demolishing the coop was his own voluntary action. And we, as onlooking lay psychologists, agree with him. By contrast, the "agency" of the tornado has none of these psychological

I am grateful to members of the Pew seminar of June 1994 at Wheaton College for comments and criticism that have improved this paper, and to Robert C. Roberts for significant help in the writing of the opening and the first section.

138

properties. It has no beliefs or desires, does not deliberate, makes no choices and forms no intentions; it cannot be praised or blamed or otherwise held responsible for clearing the chicken coop; the distinction between its doing something and its undergoing forces and influences is not categorical, as it is in the case of human actions. In the case of the tornado there is no such thing as execution, because there is no plan to execute; there is just physical movement, with its causes and effects.

Philosophers have been much exercised to explore the differences between human agency and what we might call "natural" agencies (see Macmurray, 1957; Chisholm, 1966; Langford, 1971; Evans, 1982; Davidson, 1980; Aristotle, 1985; Thomas Aquinas, 1948). But the history of psychology in the twentieth century has been, in large part, the history of an effort to blur this distinction in the name of science. For many, "science" has come to mean pre-eminently natural science, the kind of science that explains so well the actions of "agents" like tornadoes. That history has also been marked by a steady retreat from the effort to reduce human agency to natural agency, in the face of the undeniable distinctiveness of human agency. Whatever success the blurring project has had is due to the fact that humans are, to a significant extent, subject to causal forces outside their volition (or forces that shape their volition). Brain damage and extreme child abuse clearly affect and limit the agency of their victims, and such facts must be taken into account in any theory of human agency. However, common sense and Christian teaching suggest that human behavior cannot be adequately explained without reference to concepts like choice, intention, and responsibility (see Talbot, this volume, and Jones, this volume).

My primary aim is to explore from a Christian standpoint how human agency develops and what facilitates its development. To situate and further this exploration, I will begin by pointing out some features of human agency that are especially highlighted in the Bible. I will then turn to a sketch of modern psychology's attempts to account for human agency in naturalistic terms. This short chronicle will show scientific psychology moving closer and closer to the Christian view of agency, yet without attaining it. I will then illustrate the account of agency that I have been building by examining conceptually an exemplary case of human agency. And last, I shall discuss the social formation of agency from the points of view of Christianity and developmental psychology.

Notes on Agency from Scripture

We find in the Bible many narratives of divine and human actions, as well as theological/anthropological commentary (e.g. that of the Apostle Paul and much in the Gospel of John) that brings out special features of our agency in its relations to God's agency. Taken together these contain a concept of agency that is largely a common possession of all human cultures, but that is also in some ways distinctive. In the present section I shall highlight six features of the biblical concept of human agency: (1) embodiment, with its limitations and dependencies, (2) co-agency, (3) the derivation of action from inwardness, (4) the movement of the will, (5) goodness and evil, and (6) responsibility.

Features of Agency

Embodiment

In the fifth chapter of John's Gospel is a story of a severely handicapped man who desired to be healed. He lay by a pool that was known to be a site of miraculous healings, but his agency was so impaired by his condition that he could not get himself into the pool at the times the healings occurred. He needed what he lacked to obtain what he lacked. Such an example brings out our dependency on bodily functioning that we usually hardly notice, so automatically do normal bodies work most of the time. The normal course of the majority of human actions requires controlled movements of parts of our bodies. I cannot write this paper without some such movement — of my hand holding a pen, of fingers on the keyboard, of tongue and lips if I dictate into a machine. Only a limited number of actions, such as mathematical computations "in the head" and acts of imagination, can be performed without any bodily movement at all. The case of the sick man in John 5 thus illustrates dramatically a general fact about human action, namely *that we are highly dependent on the contingency of our bodies' functioning properly*.

Co-agency

It also illustrates that human actions are virtually never completely individual, but are *co-actions with others*. The sick man complained to Jesus that he had no one to put him into the healing pool. With this little bit of help, presumably, his powers of agency would have been greatly expanded, and we might think of all the actions he would have performed in the future as performed with the help of that helper on the great day of his healing. In this way, virtually all of his future actions would be co-actions with that helper. But as the story reports, no one helped him get to the pool, and Jesus healed him directly with the words "Rise, take up your pallet, and walk" (v. 8). Thus Jesus became his co-agent. In this sense of co-agency, every action that every person performs is a co-action, insofar as other agents are involved in providing the conditions of our agency.

But some actions are co-actions in a more obvious and special way. When the religious leaders persecuted Jesus for healing the man on the sabbath, Jesus responded that "the Son can do nothing of his own accord, but only what he sees the Father doing; for whatever he does, that the Son does likewise" (v. 19). We have here the picture of coordinated action, in which the Father takes the lead and the Son, watching the Father, models his own actions on those of the Father. This is a special case of a characteristic aspect of many human actions, illustrated by any example of team action. When a basketball player makes a goal, it is correct to say (and we do say), not only that the individual made the goal, but that the *team* made the goal. The individual could not have made the goal without the coordinated actions of the other team members. In cases of this sort, not only do other people supply some of the conditions neces-sary for the individual to act, but the coordinated agent or agents share in the intention to perform the particular action in question (the healing of a sick man, the making of a basketball goal). Since the mental back-ground of beliefs and desires is shared, at least in part, by the two or more co-agents (and since such a mental background is necessary to true agency, as we are arguing), we may call this kind of coordinated agency *true co-agency*.

Inwardness

Our third feature of the biblical concept of agency can be treated briefly, inasmuch as we have already illustrated it in the introduction, and it is recurrent in our whole discussion. But it is worth noting how strongly the New Testament emphasizes this point, often in connection with the word "heart" (καρδία). For example, Jesus comments that "it is from within, from the human heart, that evil intentions come: fornication, theft, murder, adultery, avarice, wickedness, deceit, licentiousness, envy, slander, pride, folly" (Mark 7:21-22). So essential is the inward side of action that its moral value is in place even in the absence of the characteristic behavior: "I say to you that every one who looks at a woman lustfully has already com-mitted adultery with her in his heart" (Matthew 5:28). And the Apostle Paul points out that even if the outward "action" is good, it may be worthless from God's point of view: "If I give away all I have, and if I deliver my body to be burned, but have not love, I gain nothing" (1 Corinthians 13:3).

Movement of the Will

A particular aspect of inwardness that seems to be especially essential to the biblical concept of agency, and which may derive, in our Western culture, from the Bible, is the *movement of the will*. This fourth feature of the biblical concept of agency is captured by a rather diverse set of verbs used by the Apostle Paul to express the human power to choose between good and evil, between the life of the Spirit and the life of the flesh (Romans 8), between the old man (ἄνθροπος) and the new (Colossians 3). This choice is available to Christians inasmuch as they have the Spirit but are also still subject to the attractions of sin. One can "set one's mind" (φρονέω) on the things of the Spirit or on those of the flesh (Romans 8:5-7); one can "yield" or "present" (παρίστημι) one's members to sin as instruments of wickedness or to God as instruments of righteousness (Romans 6:13); one can "walk" (περιπατέω, στοιχέω) or not by the Spirit (Galatians 5:16, 25); one can "seek" (ζητέω) the things above or the things on earth (Colossians 3:1); one can "kill" (νεκρόω) what is earthly in oneself (Colossians 3:5; a list of vices follows); one can "take off" (ἀπεκδύομαι; ἀποτίθημι — Ephesians 4:22) the old nature and "put on" (ἐνδύομαι) the new or, presumably, vice versa (Colossians 3:9-10, 12); etc. As I say, these choices presuppose that one is a member of the church and thus has the resources of the gospel and the Spirit available. The choice is whether to wear them or not, whether to take them up and let them work in one's life. Perhaps we could think of them as two partially formed personalities, which one can adopt, like an actor, more or less at will. The richness of Paul's vocabulary suggests that we should think of such "acts of will" not in an abstract way as a sort of spiritual grunting in the direction of the Spirit or the relaxing counterpart of such grunting, but as definite actions of various sorts, such as calling one's baptism to remembrance, reading spiritual biographies, helping out in a soup kitchen, reading Scripture, praying, or seeking out the spiritual counsel of a friend.

Goodness and Evil

On the biblical concept of agency, it is important that actions can be *good or evil*. The central biblical way of conceptualizing the distinction between good and evil actions is their conformity to God's will or lack thereof. In the Old Testament this conformity takes the form of keeping God's commandments and obeying his decrees as enunciated by the prophets. In the New Testament it takes the form of attachment to, reliance on, and service to Jesus Christ, of living as a member of Christ's body and in the fellowship of the Holy Spirit. By Christ's incarnation, death, and resurrection, and the descent of the Holy Spirit, a new order of the world in relation to God has been established, and one becomes right with God not by obeying commandments and decrees (although such obedience will inevitably follow) but by attaching oneself to the Head of that new order and taking one's place as a member of it. Right actions are ones that express this attachment and membership, and wrong actions are ones that are contrary to it. From what we noted about inwardness it is obvious that this attachment and membership have profound implications for the member's attitudes (emotions, concerns, outlook, perceptual dispositions) and not just for "behavior" in some thin sense. To be a Christian is to be a new creation. It is to have a new set of dispositions of the heart, lists of which are scattered throughout Paul's letters. In Colossians 3, for example, the list includes compassion, kindness, lowliness, meekness, patience, forbearance, forgiveness, love, peace, thankfulness, singleness of heart. Such are the traits that the Christian "puts on" (ἐνδύομαι) like a new set of clothes. The implication of the new covenant, as contrasted with the old, is that these "clothes" have been provided, are already there to be put on through the work of the Holy Spirit. The Christian virtues are first of all forms of fellowship with God. The implication for the Christian concept of agency is that the actions flowing naturally from such virtues as forgiveness, love, and peace are examples of what I earlier called "true co-agency." It is a kind of team action between God and the believer(s), although in this case the principal agent is God. This type of co-agency, in which believers consciously affirm God's involvement in their actions and consciously desire to be in God's will, is a definitive characteristic of proper human agency from the Christian point of view. It is part of the meaning of the New Testament affirmation that Christ is "in" believers; for example, so sensible is Paul of Christ's co-agency with him that Paul almost disappears as a separate agent: "I have been crucified with Christ; it is no longer I who live, but Christ who lives in me." But he goes on to distinguish himself from Christ when he says, "the life I now live in the flesh I live by faith in the Son of God, who loved me and gave himself for me" (Galatians 2:20).

Responsibility

In the introduction we noted that one of the cherished features of the everyday concept of agency is the notion that we human agents, unlike any other kinds, are *responsible* for our actions. Praise and blame, self-congratulation and guilt, are in order. While the stress on co-agency in the New Testament changes the ascription of responsibility somewhat from the common sense view, human agency still has very much the quality of responsibility. People in general are assumed to be responsible for their actions, in the sense that when they do wrong they could have done right, or at least could have done better than they did. Jews are taken to be responsible on the basis of their knowledge of God's will as expressed in "Moses and the prophets" (Luke 16:29, 31); non-Jews are responsible on the basis of a natural knowledge of God (Romans 1:20) and conscience (Romans 2:14-16). Christians have adequate knowledge of God's will inasmuch as they have the law of the old covenant as well as knowledge of the kind of life and character that are offered them in Christ. Morally, Christians are co-agents with Christ and the Holy Spirit, so that when their action is in conformity with the will of God, the credit is to be given primarily to God. (They also are to be praised for what God in Christ is doing through them.) However, when Christians' actions fall short, God is not to be blamed since God is at all times ready to work in the believer; failure is thus the result of the believer's failure to tap that moral resource. It does not necessarily follow that the Christian is *always* to blame, for factors beyond one's control may prevent a person from "putting on the new nature" (Colossians 3:10). Moreover, we must not assume that yielding oneself as an instrument of righteousness (Romans 6:13) is easy or instantaneously accomplished; more likely it is a lifelong and never-completed process (Romans 7:21). Nevertheless, the chief locus of responsibility, in Christian agency, is in this yielding, this putting on, this seeking, this setting one's mind on the things that have been accomplished, so that they may bear actual fruit in one's heart and behavior. When Christians are to be blamed for their moral failures, they are to be blamed for not putting on their new nature; and when they are to be praised, they are to be praised for yielding to God's working in them (2 Corinthians 11:23-29). Paul expresses the logic of Christian responsibility succinctly when he says, "work out your own salvation with fear and trembling; for God is at work in you, both to will and to work for his good pleasure" (Philippians 2:12-13).

Agency in Twentieth-Century Psychology

Natural Science Approaches to Agency

Due in part to the influence of Christian thought, the existence of human will and the human capacity to make responsible choices was for centuries assumed by most thinkers in Western culture. However, as the explanatory power of scientific methods became increasingly evident in physics, chemistry, and biology, the philosophy of science and the social (or human) sciences began to assume that such methods alone were capable of leading to genuine knowledge. Psychologists in particular were frustrated by the confusion that seemed to result from theological and philosophical speculation. By the twentieth century, they were frustrated also by the barrenness of subject-dependent methods like introspection when used in the service of psychological science. So modern psychologists, desiring that their research yield indisputable findings, limited their study of humans to third-person observations that could be replicated by anyone with professional training and equipment. With this methodological shift, along with the theory of evolution, humans came to be viewed as no more than intelligent organisms whose functioning results from purely natural causes, subject only to natural forces. Concepts like the will were lost since they could not easily be examined through third-person observations of the human subject. Instead, human choice came to be described in terms of cause-and-effect relations among biological and/or environmental influences that in turn (according to the more cognitive approaches) had reciprocal cause-and-effect relations with cognition.

Non-cognitive Causes of Behavior

Furthest removed from a Christian view of the person was the behaviorist explanation of "choice" as a conditioned or unconditioned response to an environmental stimulus (Watson, 1924; Skinner, 1953). The stimulus (cause) was understood to be the material agent leading inevitably to the behavioral response (effect). This explanation of behavior makes no reference to such mental states and occurrences as beliefs, desires, deliberations, efforts, acts of will, and emotions. In such a framework, since the true causal account of behavior is a mechanical impingement of a physical environment on the body of the "agent," the *experience* of choice (which would involve reference to beliefs, desires, etc.) was seen as a mythological holdover from a pre-scientific era (Skinner, 1971).

Virtually no psychologists working in the 1990s accept this picture of human agency, though we must admit that, to the extent that humans behave in direct response to environmental stimuli, their behavior can be profitably predicted in terms of reinforcement and punishment. However, such an approach has been found to be most accurate in predicting the behavior of immature adults, children, and the mentally retarded. This suggests that mature adult behavior is more cognitively complex, and more agentic, than strict behaviorism can account for.

Another influential but strongly deterministic approach to choice has been the attempt in motivation research to describe certain hypothesized internal drives that lead an organism to behave in certain predictable ways. Originating with studies of hunger and thirst (sometimes with a behavioristic slant, e.g., Hull, 1943; Miller, 1951), this orientation marked an advance over radical behaviorism by appealing to causal forces internal to the organism (though these forces were carefully operationalized, with the result that their mental character was minimized). Like strict behaviorism, this approach neglected the role of beliefs and desires in motivating and directing human behavior. The language of volition is absent in this body of work inasmuch as these researchers sought to describe in purely impersonal terms the "forces" that "push" organisms to behave in the ways they do.

From a very different standpoint, Murray (1938) and others (e.g. McClelland, Atkinson, Clark, and Lowell, 1953) analyzed human motivation in terms of certain psychogenic needs, including affiliation, autonomy, power, and achievement. They hypothesized such needs to be forces within the brain that organized human mental and behavioral activity towards changing existing situations. A primary value of this approach was its openness to the study of uniquely human motivations. However, Murray's dynamic model fell short of describing human motivation without reference to agentic conceptions.

Cognitive Influences on Behavior

Motivation research moved closer to a study of agency by focusing on cognition's impact on motivation. Some beliefs have motivational power, for example, beliefs regarding (1) reinforcement value and (2) expectancies of obtaining the reinforcement (Lewin, 1936; Atkinson, 1964). Also, though the term "action" does not figure in this research, the notion of behaving on the basis of an expectation of a certain state of affairs (goal-directed behavior) is a significant portion of the notion of action. These Expectancy X Values motivational theories recognized that certain goals have a positive attraction (or valence) within the mental system of an individual due to specific internal needs.

Attribution researchers furthered this move towards cognition by studying how one's beliefs about the internal and external causes of one's behavior (including internal attributions regarding ability and effort) influence that behavior (Heider, 1958; Weiner, 1972). Beliefs about one's effort and ability are clearly important to volition, yet oddly this approach is agnostic about the referents of these beliefs (that is, the attributed efforts and abilities themselves). Attributional beliefs are viewed simply as mental phenomena that impact human behavior. Such an approach locates some of the causal influences on human behavior in the cognitive realm, though in an abstract and impersonal way.

By the 1960s many researchers shaped by behaviorism were also beginning to acknowledge the role of cognition in behavior. Cognitive-behaviorists developed constructs like *self-regulation* and *self-control* to account for volitional phenomena, but still without appealing to volition. Mischel (1974) studied self-control, the ability of children to restrain the gratification of their own impulses; and Bandura (1986) and others have focused on self-regulation — the ability of individuals to keep themselves on task and monitor their own progress. Both self-control and self-regulation are obviously volitional processes. They presuppose the reality of goal-directed behavior and the everyday desires, beliefs, and efforts necessary to work at maintaining that behavior over time. However, Mischel and Bandura continued to avoid agentic/volitional terminology out of a (natural-science) aversion to anything that cannot be at least indirectly, but clearly, linked to observable, measurable phenomena. In spite of this aversion, we see in these researchers psychologists of a broadly behaviorist cast being pushed by volitional reality to acknowledge agentic features of human nature. More recently, Bandura (1989) has moved further, acknowledging that self-influence can determine behavior as much as external influence, and that humans are genuine agents.

More strictly cognitive is the study of decision making, a focus on the cognitive processes that assist people in arriving at decisions, such as evaluation weighting, cognitive framing, and probability judgment (Tversky and Kahneman, 1981; Payne, Bettman, and Johnson, 1992). Clearly, human action is affected by such mental processes. In this subfield we are getting very close to the study of the cognitive and volitional processes of real human agency; the literature even deploys the concept of a "decision-maker." However, natural-science goals continue to shape the inquiry, in that the processes under investigation are each supposed to explain a certain portion of the variance observed in decision making. Mental processes are not being thought of in their own terms, that is, as states and activities of responsible persons, but are construed on the model of physical forces and chemical agents, theoretically posited and indirectly observable entities appealed to in explanation of observable bodily movements.

Another set of approaches that have addressed volitional issues indirectly are those that involve the study of the capacities of organisms or computers to interact with and learn from their environment, gaining feedback which in turn impacts future interaction with the environment. Both Piaget (1954) and Gibson (1969) have explored the importance of perception to infants as they make their way around and master their world. Young children develop mentally as they act — moving within the world and learning what is constant, what changes, and how they can influence events. Drawing analogies from information processing and ethology, other researchers (e.g., Miller, Galanter, and Pribram, 1960; Carver and Scheier, 1981; Frese and Sabini, 1985) have recognized that much human behavior results from the formation of plans that guide initial behavior but are reshaped as a result of feedback received through behavior, a process that continues until the behavior results in the desired outcome (or the organism gives up). (We noted that some cognitive-behaviorists have observed similar phenomena; both groups describe the phenomena as "self-regulation.") Organismic and cybernetic researchers together recognize that most behavior is goal-directed and a function of the organism's understanding of itself and the world resulting from its planful interaction with the world. The strength of these approaches lies in their focus on the interaction of cognition and the environment.

Among natural-science psychologists, a group of Germans have probably made the most progress in describing human action (Kuhl, 1985; Heckhausen, 1991; Gollwitzer, 1986; Beckmann, 1986). This school focuses explicitly on the goal-directed, volitional processes that are involved in action, including intention formation, action control, action initiation, and commitment. Here we find natural-science psychologists producing a body of research and theory rich with insights into volitional activity and obtaining as good a picture of agency as may be possible given the methods they must use. Nevertheless, this school too prescinds from reference to the responsible self that *owns* these cognitive and volitional processes and *engages* in these cognitive and volitional activities.

Subjects, Actions, and Virtue

The above approaches differ regarding the level at which they study the causes of (or influences on) human behavior (biological, environmental, social, or cognitive). Yet they all flow from a natural-science paradigm. Most of these models make no reference to concepts like volition, and all balk at the notion of a "will," largely because such concepts cannot be naturalistically verified, from outside the subject. The bulk of this literature has thus resulted in descriptions of machine-like causal forces (like motivational drives) or mental processes (like self-regulation) that affect volition, without resorting to theoretic reference to the subject that uses (and is shaped by) those processes.

Such models have been the primary ones for studying and depicting agency-like phenomena in twentieth-century Western psychology. As a result, they have subtly led us as a culture to see humans as organismic, thinking machines (the highest thing that can be modeled from a natural-science viewpoint). But they cannot account for the unified organization of all the processes they study because they ignore the actor, the personal center of the activity who, though influenced by environment, drives, and thoughts, yet remains the unifying, original source of action.

An unfortunate consequence of this oversight is the lack, within the purview of mainstream psychological study, of a conscious, personal subject who is responsible for his or her actions. Limiting psychological study to behavior, cognition, and even volition apart from their deep relation to such things as virtue and human responsibility has contributed to a massive and culturally pervasive learned helplessness. On some level, many modern Americans are inclined to see themselves as sets of processes shaped passively by forces beyond their control, without seeing the essential connections of these processes to moral standards and others (including God) to whom they are accountable. This is a profound and practical cultural consequence of the assumption of a single (natural-science) model for the human sciences that essentially sunders virtue and knowledge.

A Christian notion of agency, then, can be distinguished from naturalistic notions by its assumption of the existence of a personal, responsible origin of human action, as well as by its recognition that human activity has, simultaneously, an ultimate, divine origin and standard. Nevertheless, the importance of natural-science approaches to volitional activity should not be minimized. They actually lend support to the Christian belief that human agency is limited and not absolute, by demonstrating that it is conditioned by a variety of environmental, biological, and cognitive factors (see Jones, this volume).

Modern and Postmodern Psychological Insights into Human Agency

There have been at least three affirmative approaches to personal choice in twentieth-century American psychology. In spite of the deterministic themes in Freud's writings, ego psychology has not been opposed to the concept of volition (Erikson, 1963; Rapaport, 1967; Loevinger, 1976; Block and Block, 1980). For example, Erikson believed that around children's second and third years, they go through a stage in which, with the appropriate support, they begin to learn to control their behavior, and develop confidence in their ability to make choices. Erikson saw this development of the will as a fundamental task of childhood (and seemed unconcerned with the metaphysical implications of his openness to the notion of a will). Unfortunately, apart from the Blocks, ego psychologists have not pursued this topic in much depth and their interest has done little to affect mainstream psychological discourse.

Of all the schools, humanistic psychology most clearly embraces the notion of the will. Psychologists of this school have argued against strict determinism and for the belief that humans are at least to some extent capable of free choices, and they have also recognized the self as the individual's unifying center (Maslow, 1968; May, 1969; Rogers, 1961). However, as with ego psychology, little empirical work has been done from this standpoint; as a result this school has made little progress in understanding human choice since the classic works of Rogers and Maslow (Rychlak, 1983, would be one fine exception). Furthermore, because of its pervasive individualism, humanistic psychology can be faulted for underestimating the positive role of the social world in the formation of human choice, as well as for undermining any transcendent claims of morality on the individual. It is also theoretically closed to the notion of co-agency that, as we have seen, is so prominent in biblical psychology.

Perhaps the most promising developments in agency psychology are the results of social constructivists who have examined agency, action, and volition and focused especially on the role of the social world in supplying the meaning and structure that make individual activity possible (Rogoff, 1990; Harré, 1984; Valsiner, 1987). Though rejecting the notion of a reified will (so, at least, Harré, 1984), this approach assumes agent causality, and takes seriously that mature human actions are incompletely determined, are intentional and goal-directed, require personal effort, and are meaningfully constructed within the conventions and beliefs of one's social community. In addition, like all postmodernists, social constructivists affirm the validity of local meanings rather than a universal set of criteria by which the understandings of all communities are judged. Such a stance makes these investigators more open to non-modern forms of discourse and agentic self-understanding (perhaps even the Christian?), but it also runs the risks of relativism. In addition, like all the twentieth-century approaches we have seen, whether naturalistic or humanistic, most social constructivists are theoretical secularists and therefore view agency as a human experience entirely reducible to processes resident in this sphere of existence.

This overview highlights various approaches to agency that can be found in twentieth-century psychology. Mainstream psychologists, shaped by the natural sciences, have been uncomfortable with the psychologically richest notion of a mature human agent and for methodological reasons have been unable to *see* human agency in all its dimensions. Introductory texts in psychology continue to neglect the topic of agency and to treat the causes of human behavior as consisting entirely of impersonal processes (i.e. biological, environmental, or cognitive). When psychologists do speak of actions, they tend to mean simply goal-directed behavior, thus expressing a concept that does not differentiate the sort of agency that a one-year-old human infant or an intelligent horse is capable of, from the sort of agency that we have found to be assumed by the Bible and that we will, in the next section, see to be basic to our everyday thinking about human persons. (I want to underscore that when I use the words "agency" and "action" without further qualification in this paper, I assume this full or rich concept, and not one of the reduced concepts current among professional psychologists.) Despite these defects in psychologists' treatment of action, our understanding of the impersonal processes that do in fact shape human agency has enjoyed tremendous progress through the psychological research of this century. Moreover, from the agentic wasteland of radical behaviorism, mainstream psychology has moved steadily closer to describing agency as it is actually experienced. Some twentieth-century psychologists have even described some of the unique characteristics of mature human agency.

In the next section, I shall use a simple story to illustrate some of the features of human agency. The orientation of my description will be Christian, but I will get valuable help from twentieth-century secular psychology.

A Story of a Human Agent

Three weeks ago, Joe received his promotion to Regional Manager at Victor Photos. He had worked long hours for three years in hope of moving up in the company. Since his promotion he has been deliberating about what to do with his large salary increase, and has been getting counseling from several local car dealers. Finally, after working out the financing with his bank, he has purchased a new jet-black Ferrari.

The Personal Contexts of Human Agency

To understand this action, one must see it within its larger contexts, and there are a number of contexts of agency worth considering: the biological, the narrative, the identity context, the environmental, the goods context, and the linguistic/rational context.

The Biological Context

Human desire is conditioned by the body. Thus the genetic, hormonal, neurological, and morphological structures of the body, along with their development, limit the range of actions within an individual's potential. This fact is an instance of the more general fact that nature limits human freedom (Ricoeur, 1966). The body also provides a motivational field that guides behavior more or less throughout the lifespan. Hunger, thirst, the sex drive, the enjoyment of pleasure and dislike of pain, differences between the sexes, as well as possible neurological abnormalities, to name a few influences, all provide contexts within which an individual's agency is experienced.

Joe possesses an average intelligence, a muscular frame, good looks, and is the beneficiary of an overall normal course of development. Certain courses of action are not easily accessible to him. For example, he never enjoyed working with numbers and would loathe the job of an accountant. However, his popularity in high school, due in some measure to his biological blessings, has prepared him well for working with people at Victor Photos.

The Narrative Context

Mature humans also act from within their historical situation, their past experiences, associations, and influences, as well as their future goals. Agents are essentially historical beings rooted in a personal, social, cultural world within which they understand themselves, their options, and their possibilities. One's past initiatives, both successes and failures, one's virtues and vices as established over time, and one's family history and other social connections influence what one attempts to achieve and also the character of these attempts. We act according to purposes and goals developed and shaped in the past and related to the persons and events that are a part of our story. Our actions express a pilgrimage from our earliest years to the celestial or infernal city. Without a history, there is no agency.

The Identity Context

One's narrative contributes significantly to the formation of one's identity, a trait itself foundational to agency (Taylor, 1985). For example, certain types of deeds, like asking for forgiveness, do not make sense given certain views of one's self. Each of us has a theory of self that guides our mature actions (Harré, 1984). Humans develop personal goals based on their (socially mediated) view of who they are ontologically and ethically, their own narrative, as well as their understanding of their capacities and potential. One's sense of self can limit the range of actions that seem plausible given one's biographically determined situation (Schutz, 1962). Mature human actions then can be seen as a form of self-definition as well as self-realization

(Gollwitzer, 1986). Christian teaching regarding human nature, union with Christ, and the Christian's possibilities for action, make sensible and possible certain courses of action that are not actual options for the non-Christian.

Joe was the firstborn of a tight-knit, blue-collar family that valued hard work and the material trappings (proof) of success. From a young age, Joe remembers his father working long hours, and he sensed that his family envisioned great things for him. Joe was never very studious, but he usually got along well with others and enjoyed lots of extracurricular activities throughout his school years. He always worked for what he had, but enjoyed spending his money, thinking his parents were too "tight." As he developed he came to see himself as someone who would be very successful in whatever he attempted. There is no doubt that Joe's history and sense of self are very much involved in his purchase of the Ferrari. Joe has a typical modern-American individualist self-understanding, and so his indebtedness to his family is not particularly evident in his narrative self-understanding. If he thought more about the ways his upbringing had enabled him to buy his Ferrari, his sense of agency would be more that of a co-agency. He would think of his action as something that *he and his parents* did. His co-agency is in one sense no less real for his failure to recognize it. If Joe were a spiritual Christian, the question of *God's* co-agency also might arise for him. Here the goods context (see below) becomes relevant to the ascription of co-agency, since it is doubtful whether God endorses the purchase of a Ferrari, which is essentially an act of self-glorification. It would be more plausible, in Christian terms, to claim co-agency with God if Joe had *resisted* the temptation to buy the Ferrari and used some of his increased income for some sort of ministry.

The Environmental Context

Every physical and social environment affords certain "action opportunities," that in turn require a state of readiness — that is, a degree of awareness of specific goals within a particular setting. Important goals may be temporarily neglected because they are not close to one's awareness at a particular time and place, though one would act upon them if they were more salient. If one is primed for a certain task, that is, if one has a certain state of readiness for it (Harré, 1984), one is more likely to initiate that type of action. The details of one's environment set limits to the actions one will attempt. Such environmental/task-based contextual factors are so interwoven with one's internal states that they are experientially indivisible and together constitute the context of mature human actions. Joe's purchase of the car involved the mundane fact that he suddenly acquired a certain income in a particular cultural context in which a large number of people admire Ferrari owners.

The Goods Context

Humans also act within a world loaded with value and meaning. Some things are important to us, others are loathed. Mature agents inhabit a "world" of desirable persons, objects, activities, and experiences; a framework of perceived goods that consists of the motives, values, or loves that form the goal-directed core of the individual; a set of criteria for distinguishing noble from ignoble actions, desires, and emotions (Scheler, 1973; Taylor, 1989). This moral framework is essential because the evaluations that flow from it are "the indispensable horizon or foundation out of which we reflect and evaluate as persons" (Taylor, 1985, p. 35). Actions aim to realize perceived goods, but it is part of a moral framework to provide ways of evaluating such perceptions as well. For example, Joe's perception of the Ferrari as a good arises out of his social background; but that background may also supply moral or religious criteria by which to evaluate this evaluation as extravagant or selfish. Thus Joe would have within him a value resource for taking action to resist his burning desire for a Ferrari.

One's perceived goods are ordered in a goal-hierarchy (Langford, 1971; Frese and Sabini, 1985; von Cranach, 1982). Particular goals are nested within larger goals which in turn are nested within the most important goals of our lives (Bruner, 1982). The largest goals of all are our "reasons for living." Nuttin (1983) suggests that we all possess a "master plan" that includes our most important goals and orients our day-to-day behavior without requiring constant, conscious attention. Such goals and plans are shaped by our past narrative and contribute to the present narrative flow of our lives. One of Joe's most important goals in life is to be highly esteemed by others. Consequently, his purchase of the car has an immediate goal of car ownership that serves a "higher" goal of possessing high-quality, expensive objects, that in turn serves his "highest" goals (he hopes) of obtaining the esteem of others and becoming "successful."

The Linguistic/Rational Context

All of the most distinctively human contexts of agency are grounded in or shaped by our ability to speak and understand language. Much of the narrative context of our actions is mediated via family and personal stories; and the stories themselves often include as central elements things that were said and thought by people, and things done that could have been done only with a planning and understanding that are enabled by the power of language. The identity context of our actions is affected not only by our family, ethnic, and national stories, but also by theories or theory-like bodies of thought about human nature and the meaning of life that we could not possess without linguistic mediation. For example, Christian faith is formed by the "word" of God — the things that are said about God and his relations to us. Psychotherapies do their work in large part by providing us ways of conceptualizing ourselves, our problems, our relationships. All philosophies of life and religious and moral outlooks (what I have called goods contexts) are examples of linguistically mediated identity-formation. Our understanding of the more immediate context of our actions is always to some extent linguistically mediated, even if we do not hear or overtly speak words that issue in action; self-talk may do so, but even in the absence of talk, we think, notice, and perceive against the background of linguistically mediated learning.

Joe's action in buying the Ferrari, then, is more fully grasped when one knows something of the above contexts. These agency contexts are notoriously difficult to examine, for Joe, let alone for "outsiders" who are not omniscient. But this difficulty must not prevent the psychologist from recognizing that human agency always occurs within such contexts. Two deeds by different people may bear a superficial, "objective" resemblance, while differing profoundly in meaning, as revealed only in light of their complete contexts.

The Process of Enactment

Actions vary in the amount of time required to carry them out. Some have been planned for years; some take years to carry out. Some medieval cathedrals, for example, took over a century to build, from conception to completion. In the following I attempt to document a sequence of sub-events and processes involved in action.

Commitment to an Action

Halisch and Kuhl (1987) suggest that action can be divided into predecision and postdecision processes. Predecision processes are largely motivational and relate to the formation of goals that are shaped by what we are terming one's agency contexts, as well as more immediate cognitive decision-making processes (Tversky and Kahneman, 1981). Predecision processes should help the agent to evaluate and clarify the goods, possibilities, and goals, and should be oriented towards obtaining relevant information. Heckhausen and Kuhl (1985) say that a decision to act is based on an understanding of the opportunity for action, the time involved, the importance of the project, its urgency, and the availability of means, all of which relate to the action's contexts. If a potential project meets certain criteria for each of these aspects, the agent decides to act.

The decision begins with the agent's commitment to act. According to Heckhausen (1991), in making the commitment, the individual has crossed the volitional "Rubicon" and a different set of processes is active than before the decision was made. The goal has become a "current concern" (Klinger, 1986), and the agent's mental resources are no longer set on an evaluation of possible goals or the seeking of more information, but instead on goal maintenance and obtaining goal realization.

Commitment to act varies in depth, a fact of interest to Christians. One can be firmly resolved to act or only mildly invested in seeing the goal realized. The degree of one's commitment can determine whether or not, under certain circumstances, the action will be taken. Weak intentions are easily overturned. Christianity, in particular, places a high premium on deep commitment to action — whole-hearted and pure, at least with regard to one's faith (Kierkegaard, 1938).

Commitment is the moment in the volitional process that is most commonly referred to when thinking about the will. The will is generally thought to be the locus of choice, and volitional analysis throughout the ages has concentrated on the step of commitment in the process of enactment. Recent research, however, suggests that choice is one small, though important, part of volitional activity. Virtuous and vicious deeds have many more dimensions than bare decision. At least as important from a moral standpoint is the contribution of one's narrative, one's identity, and the mental actions that lead to action, as well as those processes that maintain the behavior until goal completion.

When an agent commits to a particular course of action, an intention is formed. Intentions have been an important focus of study in German action research because their mental reality is another feature that clearly distinguishes mature action from animal behavior. Intentions are the goal-based cognitions that the agent has committed herself to enact. According to the cognitivist Kuhl (1985), intentions are largely cognitive structures that have volitional and affective characteristics. As a result, they can be represented in propositional form, for example, "I will visit a car dealer now." However, feelings about the goal may also be stored with the intention. For example, Joe's old girlfriend worked at one of the dealers, so Joe had a certain anxiety stored with his current intention to visit that dealer. The quality or depth of commitment regarding the action is also stored with the intention. Kuhl's observations do not mean that all of one's intentions are easily formulable by the agent; humans often act for reasons they are unaware of. However, to be mature, a human intention must be capable of being expressed propositionally.

Kuhl (1985) also says that intentions are preserved by certain self-regulatory processes (and self-control processes), including motivational control, attentional focus, and emotion control, all of which the agent uses to stay on-task. Without such meta-intentional processes, intentions can deteriorate in the face of competing action alternatives. Courses of action are often interrupted without being abandoned. In such cases, an intention is maintained as a tacit concern until circumstances and motivation permit its reactivation as a current concern.

Joe had formed a general intention to buy a flashy car long before the pay raise came along. Later, after some investigation and analysis, he formed a specific intention to purchase a particular car. Once he formed the intention, he acted consistently with it until its goal was realized. Once the deal was signed, his intention was realized and so dissolved.

The Action Itself

Actions vary in type; an action can be purely mental (working out financial details in one's head), or it can also involve behavior (asking a friend's opinion). An action may also vary in the amount of effort applied. Goals can also be obstructed, in which case the degree of commitment helps to predict whether the action will be taken. Exertion is the degree of effort applied in an action (Heider, 1958). In the face of difficult obstacles, an agent must summon increased effort to achieve the goal. Effort is highly correlated with commitment, but is also tied closely to one's identity context and one's goods, as research on achievement motivation and attribution has repeatedly found (McClelland, Atkinson, Clark, and Lowell, 1953; Atkinson, 1964; Weiner, 1972). Everyday experience suggests that effort is especially under the control of the agent; we esteem actions that involve effort.

Perseverance, of course, affects performance. Some people consistently give up more easily than others, some tend to work far longer on a hopeless task than seems best, while others have learned to persevere with wisdom. Such tendencies can be influenced by inborn factors as well as training, but appear to be relatively stable. According to the Scriptures, effort and perseverance in God-centered activities are due to the Spirit. The same self-regulating processes that maintain an intention are also required in action maintenance. One of these processes involves an agent's regular evaluations of whether the goal has been reached (Miller, Galanter, and Pribram, 1960; Carver and Scheier, 1981).

More recent cognitive theorizing has also focused on the existence of a metacognitive "processor." Some have speculated that human cognition requires an executive control center that manages the flow and processing of information beyond the individual's awareness (Brown, Bransford, Ferrara, and Campione, 1983; Ashcroft, 1989). Reading, for example, requires countless feature-detection and semantic skills, as well as certain decisions regarding interpretation and comprehension that appear to be largely beyond awareness. Human action is of sufficient complexity to require similar metaprocessing (Kuhl, 1985; Beckmann, 1986). For example, to stay on task in the face of distracting stimuli it may be necessary to refocus attention briefly on the value of the goal. Such a strategy may be used deliberately or automatically, and if automatically, the decision to engage in that sub-act will be due, according to these speculations, to the executive control center.

Some of the most vexing issues facing us in a thorough study of volition may relate in some way to the functioning of such a subconscious control center. Mature action may be due to the proper functioning of this organizing and monitoring activity-center beneath consciousness. On the other hand, when a person is indecisive, she may be entertaining too many options in an unprofitable way. That "part" of the executive responsible for monitoring wasted resources is perseverating and so performing maladaptively. Perhaps what is called weakness of will is to some extent due to problems in the agent's executive control center. The activities of this semi-autonomous, subconscious mental structure nevertheless have moral implications. Virtuous agency may to some extent require the renewal of this center.

At one point in the loan-application process, it appeared that Joe would be denied because of a poor credit record. Many options raced through his mind. He thought of walking out. But because he was deeply committed to purchasing the car, he calmed himself down and argued persuasively that things had changed in his life; he was older now, and he should be given the loan. His perseverance was rewarded.

Retrospective Evaluation

It is characteristic of mature human agency, in contradistinction from lesser kinds, that the agent evaluates his own past actions. Joe may be glad he bought the car because it did everything for his image he had hoped it would; or he may be disappointed. Thus actions are sometimes evaluated for their success in achieving an intended outcome. They may also be evaluated in moral terms. For example, Joe may, upon reflection, think that buying the Ferrari was socially irresponsible, given some other things he might have done with his money, had he bought a Chevy Cavalier instead. Or he may decide that the purchase reflected a lack of humility and a love of ostentation. Such evaluations illustrate the general facts about human agency that (A) actions are goal-oriented and thus involved in all the complexities and length of range that human goals can possess; (B) actions can be interpreted in various ways, which give them different meanings; and (C) actions have a goods context (see above). By contrast, animal actions have much simpler and shorter-range goals, and it may be doubted whether they have any meaning at all, in the present sense, since such meaning seems to depend on the powers of language and reflection.

To summarize: An action is performed out of the background of the agent's biological condition, narrative development, personal identity, linguistic/rational structures, physical environment, and a world of perceived goods (and evils). Its course begins when out of these contexts the agent commits towards realizing a specific goal, and so forms an intention. The action itself sometimes requires a degree of effort by the agent, including strategies to stay on task until the task is completed or abandoned. Finally, the agent may evaluate the action after the fact.

The last major task of this paper awaits us: to examine how human agency is fostered by the loving agency of other humans.

The Social Formation of Human Agency

Stern (1985) argues that pre-language infants can act. He believes that infant action is made possible by the development, within the first months of life, of a "core self" that includes an awareness of authorship of actions, control over body movements, and control over consequences of actions. However, we must stress the relative simplicity of such infantile actions, in comparison with adult actions set in linguistically mediated narrative and goods contexts that ground responsibility and a more-or-less accurate appreciation of co-agency. Stern seems to be employing the concept of action typical of twentieth-century psychologists, namely the "reduced" or "thin" concept of action as mere goal-directed behavior. Our concern in this section is to describe the development of a simple agent into a full agent, the gradual incorporation of sensorimotor activity into a richer, more complex order through enculturation into a world of agents.

Intersubjectivity

Before infants understand language they begin to resonate emotionally with others in their social environment (Lamb and Bornstein, 1987; Tronick, 1989). The capacity to share in the experience or understanding of another has been termed "intersubjectivity" (Stern, 1985; Schutz, 1962; Harré, 1984). Interpersonal interactions during infancy often seem to involve the sharing of attention, intention, and affect (Stern, 1985). A common interpersonal experience of a parent-infant dyad is "mirroring" (Pines, 1987; Kohut, 1977), in which the parent reflects back to the child the affect state of the child. This "state-sharing" of affect is believed to affirm the child's experience of self-coherence and unity. Intersubjectivity is also important because it is a mutual exchange of meaning. For example, as the child experiences an emotion or performs an act, the parent interprets this in a certain way and communicates this interpretation to the child. Eventually, the child's (and the parent's) emotions and actions come to be shaped by this ongoing, reciprocal exchange of meaning.

Intersubjectivity is the fundamental, interpersonal channel through which meaning and love are conveyed. Without such experiences, the child is left on his own emotionally, even though his physical needs may be completely met. Harmful intersubjective experiences may leave the child with an incomplete self-structure (Kohut, 1977), and therefore limited in his ability to act freely. In addition, intersubjectivity is the medium through which more complex, linguistic, agent-shaping meanings are shared.

Language

The importance of language to agency can hardly be overstated. Without language, the young, pre-verbal Helen Keller acted like an animal. Language opened her up to her humanity. It is the primary medium for communicating the highest qualities of human nature. It is through language that parents convey messages about the world, God, others, and the child herself. Humans talk about needs, values, goodness and sin, goals and the satisfaction of goals. Conversation makes available a world in which the young child can act, and helps the child develop a sense of her own identity. Language is thus person-formative (Harré, 1984; Levitin, 1982; Roberts, this volume, a). Of special interest are those forms of speech that are directly linked to mature action: commands, wishes, requests, exhortations, hopes, and the expression of the intentions of others. Commands and requests are instrumental in creating projects. Evaluative speech, like praise, blame, accusation, justification, and excuse, shapes human action (Harré, 1984) by creating, expressing, and reinforcing a goods context for it. Such speech motivates or discourages actions and establishes a concept of responsibility in the child (see Talbot, this volume).

The Gift of Love

Through intersubjectivity and language, parents and other caretakers give to children certain "gifts" that promote personal formation and thus make agency possible. I call them "gifts" to indicate their personal origin in the giver, the freeness with which they are provided, and the psychological transfer that occurs from one person to another. Arguably the most important is the gift of love.

From birth, infants require the care of others in their world. As Roberts (this volume, b) has noted, through interactions of care, infants come to form attachments to primary caregivers, and this capacity for attachment remains a central characteristic of human experience throughout life. In the parent-child interactions, the reliability and responsiveness of the care are especially important. Reliable, responsive, affectionate care has been found to correlate positively with more secure child attachment, greater perceived self-control, more exploratory behavior, and higher levels of social maturity in peer interaction (Kindermann and Skinner, 1988). While such correlation has not been seen in every study (Grusec and Lytton, 1988), and one must be aware of bi-directional effects, the relation between loving, sensitive parental care and prosocial, self-initiated child activity has been noted by psychologists from many different traditions, from object relations theorists (e.g., Guntrip, 1973; Mahler, Pine, and Bergman, 1975; Kohut; 1977) to more mainstream researchers (Clarke-Stewart, 1973; Baumrind, 1977; Maccoby and Martin, 1983; Hartup, 1989). For example, Baumrind found that loving, supportive, enthusiastic parental relations appear to foster prosocial actions, feelings of competence, and of agency (e.g. taking initiative and persisting in tasks). We seem to be safe in concluding that infant care that responds warmly and nurturingly to child need enhances the personal agency of the child. As we develop, we transfer our ultimate attachment to God and then derive from him a growing capacity for true agency. And as we grow as agents we grow in our capacity to transcend our merely need-based relations with others (including God) and love them from the heart, not simply from the belly.

Human attachments continue throughout life (Roberts, this volume, b). However, the term "attachment," as it is used in the psychological literature on the subject, tends to denote an asymmetric relationship characterized by dependence and some passivity. This describes well the parent-infant relation, and this relation parallels in important respects the Christian's relationship with God. However, the term may be less adequate for characterizing the child's maturing relations with others, relations which on other dimensions transcend attachment phenomena. For example, we can learn to value others and actively seek their welfare, something far beyond the capacity of an infant. Therefore, the notion of attachment should perhaps be augmented by the notion of agentic love in order to encompass the characteristics of more mature social relations.

The Gift of Law

Agency is also promoted by providing moral, conventional, motivational, and cognitive structure for the developing agent. All parents inevitably supply some structure, even if only to limit the range of options available to the child. However, much early childhood activity involves the creation of joint projects in which both parent and child participate more or less actively to realize a goal. Through taking on the tasks of others, the child learns to act within the rules of a particular culture and is given the mental "tools" to develop increasingly challenging and personally rewarding tasks (Bruner, 1982; Wood, Bruner, and Ross, 1976; Vygotsky, 1978; Valsiner, 1987; Rogoff, 1990; see Neal, this volume, on the subject of "scaffolding"). As I have noted, Christian psychology stresses that agency is co-agency: thus the believer sees in her God-centered activities both the action of God and herself as the active image of God. Though we must distinguish between forms of joint activity, constructive experiences of parent-initiated joint activity in which the parent lays down, or at least expresses, the rules governing the activity, not only promote the capacities for self-regulation that Neal stresses, but may also provide psychological precursors for the experience of Christian co-agency.

Caregivers also establish standards for performance in school, home, social relations, and in moral and religious matters. These standards govern the quality of task performance, manners, altruistic behavior, and forbidden activities. Parents communicate their expectations to the child and also model behavior that may or may not conform to those standards. These standards (and example) promote or discourage certain actions, and may become internalized and so inform the actions of maturing persons.

Children vary in their response to structure, depending on the amount of love in the home. Available research suggests that parents who have high, strictly enforced standards and provide loving support and measured assistance in their children's endeavors, will nurture children who are highly agentic and socially responsible in later years (Baumrind, 1977; Maccoby and Martin, 1983; Grusec and Lytton, 1988). Conversely, providing too much or too little structure inhibits the child's ability to act independently. The trick is to find the balance between parental authority and child initiative that allows for the child's individuality and increasing maturity (again, see Neal, this volume).

The Gift of Hope

Since limitations and moral guilt can lead to a sense of despair that restricts a child's active development, another task of caregiving is to communicate hope. The child must be equipped to see, realistically, that in spite of past failures or transgressions future action can be better. High parental expectations may discourage a child, or they may challenge him to act beyond his past performance and present accomplishments. The parents' bestowal of confidence can make the difference.

Harré (1984) defines symbiosis as the "routine supplementation of the incomplete cognitive, emotional, and intentional repertoire of one being by another through speech" (p. 93). Harré, Clark, and De Carlo (1985) give the example of a mother speaking to her infant as if he could understand her conversation with him, and answering the questions she poses. The mother is not interacting with the infant as he actually is, but with a being of her own construction; however, such interactions are more than prophetic, for to some extent they call into being the very cognitive structures they presume. In this way a mother's confidence in her child's ability to do a task can be assimilated by the child, thus enhancing his agency.

Hopes must reflect genuine abilities. Prodigy hopes expressed for a child of average ability may create feelings of deep inadequacy. But when gauged to the child's ability, the gift of hope is especially important to agency because it helps to draw the child to take the next step beyond its present "determined" limitations. The gospel of hope will flourish in the heart of a child who has been enriched with realistic parental hope.

The Gift of Faith

The term "faith" is ambiguous, referring sometimes to an attitude of trust in what God has done in Jesus Christ (Romans 5:1), and sometimes to the apostolic tradition (1 Timothy 3:9; 4:1; 5:8) known as *the faith.* These two senses of "faith" belong together and are both important for Christian agency. To give the gift of faith is to communicate an interpretation of reality: of the character of good and evil, the nature of God and the created world, and the nature of the self. But to give this gift, one must communicate these things as a believer for whom they have an encompassing and heartfelt significance. Otherwise, "the faith" will never come across to the child in the form of personal "faith." From preschool years through adolescence, opportunities abound for formal and informal communication regarding such topics.

Of special importance is instruction regarding good and evil in the child herself. In humans, God's creative (and re-creative) work dwells side by side with sin, so Christian caregivers must prepare children to know themselves as good *and* bad. This is no easy task. Discernment is needed to know what to focus the child's attention on, and when. However, over the years the child should become aware of her propensities to sin as well as her gifts and graces. Such awareness will help the Christian to distinguish the promptings of the Spirit from those of the flesh. This power of discrimination is a crucial part of Christian agency.

Finally, one of the most important messages relevant to Christian agency is that by grace and through a personal faith in Christ the child can become increasingly freed from the determining power of sin. Though there are no guarantees that a child will personally believe, we have grounds to think that the gift of faith is often communicated mysteriously through the loving, lawful, hopeful caregiving of Christian parents.

Conclusion

The creation of agency is a function of a biologically-based capacity for complex action, an agency-promoting social environment, the will of the individual, and the grace of God. God's role as the ultimate source of agency is fundamental to a Christian approach. However, Christianity also recognizes the human agent as the immediate or secondary origin who voluntarily acts according to his agency-contexts, for his own reasons, with responsibility. The last section of this paper has focused on the mediate role of other agents in one's social world in developing agency. The influence of other humans on agency can be termed "quasi-causal" (Howard, 1982). Humans cannot directly cause agency in others, but they can indirectly facilitate its development. In addition, by withholding the gifts discussed above and providing instead toxic substitutes (like hatred or too much structure), others can directly limit the flowering of agency in the developing person. Adults continue to be responsive to others' actions, but usually with less impact than in childhood.

Agency in its fullest and truest form, however, is the agency of Christ given to those he has redeemed. Yet even here, our agentic imitation of the Father is socially-mediated, for the Christian acts as a member of Christ's body, in relation with other believers. Ideally, Christians become more agentic through the communion they experience within the body. One's relationships with other believers become a special site of the manifestation of Christian agency as well as an ongoing source of the love, obedience, hope, and faith of others that help us to grow more fully in redeemed agency.

A Parental Style for Nurturing Christian Wisdom

CYNTHIA JONES NEAL

My child, if you accept my words
and treasure up my commandment within you,
making your ear attentive to wisdom
and inclining your heart to understanding;
if you indeed cry out for insight
and raise your voice for understanding;
if you seek it like silver,
and search for it as for hidden treasures —
then you will understand the fear of the Lord
and find the knowledge of God.

Proverbs 2:1-3

My son
In a secret place
our ancestors
the ones with the wrinkled faces
and white hair
left us these words:

Look long
and wisely
Is this real?
Is this the truth?

Now
listen to my words
with care

Look at things
look long
and wisely

Is this real?
Is this true?

This is how you must work
and act.

(Gerez, 1984, pp. 34-35)

OUR TRADITION HOLDS out an ideal of intelligent living, a concept of wise character formation, that has not always been exemplified in the members of the Christian community, nor always aimed at in the practices by which its younger members are nurtured. Some recent work by developmental psychologists confirms that ideal and offers guidelines for realizing it in the lives of our children. I shall first explore some aspects of the biblical psychology of agency, in particular the concept of wisdom and its relation to rule-following as applied to people under the new covenant. This concept seems to be paralleled by a distinction some psychologists have made between self-control and self-regulation, a distinction I shall rename with the more perspicuous terms "heteronomous agency" and "intelligent agency." Second, I turn to the literature on a parental nurturing style that has come to be known as "scaffolding," whose explicit purpose is to form intelligent agency in the child. I shall argue that this style is paralleled and confirmed in the New Testament theology of grace. Third, I shall present a four-phase developmental schema showing how scaffolding works in each phase.

Two Formations of Agency and the Theology of Grace

Kopp (1982) defines "self-control" as the capacity to comply with a caregiver's commands and directives in the absence of the caregiver. But self-control, as Kopp defines it, lacks intelligence of a certain sort, and she contrasts self-control with a more intelligent kind of agency that she calls "self-regulation." The self-controlled person has "internalized" the commands and directives, but treats them as though they are still external, since his response to them follows a more or less rigid S-R (stimulus-response) pattern. For example, a child playing alone says to himself,

"Don't touch that," when approaching an electrical outlet, and withdraws. He has internalized his mother's directive, but responds to it in the same kind of way he would if mother were present and saying to him "Don't touch that." A more mature agency in which similar behavior comes from a similar thought would be to think, "Outlets can give nasty shocks, so I'd better keep my hands off," and withdraw. The older child is not just responding to a stimulus, but is considering, on its own merits and out of the resources of his own intelligence, a line of reasoning. As he grows and comes to know more about outlets he will (intelligently) sometimes touch them and sometimes not, being able to measure his behavior to the particular circumstances — e.g. whether the circuit breaker has been tripped, whether the outlet cover is adequate to protect him, etc. This capacity to adjust to circumstances on the basis of *understanding*, with the subject regulating his own behavior by his own understanding, is what we call practical intelligence, and it is very different from the S-R pattern described by Kopp as self-control.

But even the child who merely follows internalized commands has *some* understanding of the circumstances of action and *some* skill for dealing with these circumstances in his own right. For example, he must be able to recognize electrical outlets, distinguishing them from his toys, so as to give himself the electrical outlet avoidance command at the appropriate time; and he must have the motor skills to avoid the outlets. And so we might be tempted to think that the later, more intelligent kind of agency is nothing but a *more ramified* understanding of the circumstances of action and *greater* skill in dealing with them. Kopp seems to take this position when she says, "What sets self-control apart from self-regulation is a difference in degree, not in kind. . . . [Self-regulation] is a distinctly more mature form of control and presumably implicates the use of reflection and strategies" (Kopp, 1982, p. 207; for critical discussion, see Diaz, Neal, and Amaya-Williams, 1990). But this is, in my view, an inadequate understanding of the qualitative shift that occurs as the child takes over the regulatory role implied in the construct of self-regulation. In addition to greater understanding and skill, the intelligent agent understands *himself* as *capable* of and *responsible* for *applying* his understanding and skill in the circumstances of life. He has a deep dispositional construal of himself as a responsible agent, as an origin of actions, as a locus of control. He has not only the understanding and skills necessary for intelligent action, but also the disposition to assume responsibility for his own thought and action. A person can be mature in years, and have considerable understanding and skill in practical contexts, and still lack this deeper sense of self that is essential to being a fully intelligent agent.

Another example illustrating the distinction between "self-control" and "self-regulation" is an incident that occurred in my daughter's third-grade classroom. The rule was that during small-group time, students were forbidden to interrupt the teacher "unless they were bleeding or dying." One day my daughter's best friend, Kelly, felt the call of nature in a big way. She could hardly stand it, she needed to visit the restroom so badly. But she knew the rule and did not feel that this need constituted an emergency of death or blood. Yet she was near tears, the need was so large. My daughter, Meghan, knew what was happening to Kelly and decided this *did* constitute an emergency and marched up to the teacher. With a piercing and accusing look, the teacher sternly asked Meghan if she remembered the rule. Meghan promptly placed both hands on her hips and announced that of course she remembered the rule; however, this was a different emergency that required the teacher's assistance immediately. Kelly was demonstrating perfect "self-control" in this situation; her behavior was a rigid response to an "external" command. Meghan, on the other hand, was able to guide her behavior "using her own head" and flexibly responded to the particular circumstances. (I am not suggesting that Meghan is always "self-regulated" — however, the story does make a great illustration!)

The distinction between these two kinds of agency is fundamental to the rest of this paper, but I want to rename it, for several reasons. First, as we ordinarily speak of "self-control," there is nothing inherently unintelligent about controlling oneself; one may do that, it seems, intelligently *or* unintelligently. And so Kopp's association of self-control with unintelligence makes for an infelicitous choice of words. Second, in our Christian tradition, one of the fruits of the Holy Spirit (Galatians 5:23) is called "self-control," and it is certainly not mechanical, or lacking in intelligence or maturity! Third, 'self-control' and 'self-regulation' don't wear much of a distinction on their faces, and it would be better to have a set of terms that are, in themselves, more distinguishing. Finally, the word "self" in these two expressions is misleading. What Kopp calls self-control is perhaps usually directed literally at the self, controlling the self with regard to internalized rules and commands, initially formulated externally to the self. Self-regulation, on the other hand, may be directed at objects other than the self. In the example from Meghan's classroom, Meghan does not regulate *herself*, but takes control of the *situation* — of Kelly and the teacher. So I would like to use the terms "heteronomous agency" and "intelligent agency" to mark our distinction. ("Heteronomous" comes from two Greek words: *heteros* = *other* and *nomos* = *law*; hence, heteronomous action is action that follows a rule as though it belongs to somebody other than the agent.)

Something like this distinction from contemporary psychology is central to the teaching of the Bible about spiritual maturity in response to God's gracious salvation. The prophet Jeremiah prophesied a new covenant:

> But this is the covenant that I will make with the house of Israel after those days, says the Lord: I will put my law within them, and I will write it on their hearts; and I will be their God, and they shall be my people. No longer shall they teach one another, or say to each other, "Know the Lord," for they shall all know me, from the least of them to the greatest . . . . (31:33-34).

In the prophesied new dispensation, which Christians take to be the reign of Christ in the church, the will of God has been so thoroughly appropriated by the people, so completely "taken to heart," that it is no longer a *heteros nomos*, but has become a law of their very own minds. (It is of course still *heteros* in that it comes from God, and not from themselves.) It is as though the very Spirit of God dwells in them (Romans 8:11), as though they have the mind of Christ (1 Corinthians 2:16). They have not just "internalized" some commands, to which they react with a sort of conformity reflex; they have become spiritually intelligent with something like the intelligence of God himself.

Paul admonished Peter not to capitulate to those making a fetish of external laws and requiring others to do the same. With Christ's death and resurrection, the developmental transition toward maturity, experiencing Christ's freedom, is what the apostle needs to preach.

> . . . when Cephas came to Antioch, I opposed him to his face, because he stood self-condemned; for until certain people came from James, he used to eat with the Gentiles. But after they came, he drew back and kept himself separate for fear of the circumcision faction. And the other Jews joined him in this hypocrisy, so that even Barnabas was led astray by their hypocrisy. But when I saw that they were not acting consistently with the truth of the Gospel, I said to Cephas before them all, "If you, though a Jew, live like a Gentile and not like a Jew, how can you compel the Gentiles to live like Jews?" (Galatians 2:11-14)

> For through the law I died to the law, so that I might live to God. I have been crucified with Christ; and it is no longer I who live, but it is Christ who lives in me. And the life I now live in the flesh I live by faith in the Son of God, who loved me and gave himself for me. (Galatians 2:19-20)

Now before faith came, we were imprisoned and guarded under the law until faith would be revealed. Therefore the law was our disciplinarian until Christ came, so that we might be justified by faith. But now that faith has come, we are no longer subject to a disciplinarian, for in Christ Jesus you are all children of God through faith. As many of you as were baptized into Christ have clothed yourselves with Christ. (Galatians 3:23-27)

And yet Paul introduces the "law of Christ" (Galatians 6:2). Is he merely substituting a new set of legalities? According to F. F. Bruce (1982), Paul is distinguishing the law as a yoke of bondage from the law of Christ as the way of freedom. Bruce cites Galatians 5:13-15, which reads,

For you were called to freedom, brothers and sisters; only do not use your freedom as an opportunity for self-indulgence, but through love become slaves to one another. For the whole law is summed up in a single commandment, "You shall love your neighbor as yourself." If, however, you bite and devour one another, take care that you are not consumed by one another.

Bruce reminds us that Jesus too had said that the whole law was summed up in the commandment to love God and neighbor, and then comments that the nature of law is deeply changed when interpreted as love. "The law of love," he says, "cannot be enforced by penal sanctions; the fruit of the Spirit, as Paul enumerates its ninefold variety — love, joy, peace, patience, kindness, goodness, faithfulness, gentleness, self-control — is not produced by legal enactments but simply because it is the nature of a life controlled by the Spirit to produce such fruit. . . . 'The Spirit's law of life in Christ Jesus', as he calls it elsewhere (Rom. 8:2), has little more than the term 'law' in common with that from which the gospel has liberated him and (he trusts) his Galatian converts" (p. 42). The personal relationship with God that characterizes Christian maturity is not a matter of consulting formulas and "doing what they say," but of living out an attachment to a God of a certain gracious character and seeing all humans as ones for whom God has acted in Christ. This is not a lawless life, since God's character orders it and that order shapes ("regulates") the dispositions of anyone who loves him; but neither is it a life bound by law in the old sense.

Behavior originating from heteronomous agency (what Paul calls "doing works of the law" — Galatians 2:16) is organized in a more or less rigid stimulus-response manner, where the internalized command is the stimulus, and the compliance is the response (I say "more or less," because obviously, there are many shades and degrees of legalistic rigidity). In contrast, to practice the self-control of which Paul speaks, there must be a wise and discerning self who is making the decisions and plans, and organizing his or her behavior to meet these goals. This is a self with some depth of understanding and a sense of his or her own responsible agency, a heart formed on the model of, and in communion with, the Lord. This is a self capable of practicing the virtues from an internal plane, one who has been "transformed by the renewing of your minds, so that you may discern what is the will of God — what is good and acceptable and perfect" (Romans 12:2). This is a self which is made possible, I believe, through a developmental process that is consistent with intelligent agency.

According to the developmental theorizing of Russian psychologist L. S. Vygotsky (1962, 1978), development originates from and is embedded within life's social and cultural context. Vygotsky believed that we draw meaning from life and develop cognitively principally by learning the shared meanings of our culture. These shared meanings are passed down through the generations. We develop the skills and understandings of our culture primarily through apprenticeships with more experienced learning partners (see also Rogoff, 1990; Rogoff, Mistry, Goncu, and Mosier, 1993). These apprenticeship relationships serve to guide us and enable us to understand more and more about our world and to develop an increasing number of skills. The family, and in particular, the parents serve as a child's first apprenticeship partners. Obviously, formal schooling, friends, and church will also play important roles. Nevertheless, the early relationship with parents, and specifically, the *manner* in which the parents teach/guide the child, has enormous influence in whether the child develops intelligent agency.

So regulation of a child's behavior is, first, a shared act, an interpersonal transaction. Since the human infant is immersed from birth in a sociocultural environment, the child's functioning and behavior are externally regulated by the adult caregiving interactions. Furthermore, intelligent agency develops within the context of adult-child interactions, especially when the caregiver sensitively and gradually withdraws from joint activity, allowing, promoting, and rewarding the child's takeover of the regulatory role. The perspective that I now offer builds on Vygotsky's theory by postulating that individual differences in intelligent agency can be expected from differences in the quality of caregiver-child interactions. Let us turn to scaffolding as a parental style for nurturing Christian wisdom.

Scaffolding

As I have noted, the concept of scaffolding derives from Vygotsky's idea that the child's agency is at first parasitic on the agency of the nurturer. Scaffolding is a form of nurture and guidance that allows the center of regulation to shift gradually and appropriately from the nurturer to the child. The process requires considerable attention and sensitivity on the part of the nurturer, who must discern when the child needs support in the forms of actual help, modeling behavior, verbal instruction, emotional safety, or demonstrated approval, and when the child is to be left to his or her own devices in these respects. The degree and kinds of intervention required from the nurturer change constantly as the child learns and develops, placing further demands of flexibility, sensitivity, and creativity on the nurturer (Diaz, Neal, and Amaya-Williams, 1990; Wood and Middleton, 1975; Wood, Bruner, and Ross, 1976). One constant in scaffolding is an underlying attitude of nurturance, care, warmth, attention, and availability to the child, though like other aspects of the process, these will vary in mode of expression as the child's needs change (Neal and Diaz, 1989; Neal, 1990).

Let me comment on the analogy that the word "scaffolding" suggests (Bruner, 1983), since it is both suggestive and flawed. The scaffolding that builders (say, bricklayers) use in constructing a building is a temporary and adjustable support for the builder. As the building goes up, the scaffolding goes up with it, enabling the builder to reach the parts that need to be worked on, and when the building is complete, the scaffolding is removed. The building corresponds, of course, to the child, and the builder corresponds to the parent or other nurturer. The scaffolding corresponds to the support that the parent gives the child, and the raising or lowering of the scaffolding corresponds to the adjustments the nurturer makes in the support of the child's activities. The removal of the scaffolding corresponds to the withdrawal of the nurturer when the child is "complete," having achieved intelligent agency. The analogy is flawed in that real scaffolding supports builders (analog: parents), while developmental scaffolding supports what is "built" (namely, children). It is also flawed in suggesting that intelligent agency is sustained in a complete absence of support from nurturers (scaffolds are *completely* removed when the building is finished, but familial and other forms of nurturing support are never, in the best cases, completely removed). The idea of radical autonomy has been attractive to modern thinkers, but it is inconsistent with Christian psychology (see Roberts, this volume a) and with some strains of developmental psychology (see Bowlby, 1982, 1988).

An analogy that is in some ways better is that of a dance. Many of us can remember holding our infants, cradled in our arms, moving in rhythm to quiet them or perhaps to stimulate them. Soon, the toddler is no longer satisfied to be cradled; she wants to be upright and participate in what the parent is doing. The dance changes with a more active partner. Eventually the preschooler prefers to stand on his parent's feet as he "dances." He participates in a rudimentary way, allowing the parent's feet to guide the action. With age the dance continues but the child now stands on his own feet. The parent still serves as the guide and yet moves *with* the child and his faltering steps, allowing mistakes to lead the parent's next step. Of course, the dance doesn't end here — adolescence breaks in! The partners must learn new steps, often with the parent allowing the adolescent to teach him or her fresh steps. The analogy of the dance is more accurate, especially for Christian psychology, since even full-grown adults "follow" or "guide" one another on the dance floor, making for a more communal picture of intelligent agency. Since the scaffolding analogy is well established in the literature, I will continue to use it, despite its flaws, and will also, from time to time, refer to the process of facilitating intelligent agency as a dance.

Appropriate scaffolding within the teaching interaction occurs when the parent effectively supports the child based on the child's behavioral cues (Neal, 1991). Adjustment involves assessing the focus of attention, the level of skill development, and the amount of responsibility the child is able to take over during the course of the interaction. If the child is not focused on the task, the first job of the scaffolder is to orient the child's attention to the task at hand. Instructing without the child's attention makes little sense. If the child is focused on the task, the parent can break the task into manageable parts, verbalize the planning strategy, and use modeling and explanations for the conceptual role of the task. Using questions, a parent can assess the level of the child's understanding of the task and instruct with greater sensitivity. The child's responses to the questions give the parent a window into the child's skills and understanding. As the child responds with correct performance, the parent takes his or her cue and withdraws, taking on a merely confirmatory role. With incorrect performance from the child, the parent can move in with further support.

An example is in order. Many of us have taught our children how to ride a bicycle. Most probably, we started them on a tricycle during the preschool years. With the advent of children's seats on adult bikes, many children have been able to enjoy riding on the back of their parents' bikes, gaining some experience of the "feel" for riding a "big" bicycle. The two-wheeler with training wheels often comes next, although to be honest, I was always concerned my child would think that riding at a slant was the normal way to ride! Finally the day comes for the solo ride. Initially we hold onto the seat and run while they get the feel of riding without training wheels. Eventually, we give them a push and run alongside without hanging on. At last, they have both the skill and the courage to go it alone.

Another pertinent example is that of supporting a child in working out a moral dilemma. It is awfully easy simply to tell our children how to resolve the issue, but that is not scaffolding, and does not optimally facilitate intelligent agency. A parent who is interested in scaffolding will encourage the child to identify all of the relevant details. Often merely the narration of a dilemma by the child will direct the focus on the salient aspects which, in turn, can guide possible actions. The parent will ask questions, look for examples of ways the child has handled similar problems, and allow the child to wrestle with several solutions and their consequences. It is completely appropriate for the parent to specify ways in which his or her values might imply certain solutions. During this discourse the parent encourages the child's thinking and communicates his or her trust that the child is capable of working on this problem. In many ways this is an asymmetrical interaction. It is one thing to help our children decide whether to report a friend who is drinking to his parent, and quite another to decide whether drinking is an option for a child under age. In other words, I am not suggesting that all children are equally equipped to make all decisions (I can't even say that about all adults!) or that there is only one acceptable solution. That is the beauty of the concept of scaffolding. Our parenting is guided by the particular child's strengths and limitations at the present point of development.

What does the Christian tradition have to say about scaffolding? I shall consider some relevant biblical texts, and suggest that the Scriptures are open, if not downright friendly, to this concept.

Proverbs 22:6 tells us, "Train up a child according to his way, and even when he is old he will not depart from it." Although recent Christian parenting literature stresses the word "train," I submit that the focus truly belongs on the phrase "according to his way." Children have inborn differences that should affect the way we relate to them if our caregiving behavior is responsive and sensitive. Children do not all have the same native endowments, nor do they all develop at the same rate; it is essential to our fulfilling our God-given responsibility to bring them up that we take account of individual differences in our training of them. Parents are mandated to train, to teach God's values and directives. However, God has designed each child and knows her from before she was born. Psalm 139 states: "O Lord, you have searched me and known me. . . . For it was you who formed my inward parts; you knit me together in my mother's womb. I praise you, for I am fearfully and wonderfully made. . . . Your eyes beheld my unformed substance. In your book were written all the days that were formed for me, when none of them as yet existed" (Psalm 139:1, 13-14, 16). We must pay as much attention to the child's ways as God has. Indeed, it is our obligation to understand the nature that God had in mind when he created our particular child.

The father in the story of the prodigal son (Luke 15:11-32) demonstrates scaffolding attributes. First, it is evident that he has clearly communicated love and care to his two sons. His welcome to the returned prodigal does not sound strained and even his response to the elder son is not judgmental or harsh. He recognizes the differences in his two sons and allows the younger to struggle and experience the results of his actions. The younger son returns with repentance and the father perceives that the appropriate response is to receive the penitent with open arms and forgiveness. His response to the older son indicates that he senses his pride and jealousy and gently discourages it.

The resurrected Jesus practices scaffolding as he speaks to the disciples on the way to Emmaus (Luke 24:13-35). He adjusts the level of his teaching to the disciples' current understanding, using questions ("What things?" he asks when the disciples innocently ask him if he is the only one who does not know what's been going on in Jerusalem during the past few days), and then he corrects their misunderstandings ("Then beginning with Moses and all the prophets, he interpreted to them the things about himself in all the scriptures"); he allows them to take the initiative ("he walked ahead as if he were going on. But they urged him strongly, saying, 'Stay with us, because it is almost evening and the day is now nearly over'"), and then finally he withdraws as they come to full knowledge ("Then their eyes were opened, and they recognized him; and he vanished from their sight").

Scaffolding in Four Developmental Phases

The chart on page 176 portrays the phases of development toward intelligent agency. The scaffolding role during each phase depicts the early regulatory role of the parent with the gradual withdrawal as the child matures.

PHASE 1: The early emotional dialogue — "the parent-child dance" and the critical role of the caregiver in the regulation of neurophysiological and emotional modulation.

During the early months of its life, the infant exhibits rudimentary forms of neurophysiological control. For example, when the incoming

Developmental Phases of Intelligent Agency	Scaffolding Role Mediating the Regulatory Role
PHASE 1	**PHASE 1**
Neurophysiological regulation	* *Neurophysiological regulation*
* Need for behavioral organization	* Engages in warm, responsive dyadic synchrony
* Need for emotional modulation	* Warmly adjusts to infant state
PHASE 2	**PHASE 2**
Attachment	*Attachment*
* Need for internal security	* Regulates internal security by providing a secure base
* Need to explore	* Responds warmly to child's growing awareness of self
* Need for mastery and curiosity	* Provides safety by adjusting environment to satisfy child's sensorimotor needs
* Language skills developing	* Serves as source of comfort and control
PHASE 3	**PHASE 3**
Emerging control, heteronomous agency	*Emerging control, heteronomous agency*
* Need to do things for self — "me do it!"	* Provides an external source of rules
* Growing awareness of rules and ability to comply	* Serves as source of support and limits
PHASE 4	**PHASE 4**
Intelligent agency	*Intelligent agency*
* Emerging capacity to plan, guide, and monitor his or her own behavior from within and flexibly according to changing circumstances	* Gives over the regulatory role sensitively and appropriately
	* Interacts warmly and nurturantly
	* Assesses the child's level of ability
	* Uses inquiry and distancing strategies
	* Breaks task down into subgoals when necessary
	* Serves as confirmatory, rather than regulatory, agent as the child shows mastery

stimuli prove too intense, the infant demonstrates certain self-soothing behaviors (e.g., thumb-sucking or non-nutritive sucking) as a form of shutting out or placing a stimulus barrier for protection. Individual differences in infants' ability to modulate arousal and wake-sleep states are quite apparent. Kopp (1982) says the caregiver role may be viewed as an assisting one.

> Although precarious states of arousal primarily give way because of maturational forces, state control is considerably aided by caregivers' social interactions and routines. Interactions help infants focus on salient features of the environment when they are alert and awake; routines provide an external buttress for endogenous control of sleep and wakefulness. (p. 203)

Research indicates that, in addition to physiological control, the dialogue that transpires between infant and caregiver plays an essential role in the infant's emotional development. Tronick describes the affective communication system that functions between the infant and the caregiver in the following two scenarios (Tronick, 1989):

> Imagine two infant-mother pairs playing the game of peek-a-boo. In the first, the infant abruptly turns away from his mother as the game reaches its "peek" of intensity and begins to suck on his thumb and stare into space with a dull facial expression. The mother stops playing and sits back watching her infant. After a few seconds the infant turns back to her with an interested and inviting expression. The mother moves closer, smiles, and says in a high-pitched, exaggerated voice, "Oh, now you're back!" He smiles in response and vocalizes. As they finish crowing together, the infant reinserts his thumb and looks away. The mother again waits. After a few seconds the infant turns back to her, and they greet each other with big smiles.
>
> Imagine a second similar situation except that after this infant turns away, she does not look back at her mother. The mother waits but then leans over into the infant's line of vision while clicking her tongue to attract her attention. The infant, however, ignores the mother and continues to look away. Undaunted, the mother persists and moves her head closer to the infant. The infant grimaces and fusses while she pushes at the mother's face. Within seconds she turns even further away from her mother and continues to suck on her thumb. (p. 112)

These early interactions are among the most profound experiences for the young infant. In the not infrequent missteps of this "dance," one

of the partners overstepped and miscalculated the intensity of her contribution, leaving the other partner needing to take a break from the
interaction. While infants as young as six months demonstrate remarkable
ability to utilize various coping strategies to deal with poor dyadic synchrony, the caregiver plays an important regulatory role. In both scenes,
the infant looks away and begins sucking the thumb. This is a coping
strategy that allows him or her to calm down and regulate his or her
emotional state. Both mothers have the opportunity to listen to the infant's
communication, then step back and wait for the child to indicate readiness
to continue the "dance." Initially, both mothers respect their infants' needs.
However, the second mother eventually intrudes upon her infant's retreat,
forcing her attention upon the child. The child withdraws further, at one
point even pushing the mother away.

These infants experience very different results from this interaction
with their mothers. The first infant learns that when he needs space to
calm down from an emotionally arousing interaction, his caregiver respects that space and waits for him to indicate readiness to continue. She
adjusts her behavior to support her child's growing yet still fragile
emotional development. Thus scaffolding provides a high quality
"dance." The second child does not have the same positive experience as
the first. This infant leaves the experience in a negative affective state,
hitting at her mom, attempting to avert all interaction. She has not been
given the necessary support and is required to regulate herself by with-
drawing from all interaction. These coping behaviors of disengagement
and withdrawal become defensive when they occur automatically, inflex-
ibly, and indiscriminately with all interactive partners.

Infants also demonstrate very early certain preferred coping strategies for the purpose of regulating their emotional state when the infants'
expectations about the interaction do not match the interaction. Some of
these strategies are: signaling behaviors (coo face, pick-me-up gesture,
fuss), focusing on something other than the parent (gazing at the bar of
the seat, looking at their own hands), self-comforting behaviors (sucking
the thumb, rocking back and forth), and behaviors whose goal is to withdraw and/or escape the interaction. When the expectations for the interaction mismatch the interaction, requiring the infant to use a coping
strategy, the infant gains some positive benefits as she repairs the mismatch. Successful repair increases the infant's sense of effectance and
competence. In addition, as the infant accumulates a history of successful
repair, she develops a pattern of coping strategies that she may bring to
other interactions with other partners (Weinberg & Tronick, 1991). The key
is for the child to perceive her own effectiveness — that she can elicit or
avert responses, determining certain experiences through her own agency.

This sense of effectance is an important milestone for the child's growing sense of self.

Obviously these coping strategies are limited and immature and the nurturer continues to need to take the primary regulatory role, reading and responding to the child's cues. I am *not* suggesting that the child's emotional development requires the parent never to miss the child's cues in an interaction. Studies show consistently that parents do miss, and not infrequently. Nevertheless, emotional development is subject to dis-regulation when the interactive failures persist without repair, when the parent is consistently unable to read cues and adjust his or her response with the result that the dyad suffers a continual and consistent inability to "dance" well. This early dance with the nurturer is a precursor to all later interactions (Tronick and Gianino, 1986).

PHASE 2: The attachment relationship and the critical role of the caregiver in the regulation of internal security.

Internal security or insecurity results from the accumulation of experiences (responsive vs. nonresponsive or rejecting; sensitive vs. insen-sitive) with the parent in the first year of life: Does the child view the parent as a secure base from which to explore and to which he or she can return when stressed or fearful? In addition to providing a sense of self-efficacy, internal locus of control, and curiosity, the quality of the attach-ment relationship provides the foundation from which all other intimate relationships are experienced (Bowlby, 1982). Bowlby (1988) defines at-tachment behavior as

> any form of behavior that results in a person attaining or maintaining proximity to some other clearly identified individual who is conceived as better able to cope with the world. It is most obvious whenever the person is frightened, fatigued, or sick, and is assuaged by comforting and caregiving. At other times the behavior is less in evidence. Never-theless for a person to know that an attachment figure is available and responsive gives him a strong and pervasive feeling of security, and so encourages him to value and continue the relationship. (p. 27)

Mary Ainsworth and her colleagues (Ainsworth, Blehar, Waters, and Wall, 1978) developed a research design which nicely illustrates this phenomenon. It is called the Strange Situation, inasmuch as the child is placed in slightly stressful situations for the purpose of assessing the child's use of the parent as a secure base. The child's behavior is assessed first with mom in a novel environment, then with a stranger with and without mom present, and finally alone, without mom or stranger. The child's response to the parent upon reunion is the most telling factor in this assessment. Results revealed three types of attachment: secure, resistant/ambivalent, and avoidant.

Children classified as *secure* easily demonstrated that for them the parent was a secure base from which to explore their surroundings. In the episode with mom present, these children readily departed to explore toys. They shared the toys with mom in an affective manner and showed affiliative behaviors to the stranger in mother's presence. When separated from the mother, some of these children displayed distress, while others did not. Distress during separation was not a key factor in discriminating secure from insecure children. The key factor was the ease with which the child was comforted upon reunion with the mother. Secure children who were distressed immediately sought and maintained contact with the mother when she entered the room. This contact effectively terminated the distress. If the child was not distressed during the separation, then upon reunion secure children actively greeted the parent, strongly initiating interaction.

Children classified as *anxious/resistant* in their attachment demonstrated a poverty of exploration upon entry into a novel situation with the mother. They evidenced difficulty in separating to explore the toys. They manifested wariness of novel situations and people. Upon reunion with the mother, these anxious/resistant children had difficulty settling down, finding comfort for their distress. They often mixed contact-seeking with contact-resistance (hitting, kicking, squirming, rejecting toys). While actively requesting to be picked up, they hit and fought to be put down. These children were unable to accept the comfort they so desperately wanted and needed.

Anxious/avoidant children readily separated from the caregiver to explore and showed little affective sharing of the toys with the parent. They evidenced no wariness of the stranger, regardless whether the mother was present or absent. What is striking about these anxiously attached children was their active avoidance of their mothers upon reunion. They turned away, moved away, and ignored their mothers.

The attachment research shows that parental warmth, nurturance, and responsivity are important to the child's development of intelligent agency. Developmental research (Ainsworth and Bell, 1974; Bell, 1970; Belsky, Taylor, and Rovine, 1984; Coates and Lewis, 1984; Gordon, Nowicki, and Wichern, 1981; Johnson, 1982; Matas, Arend, and Sroufe, 1978; Olson, Bates, and Bayles, 1984; Stayton, Hagan, and Ainsworth, 1971) corroborates the view that reciprocal interaction within a warm interpersonal relationship that endures over time (the parent-child relationship) leads to the development of a secure attachment. This, in turn, can lead to more extensive exploratory behavior, more tolerance of frustration, increased internal locus of control, and greater motivation to pay attention to and learn from the mother (Bronfenbrenner, 1975). Ellen Skinner (1986) states that

> one of the effects of interactions with a sensitive caregiver is an increased awareness of the effects one's actions exert on the environment; through prolonged experience, the child develops a generalized sense of the self as an effective agent. This sense of control in turn provides the motivational basis for sustained engagement with both the social and nonsocial environment even under conditions of difficulty, ambiguity, or novelty. (p. 360)

Mastery motivation, increased attentional capacities, positive affect, persistence in problem-solving, curiosity, and sociability are among the preschool behaviors found in children classified as secure. Insecure children, classified as resistant, are more easily frustrated, whiny, and negativistic when solving problems than either the secure or avoidant children. These children also display more dependency behaviors. Children classified as avoidant tend to show more hostile behaviors to peers and are less likely to seek help when faced with a difficult task or when physically hurt (Frankel and Bates, 1990; Matas, Arend, and Sroufe, 1978; Sroufe, 1983).

Ainsworth comments on the broader implications of the attachment research:

> It is clear that the nature of an infant's attachment to his or her mother as a 1-year-old is related both to earlier interaction with the mother and to various aspects of later development. The implication is that the way in which the infant organizes his or her behavior toward the mother affects the way in which he or she organizes behavior toward other aspects of the environment, both animate and inanimate. This organization provides a core of continuity in development. . . . This is not to insist that the organization of attachment is fixed in the first year of life and is insensitive to marked changes in maternal behavior to relevant life events occurring later on. Nor is it implied that attachment to figures other than the mother is unimportant as supplementing or compensating for anxieties in infant-mother attachment — although too little is yet known about how various attachments relate together to influence the way in which infants organize their perception and approach the world. (Ainsworth, 1979, p. 936)

In summary, when the parent has demonstrated warmth and availability, adjusting her or his behavior responsively and sensitively to the child's behavioral cues during these first two years, then the child has built, among other things, an effective repertoire of behaviors for relating to people in the environment, and a strong sense of security that leads to an inner representation of the self as valued and competent. This provides the framework upon which the child's sensorimotor activities and language development can enjoy full expression. In addition to regulating internal security the parental regulatory role provides safety by adjusting the environment to allow the child's sensorimotor activities to be expressed. The parent also serves as a source of comfort for the many spills and accidents that occur during this exciting but stressful time for the child.

PHASE 3: Emerging heteronomous agency and the parental role in providing external sources of control, support, and limits.

The distinguishing features of heteronomous agency include "compliance, and emergent abilities to delay an act on request and to behave according to caregiver and social expectations in the absence of external monitors" (Kopp, 1982, p. 206). For a child to understand parental expectations and subsequently internalize them and comply in the absence of the caregiver, she must have representational and memory capacities. Not surprisingly, in a number of studies, the single best predictor of delay of gratification was language development (Vaughn, Kopp, and Krakow, 1984; Kopp, 1982). One obvious benefit of language development is the ability to use language to control one's behavior. During the preschool years, children begin using language for the self to organize and control their behavior (Diaz, Neal, and Amaya-Williams, 1990). It is not unusual to hear children in dialogue with themselves as they play independently. What may be surprising, however, is the quality of that dialogue. For example, Marion was working with playdough one afternoon. He was attempting to build a boat to sail on an ocean. As he was constructing the ocean, I could hear him repeat in a very singsong fashion, "I need blue because water is blue, I need bluuuue 'cuz the water is bluuuue." The blue got longer as he struggled with the ocean scene. It was as if the song helped him stay on task and guide him as he worked out the scene to his satisfaction. This is a good example of a common and important way children use self-talk to guide and organize their behavior.

Parpal and Maccoby (1985) found more compliance for children three to four years old when mothers were responsive and engaged in mutual cooperative behaviors. They suggest that maternal responsiveness may function in support of compliance in two ways: (a) it induces a positive mood that elevates cooperative behavior, or (b) it enhances a child's sense of belonging to an interactive, mutual relationship, one in which the partners help each other. They also found that more "difficult" and hyperactive children showed more compliance when parents were taught to be more responsive.

A synthesis of the studies examining children's growth in heteronomous agency finds consistently that compliance and cooperation are positively related to mother's warmth, sensitivity, and gentle physical interventions (Arend, Gove, and Sroufe, 1979; Londerville and Main, 1981; Parpal and Maccoby, 1985), verbal rationales for task organization, and appropriate behavioral expectations (Kopp, 1991).

PHASE 4: Intelligent agency and the parental role of appropriate support and withdrawal as the child indicates readiness.

Intelligent agency is the child's capacity to plan, guide, and monitor his or her own behavior, adapting it flexibly to changing circumstances. The parental role is essentially to relinquish the regulatory role. Through observation the parent assesses the child's level of ability, allowing the child to work independently when possible, and using inquiry and distancing strategies. As the child shows mastery and maturity, the parent serves as a confirmatory agent in a warm and supportive atmosphere.

As I have argued throughout this chapter, scaffolding interaction is the most appropriate nurturing style to promote intelligent agency in the child. Once the parent has assessed the level of maturity and responsibility that the child can handle independently, then she guides the child to the level just beyond, which the child can partially master but only with the assistance and supervision of the parent. Vygotsky (1978) refers to this dynamic region as the *zone of proximal development*.

Rogoff and Wertsch (1984) have conceptualized the zone of proximal development as

> that phase in development in which the child has only partially mastered a task but can participate in its execution with the assistance and supervision of an adult or more capable peer. Thus, the zone of proximal development is a dynamic region of sensitivity to learning the skills of culture, in which children develop through participation in problem solving with more experienced members of the culture. (p. 1)

In judging where the child's present zone of proximal development is, the parent must be aware of two things. First, discrepancies occur between the child's definition of the task or situation before him and the parent's definition of the same thing. For example, in a discussion on faith, an adolescent son may begin philosophizing about whether there are many ways to God. To the son this may be merely an intellectual exercise, something in which teens take great delight. Embedded in the intellectual exercise are perhaps the very real questions of faith with which the boy is struggling. The father, by contrast, may think his son is rejecting the Christian faith. If the father is to judge well how he can best help his son, the father must seek to understand the intent behind the son's questions. Once the father understands the son's questioning, he can engage in a process of inquiry that allows the son to follow his arguments to their logical conclusions. The father now defines his son's questioning as honest intellectual inquiry (much as the son defines the same situation) and can guide the son through his thinking and reasoning. Often parents assume erroneously that the child is operating under the same assumptions as the adult. A clear view from both perspectives allows a parent to work from the child's level, challenging him to the next level of maturity.

The second issue essential to scaffolding is the quality of language used by the parent. We know that children use language to help guide and monitor their performance. The child internalizes the quality of the parental language and uses it as she monitors her own behavior. Ellis and Rogoff (1982) examined the effectiveness of verbal strategies employed by the adult in adult-child problem-solving dyads. They found that learners perform better when taught by adults who rely more on conceptual information than particular information. Children perform better when working independently if they first work with an adult on a related task who models effective planning behavior and verbalizes his or her strategies and problem definitions. Conceptual information has by nature more generality than mere factual information, and thus confers greater independence (intelligent agency) on the recipient. When a child must answer questions (as opposed to obeying a command), he or she is challenged to impose a cognitive structure on the task, thereby gaining an additional tool to use when working alone. In addition, when a child answers the parent's question, the parent can ascertain whether the child is understanding the task. The child's responses allow the parent to adjust the level of instruction.

Verbal teaching strategies that invite the child to reconstruct, anticipate, and attend to transformations foster children's representational abilities. Children of parents who employ distancing strategies (an inquiry approach that places a demand on the child's cognitive abilities to represent objects, events, or people) achieve more advanced levels on tasks involving memory, object categorization, and transformation (Sigel, 1982). Distancing strategies require the child to separate himself or herself from the immediate environment and impose his or her own cognitive structure upon the problem. High-level distancing strategies are open-ended or conceptual questions, whereas low-level distancing strategies include the use of commands, directives, and perceptual questions, where the answer is readily available in the child's immediate perceptual field. Examples of the first type would be, "Help me understand your reasoning behind the solution you've chosen for this dilemma," and "How can you tell when you've made the right decision?" Examples of the second type would be, "Here is what you are to do" and "Don't be a fool. Just say no."

Conclusion

What we believe about our roles as parents and the roles children play in their own development determines how we interact with our children. If we believe that children are active agents in their own development and that the role of parenting is one of preparing the young to grow in discernment and wisdom, able to hear and respond to God personally, then our parenting will emphasize discipleship rather than discipline. We will adjust more or less smoothly to the changes in our child's development, our "dance" changing as our partner matures. After having done quite well in their early regulatory roles, parents often falter in the later phases, during the time of giving over the regulatory role to the child. Christian parents are too often satisfied to terminate at the heteronomous agency phase, but this is a premature termination. Intelligent agency should be our goal for our children, and scaffolding is, I have argued, a manner of discipling children that promotes this development.

The Meaning of Agency and Responsibility in Light of Social Science Research

Stanton L. Jones

L ET US BEGIN with two examples of behaviors that might seem to belong to the categories of "unfree" and "free" behavior, respectively: consumption of alcohol by "hard-core" alcoholics — "addicts" — and television watching. First, a description by O'Leary and Wilson (1987, p. 296) of alcohol consumption by alcoholics in an unusual situation:

> [The researchers] demonstrated that chronic alcoholics could, within a free operant situation, voluntarily restrict their drinking below five ounces [of pure ethanol] per day if this moderation was positively reinforced by access to an enriched environment, as opposed to remaining in an impoverished environment. In the enriched setting a subject could earn money by working, use a private phone, eat a regular diet, obtain reading material, entertain visitors and use the recreation room, which included television, a pool table, and other games, and engage the nursing staff in conversation. Subjects drank significantly more during the periods in which the reinforcement contingencies were not in effect, even if they were allowed free (noncontingent) access to the enriched environment.

In common terminology, these chronic, skid-row alcoholics, faced with the opportunity for access to good food, entertainment, the company of nurses, and other inducements on the condition that they restrict alcohol intake to non-abusive levels, were able to choose to maintain their drinking at the mandated moderate levels.

On the other hand, consider the example of a study of television watching by adopted children, a behavior we might assume to be a function of pure volition. Plomin, Corley, DeFries, and Fulker (1990) found that the television-viewing behavior of three-, four-, and five-year-old, early-adopted children was more strongly related to genetic factors than to environmental influences. Plomin et al. reported that about 30% of the variance in child television viewing was explained by "heritability," their genetic inheritance from their biological parents, while about 20% of the variance was attributable to the shared environment of the home they had been adopted into and lived in since near birth. Anticipating the incredulity these results might generate, the authors proactively addressed the issue of "free will" (in terms hauntingly reminiscent of Jonathan Edwards) by saying:

> whether or not one watches television seems to be completely a matter of free will. . . . It is critical to recognize that genetic effects on behavior are not deterministic in the sense of a puppeteer pulling our strings. Genetic influences imply probabilistic propensities rather than hard-wired patterns of behavior. We can turn the television on and off as we please, but turning it off or leaving it on pleases individuals differently, in part due to genetic factors. (p. 376)

Granting that the television-watching behavior (or any other behavior) of children may not be a compelling example of free action, the finding that genetic factors influence such a molecular and seemingly innocuous slice of human action gives one pause as we consider the meaning of agency and responsibility in the light of social science research.

I thank Cornelius Plantinga for offering his excellent essay "Sin and Addiction" (this volume) for our consideration. It is an insightful, wise, compassionate, pastorally sensitive and intellectually rigorous discussion of some of the most difficult issues I struggle with as a Christian and psychologist.

My thoughts here are less a response to his paper than tentative reflections on a perplexing issue that he raised but did not attempt directly to resolve in his paper. Plantinga states that "To discuss addiction is dramatically to raise the hard questions of human freedom and responsibility that lie along the base of the Christian understanding of sin" (p. 245). Indeed, this question surfaces time and again in his paper. His short definition of sin as "culpable Shalom-breaking" (p. 247) is very helpful, but the precise understanding of "culpable" that is at the center of the issue of human freedom and responsibility is left unclear. In examining the relationship between sin and addiction, he asks whether the addict is a person who simply "has a bad habit of making sinful choices," is a "victim of biological and social forces," or is a "person who habitually makes bad choices" (p. 254). Plantinga comes most directly against the issues that interest me here when he introduces the concept of "tragedy," saying "the chaos of addiction comes out of particular human character and sin, but also out of the temptations and disorganizing forces resident in an addict's home and neighborhood and maybe even in her genes" (p. 256). He goes on to say:

> In fact, tragedy implies the fall of someone who is naturally great, but whose greatness has been compromised and finally crumbled by a mix of forces, including personal agency, that work together for evil in a way that seems simultaneously surprising and predictable, preventable and inevitable. . . . Addicts are sinners like everyone else, but they are also tragic figures whose fall is often owed to a combination of factors so numerous, complex, and elusive that only a proud and foolish therapist would propose a neat taxonomy of them. In any case, we must reject both the typically judgmental and typically permissive accounts of the relation between sin and addiction: we must say neither that all addiction is simply sin nor that it is inculpable disease. (p. 256)

It is precisely this question that preoccupies me: How can we understand a "mix of forces" as "determining" human action — a mix that includes personal agency but also genetic, environmental, and other causative factors — and still have a meaningful concept of personal responsibility and human agency? As my title implies, social science's findings about "determinants" of human action raise questions about how we should understand human agency and responsibility. To pursue this topic, I will briefly review how the major "schools" of psychology have dealt with freedom and determinism, discuss the impact of this issue on current Christian thought and why the issue is so important, sketch a brief theological prologue to my main points, and then wade into the body of my speculations.

Psychology, Determinism, and Freedom

In contemporary psychology, there seem to be four major "paradigms" vying for ascendancy: psychodynamic psychology, behavioral and cognitive-behavioral psychology, humanistic psychology, and cognitive-constructivist psychology. The first two seem to be uniformly deterministic in their historic presentations. Humanistic psychology has attempted to defend human freedom. Modern cognitive psychology presents a confusing message on this issue (Browning, 1987; Evans, 1982; Jones and Butman, 1991; Rolston, 1987). I shall say nothing about psychodynamic psychology, as it is outside the comfortable bounds of my expertise. I would like to comment, however, on each of the other three traditions, examining Albert

Bandura as a representative of cognitive-behavioral psychology, Joseph Rychlak as a representative of humanistic psychology, and several authors for cognitive-constructivist psychology.

Cognitive-Behavioral Psychology

As I have noted elsewhere (Jones, 1988), traditional behaviorists endorse some form of determinism — the notion that all behaviors are the inevitable results of the causally relevant conditions that preceded the behavioral event in question (Erwin, 1978). Skinner (1976, p. 185) has said that "A person is not an originating agent; he is a locus, a point at which many genetic and environmental conditions come together in a joint effect." Wolpe suggests similarly that "Delightful as it is to regard ourselves as partially free agents not entirely under the domination of the causal sequences that relentlessly channel the course of events for everything else in nature, this freedom is, alas, only an illusion. Our thinking is behavior and is as unfree as any other behavior. . . . We always do what we must do" (Wolpe, 1978, p. 444). Most cognitive-behaviorists take similar stances. For instance, Marlatt (1982, p. 333), speaking about responsibility in the development of an addiction problem, states that "an individual who acquires a maladaptive habit pattern on the basis of past conditioning and the effects of reinforcement is no more 'responsible' for his behavior than one of Pavlov's dogs would be held responsible for salivating at the sound of a ringing bell."

Albert Bandura of Stanford University has attempted to incorporate an enlarged sense of human responsibility into his approach to cognitive-behavioral psychology through his notion of "reciprocal determinism" (Bandura, 1978). He notes that the human being, though shaped by environment, reciprocally shapes and molds that environment. This concept has been well-received by the behavioral world; it seems to encapsulate a human recognition of freedom qualified by a humble recognition of the limitations and constraints on that freedom. Bandura himself believes that "It is within the framework of reciprocal determinism that the concept of freedom assumes meaning. . . . Because people's conceptions, their behavior, and their environments are reciprocal determinants of each other, individuals are neither powerless objects controlled by environmental forces nor entirely free agents who can do whatever they choose. People can be considered partially free insofar as they shape future conditions by influencing their courses of action" (p. 357).

This concept is alluring to the Christian who also believes in limited freedom. But is reciprocal determinism really adequate as an understanding or explanation of limited freedom? The essence of Bandura's position seems to be that the self system is a system of internal or cognitive "mechanisms" (p. 348) that develop through past direct or vicarious experience, judgments by others, and by logic. Once developed, through these mechanisms the person is not an illusory way station for external causes of behavior (as for Skinner), but is rather a substantive processor of the factors that combine to cause behavior. But is this real freedom? Bandura himself states that "a self system is not a psychic agent that controls behavior" (p. 348). Note that even though the proposed self system is substantive, it is still mechanically conceived, including its development and activation, as when Bandura states that "self-evaluative influences do not operate unless activated" (p. 354). Further, Bandura (1983) later clarified that there is always "sequentiality" of reciprocal influence, meaning that behavior which changes our environment is necessarily caused by the pre-existing environmental conditions processed by existing person structures. Since the person structures must in turn be caused (in terms of temporal ordering) by environmental factors acting on pre-existing bio-cognitive potentialities, it appears that Bandura's system collapses into an event-deterministic framework with an added assortment of causal processes absorbed into the person.

True limited freedom is not to be found in any of the behavioristic systems, not even in the work of Albert Bandura. The major contribution of this tradition is its understanding of how our behavior might be shaped and molded, by both the immediate and remote environments within which we live and move and have our being.

Humanistic Psychology

There are many humanistic psychologies. Joseph Rychlak of Loyola University is certainly one of the most rigorous and thoughtful adherents of this school, and he has developed an articulate understanding of human freedom. Rychlak (1979) argues that humans do not emit just *re*sponses; they also emit "telosponses." He states that "A *telosponse* is the person's taking on (predicating, premising) of meaningful items (images, language terms, judgments, etc.) relating to a referent acting as a purpose for the sake of which behavior is then intended" (p. 140). Rather than being driven by past conditioning, humans can act with reference to future goals or purposes, shaping their own behavior by taking on new understandings both of their goal and of their "referent acting." It is on the basis of their capacities to telospond that humans can be construed as having freedom or free will:

> *Free will* is a non-technical way of referring to the capacity which telosponding organisms have dialectically to alter meanings which they affirm as predications (grounding premises) in the course of behavior. We are free organisms to the extent that we can rearrange the grounds for the sake of which we are determined. Before affirmation we can speak of freedom, and, after affirmation we can speak of will (power) in the meaning-extension to follow. In short, free will and psychic determinism are opposite sides of the same coin (pp. 147-48).

Rychlak argues that freedom is a requirement of telosponding and that telosponding is the ground for freedom. Our capacities for telosponding and freedom, in turn, set the foundation for Rychlak's understanding of human responsibility:

> Personal responsibility enters the picture when the human being recognizes this selective process, a process which at heart is one of *selecting the grounds for the sake of which one will be determined* (p. 148).

To the extent that Rychlak is representative of the humanistic psychology tradition, humanistic psychology attempts to defend freedom and responsibility. Foreshadowing my later arguments, I will note two problems with this understanding. First, I believe there are problems with any understanding of human freedom that limits freedom to a subclass of human action delimited by certain criteria. Rychlak says that "We are free organisms to the extent that . . ." and that "Personal responsibility enters the picture . . . ," indicating that *when certain conditions obtain, then we are free.* I will argue later for an understanding that may allow for some unfree human behavior, but I would want to draw this circle small within the larger set of free actions, and suggest that much must be stripped away from human action for it to lack any freedom at all. Second, Rychlak's view of freedom is difficult to reconcile with an understanding of how free acts might be at the same time quite bounded; i.e., how nature and nurture might condition even acts that we want to define as free. We need an understanding of freedom that will hold in the face of understandings of our actions as influenced by factors quite beyond our control as agents.

Contemporary Cognitive-Constructivist Psychology

Cognitive psychology grew out of information-processing approaches to understanding brain/mental functioning. While some approaches to cognitive psychology have retained their ties to more deterministic and mechanistic models of cognitive functioning, others have explicitly moved into truly "mentalistic" understandings of the mind, suggesting that the mental operations of the human mind transcend mere brain processes or fundamental learning processes such as those of operant psychology (e.g., see Sperry, 1988, 1993). Cognitive psychologists such as Sperry accept that humans are originating agents. The ties between academic cognitive psychology and the cognitive therapy movement I am about to describe are exceedingly loose.

Cognitive therapy grew predominantly as an offshoot of applied cognitive-behavioral psychology, though several of the major contributors to its growth, especially Beck and Ellis, had no roots in that tradition (nor, for that matter, in academic cognitive psychology). One variant of cognitive psychology associated with Ellis and his followers is increasingly described as "rationalistic" (Mahoney, 1993), focusing on taxonomies of rational and irrational beliefs. As cognitive therapy has prospered, however, more of its practitioners have become "integrationist," drawing upon insights from the psychodynamic and humanistic traditions of psychology, and especially upon philosophical movements described variously as postmodernism, hermeneutics, deconstruction, idealism, and so forth. Recently these developments have congealed under the label of the "cognitive-constructivist" therapies. "At the core of constructivist theory is a view of human beings as active agents who, individually and collectively, co-constitute the meaning of their experiential world" (Neimeyer, 1993, p. 222). Humans are viewed as active, even proactive, in remarkable similarity to Rychlak's concept of telosponding. Some cognitive constructivists seem to emphasize the absolute lack of fixed meanings in human experience, with options of human belief termed "multiple realities" (Meichenbaum, 1993, p. 203), and also to minimize constraints on factors that shape the meaning systems of persons. Others, however, argue that it is vital to understand the factors that condition or set boundaries upon meaning. Mahoney (1993, p. 189) speaks of the "increasing importance attributed to biological and social factors in the etiology, maintenance, and treatment of psychological disorders," and of the "dynamic boundary between biological and social influences." Safran and Segal (1990) draw on conceptions as diverse as Freudian drive theory, Bowlby's attachment theory, and contemporary work on memory to understand the shaping of the "self," which they define as "an invariant pattern of awarenesses through which psychological processes are organized" (p. 59). They argue that "agency or authorship of action is the most fundamental invariant of core self-experience and consists of the sense of volition that precedes a motor act and the sense of predictability and consequences that follow actions"

(p. 60). This notion of a self is closer to what I will argue for in this paper than that of any of the other traditions in applied psychology.

Conclusion

A number of psychologists are gradually coming to recognize the vital importance of developing an understanding of human freedom that allows for real agency yet grasps the conditionedness of our existence. These efforts are being assisted by philosophers like Stephen Toulmin who have been willing to contribute to the dialogue about these matters. Discussing the role of enlightenment philosophy in setting the ground for modern deterministic understandings of the person, Toulmin (cited in Howard and Conway, 1986, p. 1241) states that

> the realm of reasons and the realm of causes can no longer, for us, be *separate* realms, like the separate Cartesian "substances" of mind and matter. Rather, human life intertwines reasons and causes in as complex a manner as it does all other aspects of the "mental" and the "material," the "human" and the "natural." If we are to heal the wounds created by the Cartesian split, and reintegrate humanity with nature, it will follow as a result that human actions, too, are performed *within* the world of natural processes; and the older philosophical barriers separating rationality from causality will have to be dismantled along with all the others. A world of nature into which humanity has been reintegrated will no longer be an impersonal, mechanistic world. Rather, it will be a world within which the human reason itself is a causally efficacious agency, within which — as the ancients recognized but the philosophers of the seventeenth century denied — we have the elbowroom that we require to exercise the autonomy that is a chief mark of our humanity.

Though I am not completely happy with Toulmin's seemingly exclusive identification of "causally efficacious agency" with the human faculty of reason, I do think he is right in identifying the split we need to heal and the vital import of agency as "a chief mark of our humanity."

The Contemporary Context for Dialogue

I am inclined to concur with the popular sense in Christian circles that the growing acceptance of psychological and other social scientific understandings of the person has contributed to a declining sense of the efficacy of human agency and a complementary rise of what is commonly described as a "victim" mindset in our culture. Christians are appropriately concerned about these developments because of the undermining effect such ideas probably have on a sense of personal responsibility and of culpability for sin.

In a compelling recent essay, psychiatrist Jeffrey Satinover (1994) sounded a strident warning about the detrimental implications of a growing psychologization of our understanding of humanity. He stated that

> a primary goal of any modern, scientific psychology has been to understand human subjectivity and behavior — including those areas that touch on morals, meaning, purpose, and value, and therefore on human motivation and choice — not in terms of ultimate purpose but in terms of prior causes. In the domain of psychology or psychoanalysis proper, this search for causes inevitably means the reduction of what appears to be a freely acting or choosing agent — man — to prior, more elementary influences. . . . [U]nwittingly and unacknowledged, the scientific study of man thus aims ultimately at his abolition as man — as free agent — and his reconstruction as mechanism. (p. 14)

Satinover goes on to argue that the "scientific method is reductive without limit. . . . From a scientific perspective there is never any room whatever for freely acting agents. . . . It is in the very nature of science and the scientific method that it cannot at all address or understand free agency" (p. 15). Satinover argues that such a reductive agenda results in "the elimination of the possibility of choice, meaning, and purpose in human existence" (p. 16). He suggests that this is a tacit goal of psychological understandings of the person. He imagines our understanding of the causes of human action to be like a triangle that is progressively being filled in from the bottom with information about the genetic, biological, environmental, psychodynamic, and other causes of human behavior, to the point where the empty apex of the triangle, which represents the unexplained residue of human action to which we may attribute the quaint designation of "free choice," is seemingly reduced to a mere dot. He lays down the last boundary that Christians must defend, by arguing that "upon reflection, we realize that the only domain of potential choice that means anything to us and which, if it exists at all, needs to be a priori free is that of moral choice" (p. 17). This, presumably, is the unfilled-in spot at the apex of the triangle, which must not be explained away by recourse to "causes."

Satinover speaks for many thinking Christians today. He is right that were the apex to be filled in with "causes" of an order lower than human agency, human beings as imagers of the Creator God, as beings endowed with dignity and value, would cease to exist. It is indeed man *qua* man who is at stake.

But outrage against researchers and clinicians who seek to understand the factors that shape and mold human experience is being oversold. Appreciation for the value of information about genetic predispositions for alcoholism and schizophrenia is remarkably missing from Satinover's essay and from much of our discourse in the Christian community. In our rush to decry society's flight from responsibility, we have too often minimized compassion for those who have experienced sexual abuse, parental neglect, unremitting marital conflict, and other unfortunate environmental conditions, and we have failed to appreciate the attempts to understand how such experiences condition the well-being of those who have lived through them. Further, Satinover and others are profoundly wrong in drawing the battle line at the point of "moral choice." We give away too much in such a strategy, and thus put ourselves in an indefensible position. As I said with regard to Rychlak, it is a mistake to try to find a tiny domain of human life that we can regard as meeting certain tight definitions for what constitutes freedom.

And yet this strategy seems common in philosophical circles. This type of resolution was attempted in a classic paper by Harry Frankfurt (1971) and the revision of Frankfurt's argument proposed by Eleonore Stump (1988). Let me say first that Frankfurt does not appear to be making his proposal for an understanding of freedom of the will as a solution to the problem of determinism. In fact he says that his solution "appears to be neutral with regard to the problem of determinism. It seems conceivable that it should be causally determined that a person is free to want what he wants to want" (p. 20). Nevertheless, Frankfurt seems to attribute the key feature of freedom of the will to the occurrence of a certain type of "volition." He distinguishes between first-order desires, which are simply desires to do or not to do certain things such as sleep, eat, or drink alcohol, and, on the other hand, second-order desires whose object is to have certain first-order desires and not others, or to rank one's first-order desires in a certain order. When an individual "wants a certain desire to be his will" (p. 10) he is having a second-order volition. Second-order volitions constitute the defining feature of freedom of the will: "It is only because a person has a volition of the second-order that he is capable both of enjoying and of lacking freedom of the will" (p. 14).

Stump (1988) clarifies Frankfurt's view by asserting that in the entire corpus of Frankfurt's writings, an individual will have freedom of the will to the degree that he meets the following conditions: "(1) He has second-order volitions, (2) he does not have first-order volitions that are discordant with those second-order volitions, and (3) he has the first-order volitions he has *because of* his second-order volitions" (p. 397). Stump then goes on to improve Frankfurt's formulation by further analyzing the acting of the will by which a second-order volition exerts control on first-order desires. She draws on Aquinas's understanding of the interaction of the intellect and the will, by which the intellect moves the will through drawing the attention of the will to the good that can be pursued by one course of action over another. Stump notes that such intellectual reasoning need be neither rational nor conscious.

Frankfurt and Stump and Satinover are right in thinking that to have a meaningful concept of human agency we must specify the minimal conditions necessary for free human choices to occur. They may also have identified paradigm exemplars of free acts. Frankfurt's concept of a second-order desire seems helpful in this regard; to have second-order desires or volitions requires that one "survey the field of options" and in the process have become conscious of the variety of behavioral options available. To the extent that human agency does require choice, such a survey of options would seem to make meaningful choice more likely. The danger in Satinover's approach is that it suggests too stark a dichotomy between those human actions in which free will operates and others in which it does not. It would seem more plausible to posit a continuum of free will in human events, such that one could be exercising human freedom in resolving existential crises, but also in such mundane choices as when to go to the bathroom.

Theological Foundations

Christian orthodoxy in the Reformation tradition generally insists on both of the two complementary elements I have hinted at already and which are essential to the position I will develop later; namely, that human agency is real *and* that the extent or nature of that agency is limited. Augustine believed that the image of God has not been completely destroyed, but that human beings have lost the liberty not to sin. Augustine taught that we cannot avoid sin without the help of God's grace. We are free to choose, but our choices are between varying degrees and kinds of sinful options (Erickson, 1983-1985). John Calvin, following the tradition of Augustine, suggests that there are three kinds of freedom, the first of which is a "freedom from necessity" which is "naturally so inherent in man, that he cannot possibly be deprived of it" (1970, Book II, Chap. II, Section 5). Calvin elaborates:

In this way, then, man is said to have free will, not because he has a free choice of good and evil, but because he acts voluntarily, and not by compulsion. This is perfectly true: but why should so small a matter have been dignified with so proud a title? An admirable freedom! that man is not forced to be the servant of sin, while he is, however, . . . [a voluntary slave]; his will being bound by the fetters of sin. I abominate mere verbal disputes, by which the church is harassed to no purpose; but I think we ought religiously to eschew terms which imply some absurdity, especially in subjects where error is of pernicious consequence. How few are there who, when they hear free will attributed to man, do not immediately imagine that he is the master of his mind and will in such a sense that he can of himself incline himself either to good or evil? (Book II, Chap. II, Section 7)

Calvin seems to assume that agency exists and to be incredulous that this reality would even need to be addressed, though he notes that Augustine was also forced to argue for the existence of some capacity for human volition in his debates with those who would deny free will on the basis of a desire to excuse sin (Book II, Chap. II, Section 8). Calvin's special burden is not to establish the existence of free will, but to argue that the exercise of that free will is bounded; i.e., "free will does not enable any man to perform good works, unless he is assisted by grace" (Book II, Chap. II, Section 6).

Positions which grant that we are responsible agents but deny boundaries on that freedom have historically been associated with Pelagius and viewed as heretical since the times of Pelagius's conflict with Augustine in the early fifth century. According to Erickson (1983-1985, p. 632), "Pelagius laid heavy emphasis upon the idea of free will. Unlike the other creatures, man was created free of the controlling influences of the universe. Furthermore, he is free of any determining influences from the fall. Holding to a creationist view of the origin of the soul, Pelagius maintained that the soul, created by God especially for each person, is not tainted by any supposed corruption or guilt." The core aberration of this view seems to lie in its ascribing to human beings a quality that properly can be attributed only to God, that of unbounded freedom: "The being of God alone is unconditioned, absolute freedom; that of the creature is conditioned, relative freedom, freedom in dependence" (Brunner, 1939, p. 262). Arminians take a more moderate position than Pelagians by arguing that our nature is in fact corrupted by the influence of original sin, but they suggest that the impact of this corruption is moderated by the exercise of God's prevenient grace, which is "a universal benefit of the atoning work of Christ (which) nullifies the judicial consequences of Adam's sin" (Erickson, 1983-1985, p. 634).

While views that have denied any bounds to human agency have been labeled heretical in the orthodox Christian tradition, views that deny or substantially restrict human agency have been afforded a place at the communion table. (It is curious, given this history, that Christians on the contemporary scene are so indignant about the denial of human agency in social science.) Jonathan Edwards is described by many as a "theological determinist." Edwards appears to have proposed that human freedom is not the power of deciding but rather the power of acting in accord with one's desires. But because of his strong emphasis on the primacy of the doctrine of God's sovereignty, Edwards suggested that the outcomes involved are not left to chance; human desires are determined by God. Reformed theology in America has been much influenced by Edwards. Louis Berkhof, answering the objection to the Reformed doctrine of the decrees of God that such decrees would be inconsistent with the moral freedom of man, responded as follows:

> Man is a free agent with the power of rational self-determination. He can reflect upon, and in an intelligent way choose, certain ends, and can also determine his action with respect to them. The decree of God, however, carries with it necessity. God has decreed to effectuate all things or, if He has not decreed that, He has at least determined that they must come to pass. He has decided the course of man's life for him. In answer to this objection it may be said that the Bible certainly does not proceed with the assumption that the divine decree is inconsistent with the free agency of man. It clearly reveals that God has decreed the free acts of man, but also that the actors are nonetheless free and therefore responsible for their acts. (1939-1941, p. 106)

The foundation for what I will now write is this dual assertion: human persons are free agents, but our agency is bounded by other causal factors. Before we move on from this consideration of preliminary theological issues, let me note that discussion of the interaction of human agency and its boundaries has gone on historically not only in theological anthropology and its influence on our understanding of the process of salvation, but also in the practical realm of pastoral psychology. Writing about the traditional understandings of different types of sin and their pastoral implications as understood in the Roman Catholic tradition of pastoral care, Benedict Groeschel notes:

> There is another sin of greater significance, even though it is without a simple term of designation owing to a fault of language. It was once couched in an almost liturgical term: "sin imperfectly committed." It

is an act or habit so ingrained and linked to self-destructive pathology, or so much a part of a person's life adjustment that freedom to act otherwise is greatly diminished. Even confessors using the severe morality of days gone by never overlooked this phenomenon. The complex issues that minimize freedom and, consequently, real responsibility were summed up in the frightening package labeled "concupiscence." (Groeschel, 1983, p. 109)

So I find myself agreeing with Plantinga that human agency must be defended as a foundation of our understanding of persons, while our capacity to exercise that agency is bounded. Specific behavioral outcomes or complex patterns of outcome are the result of interacting causative factors that include a number of elements, among which is human agency.

Agency and Causation in Understanding Human Behavior

Satinover is right that one of the goals of scientific analysis is the breaking down of complex phenomena into more elementary units that are conceptually simpler, more readily quantifiable, and potentially manipulable. This description seems true not just of the social sciences but of science in general. Satinover is also right to observe that the now widely held view — that human experience is ultimately reducible to elementary and intrinsically involuntary causes — does great violence to the most precious aspects of human existence, namely choice, meaning, and purpose. The secular social scientist, however, will criticize the naive theist for stifling inquiry into the regularities that characterize human experience. What would have fueled the search for "causes" of such phenomena as violence, homosexuality, or alcoholism were it not the firm conviction that these, indeed all, behavior patterns have causes?

If some entities can be construed as causes of important aspects of human behavior, we have reasons to try to understand these constraints on human choice. The first is simply the value of real knowledge about the human condition; understanding such causes will yield a deeper understanding of ourselves. Second, knowledge of causes of significant human events may allow us to prevent human suffering. Third, understanding causes may inform us about the process of change by which an individual could be assisted in shedding destructive behavior patterns.

Determinism is the claim that human actions are the inevitable results of antecedent causes sufficient to bring those actions into being. It is the belief that given the antecedent conditions of an action, the agent could not have chosen to act otherwise. It is the concept of determinism, seemingly justified by the growing sophistication of explanatory studies of human behavior, that has the frightening undermining effect about which Satinover and other critics of psychology have raised an alarm. I am gratified that Plantinga does not join that chorus.

Determinism comes in two versions: compatibilism and incompatibilism (Evans, 1989). Incompatibilists argue that since determinism is true, human acts are not free. If my act of rising from my chair to get something to drink is a mere reflex caused by a pre-existing physiological state of thirst combined with effective visual cues of consumption of liquid on the TV screen (packaged in a host of unspecified brain events radioed to my muscles), then it makes no sense to describe my rising and drinking as a free action. Compatibilists, on the other hand, argue that freedom is ultimately reconcilable with determinism because some of the factors that cause human behavior arise from within. If my rising and drinking is most immediately caused by a thought "the drink on that commercial looks awfully scrumptious and I think I'll just have one," then *I* have acted *freely*. After all, nobody forced me to take that drink; I did it because I wanted to. The difficulty with the compatibilist position is that the individual merely becomes a way station through which external forces flow, just as Skinner argued. The person ultimately is not an originating source of action.

Christians have a stake in denying the thesis of determinism. I used to construe the choice as one between determinism on the one hand, and the thesis that human choice is not conditioned at all by antecedent causes. But such a conclusion is neither logical nor reasonable in light of the findings of the human sciences. If determinism is the belief that given its causal antecedents, no human action could have occurred otherwise than it did, then the denial of determinism is that *not* all human actions so occur. In other words, as C. Stephen Evans once pointed out to me, the denial of determinism does not entail that there are no boundaries to human choice, but rather that there is at least one human action not utterly predetermined by event causation. The hypothesis of determinism is also falsified if there are *aspects* of human action for which free agency is a necessary prior condition.

We can distinguish two different routes for elaborating a denial of determinism. One would be to identify a class of actions that are not determined while allowing all other human actions to be determined. This seems to me to be the solution proposed by Satinover (1994) when he states that "The only domain of potential choice that means anything to us and which, if it exists at all, needs to be a priori free is that of moral choice" (p. 17); in other words, he wants to preserve moral choice as the island of agency amid a sea of determined behavior.

This view would seem to limit freedom to a small set of special acts that meet rather stringent criteria, such as being *moral* actions; non-moral choices would lack freedom entirely. But why should some particular class of actions be singled out as free? If we are free when we choose to do our duty, is it not reasonable to suppose that we are also free when we choose the color of our new carpet? And if we believe in free action at all, why should we think it is relatively rare? In everyday experience, is it not more common to regard it as remarkable for a human being to *lack* freedom than to have it? Is this not precisely what makes the addictions so fascinating to us — that we wonder how a person could come to such a state as to have so little effective agency?

The other major way to preserve human freedom is to reinterpret our understanding of causation to allow for the simultaneous operation of event causation and agent causation. Evans (1989), in distinguishing event and agent causation, says that event causation is "where one event or set of events leads to another event or occurrence. Agent causality is a causal chain in which the ultimate or 'first-cause' of the series of events is not another event, but a person, an agent." (Evans attributes this distinction to Roderick Chisholm, and more classically to the philosophy of Thomas Reid.) Evans notes that both types of causation may operate at the same time: if "a cause is a condition which contributes to an event, including, in particular, necessary conditions, then all of these factors may be causes" (p. 123). He then continues:

> Of course we have noted that a libertarian does not believe that all human behavior is free, but even where we believe genuine freedom is at work, it is always legitimate to look for other causes. The individual's free choice is one factor; there may be many forces at work which make it more likely that the individual will choose one way rather than another. So the libertarian by no means limits psychologists to choice as the sole cause of behavior. (p. 123)

This is the right direction. The next step would seem to be to begin to specify the ways in which event and agent causation might interact. Thinking analogically, the nature of this interactivity might take several forms. One option would be that event causation might constrict the range of possible choices available to the acting person. A person subjected to a degrading home environment may not have available certain response options such as positive affection, or acceptance and encouragement for his own children. The individual with a genetic predisposition toward aggression may not have available a subset of responses that involve perfect equanimity under duress. Such individuals may be able to recognize the impoverishment of their capacity to respond and to take slow, painstaking steps toward growth in these areas. The transcendence of some of their given limitations via this recognition and the efforts to overcome the limitations would be special marks of free agency — themselves dependent, of course, on already available abilities that are the slow accumulation of multiple causal factors, some "natural" (event causation) and some "free" (choices).

The second option for understanding the interaction of event and agent causation involves the differential weighting of response options, in a manner analogous to loaded dice. Agents may have a range of behavioral options to choose from, but those options might be differentially weighted. One way this might be so flows from Stump's (1988) suggestion on how the intellect moves the will. Following Aquinas, she argues that

> the intellect moves the will by presenting it with an understanding of the good. In so moving the will, the intellect acts not as an efficient cause but rather as a final cause. The will is a natural inclination or appetite for the good; and the intellect moves the will, without coercion, by showing it what the good to be pursued is in a particular set of circumstances. (pp. 399-400; footnote 8)

While elements of the tripartite stratification of the person into desires/ passion, intellect, and will, make me uncomfortable, as a heuristic model this helps us connect with a cognitive-behavioral conception of social skill (McFall, 1982; Mischel, 1973). In such a model, it is argued that response options vary in probability according to their past associations with successful social encounters, their salience in memory, the actor's acuity in discerning relevant response demands of the challenging environment, and so forth.

As an example of differential weighting, suppose I am verbally assaulted by an angry student in front of a group of his peers. I am morally responsible for my response, but there are factors that differentially weight my response options. I may have grown up in an abusive home where we returned aggression with aggression to survive; the uncanny attitudinal resemblance of the confrontive student to my abusive older brother may add fuel to my impulse to respond in kind. I may have been dealing with this background at an abstract level for years, praying for the formation of new second-order and first-order volitions for dealing with just such situations, with the result of an instant impression that this is the moment for me to display meekness. I might be short on emotional reservoirs of patience at that moment due to having been up late working on a conference paper the night before. The fact that the chairperson of the faculty committee that will decide my application for promotion next month is by my side at the moment may add a powerful incentive for a particular type of response. Finally, a series of unpleasant encounters with the same student during the previous year may leap to mind during the current confrontation. With all this background, the various response options will not be weighted equally as they are "sorted" by the human agent. And yet these various "pressures" are not the whole story, as though I were nothing but a hydraulic system in which the sum of pressures from different directions yields a mathematically calculable behavioral result. Instead, I have a concept of myself — as different from, as more than — these pressures, and as able to make *my* way *among* them, not just responding to the various pressures but also assessing them and deciding which ones to *give* weight to.

Conclusion

A Christian understanding of the person endorses the reality of agency *and* restrictions on the range of that agency. It is a mistake to tie human agency to a special limited class of human choices that incorporate special characteristics such as second-order volitions. Rather, event causation in the form of genetic predispositions, environmental influences and the like, interacts with agent causation by constraining the options available for "choice" by the agent, and by differentially weighting the choice options of the choosing agent. Genetic factors may make alcohol taste more pleasant or one's responses to rapid alcohol ingestion less aversive than for other persons. Familial modeling of aggressive methods of conflict resolution may both constrain the range of possible nonviolent responses to conflict situations and differentially weight different aggressive response options. Further, our past choices add a cumulative weight that affects our present choices by further constraining and weighting our options. Our degree of freedom and responsibility probably varies on a continuum: The individual with many predisposing and current factors that push toward a particular behavioral outcome may have very limited freedom indeed, as when an individual manifests major genetic, biological, early environmental/familial, socio-cultural, and contemporary interpersonal factors that might predict, for instance, alcoholism. But perhaps the possibility of agency can never disappear as long as we are human, though agency may, in human terms, become ever more unlikely to be used adaptively and rightly.

An individual with no such predisposing factors, with an enlarged understanding of first- and second-order desire options, and with no behavioral "momentum" from past choices in this area might have maximal freedom. Consider an individual who was reared in a condition of modest comfort, experiencing neither wealth (which one might be driven to cling to or stricken by guilt to flee from) nor poverty, who felt satisfied with her past management of money, and had felt led of the Lord to spend the last year reflecting on the Christian understanding of material possessions and wealth and how they should be managed. Such a person would possess an awesome degree of freedom and responsibility upon the surprise inheritance of a 500-million-dollar estate from an unknown relative.

Finally, I would note (thanks to a brief conversation with Robert Roberts) that freedom per se should not be regarded as an absolute value in itself, since a diminished capacity to do what is wrong (what might be called being a "slave to righteousness" — Romans 6:18) is a Christian personality ideal. I hope, for example, that some auspicious parenting and growing up with a mother and two sisters will substantially diminish my son's future freedom to abuse women.

Four areas of empirical research I keep track of are, in decreasing order, homosexuality, determinants of sexual behavior in adolescents, alcoholism, and antisocial personality disorder. In each of these areas, research continues to accumulate suggesting meaningful patterns in the distribution of these responses or response-proclivities in the population. The playing field does not appear even for all; life does not appear to be fair in terms of the behaviors toward which we are inclined; choice in these areas is influenced by identifiable factors. But as a Christian, I cannot believe all human choices in these areas are determined.

Despite widespread media reports that this research has proven homosexuality to be biologically caused, the research is actually inconclusive, with important studies as yet unreplicated and the power of important findings still in question. It is no longer credible to deny that powerful forces may direct some toward a homosexual outcome of the processes by which gender identification and erotic orientation are formed. At this time there appears to be as much evidence supporting psychologic models of causation as biologic. The best understanding of the literature would appear to favor an "interactionist" theory of causation. The traditional formulation of such a model would speak only of the interaction of environmental and biological variables. And yet two of the most prominent proponents of such a model explicitly use the concept of choice in describing the development of homosexual orientation. After discussing the ways in which genetically mediated variations in personality may influence choice, they say, "This is not meant to imply that one consciously decides one's sexual orientation. Instead, sexual orientation is assumed to be shaped and reshaped by a cascade of choices made in the context of changing circumstances in one's life and enormous social and cultural pressures" (Byne and Parsons, 1993, p. 237). I have argued for a view of agency in which the presence of non-agential causal factors is compatible with a partial, though genuine, freedom of choice. If the "cascade of choices" partially determinative of a sexual orientation are ordinary choices, then on the view I have been promoting we have every reason to think that sexual orientation, like other features of personality, is partially a result of free agency.

As psychological researchers develop ever more sophisticated mathematical models for synthesizing large amounts of data on factors that influence human action, it is becoming increasingly common to speak in terms of the "percentage of variance accounted for" by the statistical model. None of these models is very powerful as yet, and there is remarkable agreement in the field that we are much better at predicting aggregated human behavior than individual human behavior. As a result, no reasonable psychologist seems ready to boast that we shall soon be able to predict individual action with precision, nor does it seem likely that we ever will. There will always be unexplained portions of the statistical variance in individual and group behavior that libertarians can regard as the predictable result of the reality of human agency.

The Christian concept of freedom is not that of freedom from regularity, freedom from influences upon behavior, or freedom from finiteness. It simply means that in the final confluence of influences from which the behavior emerges, the human being is not merely a "locus" of impersonal influences coming together, but makes real choices among real options, influenced as the agent is by his or her history and constitution. The decision so made bears the stamp both of our choices and of the many influences that have shaped us. In the normal case, we act as we do *because* of our human agency, but not *exclusively* because of it. We act as we do because of our human freedom, but also because of the factors that shape our choices.

Attachment: Bowlby and the Bible

Robert C. Roberts

Introduction

At the end of the third volume of his magisterial trilogy on the psychology of attachment, John Bowlby declares,

> Intimate attachments to other human beings are the hub around which a person's life revolves, not only when he is an infant or a toddler or a schoolchild but throughout his adolescence and his years of maturity as well, and on into old age. From these intimate attachments a person draws his strength and enjoyment of life and, through what he contributes, he gives strength and enjoyment to others. These are matters about which current science and traditional wisdom are at one. (Bowlby, 1980, p. 442)

One version of such traditional wisdom is the Christian one, which derives from the documents of the New Testament. Bowlby's research supports the biblical view of attachment. However, his concept of attachment, though parallel to the New Testament's in several respects, also diverges in significant ways. I shall compare the two concepts, arguing that Bowlby's concept could be considerably improved by making it more like the New Testament's.

Attachment in the Bible

No word, used by any biblical author, has exactly the scope and sense that I shall here attach to "attachment." But I hope to establish that around this word we can construct a concept whose features are all biblical, though never, in the Bible, tied together quite as they are here. If this concept of attachment is, as I intend, a *psychological* concept analogous to the ones that are pivotal for standard personality theories, this may explain, in part, why the concept is not found in the Bible. The Bible is not a book of systematic psychology, any more than it is a book of systematic theology. But it does contain concepts that are psychological in a less formal sense, just as it contains analogously informal theological concepts. It is these less formal concepts I shall draw on in constructing the psychological idea of attachment.

Attachment can be to things as well as to people and to God. Because the rich young ruler (Luke 18:18) was attached to his wealth, he was saddened when Jesus told him that to have eternal life he must give it up (detach himself from it); and Jesus invited the ruler to attach himself to Jesus rather than to his "goods" ("come, follow me"). This passage suggests that attachment is a sort of emotional "dependency" — that one's emotional response is conditioned by the state of what one is attached to. Through attachment to something, one becomes subject to the vicissitudes of that thing. The ruler is saddened by the prospect of those goods' not being his, and attachment to fellow human beings is evidenced by emotional responsiveness to how they are faring. "Rejoice with those who rejoice; weep with those who weep" (Rom. 15:15) can be read as an exhortation to be attached to one another. Because Paul is attached to the Jewish people ("my brethren, my kinsmen by race") their failure to grasp God's grace occasions "great sorrow and unceasing anguish in [his] heart" (Rom. 9:2-3).

In response to this fact of human nature, the central Stoic prophylaxis against emotional distress is *de*tachment (keeping "emotional distance") from things and persons (Epictetus, 1948). Unlike Stoicism and such otherwise diverse psychologies as those of Carl Jung (1961), Albert Ellis (1977), Carl Rogers (1959), and Murray Bowen (1978), the Bible does not commend detachment as an across-the-board policy for personal maturity. Certainly, people may suffer from their attachments, as Paul does from his attachment to his fellow Jews; this is the mischief of being "vulnerable," "dependent," "subject to" the object of attachment. But then emotional suffering is not the worst thing that can happen to a person. In the biblical view, it would be far worse to have no attachments at all — to be without "love." Particular attachments are sometimes unhealthy, as in the ruler's case; but attachment to God and to one's fellow human beings is strongly prescribed (Matt. 22:34-40). This implies something about the Bible's implicit conception of human nature, a conception similar to Bowlby's: we are not essentially autonomous monads who *happen* to have fellow monads with whom it is convenient and pleasant to live in harmony and some kind of inessential, non-psychological interdependency. We are made for attachments, made to live in terms of things that are not ourselves; it is not a fault in us to have our emotional life subject to the changing conditions of our fellow humans, or to the diverse attitudes and actions of God. Attachment is an essential structure (Maddi, 1980) of human personality that calls, not for mitigation or extirpation, but for proper development.

Paul encourages church members to depend on one another for many things (see 1 Cor. 12, Rom. 12:4-5, "membership one of another" being a form of attachment), and the particular kind of attachment to Christ that the apostle Paul calls "faith" is one in which a weak person (a disciple) derives strength from a strong one (the Lord):

> Three times I besought the Lord about [a "thorn" in Paul's "flesh"], that it should leave me; but he said to me, "My grace is sufficient for you, for my power is made perfect in weakness." I will all the more gladly boast of my weaknesses, that the power of Christ may rest upon me. For the sake of Christ, then, I am content with weaknesses, insults, hardships, persecutions, and calamities; for when I am weak, then I am strong. (2 Cor. 12:8-10)

This attachment to Christ is a little bit like that of a small child to its parent, as Bowlby describes it, an attachment in which the child derives security from the ongoing presence of the parent, and thus the ability to explore with confidence. Paul is able to "go on" with his work, despite adversities, living confidently and happily and free from basic anxiety, because Christ is with him; and since Christ's being with him is the paramount blessing, he can even welcome the adversities as accentuating his dependency on Christ. The similarity between the attachment of the human person to God, and that of the child to the human parent, is suggested by Jesus' use of "Abba" ("Father") in addressing God (see Mark 14:36), a use that is picked up in the early church. Thus St. Paul: "When we cry 'Abba! Father!' it is the Spirit himself bearing witness with our spirit that we are children of God" (Rom. 8:15b-16; see Gal. 4:1-7). The theme of trust in God's fatherly watchfulness, and thus attachment to God, is forcefully struck in Jesus' discourse on the birds and the lilies in Luke 12:22-31.

In the Christian view of persons, it is a basic structural fact of our nature that we get attached to things and persons, a fact not to be resisted, as it is by many modern psychologists. But the Christian psychology agrees with every personality theory I know of, in holding that not all attachments express true human nature. So the trick, for the deepest success in human life, is to get attached *in the right way to the right things.*

Jesus says, "Where your treasure is, there will your heart be also" (Matt. 6:21), thus saying, in effect, What you are like at the center of your personality (your "heart") is a function of the kind of thing you are very attached to (your "treasure"). Thus one who is very attached to God will be a different sort of "self" than someone who is very attached to money or power. Similarly, a person who is very attached to her friends will have a different personality from someone deeply attached to her public reputation.

Of course Jesus is not merely remarking here that differing attachments yield differing selves; behind his remark is the supposition that some variants of selves are worthy, healthy, and complete, while others have missed the mark. The Christian virtues are states in which, among other things, proper patterns of attachment are worked out. For example, Christian generosity is a state of relative detachment from wealth and attachment to God, and to friends and neighbors. I shall not try here to elaborate the norms for proper attachment, but such sayings of Jesus as the following will indicate the direction: "Seek first [God's] kingdom and his righteousness, and all these things shall be yours as well" (Matt. 6:33). "Blessed are those who hunger and thirst for righteousness, for they shall be satisfied" (Matt. 5:6). "He who loves father or mother more than me is not worthy of me; and he who loves son or daughter more than me is not worthy of me; and he who does not take his cross and follow me is not worthy of me" (Matt. 10:37-38). "You shall love the Lord your God with all your heart, and with all your soul, and with all your mind. . . . And . . . you shall love your neighbor as yourself" (Matt. 22:37b, 39b). In most of these passages it is acknowledged (if somewhat indirectly) that attachment to property, to son or mother, or to neighbor, is fitting and healthy *provided* that attachment to God and his kingdom is central and overriding in one's emotional makeup.

To summarize: In the Bible, attachment is a psychological relation that a person can have to things, other humans, or God. It is evidenced in emotional responsiveness to the perceived vicissitudes of its object: say, sorrow at the loss of a physical possession, or joy at its retrieval. If the object of attachment is a human being, the response might be satisfaction if the person is perceived as doing well, or anxiety if she is threatened, or anger if she is hurt through someone's action or omission. If the other person is in the role of protector (as a parent is to a child), then attachment to the object will result in anxiety if the protector is perceived as too far away or unable to protect, and relief upon perceiving the object to be near again, or again perhaps anger at the object for not being available. If the object of attachment is God, then again one will experience joy when God's purposes are perceived as fostered, and frustration when they are hindered; one will experience anxiety if God is perceived as distant or even nonexistent, and joy and comfort when he is perceived as near, benevolently watchful, and protective. The Bible regards the attachment disposition as a fact of human nature, not to be resisted wholesale, but to be properly directed, applied, and administered. Thus selective detachment is an important strategy of psycho-spiritual growth. It is proper to be attached (in an appropriate way) to human beings and (in a rather different way) to non-personal things, and proper to be very strongly (indeed, "ultimately" or "infinitely") attached to God. Attachment to inanimate or non-human animate things ("possessions") is consistent with health, but not in the degree of strength or kind appropriate to personal objects, human and divine. To say attachment is a structural feature of human personality is to say that the human psyche is an essentially connected, relational sort of thing; it lives and gains its character, for good or ill, from its connections with things "outside" itself.

Bowlby on Attachment

What Is Attachment?

In Bowlby's theory the concept of attachment initially seems to have a much narrower scope than its Christian counterpart. The most salient subject of attachment is the infant or young child, and the object is the mother or mother substitute. Bowlby distinguishes attachment as a pattern of relating from attachment behavior; attachment is a strong disposition "to seek proximity to and contact with" the mother, especially when the child is frightened, tired, or ill. Attachment behavior, by contrast, includes all the various forms of behavior by which the child attains or maintains the desired proximity (crying, facial expression, eye contact, clinging, following, calling, etc.) (Bowlby, 1982, p. 371). This behavior is "the output of . . . a safety-regulating system, namely a system the activities of which tend to reduce the risk of the individual coming to harm and are experienced as causing anxiety to be allayed and the sense of security to be increased" (Bowlby, 1982, p. 374).

Depending on how the mother interacts with her child's attachment behavior, the child's attachment will become secure, or insecure. The quality of the attachment is a function of the quality of the mother's relating to the infant as represented in the infant's "working model" (a cognitive construct) of the mother in her relationship to the infant. The working model is a fairly accurate mental representation of the mother as she has interacted, over time, with the child. If she is represented as *reliable*, the child's attachment is secure; he is happy to be with her, and returns to her regularly as a "secure base" from which to explore, but he is able to explore away from her for periods without anxiety. If she is represented as *not wholly reliable but not, on the whole, unreliable*, the child's attachment is insecure resistant (anxious); he tends to cling to her and to be distraught when she is not very close, and explores with some anxiety. If she is represented as *quite unreliable and thus on the whole a disappointment*, the child's attachment is insecure avoidant; he may cling to her sometimes, but at others will "reject" her, even acting as if he has never seen her before (see Ainsworth, Blehar, Waters, and Wall, 1978). Personal maturity in adult life is, in Bowlby's theory, very largely a result of having had one's attachment needs well satisfied in early childhood, that is to say, having had a reliably warm and solicitous mother.

I say that Bowlby's concept of attachment "initially seems" to have a narrower scope than the Christian concept because, although he does not cease interpreting attachment primarily as an infantile system for maintaining safety through spatial proximity to the mother, he broadens the concept to include persons of all ages — to attachments that seem quite remote from any safety-maintaining function. Already in the first volume of his trilogy he expands the scope of attachment to apply to adults, though he retains the narrow conception of its function:

> That attachment behaviour in adult life is a straightforward continuation of attachment behaviour in childhood is shown by the circumstances that lead an adult's attachment behaviour to become more readily elicited. In sickness and calamity, adults often become demanding of others; in conditions of sudden danger or disaster a person will almost certainly seek proximity to another known and trusted person. (Bowlby, 1982, pp. 207-8)

Something like the safety-maintaining function is still evident in the following 1973 passage, though one can detect that the emphasis moves away from survival towards happiness, fulfillment, and the meaning of life:

> Not only young children, it is now clear, but human beings of all ages are found to be at their happiest and able to deploy their talents to best advantage when they are confident that, standing behind them, there are one or more trusted persons who will come to their aid should difficulties arise. . . . Paradoxically, the truly self-reliant person when viewed in this light proves to be by no means as independent as cultural stereotypes suppose. An essential ingredient is a capacity to rely trustingly on others when occasion demands and to know on

whom it is appropriate to rely. A healthily self-reliant person is thus capable of exchanging roles when the situation changes: at one time he is providing a secure base from which his companion(s) can operate; at another he is glad to rely on one or another of his companions to provide him with just such a base in return. (Bowlby, 1973, pp. 359-60)

And the third volume of Bowlby's trilogy ends with the statement I quoted at the outset of this chapter, which seems to widen both the kind and significance of attachments:

> Intimate attachments to other human beings are the hub around which a person's life revolves, not only when he is an infant or a toddler or a schoolchild but throughout his adolescence and his years of maturity as well, and on into old age. From these intimate attachments a person draws his strength and enjoyment of life and, through what he contributes, he gives strength and enjoyment to others. (Bowlby, 1980, p. 442)

Our concept is now very far from that of a safety-regulating control system that functions primarily to insure physical proximity to a protector. It covers the attachment of adult children to parents or grandparents whom they may see infrequently, of spouses, of friends between whom "contact" may be primarily by post and whose function as protectors one of another may be minimal or non-existent. By this broadened concept parents are perhaps typically more attached to their children than children are to their parents — at least this seems to become so as children enter adolescence. Like biblical attachment, broadened Bowlbyan attachment seems to get exemplified (depending on the vicissitudes of the object of attachment) in gratitude, hope, and joy concerning the state of the object fully as much as in feelings of anxiety about the subject's own safety, and feelings of security when the subject perceives himself as safe in the object's care.

Bowlby's expanded understanding of attachment differs from the Bible's in scope; in the Bible, meaning-determining attachments can be to sub-human beings as well as to God, while in Bowlby attachments are (it seems) always to human beings. (Bowlby does mention, in passing, attachment to pets. But in most cases these are interpreted as substitutes for attachments to humans, due to either lack or frustration [see Bowlby, 1980, pp. 174-75, 255-56]. He also mentions attachment to things and places [Bowlby, 1959].) The Bible and Bowlby agree that an attachment-need is a general structural feature of personality, and is not just phase-specific. In the biblical view our personalities are constituted by our attachments, so that our proper functioning as persons is not to be secured by eschewing attachments as such, but by attaching ourselves in the *proper* way to the *proper* objects. For Bowlby our attachment-need is properly satisfied only by human beings, while the Bible posits the need for attachment to God as well; and this latter attachment places certain restrictions on what will qualify as healthy attachments to human beings. Bowlby stresses, throughout his writings, the formative power of early attachments, while the Bible concentrates on adult attachments. In accordance with this difference, Bowlby places responsibility for the quality of the attachment almost entirely on the object (whether she is reliable, affirming, etc.), while the Bible tends to place responsibility on the subject of the attachment.

Explaining Attachment and Attachment Behavior

How did humans, as a species, come to have the attachment *need?* This is a "big" question, about the origins of human nature. But it is legitimate for personality psychology, because *any* kind of explanation may throw light on human nature and the development and constitution of personality. So the question should be asked, even if there is not much hope of an uncontroversial answer to it. Bowlby refers again and again to his functional explanation of the basic human attachment need. I want to point out an inadequacy in the explanation and then suggest that Christianity offers a more satisfactory one; at least it offers the right *kind* of explanation. Then I shall comment briefly on his causal explanation of attachment behavior.

Functional Explanation of Attachment Behavior

When we look at the kind of explanation that Bowlby favors, we begin to see why he continues to use the infant/mother relationship paradigmatic of his attachment concept — even though he acknowledges that the theory has broader implications than his initial definition would suggest. He distinguishes between

> the *causes* of a particular sort of behaviour and the *function* that that behaviour fulfils. Given the structure of a behavioural system, variables that cause it to become active include such things as hormone level and stimuli of particular kinds from the environment. The function that the behaviour fulfils, on the other hand, is to be sought in the contribution it makes to survival. Male mating behaviour can serve as an example: amongst its usual causes [given the structure of mating

as a behavioral system] are androgen level and presence of female; its function is the contribution it makes to reproduction. (Bowlby, 1982, p. 223, italics added)

The function of a kind of behavior explains, not why particular *episodes* of the behavior occur, but why a given kind of organism has acquired the *disposition* to behave in this way. But we should note that, despite the difference between these kinds of explanations, functional explanation is a kind of causal explanation; the function of the behavior figures in a causal explanation of the species disposition, whether the explanation is Darwinian or theological. That is, we ask, What caused the species to have the attachment disposition? The Darwinian answer is, Because attachment behavior promoted survival, the physical characteristics that caused instances of it tended to be passed down through the generations. The theological answer is, Because God intended human beings to live a life characterized by love of himself and of fellow humans, he created them with the attachment disposition. Bowlby advocates the Darwinian explanation.

> Among essential features of [Bowlby's theory] are that the human infant comes into the world genetically biased to develop a set of behavioural patterns that, given an appropriate environment, will result in his keeping more or less close proximity to whomever [sic] cares for him, and that this tendency to maintain proximity serves the function of protecting the mobile infant and growing child from a number of dangers, amongst which in man's environment of evolutionary adaptedness the danger of predation is likely to have been paramount (Bowlby, 1988, pp. 60-61).

> In man's environment of evolutionary adaptedness the function of attachment behaviour, which of course promotes proximity to special companions, is protection from predators, and . . . this is as true for humans as it is for other species of mammal and bird. For all ground-living primates, safety lies in being with the band. To become separated from it is to provide a more or less easy meal for a lurking leopard or a pack of hunting dogs. (Bowlby, 1973, p. 143. Bowlby goes to some trouble, in the context, to show that safety continues to be the function of attachment, even in older children and adults. See pp. 142-48.)

The causal explanation for *our* having the attachment disposition is of course that our ancestors' having this disposition contributed causally to their surviving the danger of predators, and thus to their reproducing, and thus to their passing on to us their genetically based disposition to attach.

I suggest that Bowlby emphasizes infantile attachment and its adult counterpart because this kind of attachment behavior lends itself to construal as the output of a safety-regulating system. It is a construal that enables Bowlby to give a Darwinian explanation of our attachment disposition. Attachment behavior that tends to occur in contexts of danger, preceded by anxiety and followed by anxiety reduction, is far more plausibly explained as having a safety-maintenance function than, say, the attachment behavior that consists in two friends writing each other at regular intervals because they enjoy sharing thoughts and experiences and want to keep in touch. Here a Darwinian explanation, even on the behavioral level, is much less satisfying. If we are to explain the letter-writing behavior by reference to the survival-enhancing power of attachments, we must emphasize *other* behavior, like that of the clinging infant or of the friends who seek each other out at news of an approaching hurricane; and then we must treat the letter-writing behavior as somehow secondary or even epiphenomenal, a sort of "frill" that is carried along on the original function of attachment behavior.

On the other hand if, on more Aristotelian lines (see Aristotle, 1985, 1097b22-1098a20, and Books VIII and IX), we see the letter-writing behavior as *centrally* characteristic or paradigmatic of attachments (an instance of the mature form thereof), and safety-enhancing behavior as only an early and primitive form of what reaches its fruition in true friendship, then we will not be satisfied with the Darwinian explanation. A Darwinian will think of spiritual friendship as a vestige of survival-attachment, while an Aristotelian will think of survival-attachment as a primitive prefiguration of spiritual friendship — while agreeing that survival-attachment precedes spiritual friendship both ontogenetically and phylogenetically, and contributes causally to the latter. Clearly, the adequacy of a proposed explanation of attachment is relative to one's *concept* of attachment; conceptual differences here have much to do with which cases of attachment one takes to be central and which secondary.

As regards Bowlby's concept of attachment, there seem to be two Bowlbys — the Darwinian Bowlby, who emphasizes psychological phenomena that lend themselves to construal as mechanisms of biological survival; and the increasingly humanistic Bowlby, who wishes to do justice to the multifacial emotional richness and existential significance of human attachments. Bowlby denies that the attachment disposition serves some more basic function such as ensuring a food supply to the infant (see Bowlby, 1982, pp. 210-20) — as Freudians tend to suggest. He sides with Freud against the Freudians: "Though it might easily be supposed that

Freud also held that the function of a child's tie to his mother is mainly to ensure food supply, Freud's position is in fact a little different" (*ibid.*, p. 224). Freud held instead that "the function fulfilled by the secondary drive that ties infant to mother [that is, the attachment drive] is, by ensuring the mother's presence, that of preventing the psychical apparatus from becoming deranged 'by an accumulation of amounts of stimulation which require to be disposed of' [Freud, 1959, p. 137]" (*ibid.*). Thus, in his own way, Freud opts for a more Aristotelian and less Darwinian account of the function of attachment: Its function is to promote psychic self-realization. Similarly, Bowlby wishes to make attachment a *basic* feature of human nature. "[T]o have a deep attachment to a person (or a place or thing) is to have taken them as the *terminating* object of our instinctual responses" (Bowlby, 1959, p. 13, italics added). Yet Bowlby's Darwinism pushes him hard to make the attachment object not terminating, but instrumental:

> During infancy and childhood bonds are with parents (or parent sub-stitutes) who are looked to for protection, comfort, and assistance. During healthy adolescence and adult life these bonds persist but are complemented by new bonds, commonly of a heterosexual nature. Although food and sex sometimes play important roles in such relationships, the relationship *exists in its own right* and has an important survival function of its own, namely protection. Thus, within the attachment framework, bonds are seen as neither subordinate to nor derivative from food and sex. (Bowlby, 1988, pp. 162-63, italics added)

We can see from the quasi-appositive use Bowlby makes of the second "and" in the third sentence that for him the basicness of a structure of human personality is its direct relevance to survival. Food ingestion and sexual activity are no doubt means of survival, and thus so are the drives to them; but attachment has a survival value that is not derived from its relation to food and sex. It is not a means to a means to survive, but *directly* a means to survive. The explanation of everything most basic to human nature by reference to its physical survival function is of course emblematic of Bowlby's ideological Darwinism.

But we can see also an Aristotelian tendency in him, as we see indeed in most personality theorists, to think of proper functioning in terms of a *personal well-being* of a very different order than mere survival. A person's nature determines not just a tendency to survive (or for the race to survive), but for the individual (or the community) to *flourish in a personal way*, to be actualized in the distinctively human manner. It seems to me that in defending the basicness of attachment Bowlby is protesting a reductionism that "dehumanizes" the psyche, making it basically interested in nothing more significant than the satisfaction of bodily needs. We are made for something richer and deeper than that, something found above all in our human attachments. But then the Darwinian in Bowlby cannot be suppressed, and asserts that the function of attachments is after all to facilitate physical survival — survival *is* the richer and deeper something that our attachments are for. Bowlby is in a bind. He has a richly Aristotelian concept of attachment, but the only aspects of attachment he has a functional explanation for belong to the thinner, Darwinian concept, a concept that cannot do justice to the profoundest and most important things he has to say about the relations of attachment to personality.

The Christian psychologist can explain more than the Darwinian about personality because her explanatory framework is ultimately personal: Why do human beings have the attachment disposition? Because they are created by God, who is love. That is, they were created *out of* a kind of proleptic attachment, and *for* attachment of a certain sort to one another and to their God. The Christian psychologist can acknowledge that the attachment of an infant to his mother, which consists, behaviorally, largely in keeping close to her, has a safety-regulating function. Something like an evolutionary process may indeed be the means by which God created the human race. But the Christian psychologist has an added explanatory resource that allows the deeply personal aspects of human life — of which Bowlby too feels the need to make sense — to be themselves, without "reducing" them to something explainable in terms of mere survival function.

Functional Explanation of Attachment Experience

One dimension of human personality insisted on by the Christian psychologist is inwardness (Augustine, 1961; Kierkegaard, 1992; Taylor, 1989; Matt. 6:2-6, 16-18; Matt. 15:1-9; Mark 7:14-23; Rom. 10:8; Gal. 2:20; 1 Peter 3:3-4; see also Roberts, this volume, a). When Zeanah and Anders (1987) comment that "relationships exist internally as representations, as well as externally as discrete behaviors (interactions)" (p. 238), they make an essential point of New Testament psychology. The Christian psychologist takes seriously, as something requiring development and explanation, the subjective qualities of human life, what it is like to *live* a human life, to *be* a human being, to *experience* the *meaning* of, say, attachments.

Darwinian explanations, inadequate as accounts of human *behavior*, are even less adequate in talking about the psychology of human beings *from within*. The attachment behavior of an infant has a survival function, but it is not chiefly *as* promoting his safety that the two-year-old experiences being close to mother, wanting to be close to her, feeling discomfort at being too long away from her, etc. For example, it is not as promoting his survival that the child experiences mother's return to the house after an absence. It is hard to say what the child experiences here. But it seems to me it is something like, *The world is right again. I was "lost" but now am "found."* The concept of safety shapes only part of this experience. When a child mourns the absence of mother, as described in Bowlby, 1980, chapter 1, it is not just safety he longs for (though of course he *may* think, "If Mommy were with me, I wouldn't be in such danger"). He longs, instead, for *her.* Thus his attachment to her is, in his own understanding and feeling, no more conditional on her role as protector than it is on her role as feeder or warmer. This seems to be true even of dogs, of which J. P. Scott (1987, p. 51) says, "separation distress is not a response to an anticipated future event but to an ongoing immediate event." The attachment has more the character of love, than of any sort of expediency.

At least this is what will be salient to the Christian psychologist, who starts from a biblical conception of human nature — and, by analogy, of other parts of the creation. Bretherton (1992, p. 771) says that one of the challenges of attachment theory for the near future is to develop "an experiential language akin to that used by other psychoanalytic theories of interpersonal relatedness," and we might predict that, to the degree that this challenge is met, the explanation of attachment as a mechanism of biological survival will come to seem incomplete. Stress on attachment experience would also seem to undermine efforts like that of Ainsworth (1985) to restrict the concept of attachment to cases characterized by the secure base and haven functions, and would confirm Bowlby's inclination to allow the concept to range over cases in which safety is not an issue.

If we insist on limiting ourselves to biological or physiological explanations in psychology, then we must treat the meaning of experiences as people experience them, and of personal relationships as people inhabit them, as mere epiphenomena of behavior or other bodily processes. But what right have psychologists to treat the most distinctively *psychological* phenomena as *epi*phenomena? If we are to avoid such reductionism, our explanations must be in personal terms; and if our questions are "big" ones like "Why do people, as people, have the attachment need and the experiences associated with it?" then the theological answer is superior to the Darwinian one. It is, at least, the right *kind* of explanation.

For a critique of efforts to reduce explanations in psychology to biological and physiological ones, see Guntrip, 1973, especially chapters 1-4, where he shows that the inner logic of the most enduring part of Freud's psychology presses toward liberation from biology and neurology, in the direction of a distinctively *psychological* science. But in abandoning purely biological explanations of distinctively psychological phenomena (such as "meaning and motivation that determines the dealings of persons with [one] another, and the way they change and grow in the process" [p. 46], Guntrip has, it seems to me, left himself without any way of answering the "big" kind of question that Bowlby asks about the origins of the attachment need. Guntrip does not, at least in Guntrip, 1973, offer a theological answer — or indeed, any answer at all. I do not wish to be dogmatic about the matter, but at the moment a broadly theological answer seems to me the only kind that is a real candidate.

Arguments analogous in some ways to the present one, but much more elaborately worked out, can be found in Alvin Plantinga, 1991 and 1993a. He argues, first, that the concept of proper function or well-being (of organs as well as organisms, what I have called the Aristotelian idea) is both unavoidable in biology and cannot be coherently developed in a framework of metaphysical naturalism. Second, he argues that it is highly improbable that unguided natural selection would produce an organism with cognitive faculties that fairly reliably produce true beliefs. Since serious inquirers cannot help believing that our cognitive faculties do, or at least can, track truth, it is not rational for serious inquirers to be metaphysical naturalists — e.g. to believe that our cognitive faculties have resulted from unguided natural selection.

Bowlbyan Virtue

We can see the tension internal to Bowlby's psychology in another connection. In accord with his generally Darwinian orientation, the master virtue or trait of personal maturity in his personality theory is *adaptability*, which is defined in terms of *fitness to survive*. According to Bowlby this virtue is facilitated, more than by anything else, by having, in early childhood, a mother who is an excellent attachment figure. The highest degree of adaptability or maturity of character found among a group of 34 seventeen-year-olds was "the rational altruistic," a character featuring a high degree of rationality, friendliness, and altruistic impulse, social spontaneity and liking of other people, healthy respect for themselves and for others, and firm, internalized moral principles (Bowlby, 1973, pp. 329-33). Notice that while this configuration of traits may adapt an individual to survive (so that its *evolutionary* "goal" might be personal or racial survival), survival cannot be the *individual's own* goal for, or in, having these traits. For if biological survival were his or her overriding goal, the spontaneity, the respect for others, the respect for self, the concern for others, would be undermined. To respect another individual in the way that "rational altruistic" persons do is incompatible with being motivated, ultimately, only by considerations of one's own personal survival or the survival of the human race — or indeed, even of the survival of the person one "respects." In respecting a person, one has in view the *quality* of his or her *individual* life, and that not merely as a biological organism, but as a person in some person-value terms — e.g., the person's dignity as a rational being (Kant) or as a self-determiner (Nietzsche), or the person's status as a child of God (Christianity). The concept of a person operating in the mind of the "rational altruistic" respectful person may be less well defined than any of these philosophical or religious conceptions, but it will always be incompatible with regarding the other person as merely a biological "organism" whose goal it is to survive. If we want to explain, as something legitimate and important, the moral *outlook* of the mature person Bowlby envisages, the goal we ascribe to persons must be something other than survival. And this outlook of maturity is the sort of thing that personality psychologists (as distinct from biochemists, neurophysiologists, biologists) *most* want to explain.

The question about the function of attachment raises a more general issue of comparison between object-relations psychology and Christian psychology. If we ask, What are object-relations (that is, intimate personal relations) *for?* Bowlby's most basic answer is: For the survival of the race, via the survival of the individual. This answer is in uneasy tension with Bowlby's humanistic concern with psychological maturity and happiness. He is, after all, a psychotherapist, whose goal (function) is to help his clients find fulfillment. In this Bowlby is like the object-relations psychologists. Contrasting the object-relations answer to the question with that of Heinz Hartmann (1959), who says "that psychoanalysis is interested in object-relations because they are essential to biological equilibrium," Harry Guntrip comments that

> Without a good mother-infant relationship, the neonate human organism may die, but that is the reason for biology being interested in human object-relations. Psychoanalysis is interested in these relationships for quite different reasons, namely that they are crucial for the achievement of reality and maturity as a person-ego. (Guntrip, 1973, p. 109)

Christian psychologists, starting as they do with a view of the universe in which relationships of nurturing, support, and attachment are fundamental to the very nature of God and God's program of creation, regard object-relations as not only for biological survival and the achievement of ego reality, but also as fundamentally important *in themselves*. They are, ultimately, not instrumental to anything; they are their own function.

When they are not as they should be, we have not only sick bodies and sick psyches, but sick communities and indeed a sick universe. From a Christian point of view it is dangerous to see right relationships as functioning primarily as instruments or expedients to personal well-being. The danger here is a kind of egoism or perverse individualism. The encouragement to see relationships in this way seems to be one of the liabilities of modern psychotherapy, even if it is not always part of official doctrine. The therapeutic relationship is often one in which the object relation is quite intentionally regarded as instrumental to the psychological well-being of the client and, as Robert Bellah and his colleagues point out (Bellah et al., 1985), this feature of psychotherapies is probably a significant contributor to the widespread egoism of our culture. (For an evaluation and qualification of their thesis, see Roberts, 1993.)

The Causal Explanation of Attachment Behavior

We have discussed at some length Bowlby's functional explanation of the attachment need in human beings. Let us now look briefly at his causal explanation of attachment behavior. His basic concept is that of a *control system*, that is, some structural state of the organism such that, when it undergoes impingements of a certain sort, it responds with an adjustment designed to keep the organism within certain physiological or environmental parameters.

> An obvious way to conceptualize the behaviour observed is to postulate the existence of a control system within the central nervous system, analogous to the physiological control systems that maintain physiological measures, such as blood pressure and body temperature, within set limits. Thus the theory proposes that, in a way analogous to physiological homeostasis, the attachment control system maintains a person's relation to his attachment figure between certain limits of distance and accessibility. (Bowlby, 1988, p. 164)

Attachment behavior is the output of such a system. The central nervous systems (CNSs) of mother and infant are such that, if the infant moves too far away from the mother, she emits retrieving behavior, and if a certain amount of time has passed without his "checking in" with mother, the infant feels the need to go to her, and does so. Thus Bowlby offers a physiological explanation of attachment behavior. The reference to the structure in the CNS appears to be speculative (it is "postulated," as he says). However, it seems plausible, and unobjectionable from a Christian point of view, that there should be a physiological basis for attachment behavior, and for the extended phenomenon of attachment that Christian psychology sees throughout human life. But the cybernetic version of this that Bowlby proposes seems to apply better to infants (whose behavior we take to be largely determined by hard-wiring) than to older children and adults, in whom the behavior, while still having a physiological *base*, is far more determined by social construction, individual judgment, deliberated attitudes, philosophy of life, etc. So the Christian psychologist's objection to Bowlby's proposal that attachment behavior is physiologically determined really turns on our earlier objection that when Bowlby is wearing his physiological hat he narrows unduly the concept of attachment, and that when he acknowledges the broader, psychological concept, his physicalism no longer serves him plausibly. We acknowledge, of course, that attachment behavior even of the maturest and most distinctively human kind is based, in some way or other, in our physical constitution. And our learned attachment behavior (say, our "style" of interacting with our dearest friends) is for the most part "automatic" and determined at least in significant part by states of the CNS that have been put there by the learning process.

I do not think, however, that the Christian psychologist will want to admit that our behavior is entirely determined by physiological processes. The concept of agency to which Christians are committed, and to which Bowlby's more humanist side also is committed, seems to require that, to an extent, *we* are in control of our bodies and our behavior (see Jones, this volume, and Johnson, this volume). The concept of agency is far too complex and subtle to discuss in any detail here, but the recent philosophical literature that locates agency in self-identification, in what Frankfurt (1988) calls second-order desires, and in what Taylor (1985, 1989) calls strong evaluation in terms of evaluative frameworks (see Talbot, this volume), seems to point in the right direction.

Bowlbyan and Christian Maturity

God as Attachment Figure

For the humanistic Bowlby, the importance of the vicissitudes of attachment in childhood is their effect on the personality of the resultant adult. Perhaps the most important kind of effect, in Bowlby's view, is the implicit expectations of support from other people that early experiences with attachment figures promote or discourage.

Thus an individual who has been fortunate in having grown up in an ordinary good home with ordinarily affectionate parents has always known people from whom he can seek support, comfort, and protection, and where they are to be found. So deeply established are his expectations and so repeatedly have they been confirmed that, as an adult, he finds it difficult to imagine any other kind of world. This gives him an almost unconscious assurance that, whenever and wherever he might be in difficulty, there are always trustworthy figures available who will come to his aid. He will therefore approach the world with confidence and, when faced with potentially alarming situations, is likely to tackle them effectively or to seek help in doing so. (Bowlby, 1973, p. 208)

This sketch of personality maturity is strikingly at odds with the ones offered by many psychologists today, whose personality ideals tend to picture maturity as a matter of detachment from others, autonomy, and emotional independence. For these psychologists the great vice to be avoided is "enmeshment" with others (emotional dependency), but Bowlby says the mature person knows he can depend on others, and has a pretty good idea of where to find them. He is *self*-confident because he is confident that *others* will always be there for him. Proper attachment is not just a phase people pass through on the way to individuation; it is an irrevocable structure of personhood, an abiding feature of true individuation.

In this claim Christian psychologists will agree with Bowlby. But they will see something immature about the person Bowlby sketches as ideal. Is it not unrealistic, in many circumstances, to think there are other human beings who will support one and come to one's aid in time of need? This may be often so, but it is not the sort of generalization on which to build a character-ideal, because it depends on circumstances that may not obtain. Arguably, there are inevitable situations, such as one's own death, in which human help is always at best second-rate. If we affirm, with Bowlby, that by nature we need attachments with persons beyond ourselves, and note, in addition, that human attachments fall short of what we need, it follows that we need another, higher, and more essentially reliable object of attachment by reference to which we can qualify our dependency on human objects. And if, as Christian psychologists believe, the human constitution contains an essential Godward tendency, it will be not only inexpedient, but also a violation of the very order of things to depend on human help to the extent that Bowlby envisions.

The Christian psychologist will grant that the ideally mature person is *willing* to accept support and aid from his fellows, and to do so with gratitude and without humiliation; but he does not always *expect* to get help from others. Furthermore, he has an attachment need that cannot be satisfied by such others. Part of growing up is coming to the deep realization that in our own finite realm all human support will ultimately (indeed, necessarily) prove undependable. Søren Kierkegaard (1987, vol. II; 1980b) has this in mind when he speaks of despair as required in the process of psychological maturation. Christians advocate such despair not just because people and circumstances are so unreliable, but because we feel that it fits our nature poorly to rely ultimately on anything but God. God is the ultimate and absolute "attachment figure" for the mature personality; God is the one to whom thanks can be offered in *all* circumstances (1 Thess. 5:18), the one who comforts us in *all* our afflictions (2 Cor. 1:4). The first commandment is that you shall love the Lord your God with all your heart . . . and the *second* is that you shall love your neighbor as yourself (Matt. 22:37-40). He who loves father or mother, son or daughter, more than Christ is not worthy to be Christ's disciple (Matthew 10:37-38). Attachments to other humans are thus compatible with personal maturity, but only when secondary to the attachment to God.

Perhaps the major thesis of Bowlby's entire psychology is that the quality of our early attachments strongly affects our later capacity for mature attachments. What might the Christian say about this? Trust is as important to the Christian psychologist as it is to Bowlby, assuming the ordering of attachments sketched in the above paragraph — a qualified, relative but real trust of people, and an absolute trust of God. The Christian psychologist has reason to agree with Bowlby on the centrality of trust for the mature personality, and to accept the massive evidence he has garnered to the conclusion that trust in mature life is deeply affected by the trustworthiness of one's early attachment figures. Thus the good mother is a deputy of God, one who engenders in her child an implicit sense of the trustworthiness of the universe which, when he is more mature, he can direct to its proper Object. (On God as perfect attachment-figure, see Kaufman, 1981.) Other things being equal, people who have not enjoyed good mothers are at a spiritual disadvantage. On the other hand, to make human beings the ultimate object of one's trust, as Bowlby proposes, is not fitting, and so it is important to have experiences that remind us of the limits of human trustworthiness, and thus facilitate the "despair" that Kierkegaard (1987, vol. II; 1980b) talks about. The conjunction and interconnection of these features of the Christian psychology fit it to resolve what we might call "Kirkpatrick's paradox."

Kirkpatrick's Paradox

Kirkpatrick (1992) distinguishes two seemingly contrary hypothetical effects of early patterns of attachment on the God-relationship. The *compensation hypothesis* is that attachment to God is a compensation for frustrated attachment to humans (especially one's mother). It predicts that religiosity will vary inversely with the quality of parental relationships. The *correspondence hypothesis* — that the quality of one's relationship with God reflects the quality of one's early attachments, since the God-relationship is modeled on the human one — predicts that the less frustrating one's early attachments were, the better will be one's relationship with God.

Kirkpatrick (1990) found support for the compensation hypothesis in a study in which sudden religious conversions occurred four times more frequently among subjects who reported avoidant maternal attachments than among subjects reporting secure or resistant attachments. Several other indicators of religiosity followed a similar pattern among subjects whose mothers were nonreligious, though if the mothers were religious, the quality of attachment showed no effect on religiosity. In a later article (1992) Kirkpatrick reviews the evidence for the correspondence hypothesis, such as studies that show loss of faith to be associated with poor parental relationships and anthropological studies that show strong correlations across cultures between nurturing parenting styles and benevolent gods, and between "rejecting" parenting styles and malevolent gods. Thus there seems to be evidence for both kinds of effect, and this fact creates what I am calling Kirkpatrick's paradox. A Christian psychology has ways of resolving the seeming contrariety between these effects.

A Christian psychology posits both analogy and difference between attachments to human figures and attachment to God, and a need for both kinds of attachments. Thus it is unsurprising if one kind of attachment sometimes substitutes for the other, though on the Christian view neither kind of attachment is a fully *adequate* substitute for the other. Lack of an adequate God-relationship can be (partially) compensated for by satisfying human attachments, just as lack of adequate human attachments can be (partially) compensated for by an attachment to God. Also, by way of analogy between the two kinds of attachment, the two kinds of attachment figures can be modeled on one another. Following Bowlbyan cues, Christian psychology will take optimal psychic development to involve modeling of the God-concept on human attachment figures (though one could argue, following Kohutian cues [Kohut, 1977], that the child's early concept of a parent as an omnipotent and perfect caretaker is modeled on the child's innate concept of God). So parental figures will be an important source of our knowledge of God; other things being equal, having better attachment figures prepares the child better for an adequate God-concept and -relationship. Thus the Christian psychology predicts that both the compensation hypothesis and the correspondence hypothesis will be empirically borne out.

Though Christians agree with the many psychologists who have pointed out that belief in God often functions as a compensation for deficiencies in human relationships, they will not agree that "to the extent that religious beliefs serve a compensatory role vis-à-vis [human] attachments, an agnostic or atheistic stance would be expected to result from a history of satisfactory (secure) attachment relationships" (Kirkpatrick, 1992, p. 17). The assumption behind such an expectation is that humans have no particular and distinctive need for attachment to God — that our attachment needs can in principle be met by human relationships alone. If, as the Christian hypothesizes, we need both kinds of relationships, we would expect that some people who are very secure in their human attachments will still feel the need for God. Even if the compensation effect is universal among human beings, the compensation, when working optimally, may be merely developmental, in the way that, according to Kohut (1977), the developmental mechanism of transmuting internalization is a compensation for "failures" on the part of self-objects. In other words, just as even the best self-object "fails" the child at certain points, and this "failure" is in the child's developmental interest as needed to trigger his autonomy, so a natural stage in the development of attachment to God is the frustrated realization that one's human attachment figures are not just accidentally, but intrinsically, inadequate — that they have in fact been treated (falsely, though necessarily) as substitutes for God.

Why do subjects with rejecting mothers who are *not religious* tend so much more often to find compensation in the God-relationship than children of *religious* non-nurturing mothers? The religious mother, we may suppose, is associated with God in two ways in the mind of her child, the non-religious in only one. In addition to the natural tendency to model God on the mother, the children of religious mothers are exposed to a historical, verbally and behaviorally articulated association of their mothers with God. If both the correspondence hypothesis and the compensation hypothesis are true, then the non-nurturing mother will have *two competing effects* on her child: If the mother is non-nurturing, the child is, on the correspondence hypothesis, more likely to conceptualize God as non-nurturing, and thus to be *deterred* from finding compensation in God for his non-nurturing mother. But if the mother is non-nurturing, the child will also have, on the compensation hypothesis, an extra *impulse* to trust in God, that may overpower the tendency to conceive God as non-nurturing. (We assume that many kinds of social influences affect the child's God-concept, not just the correspondence effect.) But if the mother adds to the normal operation of the correspondence effect by setting herself up as God's associate (talking about God, advocating God, praying to God, claiming God's approval, etc.), she may increase the correspondence effect enough to override the compensation effect in the child's psyche.

In accordance with the fuller concept of attachment that I have been endorsing, the Christian psychologist will want to measure the adequacy of attachment to God on more dimensions than just the secure-resistant-avoidant continuum. A person might have a secure relationship with God which was nevertheless quite immature, or an insecure one that was mature in some ways. As attachment figure, God is more than just comforter or protector. God is also a model, an object of admiration, a commander, a judge; and the maturity of one's attachment to him may vary along these dimensions — in terms, e.g., of how seriously one desires to be like him and succeeds in being so, of how deeply one appreciates God's goodness and beauty, of how obedient one is, of how reverently one regards God as moral observer.

Summary

We have seen that, taking as our standard a concept of attachment constructed from the Bible, the concept with which Bowlby "starts" (both in terms of his conceptual framework and also, it seems, chronologically) is narrower than the Christian concept. Central for Bowlby is a kind of attachment characteristic of infancy and early childhood, characterized by the maintenance of physical proximity between child and mother. On whether the child's need for attachment is well satisfied at this early stage depends much concerning the child's later personality development — his self-confidence as an agent, his ability to trust other people, his disposition to respect others, and his altruism in behavior and attitude. The Bible, by contrast, focuses more on attachments in adulthood and emphasizes strongly the significance of attachments to beings other than humans — in particular, possessions (wealth) and God. The initial narrowness of Bowlby's concept is mitigated to some extent by his increasing acknowledgment that attachments are, throughout the life cycle, deeply important to human beings, indeed the very stuff of life's meaning. The more we emphasize, with the Bible, the attachments of our adulthood and their subjective meaning, the less plausible is Bowlby's explanation of attachment in terms of its survival function and the causal efficacy of the postulated attachment "control system" located in our central nervous system. If we emphasize adult attachments and their depth of meaning, both humanistic and theological explanations seem far more apposite. Christian psychology agrees with Bowlby on the basicness of the attachment disposition; it is not just phasic, but fundamental to human nature. Good early attachments prepare us for mature personality, not only by enabling us to trust that other human beings will generally be there for us when we need them, but by readying us to trust God.

Kenosis as a Key to
Maturity of Personality

Jean-Marc Laporte, S.J.

Introduction

The theme of attachment and detachment is central to any Christian account of the nature of persons and the shape of mature human personality. It seems clear that both detachment and attachment are prescribed by the Christian tradition; so I shall not aim to decide between these two processes or moments in personality development, but rather to explore how both are pursued and how they relate to one another. For Christians, the paradigm case of self-emptying love, and also of perfected personality, is Jesus Christ in the saving work of his incarnation, cross, and resurrection. Here we see a detachment which is both enabled and motivated by Christ's attachment to God the Father. The Apostle Paul models his own growth as a person on Christ's self-emptying (*kenosis*), and interprets that detachment for us both by his own life and by his commentary on Christ's act.

The emptying out of kenosis is at the heart of all personal reality — that of Christ and our own. In the end, rather than finding Paul and Jesus adequate in terms of contemporary models, we will judge contemporary models in terms of the kenosis which is at the core of gospel revelation. Christ reveals to us the mystery not only of God but of our own selves. "Kenosis" is the noun form of a mysterious verb found in Philippians 2:6-11 which expresses with the image of emptying out — akin to the image of outpouring/inpouring of the Spirit found in Joel 2:28 and Romans 5:5 — a foundational stance of Christ, and of those who follow him. That stance is a surrender of our prerogatives, real and imaginary, as we live with and for others. This surrender will lead us to discover and fulfill our true selves, like the grain of wheat in John 12 that bears fruit through dying to its self-enclosed reality as a grain. As a systematic theo-

229

logian I have long struggled with the theme of *kenosis*, which I have always considered singularly able to constellate and illuminate many areas of theology, notably the theology of grace, christology, and the Trinity. I treated it explicitly in a brief article some twenty years ago (Laporte, 1974); and it is a *leitmotif* in my book on the theology of grace (Laporte, 1988).

The main burden of my paper is to explore this biblical theme as a source for Christian psychology. But before I do so, I shall first sketch a backdrop in modern psychology by commenting on the work of the philosopher Herbert Fingarette and the psychiatrist R. D. Laing.

A Backdrop

Fingarette and Laing do not give clear evidence of any Judeo-Christian commitment, and they fail to achieve the clarity of Christian revelation on the human situation. But they are sensitive to contemporary values which are the profound traces of Judeo-Christian thought in our post-Christian culture. Some psychologists may want to rub Christian influence off our conception of persons as superficial and ephemeral, but they will find that it is no lightly applied veneer but something that has penetrated that conception in depth.

Fingarette

Fingarette's *The Self in Transformation* (1965) contains seven essays on the various phases of self-transformation, culminating in mystic selflessness. The last two chapters of his book are especially germane to our concerns, but we need to begin with a few considerations from his first two chapters.

Fingarette introduces the theme of freedom towards the end of his first chapter, and in doing so moves toward an insight already expressed by Augustine. For Augustine, freedom at its deepest is not simply saying yes or no out of one's arbitrary whim (freedom of choice), but is a response that comes from the deepest self, a response that is voluntary and free only insofar as it is seen to be the only possible and fulfilling response a person can make (freedom of autonomy). Freedom and coercion are always opposed, but at times freedom and necessity go together, as when a person surrenders to the inevitability of resting in God when God graciously becomes present face to face. In this vital matter, the bipolarity of detached self-control and readiness to respond emotionally to what is attractive is not a simple matter of quantitative dosage. I will be detached, autonomous, self-reliant, and on the path of achieving distinct self-identity to the extent that I savor the taste of my own self-in-relation and surrender to what emerges from my depths. Prototypic freedom is not the willful "I will not serve" of Lucifer but the willing "Let it be done to me according to your word" of Mary.

In his second chapter, Fingarette deals with the crucial choice by which persons begin to move effectively towards the personal maturity and integration which is the goal of all human striving, and which in some cases is facilitated by therapy. That choice is not to do this rather than that out of a will that is self-originating, self-controlled, and autonomous. It is a "surrendering to" rather than a "fighting against" the new self which is being born within (Fingarette, 1965, pp. 104-5). Real choice does not merely consist in freely taking an initiative but involves the willingness to let go and enter into a process of integration in which eventually a meaningful pattern emerges, which one cannot but choose because of its powerful attraction and consonance with who one is (pp. 55-56).

Responding to the word spoken from beyond myself as well as to what emerges from my depths evokes two further Augustinian bipolarities. God is both higher than the loftiest part of myself and more intimate to me than I am to myself. Moreover, human freedom in its magnificent complexity is totally sustained and empowered by divine grace, a grace which does not oppress me but liberates me to be myself. As Augustine puts it, my will is free to the extent that it is sound, and sound to the extent that it is under the impact of grace. And that grace works from both within and without.

In the penultimate chapter of his book Fingarette puts before us models of human beings who have managed to achieve a proper integration of attachment and detachment in their own lives, and as a result are able sympathetically and creatively to prompt integration in others. The enlightened agonist (to use a classical term which evokes the liberated person who chooses to return to the cave to draw others out of their shadowy existence) and the effective therapist (to return to our contemporary situation) are able to combine deep emotional consonance or attachment with the persons who are the objects of their therapeutic concern even as they maintain the most scrupulous objectivity and distance. Indeed, it is only to the extent that therapists/agonists are objective, and refuse to be drawn into the personal lives of those they care for, that their healing intervention is profoundly in harmony with those others and therefore effective. They refuse to be embroiled in attachments spawned by their own neediness and lack of integration so that they can participate in the one form of attachment that is called for — compassionate respect for the mystery of the other as other. In this perspective, detachment and attachment are not in inverse but in direct proportion to each other. The goal is compassionate objectivity (p. 245), a *coincidentia oppositorum* which encompasses emotion and self-control, attachment and detachment.

Fingarette speaks especially to the situation of the therapist. The type of detachment a therapist must exercise does not without further ado apply to all human relationships. A personal friend is involved in my life in a sense in which a therapist is not. But even here detachment is needed; friendship is not a licence to meddle, to intrude, or to stifle, as sometimes happens. In a relationship which by definition aims at profound intimacy — such as that between spouses — the secret of success is allowing one's partner the space within which he or she can be himself or herself. Earlier stages of love generally are characterized by an intensity and an urgency of attachment which excludes all detachment, but those features may well be the evidence of an inappropriate investment of the self in what appears to be the other but which is in some respects an aspect of the self projected outwardly. Recent reiterations of this are to be found in the work of Scott Peck and Thomas Tyrell (Peck, 1993, p. 108; Tyrell, 1994a, 1994b). Tyrell's two books trace the human love journey from the urgency of infatuation to the loving and contemplative acceptance of the other which character-izes mature relationships.

But though therapists must eschew undue involvement with their clients, they must take an emotional interest in them. From a stance of objectivity, therapists are to be profoundly present to their clients. The attachment they are to avoid is not an empathetic presence to the other, but a clinging to the other, an investing the other with unwarranted significance in resolving the therapist's own inner conflicts and needs (Fingarette, 1965, p. 267). Indeed, therapists are called to a deep identity with the other, not clinging to their own "unvarying self," but becoming "servant of all" and "last of all" (p. 268). A sort of *kenosis* allows therapists to be concerned with their clients for the clients' own sake, and thus allows therapists themselves to become more genuine as persons.

> . . . the detachment here involved is not a rejection of personal relation-ships. It is a detachment from the psychic clichés which keep us in alienation. This detachment is the essential ground out of which rela-tionships among genuinely autonomous individuals can arise. Indeed, it is not only the ground out of which genuine personal *relationships* arise; it is the ground out of which the *person himself* emerges. (p. 272)

The point is that, once we are able to let go from constricting patterns in which our attachment to others expresses our own insecurity and our own need to control aspects of ourselves which are as yet unintegrated, we are then both detached and attached — detached from what in ourselves hinders authentic relationships and becomes a screen between ourselves and others, and attached to others with a "disinterested" love which leaves them free to be themselves. We are then far from a superficial approach to attachment and detachment which sees them in some kind of quantitative balance; we are closer to an approach in which attachment and detachment are both to be affirmed within the mature and well-balanced Christian (Roberts, this volume, b).

The Christian recognizes that the only power in which we are able fully to achieve a love which affirms the mystery of the other as other is God's love. Our loving relationship with God enables us to counter our sinful proneness to invest in a created reality, human or less than human, a significance for our fulfillment which only God deserves. Though we fail, through God's grace we can repent, learn from our failures, and continue on the right path.

Laing

In his *The Divided Self* (1965), R. D. Laing seeks to develop an existential-phenomenological understanding of psychic health and disease. At the root of his outlook is the thesis that each human person

> is at the same time separate from his fellows and related to them. Such separateness and relatedness are mutually necessary postulates. Personal relatedness can exist only between beings who are separate but are not isolates. We are not isolates and we are not parts of the same physical body. Here we have the paradox, the potentially tragic paradox, that our relatedness to others is an essential aspect of our *being*, as is our separateness, but any particular person is not a necessary part of our being. (p. 26)

Psychic health and disease, and healthy and unhealthy relationships, are rooted for Laing in ontological security and insecurity. For the ontologically secure person, the person who senses his or her self-presence in the world to be real, alive, whole, and continuous (p. 39), relatedness is potentially gratifying (p. 42). Ontologically insecure persons are preoccupied with survival. For them, relations are an unwelcome impingement. The often painful circumstances of life are a threat to their identity rather than a challenge to their development. In sum, a lively sense of one's own autonomy and of one's self-identity contributes to one's ability to relate to others in depth and to let go of one's preoccupation with self and enter into fruitful interaction with others:

Thus, instead of the polarities of separateness and relatedness based on individual autonomy, there is the antithesis between complete loss of being by absorption into the other person (engulfment) and complete aloneness (isolation). There is no safe third possibility of a dialectical relationship between two persons, both sure of their own ground and, on this very basis, able to "lose themselves" in each other. (p. 44)

Thus two patterns of detachment emerge: the detachment of the ontologically insecure person, which is an isolation by which one wards off the other who poses a radical threat; and the detachment of the onto-logically secure person, which is a healthy sense of one's own separate identity enabling one to relate and be attached to others with genuine and fruitful mutuality (pp. 52-53). Similarly, there are two patterns of attach-ment: that of the ontologically secure person, for whom relationships are key to personal growth in interaction with genuine others; and that of the ontologically insecure person, for whom the other is part of his or her system of unhealthy self-protection and self-definition. Again, Christian revelation will offer greater clarity on the self which is attached and detached: for according to it we are not dealing with amorphous selves who may or may not be distinct from each other and from the divine Self, but with distinct human selves created with an emptiness which only fellow humans and a transcendent God can fill.

Fingarette has evoked for us the enlightened agonists of antiquity and the attached yet detached therapists of our own day. Laing offers parallel thoughts on ontological security and insecurity. Does the gospel present us with similar models for our own personal integration and our action for others?

Jesus and Paul

Paul of Tarsus

"Take me for a model, as I take Christ" (1 Corinthians 11:1). The very fact that Paul puts himself forward as a model raises a question: Does his boast come out of a serene sense of his own integration, or are there elements of posturing at work here based on traces of ontological insecurity, of inappropriate clinging in his make-up? Other passages where Paul reflects on himself and on his own relationship to his communities would indicate a tendency, probably arising from Paul's culture, but also from his own psychic make-up, to heighten rhetorically the vicissitudes and achieve-ments of his own life. We need not subject him to analysis two thousand years after his death to suppose that while he is an inspiring model of integration as apostle and as human being, he remains, as he himself avows, an earthen vessel — fragile, imperfect, and incomplete.

Still, Paul's utter honesty, his refusal to mask his personal struggle with sanctimonious clichés, shines through abundantly. Attachment and detachment in their attractive coincidence are present in his life and ministry. The model of the enlightened agonist which Fingarette puts before us applies to Paul, who is deeply affected by what happens to the people and the communities that the Lord has sent his way; who responds with gratitude, with affection, with anger, with exasperation, with deep compassion; and who struggles with them, chides them, boasts, and makes a point at times with overkill. But at the same time an inner core of serene disinterestedness enables Paul to overcome his initial exasperation and respond to individuals and communities with a genuine respect for who they are and where they come from, a respect which empowers and liberates. He deeply cares for each community he has founded, and his message to them is not the repetition of the same formula but the imparting of a revelation which, though one, is variously applied in accord with their needs and situations. J. C. Beker (1982) develops this point at length. He discerns a core and a coherent approach in Paul's message, but the contingent circumstances of Paul's different communities lead to often profoundly differing imperatives. Paul's constant concern is to develop a theology which will bring persons of differing backgrounds and temperaments to respect each other and form the body of Christ in these communities.

The epistles which give us the best glimpse of the quality of Paul's apostolic presence are 1 and 2 Corinthians. He makes himself vulnerable, relinquishing the trappings of strength to come to this varied community as a slave who totally identifies with its members in their struggles. But such radical attachment to others is made possible by the strength which is being renewed within him day by day, through the light of God shining in his mind. Out of this inner security he can allow difficulties to beset him on all sides without fear of being swamped. He can insert himself in the not-yet of the unredeemed world, knowing that in his heart the already-now of God's grace has established a beachhead. He is like Christ who "was rich, but became poor for your sake, to make you rich out of his poverty" (2 Corinthians 8:9). At the heart of his compassionate objectivity is his utter attachment to God in the Spirit of Jesus Christ.

Jesus of Nazareth

While Paul is an example of authentic human struggle towards that elusive point where genuine attachment and genuine detachment beautifully come together, Christ is the prime exemplar of the successful outcome of that struggle. He is a person just as given to spontaneity of emotion as Paul, free in his relationship with others, touched by the unique worth of all those who cross his path, and open to them in creative ways which go beyond the religious and social taboos of his culture. Through the Gospels we witness the temptations in the desert, the agony in the garden, and numerous encounters with his followers, whose limitations were painfully obvious to him. But then there is the deep serenity and simplicity, the openness and respect with which he approaches all sorts of people, and the unparalleled healing and integration he brings about in their lives. If we look for the enlightened agonist, the effective therapist *par excellence*, we find them in the life of Jesus, who achieves unsurpassed compassionate objectivity because of his absolutely unswerving attachment to the God he called *Abba*. He is free from the insecurity, the smokescreens, and the self-serving behaviors that mar our own presence to one another. This allows him to be a man totally for others, entering into the texture of their lives, having compassion on the multitudes, and risking his own life in the process. The outcome of his ministry is a death in which he shows ultimate vulnerability to the negative forces that emanate from sinful human nature, but also a resurrection in which his "disinterested" love, grounded in his unbreakable commitment to God, triumphs over the evil to which we are prone.

In setting out the above we are treading on humanly impossible terrain. Christ is like us in all things but sin. How can there be struggle, temptation, or learning through experience which is not inwardly characterized by the reality of sin? This is something which eludes our human awareness. But we believe it of Christ, the archetype of our faith. His innocence was not a shielding from human iniquity and opaqueness. Rather it allowed him to experience them so deeply that he was able to gain definitive victory over them, not only for himself but for us.

Let us turn now to one of the classic hymns of Christian antiquity, the *Carmen Christi* of Paul's letter to the Philippians, 2:6-11:

> [Christ Jesus] who, though he was in the form of God, did not regard equality with God as something to be exploited, but emptied himself, taking the form of a slave, being born in human likeness. And being found in human form, he humbled himself and became obedient to the point of death — even death on a cross. Therefore God also highly

exalted him and gave him the name that is above every name, so that at the name of Jesus every knee should bend, in heaven and on earth and under the earth, and every tongue should confess that Jesus Christ is Lord, to the glory of God the Father.

Much exegetical ink has been spilt on this text. I will go straight to an interpretation which makes sense in relation to the text itself and to its context in other Pauline writings and what they tell us about Paul's life and ministry. The passage speaks of a humiliation followed by an exaltation — a hiddenness followed by a recognition — much after the pattern of the suffering-servant song of Isaiah 52:13 to 53:12. No interpretation of the first verses of this passage has gained universal acceptance. Yet I make bold to offer an approach rooted in the work of certain exegetes and which is coherent with the broader context of Paul's writings:

- The passage does not speak of a process by which Christ Jesus exchanges his pre-existent divine nature for a human nature, getting the divine nature back at the exaltation. The emptying out *(kenosis)*, the assumption of the form of a slave of which the passage speaks, takes place *while* Christ Jesus is, and continues to be, in the form of God.
- Christ Jesus divests, empties himself out of what the NRSV translates as "equality with God": more literally "his being God's equal." However, "equal" in the Greek is not an adjectival form but an adverbial one. This suggests "his being equalled to God" as a more precise translation. What he chooses not to cling to is not so much his inner identity as his status in the eyes of others, his entitlement to recognition. Rather than exploit that status, he takes on the form of a slave which prevents that recognition except to the eyes of faith.
- Though the form of the slave is diametrically opposed to the form of God, his taking it on paradoxically reveals what God is rather than hides it: a God not of arbitrary power but of love, a God strong enough to assume weakness.
- As a broader interpretation of these verses, Barth's comment is on the mark: "[T]he Son of God does not give away his equality with God, does not give it up, but he does let go of it" (Barth, 1962, p. 62).
- This interpretation of the kenotic gesture offers a satisfactory counterpart to the exaltation which takes place in the second half of this hymnic passage: the recognition, the bestowing of a name, by which the abiding reality of Jesus can be spoken and celebrated for what it is. The transition in this passage is from the hiddenness of the

slave to public acclaim as Lord. The mystery of Christ with God —
his ontological security, if you will — remains the same throughout.

Texts which offer parallels to the above interpretation are numerous in the
New Testament. One might invoke a classic synoptic text, Mark 10:45,
which tells us that the Son of Man has come to serve and not to be served,
and a corresponding passage from John about the grain of wheat which
must fall into the ground and die before bearing much fruit (John 12:24).
The two texts I offer for more detailed consideration are from Paul.
    The first of these presents a kenosis more directly parallel to that
proclaimed in Philippians 2:6-11:

> In the same way, the Lord commanded that those who proclaim the
> gospel should get their living by the gospel. But I have made no use
> of any of these rights, nor am I writing this so that they may be applied
> in my case. Indeed, I would rather die than that — no one will deprive
> me of my ground for boasting! If I proclaim the gospel, this gives me
> no ground for boasting, for an obligation is laid on me, and woe to me
> if I do not proclaim the gospel! For if I do this of my own will, I have
> a reward; but if not of my own will, I am entrusted with a commission.
> What then is my reward? Just this: that in my proclamation I may make
> the gospel free of charge, so as not to make full use of my rights in the
> gospel. For though I am free with respect to all, I have made myself a
> slave to all, so that I might win more of them. To the Jews I became as
> a Jew, in order to win Jews. To those under the law I became as one
> under the law (though I myself am not under the law) so that I might
> win those under the law. To those outside the law I became as one
> outside the law (though I am not free from God's law but am under
> Christ's law) so that I might win those outside the law. To the weak I
> became weak, so that I might win the weak. I have become all things
> to all people, that I might by all means save some. I do it all for the
> sake of the gospel, so that I may share in its blessings. (1 Corinthians
> 9:14-23)

Though Paul is entitled to certain prerogatives as an apostle, he does not
take advantage of them, and he enjoins those who are enlightened to
follow his example, letting go of their higher knowledge about the non-
existence of the idols to which certain meats had been sacrificed and
becoming more compassionate towards those who are scrupulous about
partaking of those meats (1 Corinthians 8). The kenosis Paul undertakes
here is letting go of his rightful prerogatives in the interests of greater
apostolic efficacy and of building up the community. He who is free

becomes a slave for the sake of the gospel, just as in the Philippians hymn the one who is in the form of God takes the form of a slave.

What is the general pattern at work here? I will quote from an earlier article:

> Running through all these manifestations of the kenotic imagery is the same dynamic structure: Though strong in being "x" and rightfully possessing the prerogatives which come from "x," Christ emptied himself out ("I have emptied myself out, empty yourselves out") to become "y," to be identified with "y." (Laporte, 1974, p. 18)

The self-divestment that Paul refers to is relative rather than absolute. He can assume the weakness and frailty of those to whom he is sent because of an inner source of loving strength and freedom which he has received. He does not give up this inner strength in becoming weak, but he becomes weak in the assurance that his weakness will never, in spite of appearances to the contrary, swallow up and bring to nought this inner source (2 Corinthians 4:8). One divests oneself of the self as *object:* the self as *subject,* which does the divesting, remains intact, indeed is enhanced by the gift of itself (Laporte, 1974, p. 18).

In a second text Paul evokes a form of kenosis which does not correspond in the same direct way with that celebrated in Philippians 2:6-11. This kenosis Paul underwent at the beginning of his Christian life when he received the gift of justification through faith. He totally let go of all the false credentials and prerogatives to which he clung as someone circumcised, who belonged to the race of Israel and the tribe of Benjamin, who was a zealous Pharisee persecuting the church and blameless according to the law:

> Yet whatever gain I had, these things I have come to regard as loss because of Christ. More than that, I regard everything as loss because of the surpassing value of knowing Christ Jesus my Lord. For his sake I have suffered the loss of all things, and I regard them as rubbish, in order that I may gain Christ and be found in him. (Philippians 3:7-9)

This second form of kenosis is chronologically prior to the first. Paul first divests himself of the false prerogatives and entitlements of his earlier life in order to be found in Christ. Being found in Christ, and finding in Christ a new ontological security, he is able then to imitate the self-divestment of Christ, letting go of the genuine prerogatives and entitlements that flow from his new status in Christ and his new call to apostleship.

Christ Jesus did not have to achieve by a prior kenotic letting go that state in which he could take on the form of a slave for our sakes. In a phrase which adumbrates the Prologue of John's Gospel and the mysterious existence from the beginning of the Word within the bosom of God, the much earlier Philippians hymn tells us that Christ was from the beginning in the form of God. With us there is a prior conversion by which we enter into the state in which we are sufficiently secure — not in ourselves but in God — to be able to let go of ourselves in compassionate service of others. That conversion is from the idols, the securities to which we desperately cling, or, in the language of Laing and Fingarette, from the clichés and neurotic patterns which keep us from being our authentic selves and which maintain in us a false sense of security. Justified by God's grace, our authentic selves are liberated and, little by little, in the power of the Spirit, what has taken place in our hearts begins to permeate our bodies, our lives, our world, making of us agents who reach out with "disinterested" compassion. We can let go of ourselves in service, after the example of Christ's kenosis, without fear that in the process we will be stripped of our redeemed selves.

A way of reading this in terms of attachment and detachment is as follows: (A) Detachment in its illusory form is a self-enclosure, a self-containedness which vigorously assails any inclination to put myself in a position of vulnerability toward others, for fear that I will be assailed in my own deepest identity. Genuine detachment occurs out of a secure self-possession which makes attachment and vulnerability possible. (B) Conversely, illusory attachment does not respect the other as other but serves as a way to shore up some inner weakness or insecurity in oneself; it may be stifling or manipulative, and in all cases will be ineffective. By contrast, genuine attachment is ultimately "disinterested," giving others "space" to be who they are and to follow the unique path of their own fulfillment.

The ultimate pattern of proper human personality is to be found in the kenosis of Christ, a gesture of love in which both attachment and detachment are found at their best and most effective. It is a pattern in which we are detached from idols and all that inhibits a proper love of God and neighbor, and indeed a proper love of self, and in which we are passionately attached, as our Lord was, to the things that are worthy of our spiritual nature: God, and all our human neighbors, for God wants to grace them with the righteousness of his kingdom. It is a pattern for which we strive, and which we never fully attain. It is the pattern of incarnation according to which our being and our action are embodied in a genuine reaching out to others.

Conclusion

When we contemplate the dynamic movement of kenosis, we are entering into a mystery rather than seeking to master a mundane reality using an exact scientific method. Mystery is allergic to quantitative dosage, as if there ought to be so much human freedom and so much divine grace, so much vulnerability and so much autonomy, so much attachment and so much detachment, etc. Rather, both extremes of these bipolarities are to be affirmed wholeheartedly, and it is as enriched by the other that each is to be found in its most authentic form. The supreme example of kenosis is Christ Jesus, and the best of classical christology has always refused a dosage that would not allow him to be too human lest his divinity be impaired, or too divine, lest his humanity be rendered incredible. Rather we seek to re-echo the resounding rhythms of the Chalcedonian declaration: totally human, totally divine, perfect God and perfect man, born of the Father before all ages, born of Mary in these last days, and both of these in the unity of one person, God the Son, the Word made flesh. This paradox of humanity and divinity, of Jesus' human vulnerability that brings out rather than snuffs out the divine spark at the core of his being, is present implicitly in Scripture, and it is the main gist of the early ecumenical councils, which for all their incompleteness shape Christian belief. We have seen that this central element in the Christian revelation has momentous implications for our view of persons, their nature, and their psychological maturity. The movement away from self out of love of the other and for the other's sake is characteristic of the divine nature; and human personality, being an image of God, requires the same movement if it is to come to maturity.

The kenosis theme is a member of a family of themes that the Christian tradition to which I belong can offer for the enrichment and correction of contemporary psychology. In closing, I briefly mention four other members of the family:

Virtuous Action

The theme of spontaneous action, coming from the converted heart — prompt, easy, regular, done with a sense of joy and fulfillment — emerges in Paul. For him the unction of the Spirit empowers Christian discipleship and makes it joyful in the midst of trials and sufferings. It is further developed in Augustine. For him the hallmark of Christian maturity is a deep love of God which enables us to do what we will, confident that our spontaneous inclination is in harmony with God's will for us. It finds further development in Thomas Aquinas's doctrine of the virtues. For Aquinas, to act virtuously is to act by an instinct which is either acquired by dint of practice or received as God's gift.

These two paths to virtue, human practice (acquired virtues) and divine gift (infused virtues), do not play an equal role for Aquinas. One cannot acquire the virtues significant for human fulfillment without the prior gift of grace that overcomes the moral powerlessness which is our native inheritance. In other words, grace heals our wounded human nature while it raises us up to communion with God. Infused virtues are needed, not to replace acquired virtues, but to make their acquisition possible.

Once we are endowed with the requisite virtues, we can do the right thing without having to exercise deliberate control or to go against the grain, forcing our action in a direction contrary to our spontaneous attachment and precariously struggling each time against temptation instead of doing what is right with a sense of ease, security, and eagerness. This is not to deny the role of a detached awareness of, reflection on, and control of one's spontaneous attachments. To the extent that we are on the way to virtue rather than totally permeated by it, we will be tempted and must struggle, and we need to move deliberately away from attachments that are not yet ordered Godward. But the result of this combat, under God's grace, is a personality whose passions are ordered, spontaneously rejoicing where joy is called for, angry in the face of genuine injustice, grieving where there is genuine cause for sorrow, and loving where the beloved shares God's own loveableness. In the process of achieving this, attachment and detachment appear to be sequential. We must keep our distance from our own spontaneous urges, discerning their direction, shaping them deliberately; but the purpose of this phase of our existence is to come to the point of being able to surrender to these urges with a sense of trust — to love and do what we will.

Indifference

The theme of attachment and detachment clearly emerges in the *Spiritual Exercises,* the major spiritual writing of Ignatius Loyola, who founded the religious community to which I belong, the Society of Jesus. He advocates detachment in the sense that Christians are to be indifferent to all the positive and negative factors affecting their life and their endeavours — to success or failure, to long life or short life, to health or sickness, and to recognition or obscurity. But this indifference is active rather than passive, grounded in a passionate attachment to God's will and to the mission God entrusts to each one of us on earth. That prevailing attachment relativizes all else. It makes it possible that those attachments to what is not God be rightly ordered inasmuch as their objects are means that lead to God, that is, are shaped within us in response to the call of Christ as it emerges in the Gospels and in the movement of the Spirit uniquely touching the heart of each person. The *Spiritual Exercises* are a school of well-ordered affectivity. The methodical self-control, the *agere contra* advocated by the *Exercises*, is no more and no less than a means to this end. We are far from a straitjacket spirituality that exhorts us to a relentless and unbalanced detachment.

Trinitarian Theology

The earlier tradition of the Western Church, grounded in the ecumenical councils, discerns in persons an essential bipolarity. Persons are just as much characterized by relationship as by subsistence (see Vitz, this volume). Subsistence means that persons, including the divine persons of Father, Son, and Holy Spirit, have their own being in themselves, their own autonomy, their own distinctness, and the detachment by which they remain themselves. Relation means that persons by definition are in relation to other persons. Though we humans may not be essentially related to any other human individual, we are essentially related to God, and without relations with some significant other human persons, our human development is totally stymied. To use the Latin tag, persons are *esse ad* (being towards another) as much as *esse in* (being in themselves). They are, as we are reminded in the evocative essay of Norris Clarke, heteronomous, attached, given to kenotic outreach in which they find themselves by losing themselves in the other (Clarke, 1993). Indeed, when one seeks within the classical Western tradition to define what distinguishes the persons within the Trinity, one comes up with the axiom that all is one in the Godhead except where there is the mutuality of relationship. Could not this scholastic approach to the divine persons also apply to human persons, *mutatis mutandis?*

The Vulnerable God

A fourth theme has emerged in recent years. An earlier classical theology stressed the timelessness of God, God's perfection and incorruptibility, and God's not being affected by the vicissitudes of creaturely existence. But in recent years the counterpoint to this is being heard: God is a kenotic

God able personally to take on the sufferings of creation, to heal them not as a *Deus ex machina* coming from outside but as someone who has pitched his tent in our midst. The point is not to move from a rigid classical approach in which the detachment of God is uppermost to a fluid Process position in which God is all attachment and vulnerability to the limitations of creation. Instead, the point is to retrieve the paradox at the heart of the Christian affirmation of God as love. It is precisely the fontal plenitude of God which allows God to be intimately present and involved with creation without any underlying self-seeking, manipulation, or impingement. God being God, we can be ourselves. And, seeking to be perfect as our heavenly Father is perfect, we haltingly try to give others the space they need and deserve in order to be their authentic selves out of the God-given taste we have of our own authenticity with and under God. Emptying out is at the heart of God; mirrored in our world, it appears as compassionate objectivity.

Sin and Addiction

Cornelius Plantinga, Jr.

O NE RESPECTABLE WAY to sharpen our vision of a big, messy reality is to compare and contrast it with its conceptual neighbors. Thus, a person who wants to understand human sin will at some point ask about its relation to such neighboring realities as crime, disease, folly, and immorality. The goal is to isolate and define sin by locating and illuminating the borders it shares with its neighbors.

Nowhere is a border survey more helpful and more needed than in the case of sin and addiction. For here the borders are long, disputed, and sometimes absent. Principally, to look at addiction is to look at significant dynamics of sin. Moreover, to discuss addiction is dramatically to raise the hard questions of human freedom and responsibility that lie along the base of the Christian understanding of sin.

To identify these dynamics, raise these questions, and thus to deepen our understanding of the nature of sin, is the project in this essay. To pursue it, I will offer a definition and description of sin, do the same for addiction, and then spend the rest of the essay working out the relation between them.

I want to thank the members of the Pew seminar on persons, and especially Al Howsepian, for helpful criticisms that I have used to prepare the final draft of my essay. This essay, presented to the conference in June 1994, was published as parts of chapters 1, 5, and especially 8 of *Not the Way It's Supposed to Be: A Breviary of Sin* (Eerdmans, 1995).

Shalom and Sin

The Biblical Concept of Shalom

As the great prophets of the Bible knew, sin has a thousand faces. The prophets knew how many ways human life can go wrong because they knew how many ways human life can go right. (You need the concept of a wall on plumb to tell when one is off.) These prophets kept dreaming of a time when God would put things right again (see, e.g., Isaiah 2:2-4; 11:1-9; 32:14-20; 42:1-12; 60; 65:17-25; Joel 2:24-29; 3:17-18).

They dreamed of a new age in which human crookedness would be straightened out, rough places made plain. The foolish would be made wise, and the wise, humble. They dreamed of a time when the deserts would flower, the mountains would run with wine, weeping would cease, and people could go to sleep without weapons on their laps. People would work in peace and work to fruitful effect. Lambs could lie down with lions. All nature would be fruitful, benign, and filled with wonder upon wonder; all humans would be knit together in brotherhood and sisterhood; and all nature and all humans would look to God, walk with God, lean toward God, and delight in God. Shouts of joy and recognition would well up from valleys and seas, from women in streets and from men on ships.

The webbing together of God, humans, and all creation in justice, fulfillment, and delight is what the Hebrew prophets call *shalom*. We call it peace, but it means far more than just peace of mind or ceasefire between enemies. In Scripture, shalom means *universal flourishing, wholeness, and delight* — a rich state of affairs in which natural needs are satisfied and natural gifts fruitfully employed, a state of affairs that inspires joyful wonder as its Creator and Savior opens doors and welcomes the creatures in whom he delights (Wolterstorff, 1983, pp. 69-72). Shalom, to put it simply, is the way things ought to be.

In biblical thinking, we can understand neither shalom nor sin apart from reference to God. Sin is a religious concept, not just a moral one. When we are thinking religiously, we think of the defrauding of one's business client, for instance, not merely as an instance of lawlessness, but also of faithlessness; and we think of the fraud as faithless not only to the client, but also to God. Criminal and moral misadventures qualify as sin because they offend and betray God. Sin is not only the breaking of law, but also the breaking of covenant with one's Savior. Sin is the smearing of a relationship, the grieving of one's divine parent and benefactor, a betrayal of the partner to whom one is joined by a holy bond.

Hence a usual biblical analogy: idolatry is adultery. And adultery itself desperately strains more than one union: the adulterer at once breaks human and divine covenant. In fact, in the most famous of the penitential psalms, by tradition a psalm David wrote after his adultery with Bathsheba, the author views his sin primarily, perhaps exclusively, as a sin against God:

> Have mercy on me, O God,
>   according to your steadfast love;
> according to your abundant mercy
>   blot out my transgressions.
> Wash me thoroughly from my iniquity
>   and cleanse me from my sin.
> For I know my transgressions,
>   and my sin is ever before me.
> Against you, you alone, have I sinned
>   and done what is evil in your sight.
>   (Psalm 51:1-4, NRSV here and in succeeding references)

A Definition and Characterization of Sin

All sin has first and finally a Godward force. Let's say that *a* sin is any act — any thought, desire, emotion, word, or deed — or its particular absence, that displeases God and deserves blame. Let's add that the disposition to commit sins also displeases God and deserves blame, and let's therefore use the word *sin* to refer to such instances of both act and disposition. Sin is a culpable and personal affront to a personal God.

But once we possess the concept of shalom, we are in position to enlarge and specify this understanding of sin. God is, after all, not arbitrarily offended. God hates sin not just because it violates his law, but, more substantively, because it violates shalom, because it breaks the peace, because it interferes with the way things are supposed to be. (Indeed, that is why God has laws against a good deal of sin.) God is for shalom and *therefore* against sin. In fact, we may safely describe evil as any spoiling of shalom, whether physically (e.g., by disease), morally, spiritually, or otherwise. Moral and spiritual evil are agential evil, that is, evil that, roughly speaking, only persons can do or have (on agency, see Jones, this volume; Johnson, this volume; and Talbot, this volume). Agential evil thus comprises evil acts and dispositions. Sin is any agential evil for which some person (or group of persons) is to blame. In short, sin is culpable shalom-breaking.

The Bible's big double message is creation and redemption. Sin intervenes, but never as an independent theme. St. Paul, the Bible's chief theologian of sin and grace, therefore speaks of sin in terms of what it is *against.* Sin is anti-law, anti-righteousness, anti-God, anti-Spirit, anti-life. Paul's message is that God has shown free and lavish grace to sinners in the death and resurrection of Jesus Christ. Faith in this God, in this Christ, and in their grace is the only hope of human justification. Accordingly, grace, faith, and righteousness, together with the means of expressing and acquiring them — cross, resurrection, Spirit, justification, baptism into Christ — these topics cluster in the center of Paul's interest. As for sin, Paul knows that sin lures, enslaves, and destroys, that Christ died to redeem us from it, and that our sin must therefore be dreadful, but he never does tell us exactly where sin comes from. Nor does he try to define the nature of its power and transmission (Westerholm, 1988, p. 160).

Perhaps one reason for this omission is that, in the biblical world view, even when sin is depressingly familiar, it is never normal. It is finally unknown, irrational, alien. Sin is always a departure from the norm and is assessed accordingly. It is deviant and perverse, an *in*justice or *in*iquity or *in*gratitude. Sin in the Exodus literature is *dis*order and *dis*obedience. It is faithlessness, lawlessness, Godlessness. Sin is both the overstepping of a line and the failure to reach it — both transgression and shortcoming. It is a missing of the mark, a spoiling of goods, a staining of garments, a hitch in one's gait, a wandering from the path, a fragmenting of the whole. It is what culpably *disturbs* shalom. Sinful life is only a half-depressing, half-ludicrous caricature of genuine human life (Bromiley, 1988, p. 519).

So the biggest biblical idea about sin, expressed in a riot of images and terms, is that sin is an anomaly, an intruder, a notorious gate-crasher. Sin does not belong in God's world, but somehow it has gotten in. In fact, sin has dug in, and, like a tick, burrows deeper whenever we try to remove it (Bromiley, 1988, p. 522). This stubborn and persistent feature of human sin can make it look as if it has a life of its own, as if it were an independent power or even a kind of person. Indeed, St. Paul uses language that suggests as much, as when he says that sin "exercised dominion in death" (Romans 5:21), that "sin deceived me and . . . killed me" (7:11), that "if I do what I do not want, it is no longer I that do it, but sin that dwells within me" (7:20).

Still, one must always read on. Victory passages typically follow the big Pauline sin passages, and these (especially Romans 8:31-39, where all the trumpets are sounding) present the main biblical teaching: sin is a fearfully powerful spoiler of the good, but it cannot finally overpower either the original or renewed project of God in the world.

Why not? How do we explain that sin is both dominant and doomed, both a "power" and a "nothing," both formidable and negligible? "The works of sin are real enough," says Geoffrey Bromiley, "but they carry no solid achievements" (Bromiley, 1988, p. 519). Why?

The reason is that sin is a parasite, an uninvited guest that keeps tapping its host for sustenance. Nothing about sin is its own; all its power, persistence, and plausibility are stolen goods. Sin is not really an entity, but a spoiler of entities, not an organism, but only a leech on organisms. Sin does not build shalom: it vandalizes it. Like a parasite, sin attaches the life force and dynamics of its host and converts them to some new and destructive use. Sowing and reaping, human longing, children's natural trust of their parents — such things belong among the springs and roots of a good creation. Sin does not remove these things; it attaches and turns them. In this way and others, sin invites comparison with addiction, another persistent, parasitic, and exasperating human malady.

The Wide World of Addiction

A Definition and Characterization

Addiction is a complex, progressive, injurious, and, often, disabling attachment to a substance (alcohol, heroin, barbiturates) or a behavior (sex, work, gambling) in which a person compulsively seeks a change of mood. The addictor might be a good staple of life, such as food and drink, or a slimy little vice, such as voyeurism. It might be almost anything, if one defines addiction loosely enough. Indeed, addiction writers in recent decades have impressively lengthened the list of possible addictors so that it now includes not only alcohol and other drugs, but also sex — and not only sex, but also love and romance (Schaef, 1989, p. 3). Also on the growing list are shopping, religion, exercise, video games, money, and going to the movies. One writer who follows the trends in fashionable dependencies cites a confession in Pittsburgh of "sewing or fabric addiction" (McKenzie, 1991, p. 325).

Leaving aside the question how seriously to take some of the more exotic addictions, we are safe in assuming that the genesis of addictions, and the number and blend in them of contributing factors (chemical, neurological, psychological, cultural, social, spiritual), vary among addictors and from one addict to another. Furthermore, addictive dependencies range along a spectrum from mild to devastating (Peele, 1985, p. 2; Hart, 1988, p. 40). By themselves such variables guarantee the complexity of the addictive phenomenon, but, in addition to this, some addicts also struggle with cross-addictions and multiple addictions. Some even appear to get hooked on the cures for their addictions. (In certain cases, government methadone prescriptions are roughly as helpful to heroin addicts as school suspensions are to truants.) Recovering addicts often come to believe that their addictions, whether single or grouped, whether predominantly chemical or psychological, include a spiritual dimension that can only be called "demonic."

No matter how they start, addictions eventually center in distress and in the self-defeating choice of an agent to relieve the distress. In fact, trying to cure distress with the same thing that caused it is typically the mechanism that closes the trap on an addict — a trap that, as just suggested, might be baited with anything from whiskey to wool.

But what moves an addict to the bait? At every stage, addiction is driven by one of the most powerful, mysterious, and vital forces of human existence. What drives addiction is longing — a longing not just of brain, belly, or loins, but finally of the heart (May, 1988, p. 3).

Because they are human beings, addicts long for wholeness, for fulfillment, and for the final good that believers call God. Like all idolatries, addiction taps this vital spiritual force and draws off its energies to objects and processes that drain the addict instead of filling him. Accordingly, the addict longs not for God, but for transcendence; not for joy, but only for pleasure — and sometimes for mere escape from pain. Some therapists believe that addicts can get high even on the vapors of guilt, or, less simply, that desire, pleasure, guilt feelings, and a Nietzschean will to power sometimes run together into a high-octane blend that fuels addiction (Lenters, 1985, pp. 15-17).

In any case, addiction taps into longing the way a blackmailer might garnish your wages. Every time you meet a demand, it escalates. Every time you recover self-respect, the will to love, or any other vital resource, it gets sapped away by this parasite.

Of course, people who are attached to cigarettes or to a cocktail at the end of every workday may not recognize themselves as players in such a drama. Some persons use, or even abuse, such substances as alcohol without becoming dependent on them. Some persons develop mild dependencies, but not full-blown addictions. In some cases, genuine addictions can remain, or remain for a time, at a minor-league level.

But to a big-league addict, addiction feels not only parasitical, but also wily and perverse. It feels demonically alive, as if not just something, but some*one*, were trying to lure, hook, and land him — someone who first successfully tempts him and then accuses him of weakness for having succumbed. As the "Big Book" of Alcoholics Anonymous says, addiction is "cunning, baffling, powerful, and patient" (Schaef, 1989, pp. 25-26); a victor over every ordinary attempt to conquer it, a demon that rushes to fill vacuums, a dismissed shadow that keeps threatening to return. Thus, an addict who repeatedly makes and then breaks contracts with himself; who finds his longings narrowing and hardening into an obsession with things he knows will devastate his work, self-respect, relationships, and bank account, and who yet seeks compulsively to satisfy those longings; who thus finds his will split between wanting to banish an addictive substance from the earth, and wanting to protect his private cache of it; whose addiction, as it moves through mild and moderate stages, first enthralls him in one sense of the word and then in the other — an addict like this often comes to believe that his "struggle is not against enemies of blood and flesh, but against . . . spiritual forces of evil" (Ephesians 6:12).

What follows is that treatments, like areas of addiction research, must typically be multilevel. Accordingly, a psychiatrist might initially take a medical approach to an alcoholic addiction, then a psychological one, and then a family systems approach. Following Alcoholics Anonymous, she may all along attempt as well to help her patient regain a measure of spiritual hygiene. If she is a Christian, she may also undertake, or propose, ministries of prayer, healing, or, in extraordinary cases, even of exorcism (Peck, 1984, pp. 182-211).

Descent and Ascent in the Spiral of Addiction

In 1983, Patrick Carnes published *Out of the Shadows*, a pioneering book about sexual addiction that tells us as much about addiction in general as it does about sexual addiction in particular. In his book, Carnes describes people caught in a cycle of delusion ("Sex is my most important need"), obsession (hours-long waits in a voyeur's blind for a seconds-long glimpse of nudity), and ritual behavior ("special routines" favored by voyeurs, molesters, and flashers). These pleasure-seeking behaviors, once indulged, leave the addict with a residue of despair. Predictably, what traps him, what converts him from a mere delinquent into an addict, is that he tries to relieve the despair by indulging his obsession all over again, thereby initiating a new round of addiction.

Carnes notes that sexual addicts often experience a tolerance effect. Whatever comforts they find in pornography, for instance, eventually pale. So the addict graduates to the hands-on experience of non-therapeutic massage, and perhaps then to surreptitious, and clearly illegal, groping of strangers on crowded buses or subway trains. The escalating risk of these adventures enhances the addict's mood change, the "high" he seeks, and thus compensates for the tolerance effect.

Of course, addicts try, often desperately, to manage their problem. They reproach themselves, confess their sins to God, make and break resolutions, set ever new dates for one last fling. They struggle to deal with the depressing accompaniments of their secret life — lies, deceptions, scapegoating, alternating rage and self-pity, isolation, fear of discovery, the loss of real intimacy with loved ones. But all this is uphill work, in part because the spiritual forces arrayed against an addict include various temptations that society approves. A heavy gambler, for instance, may discover that his state government and even his local church have a game they would like him to play. An alcoholic who turns a magazine page may face a gin advertisement that has been crafted by an excellent mind. Similarly, a sex addict who views a TV newscast may meet a segment that seemingly has been shaped and shot as much to titillate as to inform. Typically, nobody in these settings protects or disabuses the vulnerable. Nobody plays the role of country priest, reminding the addict that pleasure often masks anguish. The result is that under such circumstances the addict, who desperately needs to deny himself in order to survive, may feel surrounded. How can he prevail against all these foes who pop up everywhere, and who seemingly share scouting reports of his weaknesses?

In general, the addict must make his way in a sensate society which assumes everybody's fundamental right to gratify at least five of their senses and which discourages self-denial as foolish, perhaps even impious. For the self is a sacred object (see Roberts, 1993, p. 304).

> Holy, holy, holy is the self of hosts
> Of TV talk shows, and of all their guests.
> The whole earth is full of their glory.

Yet, the same culture that encourages self-indulgence also punishes the indulgent with scorn fit for a failed god. This is another demonic dimension of addiction. As Gerald May has observed, the addict's repeated failures of self-mastery devastate his self-esteem in part because he lives in a culture that teaches him that we are our own creators (May, 1988, p. 3). A person who has succumbed to an addiction thus imagines a derisive question coming at him from his culture: What kind of moron creates but cannot control himself? (What kind of carmaker cannot drive his own product?)

When her attempts at self-management fail, as they usually do, and when her self-esteem plummets, as it always does, the addict feels compelled to seek solace in her obsessive behavior, and thus cycles down one more level. In this way, addictions flourish by feeding on human attempts to master them (May, 1988, p. 42).

According to Carnes, the sex addict's secret life may eventually get exposed in a way that is dramatic enough to nudge him forcefully toward full disclosure. The exposure event is thus a severe mercy, a potent bearer of shame and grace. "A moment comes for every addict," says Carnes, when

- The squad car pulls into your driveway and you know why they've come.
- Your teenage son finds your pornography.
- You have a car accident while exposing yourself.
- The money you spent on the last prostitute equals the amount for the new shoes your child needs. (Carnes, 1983, pp. v-vi)

What now? An addict stands a chance of recovery only if he is finally willing to tell himself the truth. The only way out of the addict's plight is *through* it. He has to face it, deal with it, confess it. With the firm and caring support of people important to him, he has to rip his way through all the tissues of denial and self-deception that have "protected his supply." The addict has to take a hard step, the first of the famous twelve steps. Paradoxically, he must help himself by admitting that he is helpless. He must perform the courageous, difficult, and highly responsible act of acknowledging the hopelessness and wholesale unmanageability of his life. The addict must abandon "the uncanny game of hide-and-seek in the obscurity of the soul in which it, the single human soul, evades itself, avoids itself, hides from itself" (Buber, 1953, p. 111). Only then is the way open for his return to a tolerably healthy life — a return that is likely to take time, vigilance, and the support of a number of other human beings, some of them professionals.

Carnes has much else of interest to say, including observations about the role of family systems in dependency and co-dependency, about the addict's awareness that his behavior pattern is perverse (a three hour wait for twenty seconds of nudity is "insane even to the voyeur"), and about multiple and typically paired addictions (sex and food, gambling and alcohol). But Carnes is clear from the outset that the behaviors of addicts are not chosen: "For the addict there is no choice. . . . The addiction is in charge." Sex addicts "have no control over their sexual behavior" (Carnes, 1983, p. ix).

Sin or Symptom?

Here the inevitable question arises. In his accounts of peepings, flashings, and uninvited fondlings, isn't Carnes actually describing *sin* — and, as a matter of fact, some pretty greasy examples of it? When people habitually pay prostitutes to talk dirty to them on the telephone and then, once a month, guard their telephone bill from prying eyes; when they prowl public restrooms, hunting for anonymous sex; when they sacrifice the happiness of their children in order to indulge private sexual preoccupations that are increasingly dangerous, time-consuming, and expensive —

when they do these things, why not simply call the whole works sin? Why import the language of addiction, the kind of language that makes a john look like a victim?

These questions suggest our main one: What really is the relationship between sin and addiction?

In trying to state this relation we may begin by simply noting that addictions often do include morally wrong thoughts, words, and deeds. No serious person, Christian or otherwise, wants to defend self-destructive drug abuse, for instance, or incestuous fantasizing, or habitual lying to oneself and others. These acts wreck shalom, at least for the addict and usually for a number of others who get entangled in the addict's web. These acts are plainly wrong, whether or not they fit into an addictive process, and people therefore ought not to do them.

But the question before us is whether these things, when they *do* fit into a pattern of addiction, are instances of sin — that is, whether the persons who do them are culpable, whether they deserve blame and reproach, whether the solution to the problem their behavior raises is repentance or therapy or both.

Carnes says that sexual addicts lack choice, that "the addiction is in charge." But this is by no means a settled conclusion of expert observers (Gerald May, for example, appears to demur) and would, in any case, be an extraordinarily hard conclusion to back with evidence. Addicts can't help it, says Carnes. But how does he know? Given self-deception as ingredient in the addictive process, addicts themselves may not be the best witnesses on this topic. And who else *could* be an authoritative witness? Few of us, after all, can gauge the potent and subtle workings of will and choice even in ourselves, let alone in others. What we can see in addicts is a pattern of destructive delusion, obsession, and behavior. What we cannot see is the extent to which a person has control, the extent to which a person chooses her poison, and the degree to which her poisonous choices have been determined by various other factors. What we can see is that some addicts do, in fact, make constructive choices. They do stop their destructive behavior. What we cannot see is why others do not.

Is an addict a person who has a bad habit of making sinful choices? Or is an addict the victim of biological and social forces she may resist, but is, at least for a time, powerless to overcome? Or, conceivably, is an addict a person who habitually makes bad choices just because of such forces or who, perhaps, awakens such forces by making bad choices? Are some addictions, like some neuroses, in effect the addict's self-condemnation and self-sentence for bad behavior (Mowrer, 1989, p. 82)? Are certain alcoholics, for example, busy with the undeclared project of drowning not just their sorrows, but also their guilt? Or are addicts shortcut artists —

people who want gratification "without effort, pain, or labor" (Van Kaam, 1987, p. 251)?

Of course, even if an addict does eventually lack the power to choose and to act contrary to the tug of his addiction, he may still bear responsibility for the moral evil he does, and this moral evil might therefore count as sin. Perhaps he addicted himself. Perhaps he misbehaved at a time when he *did* have the power to choose and act well. If he is like other human beings, his habit has a pre-history of choices and deeds. The habit that binds him is a chain of his own acts. Perhaps he made himself an alcoholic, for example, by self-indulgently drinking too much for too many years. In short, to be physically and psychologically hooked on some substance or behavior pattern is not necessarily to be let off the hook morally. (Being high on crack cocaine is typically no excuse for running down pedestrians with your motorcycle.) Involuntary sin may still be sin (Adams, 1985, passim).

We are further, and maybe more significantly, responsible for what we do with our addictions once we have them — whether we seek help for them, for example, whether we wear them as merit badges (certain subcultures admire men who can hold a lot of liquor), or whether we use one addiction as an excuse for another. In any case, addicts who are serious about recovery must at some point take responsibility for the wreckage that surrounds their addiction and for the salvage work that now needs to start.

Suppose we assume that sinful behavior sometimes triggers the addictive process, or emerges from it, or both. Addictions do typically include patterns of moral evil, after all. No doubt these moral evils are sometimes sin. Lying, gluttonous eating and drinking, beating up one's spouse while blaming her for provoking the beating, and engaging in the sexual rituals Carnes describes are prima facie sins. They are immoral acts that are, for all we know, chargeable to those who do them.

Still, none of us knows the degree to which other human beings bear responsibility for their behavior, the degree to which they "could have helped it." That is one important difference between us and God. So even if, for the purposes of discussion, we call an addict's immoral acts sin, we do so provisionally. Perhaps, if we had all the facts, we might downgrade some of these acts to the more general status of moral evils. Indeed, when one observes the rifts and scars of children whose parents took turns slapping, deriding, ignoring, bullying, or, sometimes worse, simply abandoning them; when one observes the wholesale life misman-agement of grownups who have lived for years in the shadow of their bereft childhood, and who attempt with one addictor after another to relieve their distress and to fill those empty places where love should have settled, only to discover that their addictor keeps enlarging the very void it was meant to fill (Wakefield, 1988, p. 200); when one knows people of this kind and observes their nearly predictable character pathology, one hesitates to call all this chaos sin. The label sounds smug and impertinent.

Addiction as Tragedy

In such cases, we want to think inside some broader category, perhaps the category of tragedy. Like the fallenness of the human race, the chaos of addiction comes out of particular human character and sin, but also out of the temptations and disorganizing forces resident in an addict's home and neighborhood, and maybe even in her genes. The serpent is both within and without (Duffy, 1988, p. 615). Family habits, cultural expectations (e.g., *machismo*), the behavior patterns of parents, the spiritual forces generated by television advertising and rock videos, and a host of other factors combine to exert pressure on candidates for addiction. If the pressure is strong enough, a person may surrender to it and enter the deadly spiral of dependency.

To think of addiction as tragic is to focus not simply on an addict's patterns of behavior, but also on the person who behaves this way. Tragedy implies the weight and worth of its central figures. Tragedy is never the fall of simple victims or villains; these falls are dramatically uninteresting and untragic. Tragedy implies the fall of someone who is responsible and significant — a person of substance, not just of substance abuse. In fact, tragedy implies the fall of someone who is naturally great, but whose greatness has been compromised and finally crumbled by a mix of forces, including personal agency, that work together for evil in a way that seems simultaneously surprising and predictable, preventable and inevitable. A tragic figure is, in some intricate combination, both weak and willful, both foolish and guilty. We therefore want to accuse him and also to sympathize with him. (Think, for instance, of Shakespeare's King Lear, and his feather-headed demand that his daughters declare their love for him.) In tragedy, sin is surely one of the forces at work, but by no means the only one and sometimes not even the most obvious one.

So it is in the phenomenon of addiction. Addicts are sinners like everybody else, but they are also tragic figures whose fall is often owed to a combination of factors so numerous, complex, and elusive that only a proud and foolish therapist would propose a neat taxonomy of them. In any case, we must reject both the typically judgmental and typically permissive accounts of the relation between sin and addiction; we must say neither that all addiction is simple sin nor that it is inculpable disease.

These simplicities have historically been attached by turns to alcoholism, for example, but neither seems at all adequate (Fingarette, 1988, p. 111; Peele, 1985, pp. 28-45).

Remarkably enough, at the end of the day it might not matter very much how we classify the damaging behaviors of addicts. Whether these behaviors amount to sin or symptom, the prescription for dealing with them may turn out to be just about the same. Nobody is more insistent than Alcoholics Anonymous that alcoholism is a disease; nobody is more insistent than A.A. on the need for the alcoholic to take full responsibility for his disease and to deal with it in brutal candor. Moreover, nobody is more insistent that the addict must admit helplessness and therefore surrender his life to God, or to a "higher power." The idea is that those who surrender shall be free — or, at least, free for today.

A Feminist Challenge to the Twelve Steps

People often notice that the twelve steps of A.A. look like phases in the Christian program of renewal. You admit powerlessness, give yourself over to God, confess wrongdoing, make amends, seek growth in grace, and then witness to others. Through every phase, you consciously depend on the will and power of God.

But nowadays new voices — proponents of Rational Recovery, for instance, and certain feminists — are asking the old questions about the paradoxical character of this program. How can a new surrender help the old one? If dependency was the problem, how can it also be the solution?

Charlotte Davis Kasl speaks for those feminists who suggest that the twelve steps of recovery programs have traditionally been stated in a way that misses the special needs of women. In particular, the twelve steps assume that recovery begins with the admission of powerlessness over an addictor and then with surrender of will and lives to the care of God. But this recipe will not work for many contemporary women, says Kasl. Why not?

> The steps were formulated by a white, middle-class male in the 1930s; not surprisingly, they work to break down an overinflated ego, and put reliance on an all-powerful male God. But most women suffer from the *lack* of a healthy, aware ego, and need to strengthen their sense of self by affirming their own inner wisdom. (Kasl, 1990, p. 30)

Kasl goes on to make the general claim that if they are to find health, women must stop depending on other things and persons altogether, including God. Instead, women must "awaken the wisdom that is within" by asserting and exercising their own power to take charge of their own lives. For help in this program, women may appeal to what Kasl calls "the universe/Goddess/Great Spirit," but this is apparently a skinny being whose slight status invites little by way of trust or worship.

The feminist recoil from the twelve-step program suggests a cluster of interesting questions that deserve more attention than I can pay them here. For now, suppose that sin sometimes takes the complementary forms of macho pride and passive subservience, of self-idolatry and other-idolatry, of self-exaltation and self-abnegation (Migliore, 1991, pp. 131-33). To what degree do traditional male and female gender roles express these forms? Accordingly, to what degree must Christians take their audience into consideration when preaching humility? Who needs to hear this sermon? Big people or little people? Those who strut or those who slouch? And how about the empowerment message of Scripture — the "I can do all things," and "you are more than conquerors" message? Who needs to hear *this* sermon? Flourishing chief executive officers? Or those harassed folk whose tenderest hopes keep getting shredded and tossed back at them like confetti?

Unhappily, though Kasl raises a vital question, namely, whether over- and underinflated egos may need prescriptions that are properly adjusted for inflation, her own analysis of the predicament of addicted women, and her advice to them based on this analysis, seem hardly less peculiar than the tradition she rejects. One peculiarity is that though Kasl thinks women tend to suffer from powerlessness, she does not want them to say so. She does not want them to begin their recovery by admitting bondage to some addictor. Why not? Apparently because such an admission would simply reinforce the general feeling of powerlessness from which women suffer. So Kasl recommends self-assertion instead — the "I can" as substitute for the "I can't." What women need is self-help and self-affirmation, she says, with no reliance on "something external" to lift or restore them (Kasl, 1990, p. 30).

And here we have a second peculiarity. How realistic is this revised program? After all, as Kasl readily observes, independent and over-inflated males are just as likely to get addicted as women. Hence an obvious question: If independence has not worked for men, why is it likely to work for women?

Perhaps Kasl would reply that men suffer from a surplus of independence and women from a deficit so that, in the interests of a balance of trade, men need to lose independence and women to gain it. Fair enough. Still, if the goal of women's therapy is something in between male aloofness and female enmeshment — a nicely balanced ego that is neither macho nor minnow — the move toward restoration of this balance is going to take strength. The assertion of sound and sacred personhood will take courage. Where are these blessings to come from? To tap the self as their source is to write a check on the same account that Kasl says has been overdrawn.

Kasl and other feminists may have hold of a significant difference in the way that traditional gender roles play out with reference to addiction and other human troubles. If so — if males tend toward self-idolatry and females toward other-idolatry — then, as Mary Stewart Van Leeuwen proposes, surely the right move for both is to quit their idolatries and turn to God (Van Leeuwen, 1990, pp. 247-50). But this is the move Kasl rejects in favor of total self-reliance, the very flaw A.A. was set up to combat.

In any case, for women to exchange their form of idolatry for the masculine one hardly looks like an improvement. It looks more like an infection caught from sleeping with the enemy.

Overlapping Circles

Given the relevant qualifications, let us say that addictions often include sin — or, putting matters the other way around, that some sin displays the addictive syndrome. Suppose we imagine sin and addiction as significantly overlapping circles. On the ends, in the quarter moons where the circles do not overlap, we have examples of addiction that include little or no actual sin by the addict himself and examples of sin that betray little of the addictive process. Cases of intra-uterine addiction, for example, belong in the former category, as do any other chemical or process addictions innocently contracted — as when a clinically schizophrenic or depressed person slides into substance addiction while seeking relief from sickness. (Perhaps some addictions in these cases qualify as *physical* evils rather than as moral ones.)

In the latter category belong sins that hang around on the listless side of human life, particularly those that include little by way of mood change, or of yearning for it. A person, for instance, who wholly neglects her aged parents because she finds them boring may present symptoms of sloth and filial ingratitude, but not of addiction.

Sin and addiction overlap wherever sin displays the addictive syndrome, wherever sin shares with addiction certain typical dynamics. What we might call minor-league addictions display at least a few of these dynamics, while major-league addictions display many more, or more intense forms, of them.

Dynamics of Addiction

(1) Repetition of pleasurable and therefore habit-forming behavior, plus escalating tolerance and desire

(2) Unpleasant aftereffects of such behavior, including withdrawal symptoms and self-reproach

(3) Vows to moderate or quit, followed by relapses and by attendant feelings of guilt, shame, and general distress

(4) Attempts to ease this distress with new rounds of the addictive behavior (or with the first rounds of a companion addiction)

(5) Deterioration of work and relationships, with accompanying cognitive disturbances, including denial, delusions, and self-deceptions, especially about the effects of the addiction and the degree to which one is enthralled by it

(6) Gradually increasing preoccupation, then obsession, with the addictor

(7) Compulsivity in addictive behavior: evidence that one's will has become at least partly split, enfeebled, and enslaved

(8) A tendency to draw others into the web of addiction, people who support and enable the primary addiction. These "co-dependents" present certain addictive patterns of their own — in particular, the simultaneous need to be needed by the addict and to control him. The co-dependent relationship is thus one in which primary and parasitic addictions join.

Where in the family of sins do we find displays of this syndrome? Not surprisingly, we typically find them among such appetitive sins as avarice, gluttony, and lust — the sins that exhibit some combination of exaggerated and misplaced longing. Healthy people keep a rein on their longings. Healthy people enjoy the freedom that is born of contentment (a "freedom from want"), which is, in turn, owed to a sturdy and persistent discipline of desire. Healthy people deliberately note, for instance, how many material goods they can do without, and then take extra pleasure in the simple and enduring ones they possess. They make it their goal, most of the time, to eat and drink only enough to relieve hunger and thirst, not to sate themselves. They integrate their sexual desire into a committed relationship, bonded by vows and trust.

These disciplines are, of course, by no means easy to acquire or to preserve, and failures in them are drearily familiar to all of us. (In these respects, the discipline of desire resembles mastery of a foreign language or of a musical instrument.) But a disciplined person cuts losses and tries to contain failure. She knows the traps that lie in the shadows of failure and purposely tries to skirt them (the all-or-nothing trap, for example, in which a dieter who has just fallen off the wagon by mouthing a handful of peanuts concludes that she might as well now eat the whole can). Everybody fails. But for whatever reason, the candidate for addiction gives in to failure, seeks deadly comfort from the same kind of thing that caused the failure, and thus begins a war against herself that is likely to take a lot of skilled, compassionate, and expensive help to stop.

Unsurprisingly, given the overlap between sin and addiction, the-ologians report such wars just as often as therapists do. At the center of his *Confessions,* St. Augustine ponders the bondage of the will, "the force of habit, by which the mind is swept along and held fast even against its will" (Augustine, 1961, 8.5). Scripturally, Augustine is moving among those Pauline passages (Galatians 5:17, Romans 7:22-25) that speak of the war between flesh and spirit, that inner war we lose whenever we will what is right, but do what is wrong. Experientially, Augustine is talking about his long battle with lust. The fearful, inexplicable, and, finally, eerie dynamic of moral evil, he says, is that we enslave ourselves to it. As in all tragedy, the enemy is within as well as without. We know we are doing wrong, we want not to do it, and still we do it. The reason is that at some other level of our being we *do* want to do it. Giving in to that want at that level leaves a bondage we both create and resent. Each wrong choice forges a link in the chain that binds us:

> I was held fast, not in fetters clamped upon me by another, but by my own will, which had the strength of iron chains. The enemy held my will in his power and from it he had made a chain and shackled me. For my will was perverse and lust had grown from it, and when I gave in to lust habit was born, and when I did not resist the habit it became a necessity. These were the links which together formed what I have called my chain, and it held me fast in the duress of servitude. (Augustine, 1961, 8.5)

Passages like this one from a father of the Christian church might be just as likely to appear in the confessions of a contemporary alcoholic or food addict, for Augustine's chain runs right through the dynamics of addic-tion. These are the dynamics of appetitive sin in particular, the kind of sin likeliest to display the classic addictive syndrome, likeliest to chain its subjects to their own sin so that they become at once its agents and victims.

But all sin shares with addiction at least a few of the dynamics on the list, as well as certain other common profiles. For example, even when they do not display the full addictive syndrome, many forms of sin include patterns of self-seeking, childish impatience with delayed gratification, and refusal to accept reasonable limits on behavior. In addition, sin, like addiction, tends to split and bind the will, to work itself into a habit of the heart, and to hide itself under layers of self-deception. Moreover, people often commit sins in order to relieve distress caused by other sins: they may lie to prevent a humiliating exposure of their thievery, for example, and then lie again to prevent the discovery of their first lie. Hence the familiar spiral shape of certain patterns of sin.

In these and many other ways addiction extends a tradition familiar to all of us, including all of us who would never dream of calling ourselves addicts (see Howsepian, this volume). In important respects, "the addiction experience is the human experience" since we all "have a habit" where sin is concerned (Lenters, 1985, p. 4). Addiction shows us how the habit works, where it goes, and why it persists. In fact, we might think of addiction as a lab demonstration of the great law of returns — the law of longing and acting and the forming of habits that lead to renewed longing.

Addiction is a dramatic portrait of some main dynamics of sin, a stage show of warped longings, split wills, encumbered liberties, and perverse attacks on one's own well-being — some of the same dramatic machinery that moves the general tragedy of sin forward. Addiction shows us the progressive and lethal character of moral evil, the movement of corruption that Patrick McCormick calls "a conversion unto death" (McCormick, 1989, p. 152).

For addicts this conversion begins and ends in an act of surrender — first to appetitive failure and then, in recovery, to God. The "theology of addiction," as Richard Mouw observes, is all about giving in, about "giving oneself over" (Mouw, 1988, p. 41). Addiction is about our hungers and thirsts, about our ultimate concern, about the clinging and longing of our hearts, and about giving ourselves over to these things. When it is in full cry, addiction is finally about idolatry. At last, the addict will do anything for his idol, including dying for it. According to Mouw, there comes a point in the life of every alcoholic in which he sings his own version of Martin Luther's hymn: "Let goods and kindred go; this mortal life also; I'm going to get loaded" (Mouw, 1988, p. 42).

The mix of wilfulness and despair, defiance and futility in the texture of addiction rules out simple ways of addressing it. Indeed, redemption from addiction must eventually be as multifaceted and protracted as redemption from sin and its miseries. But the first question for addicts and for all sinners is plain and urgent: In whose name is your help? Who or what is your only comfort in life and in death? To whom, or to what, do you ultimately belong?

The addict who turns to God has made the big and right decision.

That is because "the hardness of God is kinder than the softness of man, and His compulsion is our liberation" (Lewis, 1955, p. 229). But no mere decision is enough. Like all sinners, the addict also needs painfully to unlearn old habits, to dismantle old scenarios, to pay old debts, and then to move steadfastly along the road to recovery one small, secure step at a time, always aware that the self we want to recover is never wholly at our disposal. "Evil," says Diogenes Allen, "is one of the ways we learn that we ourselves are a mystery; for we are not in full control of ourselves and cannot find any method of gaining control" (Allen, 1986, p. 135). The addict therefore needs not just to turn to God, but also to walk with God, lean on God, cling to God, come to have the sense and feel of God, refer all things to God. Addicts need not just the God who forgives, but also the God who heals; not just the good Pardoner, but also the Great Physician. Like all sinners, the addict needs spiritual hygiene. For just as sin, addiction, and misery typically go together, so do confession, healing, and the long process of redemption. We need redemption not just from our sins and addictions, but also from their miseries — particularly those miseries that occasion more sin and deeper addiction. As all recovering sinners know, this process of healing and liberation, this "conversion unto life," this set of lessons to teach us how to dance again, will prove to be as cunning, baffling, powerful, and patient as addiction itself.

Sin and Psychosis

A. A. Howsepian

The savage danger of madness is related to the danger of the passions and to their fatal concatenation.

Michel Foucault, *Madness and Civilization* (1973, p. 85)

Concupiscence does not altogether fetter the reason, as drunkenness does, unless perchance it be so vehement as to make a man insane.

St. Thomas Aquinas, *Summa Theologiae* (II-II, 150, 1, ad 3)

OUR VIEWS ABOUT mental illness reveal, in a fundamental way, what we take mental health and human flourishing to be. Some mental disorders are considered more serious than others because we regard them as striking closer to the core of our humanity. Systems of psychiatric disease classification are designed to reflect, among other things, our view of their relative seriousness. Variant classifications of mental disease express variant understandings of our very nature as persons. It stands to reason that Christians, who have a distinctive conception of human nature and of a flourishing human life, will want to think critically about proposed schemes for classifying deviations from such flourishing. I want to rethink the category of psychosis in light of the Christian concept of sin. I shall argue for a concept of psychosis which (1) involves disordered appetite (desire) as much as disordered belief, and (2) derives the scope of its applicability from the Christian notion of a well-ordered mind.

Classifying Mental Disorders

For over one hundred years, psychiatry has labored to classify mental disorders. In the past fifty years, this has led to multiple, and often far-reaching, revisions of both the mental disorders section of the *International Classification of Diseases* and the American Psychiatric Association's *Diagnostic and Statistical Manual of Mental Disorders* (*DSM I*, 1952; *DSM II*, 1968; *DSM III-R*, 1987; *DSM IV*, 1994). Classification has at least three goals: (i) to guide scientific research; (ii) to facilitate communication among researchers and clinicians; and (iii) to enhance physicians' control of diseases. This last goal is the most important. The comprehension, treatment, and prevention of a disease often depends on its being properly classified.

Understanding the various mental disorders requires sensitivity to varying *degrees* of psychosocial disintegration. The degree of impairment resulting from a dysthymic disorder (a form of chronic low-grade depression) is generally less than what results from a major depressive episode; similarly, someone suffering from schizotypal personality disorder is less dysfunctional than someone with full-blown schizophrenia. Doctors regularly take account of a patient's degree of local or global impairment in making decisions about *triage,* and the same consideration often figures into how the disorder gets classified.

Anxiety and personality disorders are much commoner than the so-called *psychotic* disorders, but the latter have received more attention. This is at least partly due to the severer psychosocial disintegration that is characteristic of the psychoses. It may also be due to the early Christian supposition that some of those who appear mad are possessed by demons. Again, the psychoses may have received more attention because of the novel behavior of the mad, e.g., aggressive or defensive responses to hallucinated threatening voices, or bizarre posturing of one's limbs out of conviction that any change in posture will destroy the solar system. Finally, psychopathologists may have focused on the psychoses because, until quite recently, we have been hardly able to control them.

In the current systems of psychiatric disease classification, psychosis is almost always classified as a variety of disordered *believing.* I am critical of this classification, and shall argue that this mistake can best be appreciated and redressed by thinking about addiction. Although the concept of addiction has notoriously resisted precise analysis, one promising line of conceptual development is found in Graham Oddie (1993). According to Oddie, "an addiction is a resilient disposition to form resilient desires with the dissatisfaction properties" (p. 383) — in other words, addictions involve disordered *desiring.*

My primary thesis is that psychoses caused by disordered desiring should be recognized in any system of psychiatric disease classification. I assume the broadest and most general traditional definition of psychosis as primarily and essentially a loss of contact with some significant feature of reality. Addictions are then best understood as species of psychosis, and this reclassification has profound implications for how psychiatry views human nature, psychological well-being, and the organization of the self.

Many psychopathologists do not consider every expression of *psychoticism* to be psychotic. "Psychoticism," as it has been invoked, for example, in the context of standard psychometric tests such as the Minnesota Multiphasic Personality Inventory, encompasses a broad, gradable spectrum of human experience that ranges from mild interpersonal alienation (as it might be expressed, for example, in one's self-reported feelings of loneliness) to full-blown "psychotic" disorganization. The traditional understanding of psychosis focuses almost exclusively on disordered cognitive processes that typically result in aberrant belief-fixation, but psychoticism also traditionally embraces a spectrum of psychological characteristics that is sensitive to the organizational structure of one's appetites.

My secondary thesis is that the tendrils of psychoticism, so understood, capture not only clinical syndromes of grossly disordered appetition, but also those disorders of appetite, thought, and action which together constitute the basic human affliction that Christians call sin. All sinful activity, in other words, is a basic expression of deep psychoticism. Despite initial appearances, this reconceptualization of sin and addiction is not counterintuitive, for it agrees with our broadest and most general understanding of what it means to be psychotic. (In spite of the fairly widespread distinction between psychosis and psychoticism, I shall generally use these terms interchangeably, for the fact that the notion of psychoticism is sensitive to appetitive disorganization will help me liberate the concept of psychosis from the almost exclusive suggestion of doxastic disorganization — that is, disordered beliefs.)

Finally, I shall attempt to show how this reconceptualization of sin and psychosis may be recruited to meet a recent and significant challenge to contemporary psychiatry by those who are eager to dispense with a taxonomy of mental illness altogether. (See, for example, Szasz, 1961. For a critique of Szasz, see Fulford, 1989.) Along the way, I shall direct attention to a historical conceptual heritage that modern psychopathologists have ignored, which profitably views the appetites themselves as proper objects of rational evaluation.

The Place of Delusion in Psychosis

The concept of psychosis continues to shape the basic contours of psychiatric theory. Thus, the numerous diagnostic categories situated under the rubric "Schizophrenia" or "Delusional (Paranoid) Disorders" in the *DSM III-R* are located there partly because these disorders share psychotic features. Other related but nonpsychotic disorders, such as paranoid, schizoid, and schizotypal personality disorders, are classified elsewhere, although they share a number of symptoms with both schizophrenia and the delusional disorders.

The concept of psychosis also exerts considerable practical influence in the clinical context. Psychotic individuals are more readily hospitalized than those who are not; and whether hospitalized or not they are typically treated differently from their counterparts who may be afflicted with a relevantly similar but nonpsychotic disorder. The severity of a psychiatric disorder is often measured by the presence or absence of psychosis: its presence is generally taken to be more ominous than its absence; and, conversely, its amelioration is typically taken to point toward recovery. The schizophrenias, for example, have been termed the "cancers of mental illness," not so much because they almost always resist treatment and are chronic or terminal, but because of the disabling "psychotic" disintegration of the self that marks them.

Historically, the hallmark of psychosis has been delusion, which has traditionally been understood as a variety of disordered believing — typically as a culturally inexplicable, incorrigible, false believing (see Harré and Lamb, 1986). Delusional belief is almost universally recognized as a *sufficient* condition for ascribing psychosis; while (e.g.) the presence of hallucinatory phenomena not accompanied by delusional beliefs (as might occur, for example, during bouts of conversion hysteria) is considered not sufficient for ascribing psychosis.

Has delusional belief also been considered *necessary* for psychosis? It seems not, though non-delusional conditions historically classified as psychotic are at best non-paradigmatic examples. In what I shall call the "dominant traditional" view — a view from which Fulford (1989) properly dissents — psychosis appears to *require* delusional belief. Nevertheless, psychic disorganization of sufficient severity, in what appears to be the *absence* of delusions, has prompted the psychiatric community on various occasions to categorize (e.g.) symbiotic psychosis, profound "vegetative" depression, Korsakoff's syndrome, catatonic excitement and stupor, alcohol withdrawal delirium, and psychotic rage reactions as psychotic, even though none of these is essentially associated with delusion as traditionally understood. The *DSM III-R*, for example, retains conceptual space for psychosis in the absence of delusions: "The term *psychotic* is sometimes appropriate when a person's behavior is so grossly disorganized that a reasonable inference can be made that reality testing is markedly disturbed. Examples include markedly incoherent speech without apparent awareness by the person that the speech is not understandable, and the agitated, inattentive, and disoriented behavior seen in Alcohol Withdrawal Delirium" (p. 404).

It might initially appear that the common element in the aforementioned disorders — the element that qualifies them as *psychotic* — is not delusions as such but a more general malfunction in those cognitive processes that play essential roles in producing stable, veridical beliefs. The rapidity of mental-state changes that occurs in hyperexcitable states, the profound mental sluggishness characteristic of deeply vegetative depressive states, and the intense foci of anger that dominate reactions of psychotic rage, for example, seem both to prevent the formation of those relatively stable non-veridical doxastic states that comprise most delusions and also to preclude the proper conformation of a critical subset of one's beliefs to the contours of reality. So it may seem that, in its broadest characterization, to be psychotic is to be out of touch with some critical aspect of reality in at least one of two general ways, namely, either by *fixing* certain contranormal (delusional) beliefs or by being *unable to fix* certain normal beliefs. In either case, the emphasis is doxastic, for it relies on there being a disruption in the cognitive mechanisms required for fixing certain kinds of *beliefs*.

So does the concept of psychosis essentially and primarily involve the presence of some sort of doxastic disturbance? Must the psychotic either fail to fix certain beliefs (call this the "negative doxastic condition") or, more typically, fix a certain class of inappropriate, although not necessarily false (see Fulford, 1989, 1991), "delusional" beliefs (call this the "positive doxastic condition")? Any conception of psychosis that gives primacy to either of these doxastic conditions can be called a "doxa-primary conception of psychosis" (DPCP).

DPCsP, although quite popular among psychopathologists, do not appear to tell the whole story about the fundamental nature of psychosis. We have good reason to think that in its most general sense, psychosis is essentially marked not by a primary reality-dislocating doxastic disturbance, but by a more broadly construed disposition to become *detached* in one way or another from certain critical features of reality.

Thus, Eric Marcus (1992, p. 8) conceives of psychosis as "a psychic disturbance in . . . reality-based control"; Edith Jacobson (1967, p. 20) speaks of the psychotic individual as having "give[n] up" reality; Sigmund Freud (1961, p. 151) judged the psychotic ego to have been "torn away from reality"; and the *DSM III-R* defines "psychosis" in terms of a "[g]ross impairment in reality testing." (The definition continues "and the creation of a new reality." But if there are, as there appear to be, psychoses wholly dominated by the negative doxastic condition, then this addition is improper.) Although what typically follows such broadly framed construals of psychosis is a DPCP, such a narrow conceptualization of psychosis is not entailed by any of the aforementioned characterizations. For there are other, non-doxa-primary ways in which one can become psychotically detached from reality.

Consider again the concept of delusion. Contrary to popular belief, delusional beliefs are not necessarily false. Hence, the content of an occurrently held delusional belief is not what is essentially disordered; rather, what is primarily disordered are those cognitive processes that only typically happen to produce wildly non-veridical beliefs. The *DSM III-R* locates this disturbed cognitive process in the psychotic's inability to make proper inferences — "When a person is psychotic, he or she incorrectly evaluates the accuracy of his or her perceptions and thoughts and makes incorrect inferences about external reality, even in the face of contrary evidence" (p. 404) — but this is a mistake. Surely one could both be psychotic *and* infer impeccably from seriously defective premises that one takes as basic.

It is possible, as I (and Fulford, 1989) see it, for a person to have many and varied beliefs, to have only true beliefs, and yet to be psychotic. What is disordered in such a person is not the *content* of her beliefs — they're all true accidentally, but true nonetheless — but the neuropsychic *mechanism* that mediates belief fixation. In such cases, this mechanism malfunctions so that even if her circumstances had been relevantly different, her beliefs might have remained essentially the same. There is a rigidity to some subset of this person's beliefs because of a dispositional insensitivity in some of her belief-forming mechanisms to the reality of her circumstances. Even on the dominant traditional view of psychosis, one's suffering from impaired "reality testing" does not entail that any of one's beliefs are actually false, but only that some of one's reality-monitoring doxastic mechanisms are insensitive to certain features of what is real and, hence, are defective in a way in which some subset of one's beliefs *typically* turn out to be false.

Such an insensitivity of one's reality-monitoring mechanisms to certain features of what is real falls under the broadest and most general sense of psychosis as involving a disposition to become detached from certain critical features of reality. But a disposition to become detached from reality in this sense can involve *either* a doxastic *or* an appetitive dislocation of one's self from certain facets of what is real; it includes, for example, states of emotional independence and aloofness in which one does not care for, love, or take any interest in certain features of reality. To be detached from something involves, as Roberts (this volume, b) suggests, not having one's emotional responses conditioned by that thing. It involves, in other words, not being "subject to the vicissitudes of that thing" (p. 207). So there are non-doxa-primary ways in which one can become psychotically detached from reality.

Both the present broad construal of psychosis and doxa-primary conceptions rely conceptually on metaphysical judgments, that is, judgments concerning the nature of *reality*. What counts as an impairment in reality testing varies with one's concept of reality. Christian psychopathologists will diverge from their non-Christian counterparts in their diagnostic judgments concerning the presence or absence of psychosis insofar as they differ in their respective ontologies (Roberts, this volume, a; Vitz, this volume; Griffiths, this volume). But this divergence should not cause alarm; rather, it should be expected and welcomed. It is, as I see it, quite appropriate for Christian psychopathologists, as well as other Christian practitioners and scientists, to appeal to *all* that they know — whether by reason, by experience, or by faith — in forming judgments concerning what is real and, consequently, in devising diagnostic systems that reflect the variety of ways in which one may become detached from what is real.

The Place of Desire in Action and Life

The psychopathologist's traditional, almost singular, characterization of psychosis in terms of belief states is, on its face, puzzling. Why are beliefs privileged in this way? We are, after all, not only believing creatures; we are also desiring creatures. In fact, defenders of one of the most influential contemporary theories of human action (Davidson, 1980; Goldman, 1970) — the theory which Fred Dretske (1992, p. 2) calls the "orthodox view" — posit that belief-desire *pairs* causally contribute to every human action. And it seems intuitively clear that desires and emotions are as much a way of relating to reality — getting it right or wrong — as beliefs.

Moreover, how we act is, on several accounts of religious and philosophical anthropology, intimately related to who we *are*. "A good tree," Jesus said, "cannot produce bad fruit, nor can a rotten tree produce good fruit" (Matthew 7:18). According to traditional Christian anthropology, our actions are reflections of our *selves*; and if it is also the case, as in Davidson's "orthodox" account, that our actions are causal consequences of our desires, then it is plausible to suppose that our desires, as well as our beliefs, are reflections of our selves. In fact, many of the most influential theories of the self have considered desire dispositions to be *essential constitutive features* of our selves (see, for example, Frankfurt, 1988).

Desires, of course, come in various strengths and persist for various durations; they can be strong or weak, fleeting or permanent, or somewhere in between. In addition, they can be occurrent or dispositional, thin (bare appetitive forces) or thick (richly informed with reason), ego-dystonic or ego-syntonic, loosely tied to the periphery or firmly anchored to the core of one's self. According to Aristotle's *Nicomachean Ethics*, not only are the appetites essential core constituents of human selves, generically considered, but the proper organization of desire, thickly construed, plays a pivotal role in the constitution of mature, flourishing, properly functioning human beings. (For a clear and concise introduction to Aristotle's *Ethics*, see Lear, 1988.) Aristotle's moral virtues are, most fundamentally, sets of passions, properly ordered by reason. Excellent or virtuous character, therefore, is a complex intertwining of those doxastic and appetitive dispositions by which one performs well the functions distinctive to human beings. Thus, to evaluate a human action — and the human self from which it comes — one must consider the structure of the passions that seek the end that the action aims at. An excellent human act, Aristotle argues, is conatively seamless; it is performed neither with regret nor with any other internal divisions in its motivating principle. Not surprisingly, a similar view is held by Aquinas (1948, 1a2ae, 56, 59, 69).

Aristotle distinguishes four character types, *viz.* the virtuous, the vicious, the weak-willed, and the self-controlled. Having a virtuous character is a prerequisite for human flourishing; the other character types represent varieties of denuded or deformed humanity. For instance, although the self-controlled reliably perform the right actions, they do so only from within a conative matrix of internal struggle. Someone who abstains from alcohol only by regularly overcoming intense cravings for rye whiskey is sometimes called a "dry drunk." Such a person is self-controlled, rather than temperate (temperance being the virtue of desiring just those bodily pleasures which it is good to fulfill). While such a self-controlled person consistently performs numerous daily *acts of temperance*, i.e., numerous daily refrainings from drinking alcohol, such a person does not, in those instances, *act as a temperate person would do,* for such a person would not have the dry drunk's desire for too much whiskey.

This distinction between performing acts characteristic of a virtue and acting fully virtuously is important. (Aristotle's only explicit example of it involves distinguishing acts of justice from acting as a just man would.) Early in our development we do not act from virtue, because we have not yet developed a virtuous character from which to act. Yet, during those times we are able to perform acts characteristic of the virtues, i.e., we can imitate the actions a virtuous person would perform in similar circumstances. To become virtuous we must traverse a developmental period during which we again and again, in the varying circumstances of life, perform *simulacra* of fully virtuous acts, for only so can we develop those traits, with their attendant habits of judgment, which enable us to act virtuously. The Aristotelian model for moral development, therefore, privileges "acting virtuously" — a kind of acting grounded in rational desires — over mere "acts of virtue" in a thinner sense and, hence, this model privileges acting temperately (i.e., acting from the characterologi-cally grounded disposition of temperance) over the performance of mere acts of temperance. The deficiency of the dry drunk, as compared with the temperate person, is that some of her desires have not yet been con-formed to the standards of reason.

Ways that Appetites Can Disconnect Us from Reality

Any well-formed and exhaustive taxonomy of human dysfunction must acknowledge that profound self-disintegration can take the form of dis-ordered desire. Addictions are the paradigms of such disorders. The psy-chiatric community should take up the task of carving out conceptual space for appetitive disorders of psychotic proportions. I want to look first at ways in which appetites can be delusional, and then at another way they can disconnect us from reality.

Desires can be delusional in at least two ways. The first derives from the fact that we can have beliefs about our *desires*, the second from the fact that we can (and typically do) have beliefs about the *objects* of our desires, beliefs that are conceptually connected to the desires themselves. Or to put the matter another way, the first derives from the fact that desires are properties of a subject (person), and the second from the fact that desires are for an object under some description. Let us look at an example that illustrates each of these forms of appetitive delusion.

Consider a sex addict. He has the impression that sex is his most important need. Perhaps this impression is overwhelmingly vivid and possessed of impressive verisimilitude when he is presented with an en-ticing sex object and has been a while without having intercourse. This self-impression (for it is an impression *about himself*, a reflexive impression) has a vivacity and verisimilitude rivalling that of a sense impression — say, the visual impression that there is a red Chevrolet station wagon before him, in good light. In other words, it's an impression that it may be hard not to believe. But if our addict can get "outside" his appetite and the impression it carries, get a perspective on it that is informed by a saner order of values, he may *not* believe it, despite the power of the impression. (If you have some reason to think your impression of a red Chevy is a hallucination, you may not believe it either, despite its vivacity and experiential verisimilitude.) The perspective that the addict will have to take in order not to be deluded by his appetite is constituted of a set of considerations about his own life — what is valuable and therefore desirable in it. For example, if the consideration that his relationship to his wife and children is of great value can come to have some "weight" for him — if he can have a bit of *impression* of this value — then he may not be deluded by the impression generated by his addiction. In this case, though he is an addict and has disordered appetites, he is not psychotically addicted, because he has resources for doxastically resisting the false impression created by his appetite. An addict who does not have these impression-resources, but instead is impelled headlong into a state of belief that his present sexual appetite is the greatest need and most important desire of his life — this addict is psychotic, at least for the perhaps brief time that the addictional appetite holds sway over him. We can distinguish two versions of this sort of delusion, one in which the delusion comes and goes with episodes of appetite (once the appetite is satisfied, the addict reverts to awareness that the appetite's reflexive proposition was false all along); and another version in which the addict is dispositionally convinced of the truth of the delusive proposition, and does not have episodes (or not very frequent ones) of insight.

The second kind of appetitive delusion is related to the first, but is not a delusion about the addict himself but about the object of his desire. Desire, as Aquinas teaches, posits the goodness of its object. It may also posit the axiological indifference of objects other than that of the desire. So our sex addict, for example, may not only believe that intercourse with this present woman is *his* greatest *need*; it may also look to him like *the* greatest *good*. Now I admit that these two perceptions may be phenomenologically indiscriminable for the addict, yet I think there is a difference between them which we, as analysts of the mind, may discern. There is certainly a conceptual difference between the two objects. But we can see the importance of this dimension of addictional delusion by considering what truths are rendered inaccessible and unrecognizable to the addict by the working of his appetite on his cognitive powers. For in the moment of appetitive delusion the addict cannot see the value of his family life. He cannot see its moral beauty. He cannot see his duty. And most essentially, for the Christian psychologist, the appetitively deluded person cannot see God; God "does not exist" for him. It is of course possible for people who do not perceive God to believe in God nevertheless; but the person I intend to be describing at the moment is so completely "contained" in his appetite, so completely unable to see beyond it and its present object, that he cannot even believe in this rather attenuated sense. If God is real, and indeed the best thing in the universe, then somebody who has been rendered, by his disordered appetite, unable even to believe that he exists, is psychotic. (An Aristotelian implication of the above considerations is that some things cannot be perceived without being cared about. God is one of these, and the value of family life is another. This connection between perception and caring is basic to the possibility of the appetitive delusions that I am calling attention to.)

So we can be deluded about our desires and about the objects of our desires (or non-desire, as in the last-mentioned case), in the sense that false beliefs about these things are generated by severely disordered appetite. But if we allow the wider conception of psychosis that I commended in the section "The Place of Delusion in Psychosis," a conception in which the alienation from reality need not take a doxastic form, we can perhaps find a third way to conceptualize the alienation by disordered appetite that we call psychosis. The sex addict's all-consuming appetite is a form of psychosis not only because it deludes (generates false beliefs and disbeliefs) but also because it alienates its subject from reality — his own and that of the universe in which he lives.

We would certainly distort the mischief of psychosis if we stressed exclusively its doxastic implications. The psychotic "suffers" in ways that are not captured by saying that he believes false propositions and disbelieves true ones. It is not just his beliefs about reality, but his whole intercourse with it, that is disrupted. Desires can be reasonable in at least two senses. The first sense is visible in our previous discussion. Desires make "statements" about the importance, value, or desirability of their objects, in the sense that they are, or create, impressions of the value of their objects which may be believed or not believed, just as sense impressions can be believed or not believed. When the impressions that desires involve are veridical — when the object has the value that the desire attributes to it — then the desire is reasonable; when it gives a distorted impression of the value of the object, it is unreasonable. The second sense is related to the first, but distinguishable from it. Desires (or more broadly, concerns) connect us with reality in a variety of ways for which there are norms for human beings. It is good, and part of the flourishing human life, to have bodily appetites — to desire food, sexual contact, environmental temperature within a certain range, etc. A person who is "insensitive" to these goods is, as Aristotle says, not flourishing. Other concerns are less "bodily." A concern for the well-being of one's own offspring is also part of the flourishing life, which we also share with the nonrational animals.

But we have a form of life that requires still other desires and concerns. In the Aristotelian tradition it is part of mature human nature to desire the truth about the world, to have friends, and to be concerned about one's political community. To these concerns Christianity adds that a flourishing life includes a love of one's neighbor and a love for God that supersedes, in principle, all other concerns. We can see that concerns connect us in a variety of ways to features of the world in which we live, and that to be healthy is to have a variety of concerns and kinds of concerns, all arranged in some kind of interconnected balance.

Against this background, it is pretty obvious why the sex addict is not flourishing. It is not just that he has false beliefs about the world and himself, but that his inordinate appetite for sex cuts him off from many goods to which the normal person is connected by proper concerns, loves, attachments, and desires: his family, his political community, objects of intellectual pursuit, objects of beauty, his neighbor, and his God. In one translation of Plato's *Apology* (Rouse, 1956), Socrates speaks of his mission as that of getting each Athenian who would listen to him to achieve "the proper order of his care" (36C). Cares connect us with our world, but they have to be properly ordered to their objects and to one another. Addicts live an unnatural life, a life at odds with the design-plan for human beings, because their addictional desires are not only poorly ordered to their objects, but disrupt the other ways in which the normal person is connected, via desires and concerns, to reality.

The Ubiquity of Psychopathology

Suppose I am right: suppose addictions are in fact sometimes psychotically disordered appetitive states. What follows? Isn't our victory merely verbal? Apart from classifying these disorders differently, won't we proceed with business as usual? We won't, for example, treat addicts with antipsychotic (or neuroleptic) medications as a result, will we?

Perhaps we will and perhaps we won't. We know, for example, that certain mood disorders can only be treated optimally when their psychotic component is recognized and neuroleptics are added to the treatment regimen. But we also know that not all individuals afflicted with psychoses are amenable to neuroleptic treatment. In fact, some paradigmatic psychoses typically fail to respond to neuroleptics, e.g., classical paranoia and some induced psychotic disorders. Whether a subgroup of addicts might best be treated with traditional antipsychotic medications is an empirical question that I won't pursue right now. A therapeutic response to "antipsychotic" medications is neither necessary nor sufficient for being psychotic; just as a therapeutic *non*-response is neither necessary nor sufficient for being *non*-psychotic.

A deeper objection to classifying addiction states as psychotic goes like this: the breadth of the principles that sanction this reclassification would qualify a myriad of other conditions, which are currently considered non-psychotic, as psychotic. But surely there could not be so much psychosis amongst us, could there?

This objection parallels a commonly voiced objection to what is taken to be the over-sensitivity of psychoanalytic diagnostic criteria to the presence of psychopathology. The fine-grained classificatory schemes peculiar to psychoanalysis are often thought to entail a "thesis of the ubiquity of psychopathology." According to this thesis, *everyone*, with the possible exception of the unborn, is psychopathologically afflicted. On this model, there are no psychopathological false negatives, because there are no psychopathological negatives, though there can be misdiagnoses of particular cases. (For a thoughtful response to this objection to psychoanalysis, as well as a fascinating defense of the thesis, see Berger, 1991.)

Psychoanalysts tend to regard addictions not as diagnostic entities in themselves, but as symptoms of some deeper dysfunction. I find this view compelling: Addictionologists who identify addictive symptoms with "addictive disease" fail to notice the disordered underlying psychic structures that generate the symptoms. (See Berger, 1991. For some non-analytic exceptions to this rule, see Shedler and Block, 1990.)

Although psychiatrists and psychologists almost unanimously deny that a *single specific* pathological structure is common to all non-organically affected addicts, many affirm the presence of varying degrees of antecedent general pathology in most or all substance-abusers (see Sutker and Allain, 1988; Shedler and Block, 1990; Weiss, Mirin, Griffin, Gunderson, and Hufford, 1993; DeJong, Van den Brink, Harteveld, and Van der Wielen, 1993). Leon Wurmser (1978) states, for example, that "[t]here is ample, but chaotic, unsystematic, scattered evidence for the clinical adage that heavy drug use is the consequence of, not the origin for, severe psychopathology" (p. 67). He couches his understanding of addictive disorders in a rich theory of neuroses in which "part identities" are bred as a result of internecine superego conflicts (which he calls a "superego split"): "It is as if for a brief moment another personality, another consciousness, took over and steered all behavior in the direction of some primitive wish fulfillment" (p. 185; see also Wurmser, 1985). For both theoretical and inductive reasons, the psychoanalyst expects to find layers of pathological structures in the course of analysis and, in the light of this expectation, employs subtle tools of psychic excavation in an effort to uncover that pathology which his discipline takes to be ubiquitous.

Something about this view is deeply right. For the Christian, the paradigmatic example of mental health is our Lord Jesus Christ. To the extent that we lack his wisdom, courage, compassion, justice, charity, and overall appetite-organization, we are psychopathological; and this includes everyone, for according to revealed truth everyone except for Christ (and perhaps Mary, the *Theotokos* or God-bearer) suffers from the appetite-disordering ravages of original sin. The Christian psychopathologist feels quite at home here, for he too embraces a version of the ubiquity thesis, although usually under other names ("total depravity," "original sin," "original guilt," "sin nature," etc.).

Consider alcoholism again. Long-term abstinence can be achieved in many ways, but none is adequate, psychoanalysts contend, if the character defects that underlie the alcoholic's addictive symptomology are neglected. Because most analysts do not recognize addictive disorders as distinct diagnostic entities, they do not tailor their diagnostic schemes or therapeutic interventions to the prominent appetitive symptoms that dominate these syndromes. (Brickman, 1988, dissents.) Rather, they take the addict's underlying psychic structure to be disordered, and to reflect a pre-existing, perhaps pre-oedipal, psychopathology. This underlying structure causes what Louis S. Berger (1991, p. 117) calls the addict's "preemptive, impervious need to avoid unbearable tensions and psychic pain." If the analyst's goal — integrative well-being — were attainable, then moderate social drinking would be a genuine possibility for the recovered alcoholic. This surprisingly controversial suggestion has been forcefully advanced by D. L. Davies (1963).

Sin and Psychosis

The experiential and behavioral similarity between addiction and sin is striking. Cornelius Plantinga (this volume) recognizes the depth of this similarity, even stating that certain appetitive activities can themselves constitute sinful acts. He notes that some sin is independent of addiction (e.g., certain cases of sloth) and some addiction is independent of all except original sin (e.g., cases of intrauterine addiction), and says the relationship between sin and addiction involves "significantly overlapping circles" (this volume, p. 259), the overlap occurring in those areas in which sin (especially *appetitive* sin) displays what Plantinga calls "the dynamics of addiction" (this volume, p. 260).

This is illuminating. It highlights both the psychopathological nature of sin and the spirit-corrupting nature of addiction by pointing out that, in addiction as in sin, one's appetites are fused to perceived temporal goods and, consequently, fiercely rent from one's ultimate end. In this manner, addictive disorder (like the disorder of sin), in virtue of an underlying reality-rupturing psychic disturbance, tends to express itself in wild, episodic, and explosive surges of disordered desire, which detach one both from that which *is* most real and from that which *makes* one most real.

We are, according to the Christian tradition, the heirs of corruption resulting from the sin of our progenitor, Adam. To say our sin state pathology is pre-oedipal is, therefore, true but massively understated. We have, it appears, been afflicted from conception (although not, at that stage, *psycho*pathologically afflicted). We have been conceived in corruption, although in a way whose distinctive psychopathological manifestations in the phenomenology and behavior of sinning do not become evident until much later in our lives, just as, according to psychoanalytic theory, the addictive symptomology associated with the intrapsychic disturbance that underlies addictions does not, in the typical case, declare itself until well after the oedipal period. Addiction and sin both originate in primitive pathologies that tend to erupt in protean maladaptive guises. The various kinds of sinning and the various kinds of addiction can all be traced to that distinctive self-disintegrating human insult we Christians call sin — a wounding so deep, so acute, and so inflamed that it dehisces as soon as any purely natural attempt is made to close it. The fundamental problem to be remedied in both cases is the underlying state, not the superficial expression of it. For the alcoholic to stop drinking alcohol is merely a first step, just as to stop sinning in some particular way is merely a first step. Full healing demands a complete inward reordering.

In human beings sin is an impulse toward self-destruction; a morbid drive toward death fueled by that destructive psychic energy whose source is original sin. It is an impulse that cuts us off from the very source of reality, from the most real of beings — from the personal ground of all reality, from Him who is most real. To sin, then, is to place oneself out of touch with the only feature of reality that ultimately matters. Plantinga says it well: the essence of sin is brokenness and betrayal; it is most fundamentally a "breaking of covenant with one's Savior [and] a betrayal of the partner to whom one is joined by a holy bond" (this volume, p. 246). In sum, he says, "sin is culpable shalom-breaking" (p. 247), a culpable disordering of the universal flourishing, wholeness, and delight for which we were created. So construed, sinful acts are psychotic — acts which, by virtue of their disordered psychic wellspring, place one out of touch with reality at its deepest and most personal level. The sinner and the psychotic belong in the same diagnostic category. Having taken this step, we have gone beyond a generally characterized thesis of the ubiquity of psychopathology to the thesis of the ubiquity of *psychosis*.

We Are All Psychotic

My central point is partly terminological, but far from being *merely* ter-minological. Historically, changes in nomenclature by themselves change both our conception of, and our interrelationships with, other human beings. The general claim that changes in the classification schemes in which human beings are situated can alter social perceptions and, con-sequently, interpersonal relations, is neither novel nor controversial. It is a fact recognized and elaborated by, among many others, Michel Foucault (1973) and "psychopathology eliminativists" like Thomas Szasz (1961) and Theodore Sarbin (1967; see also Sarbin and Juhasz, 1978).

Szasz denies that anyone is mentally ill. Sarbin agrees, and adds that no one in any ordinary sense hallucinates. According to Szasz, people who are thought to be suffering from mental illness are merely having certain "problems in living." According to Sarbin, those believing them-selves to be hallucinating are merely falsely believing that they are being appeared to in a perceptual sort of way. The upshot is that the so-called "mentally ill" and those who are "hallucinating" are really a lot more like the rest of us than we thought. All of us have believed falsely at some time or other, and all have experienced various problems in living; whereas (if we retain the old classificatory scheme) not all of us have (while awake) hallucinated well-formed images and distinct voices nor suffered from what psychopathologists presently call "mental illness."

In a deep and interesting way, Szasz and Sarbin are attempting to alter our social perceptions by reclassifying those who are presently called "mentally ill" into less remote and more humane taxonomic categories, categories which affirm that the "mentally ill" are fit to enjoy the social goods accorded to "normal" members of the community. The intended result is to make individuals who presently appear alien and frightening to us appear more familiar and less frightening. Szasz and Sarbin insist that they are moved by both practical and theoretical considerations, and hence that their versions of eliminativism conduce not only to a more stable society but also to a more veridical conception of humanity.

The direction in which Sarbin and Szasz would like to take us is both laudable and profoundly troubling. I applaud their vision of a society that respects and welcomes the active participation of those who are presently classified as mentally ill. It is both true and tragic that many who have been labeled mentally ill have suffered indignity as a result of social misconceptions of their unfortunate plight. Many have been treated cruelly, ostracized from civil society, and looked upon as something less than human — as aliens, novelties, Bedlamic curios, and foci of animality, passion, and unreason.

But this situation can be remedied in more than one way. One remedy ought to be especially appealing to Christians, for it retains what we understand, by the light of reason and of faith, to be the core insights of a true conception of humanity, namely, the traditional Christian view of human nature as fallen and redeemable. This rich and thick anthropology is informed by all we know — whether by empirical investigation, casual observation, or special revelation. (See Alvin Plantinga's [1990] words encouraging us to avail ourselves of *all* that we know as Christians — whatever the source of our knowledge — in our attempts to understand the mysteries the world presents to us.)

Szasz's and Sarbin's reclassification seems to me wrongheaded; and its error is deep, pernicious, and instructive. From a Christian point of view, the fragmented, disorganized, and detached psychotic self is ubiquitous. This ubiquity is, at its deepest, traceable to the corruption we have inherited, and with which we identify in every act of sinning. If so, then it is not, as Sarbin and Szasz argue, that those who are presently called mentally ill are in reality a lot more like us than we imagined, but *we* are a lot more like *them*.

To possess an even rudimentary understanding of the nature and pervasiveness of sin is to understand that we are all deeply disordered, psychically disintegrated, psychopathologically constituted and, to that extent, out of touch with what is most real. It is to appreciate that we are afflicted in psychotic proportions. At just this point Cornelius Plantinga's deepest insight into the relationship between sin and addiction surfaces. He writes,

> [E]ven when they do not display the full addictive syndrome, many forms of sin include patterns of self-seeking, childish impatience with delayed gratification, and refusal to accept reasonable limits on behavior. In addition, sin, like addiction, tends to split and bind the will . . . and to hide itself under layers of self-deception. Moreover, people often commit sins in order to relieve distress caused by other sins. . . . Hence the familiar spiral shape of certain patterns of sin.
>
> In these and many other ways addiction extends a tradition familiar to all of us, including all of us who would never dream of calling ourselves addicts. (this volume, pp. 261-62)

Plantinga continues, borrowing from William Lenters (1985), "In important respects, 'the addiction experience is the human experience' since we all 'have a habit' where sin is concerned" (Plantinga, p. 262). So too, I have suggested, the psychotic experience is the human experience, since we have all, in virtue of sin, dissociated ourselves from our ultimate end, and thereby dislocated our selves from the very font of reality.

Reflecting on addiction — on gross appetitive dysfunction — enables us to see that the notion of psychosis has a broader extension than previously believed. Reflecting on sin — on gross spiritual dysfunction — enables us to see that the notion of sinful acts as psychotic acts, and of sinful selves as psychotically disorganized selves, reaches out and snares each one of us. If both the psychoanalytic thesis concerning the ubiquity of psychopathology and the Christian faith are true, then Szasz and Sarbin do not merely err, but interestingly reverse the truth. The Christian psychopathologist does well to side with the psychoanalyst in this debate. Both the theoretical and the practical advantages of doing so far outweigh the advantages expected by Sarbin and Szasz. For the specially revealed fact of the matter is that we are all sinful beings, rent from the thickest fabric of reality, and to that extent are all psychotic — beings whose only hope for healing begins with the recognition that our deepest desire can be fulfilled only by a primary attachment to that personal ground of all reality who is God.

The Therapy of Adversity and Penitence

Walter Sundberg

No tree stands firm and sturdy if it is not buffeted by constant wind; the very stresses cause it to stiffen and fix its roots firmly. Trees that have grown in a sunny vale are fragile. It is therefore to the advantage of good men, and it enables them to live without fear, to be on terms of intimacy with danger and to bear with serenity a fortune that is ill only to him who bears it ill.

Seneca, "On Providence"

If we have one character defect that is abhorrent, it is the way we hate and pick on ourselves. That is simply not tolerable nor acceptable any longer. . . . We can nurture ourselves and love ourselves. We can accept our wonderful selves, with all our faults, foibles, strong points, weak points, feelings, thoughts, and everything else. It's the best thing we've got going for us. It's who we are, and who we were meant to be. . . . We are the greatest thing that will ever happen to us. Believe it. It makes life much easier.

Melodie Beattie, *Codependent No More*

Almighty God, Father of our Lord Jesus Christ, Maker of all things, Judge of all men; We acknowledge and bewail our manifold sins and wickedness, Which we, from time to time, most grievously have committed, By thought, word, and deed, Against thy Divine Majesty, Provoking most justly thy wrath and indignation against us. . . . Forgive us all that is past; And grant that we may ever hereafter Serve and please thee In newness of life. . . .

The Book of Common Prayer

Adversity and Morality

Neither the intricacies of theology nor the securities of denominational affiliation guarantee the understanding of religious things. Nor are they always necessary. Sometimes one encounters weighty ideas concerning God and human character that are embedded in the human race, common coin we carry in our collective pocket whether inside or outside a religious community.

Until quite recently, one such common idea, says Charles Sykes in his bestseller, *A Nation of Victims*, was the notion that "adversity" is "the centerpiece of the moral order." The inherited wisdom of generations portrayed the world, not as an arena for human "wish fulfillment" or "self-actualization," but as a testing ground. Calamitous events were accepted as an inevitable part of normal life. The purpose of these events was to challenge human character to become tougher material in a more deeply human shape. "Both classical and Christian societies were cultures of consequence and responsibility" (Sykes, 1992, pp. 45-46).

From its roots in classical culture, the notion that adversity has ennobling significance was vital in the development of the modern secular political tradition beginning with Niccolò Machiavelli and including such thinkers as Thomas Hobbes, Baruch Spinoza, John Locke, Montesquieu, David Hume, Adam Smith, and the founders of the American Republic. The path to self-government that these men charted was hewn on the belief that humanity must make its way in a cold world and that earthly existence is its own end. To realize that one is on one's own can be frightening, but it is, according to these authors, also liberating. It encourages humanity to shape communal life not in slavish obedience to inherited institutions or the blinding light of some utopian dream, but in the realistic appraisal of the human condition. The argument for freedom through adversity that these great minds advanced in a series of classic treatises from *The Prince* to *The Federalist Papers* is summarized by Allan Bloom:

> Unprotectedness, nakedness, unsuccored suffering and the awfulness of death are the prospects that man without illusions must face. But, looking at things from the point of view of already established society, man can be proud of himself. He has progressed, and by his own efforts. He can think well of himself. And now possessing the truth, he can be even freer to be himself and improve his situation. He can freely make governments that, untrammeled by mythical duties and titles to rule, serve his interests. (Bloom, 1987, p. 163)

With the adversity of nature as the measure of things, humanity seeks "freedom": that is, the unfettered use of the "distinctive faculty" of reason to improve its circumstances; to seek happiness where it can find it; and to secure that happiness for as long as possible. "Autonomy," admonishes Bloom, echoing the political philosophers of modernity, "does not mean, as is now generally thought, the fateful, groundless decision in the void, but governing oneself according to the real" (*ibid.*, p. 164).

These claims are not startling or unusual. The idea that human character is shaped by adversity and people should work hard in the face of it has been common teaching through the ages. A casual perusal of Bartlett's *Familiar Quotations*, for example, yields a cloud of witnesses. "Fire is the test of gold," writes Seneca, "adversity of strong men." "Calamity is man's true touchstone," assert the Jacobean dramatists Beaumont and Fletcher. "The natural measure of [character]," states Ralph Waldo Emerson, "is resistance of circumstances." Pithy quotations of this type can be multiplied with ease.

While acceptance of adversity as an opportunity for stoical moral instruction is a general characteristic of the modern secular political tradition, it is by no means confined there. It also has deep religious roots. This is clear in the biblical legacy of Western culture. The Bible connects adversity to penitence as paths to spiritual growth, for it teaches that adversity in human life is *deserved* because it results from our own sinful behavior in rebellion against almighty God. "You love evil more than good," says the Psalmist, "and lying more than speaking the truth. . . . But God will break you down forever; he will snatch and tear you from your tent; he will uproot you from the land of the living" (Ps. 52:3, 6). "God looks down from heaven on humankind. . . . They have fallen away, they are all alike perverse; there is no one who does good, no, not one. . . . [T]hey shall be in great terror, in terror such as has not been" (Ps. 53:2-3, 5). In Thomas Cranmer's *Book of Common Prayer* — the power of which in part comes from its ability to echo the familiarity of the Scriptures — the congregation confesses its sin:

> We have erred and strayed from thy ways like lost sheep. We have followed too much the devices and desires of our own hearts. We have offended against thy holy laws. We have left undone those things which we ought to have done; and we have done those things which we ought not to have done; And there is no health in us.

If we are uprooted from our land, experience great terror, or have no health within us, we must realize that we have ourselves to blame. Far from being an excuse to escape personal responsibility, adversity is a sign of personal responsibility misused. Acceptance of responsibility is the first step on the path to eternal truth and personal integrity.

The Bible also teaches that adversity is an opening for the gift of faith. The tribulations and hardships of life disclose the ultimate meaning of human existence in so far as they weaken allegiance to the world and the flesh and can be the occasion for spiritual regeneration. "For during a severe ordeal of affliction," says Paul, commending the example of the churches of Macedonia to the Corinthians, "their abundant joy and their extreme poverty have overflowed in a wealth of generosity" (1 Cor. 8:2). "For a little while," writes the author of First Peter to the oppressed Christians of the second generation of the faith, "you have had to suffer various trials, so that the genuineness of your faith — being more precious than gold that, though perishable, is tested by fire — may be found to result in praise and glory and honor when Jesus Christ is revealed" (1:6-7). For the Prodigal Son who had squandered his father's inheritance, the test came when "there arose a severe famine" that caught him up short. Then he found himself eating with the swine "and no one gave him anything." A change of heart followed from these calamities: "I will arise and go to my father, and will say to him, 'Father, I have sinned against heaven and before you'" (Luke 15:14-16). It is no wonder that Francis Bacon, in another nugget quoted in Bartlett's, claimed that "adversity is the blessing of the New Testament."

This recognition of the function of adversity was especially characteristic of the children of the Reformation. Whatever else Protestants taught (and whatever divided them), they all preached alike that adversity is within the gracious purposes of almighty God. Adversity forces believers to confront their limitations. It summons them to rise above their difficulties to seek the greatness of spiritual life. "At the heart of the Protestant ethic was the insistence that man labor incessantly to improve himself; only through such efforts could man realize the meaning of life and his place in the order of things" (Sykes, 1992, p. 47).

The inseparable connection between adversity and religion has been so much a part of the tradition of Western thought that even the severest skeptics of orthodox Christian faith have recognized it. When Deists in the eighteenth century tried to make Christianity acceptable by transforming it into an ideal construct of a humanizing, life-enhancing "natural religion" grounded in universal principles of rationality and dedicated to the fostering of human happiness, David Hume responded by offering a sober (if cynical) account of the "natural history" of religion's origins. "Men," he wrote, "are much oftener thrown on their knees by the melancholy than by the agreeable passions." They turn to God not when prosperity rules life but when they are in trouble:

> Every disastrous accident alarms us, and sets us on enquiries concerning the principles whence it arose; Apprehensions spring up with

regard to futurity; And the mind, sunk in diffidence, terror and melancholy, has recourse to every method of appeasing those secret intelligent powers, on whom our fortune is supposed entirely to depend.
(Hume, 1957, p. 31)

For good or for ill, says Hume, adversity is the path to an encounter with
the reality (or the illusion) of the divine.

Aversion to Adversity

Adversity molds character and deepens religious faith. While this may be the
wisdom of the ages, it is not the wisdom of *our* age. "Nothing perhaps
separates modern man from his forebears more definitely than his attitude
toward adversity" (Sykes, 1992, p. 45). We live in a "therapeutic culture,"
in which the personal fulfillment of individual fantasies and desires is the
stated goal. The therapy industry is a child of post–World War II affluence
in which the self is no longer conceived to be a fixed reality constrained
by its obligations and the limitations of the human condition. Its New
Personality has "a single war cry . . . I DESERVE." Quoting Bernie Zilbergeld's *The Shrinking of America: Myths of Psychological Change* (1983), Sykes
lets the New Personality speak: "'I deserve love. I deserve to be trusted.
I deserve freedom. I deserve friendship. I deserve respect. I deserve sexual
pleasure. I deserve happiness'" (p. 41). Adversity is to be avoided, not
embraced; it is not "normal." It is the agent of subjugation and repression,
not illumination and moral progress.

The aspirations of the New Personality created by the therapeutic
culture come at a heavy price. Fulfillment demands "tearing out by force
the mores and norms that [stand] in its way" (p. 50). When the New
Personality does not get its way, it dons the mantle of victim. If nothing
else, the claim that one is a victim releases the New Personality from blame
and obtains attention and sympathy for it. So dominant is this attitude,
especially in the influential precincts of the Knowledge Class, that we are
in danger of becoming "a nation of victims."

The careful scholar may wince at Sykes's sweeping generalizations,
but there is no denying the explanatory power of his thesis. One needs no
more than a nodding acquaintance with current affairs to see its relevance.
For example, since the publication of Sykes's book, we have endured the
sordid spectacle of the trials of Lorena Bobbitt and the Menendez brothers.
In both cases, where the facts of the actual crimes were not under dispute,
the defendants were successfully portrayed as victims by a bevy of paid
therapists who convinced one jury in its entirety and a portion of the other

to reject the prosecutors' most serious charges. After recounting the dismal facts of both trials, Walter Berns, George M. Olin University Professor at Georgetown University, concludes that these juries, and an increasing portion of American society, believe in "the gospel according to Oprah Winfrey, Phil Donahue, Sally Jesse Raphael, and Montel Williams: that 'everybody has a psychology,' and everybody is a victim. . . . Woe to the criminal-justice system that travels down this perverse and awful path" (Berns, 1994, p. 29).

In trials such as these we face nothing less than the legal sanction of the therapeutic culture and the rejection of adversity as a normal condition and penitence as a healthy response. If this happens not just in isolated cases but to a widespread degree (and who is to say that it will not?), then the time-honored truths of our intellectual and religious heritage concerning adversity may no longer be common, but may come to be treated as suspicious ideas that are unjust, illegitimate, perhaps ultimately illegal.

To this situation the church itself may be captive. Consider the argument of a disturbing sociological essay by Marsha G. Witten: *All Is Forgiven: The Secular Message in American Protestantism.* The book analyzes forty-seven sermons on Luke 15:11-32 (the parable of the Prodigal Son) preached by pastors of the Presbyterian Church (U.S.A.) and the Southern Baptist Convention. Witten, who claims no religious affiliation herself, finds in her sample sermons a watered-down Protestant faith accommodating itself to the desires and fantasies of the New Personality. "The transcendent, majestic, awesome God of Luther and Calvin — whose image informed early Protestant visions of the relationship between human beings and the divine — has undergone a softening of demeanor . . ." (Witten, 1993, p. 53). The way God functions in the sermons is largely "therapeutic"; his purpose is to relieve "negative feelings, especially anxiety and doubt" and to do so as painlessly as possible (p. 35).

> God's love [intones a Presbyterian preacher] has no strings attached to it. It cannot be earned. It cannot be shut off, deterred. It cannot be escaped. God loves us as we are. God loves us for what we are and in spite of what we are. There is nothing we can do to make God love us less. God loves us when no one else does. God loves us when we are unlovable. God loves us when we cannot stand ourselves. (p. 37)

Not judgment but unconditional acceptance is the norm. Another Presbyterian puts it this way: "[This is] what God is saying to you. It's not 'Go to your room.' It's come to the party!" (p. 39). Yet another preacher compares the wonder of God's love found in the parable to the feel-good reaction of

Walt Disney movies such as "Dumbo" and "Pinocchio." The happy story of the Prodigal Son may not "jibe with the world in which we must make our way from day to day," but it matches the magical message that Jesus offers us. On this last sermon, Witten comments laconically:

> God's incomprehensible actions, his supernatural qualities, belong to the world of myth and fairy tale, to children's fables, to bedtime stories and their modern Technicolor equivalents. So disenchanted has modern life become that only if one suspends one's critical judgment, turns off one's practical cynicism about the "real" world, views things from the magic point of view of a toddler, and relaxes the discipline of one's cognition, can one tune into a story of an elephant that learns to fly, a puppet that becomes a human being, or a God who so loved the world that he dies for it. (p. 47)

It would appear that the tough realism of traditional wisdom regarding the function of adversity in life is a thing of the past. Perhaps the New Personality, crying "I DESERVE," has taken the Father of the Prodigal Son captive. If so, then we should read the parable this way: "The younger son gathered all together, journeyed to a far country and there wasted his possessions with prodigal living. . . . And there arose a severe famine in that land, and he began to be in want . . . and no one gave him anything. But when he came to himself, he said 'This is not fair. I do not deserve this. I am a victim.' . . . And his father saw him and had compassion, and ran and fell on his neck and kissed him." All, indeed, is forgiven.

A Proposal

Psychiatry and psychology have contributed much to the humanitarian impulse of Western culture since the nineteenth century and they are no doubt here to stay. But their enormous success has certain undeniable costs for which the critical concept of the "therapeutic culture" is a legitimate description. If the "therapeutic culture" is reasonably portrayed by Sykes, Berns, and Witten; if it affects the popular perception of both the nature of humanity and the meaning of human life; if it threatens the preaching of Christian faith by ignoring judgment, discouraging penitence, and cheapening grace; how should we respond? I would argue that to counter the influence of the therapeutic culture in the church we must reaffirm the time-honored connection between the experience of adversity and Christian faith.

One could demonstrate this connection at work in any period in church history by reference to major theological figures. It is especially apparent in the sixteenth century. The sixteenth century — the Age of Reform — is the century of origin of the Protestant tradition in the West. It also reshaped the character of Roman Catholicism. Both Protestants and Catholics continue to live under its shadow. It therefore carries an indisputable weight for our reflections. The Age of Reform represents a different theology from much that is current — so different that even a non-religious sociologist like Marsha Witten can recognize the great reformers to be out-of-synch with contemporary accommodationist preaching (p. 53).

Luther

In Charles Sykes's above-quoted lament for a bygone era, he alludes to "the heart of the Protestant ethic" in which man labors "incessantly to improve himself" (Sykes, 1992, p. 47). Talk about the Protestant ethic has been common ever since Max Weber analyzed the phenomenon in *The Protestant Ethic and the Spirit of Capitalism* at the beginning of the twentieth century. Certainly the notion of a Protestant ethic has been subject to vigorous debate. However this debate is waged, the question on which it focuses is the character of the people that the Protestant movement creates and the historical effects that this character produces.

In its origin, the Protestant ethic took its bearings from traditional Christian piety which "was based," according to Karl Holl, "upon the idea of judgment, a verdict that God would one day render concerning the person's worthiness or unworthiness" (Holl, 1977, p. 17). Martin Luther's theology begins in the candid acknowledgment that we are in rebellion against God; indeed, that we want to be gods ourselves, taking control of all aspects of our lives so that we can get our way.

Luther expresses this concept arrestingly in his early "Scholastic Disputation" of 1517: "Man is by nature unable to want God to be God. Indeed, he himself wants to be God, and does not want God to be God" (*Luther's Works*, vol. 31, p. 10). This is the seat of our unworthiness, the chief evidence in our character that we are enmeshed in a web of sin. Only by facing up to our predicament can we establish a right relationship with our Creator. The function of adversity in life is to instruct us that we are not gods who are able to control all things for the purpose of our desires. In adversity God forces us "to let God be God."

In his exposition of Psalm 90 — which teaches that God "turns us back to dust," that he sweeps us away "like a dream," that he knows our "iniquities" and our "secret sins" — Luther finds the *locus classicus* in the

Bible on the meaning of adversity. He speaks of Moses (the traditional author of Psalm 90) as having the "peculiar divine mission to teach the Law among people." The "office" of lawgiver made Moses "a minister of death, sin, and damnation. His aim is to terrify the proud and to set squarely before the eyes of those who are smug in their sins their terrible condition" (vol. 13, p. 79). In this regard, "Moses rightly refers death to God Himself. He wants to warn us not to look frantically for help any-where except to Him who has caused the evil" (p. 97). Referring to verse 8 ("Thou settest our iniquities before Thee, the sins unknown to us in the light of Thy countenance"), Luther asserts:

> this is the climax of the drama which God enacts with us. His intention is that we play our part in full awareness of our sins and of death. Yet it is not an evil thing . . . to have this awareness, to complain about our miseries, and to conclude that there is nothing within us but damnation. Indeed, one should complain and sigh this way. One should also try to arrange and govern one's life in accordance with such sighing. Then it will happen that one becomes aware of salvation. (pp. 116-17)

The harsh "drama" of life is directed to the "climax" of an unrelenting encounter with adversity. Adversity, rightly understood, begets the "sigh-ing" of penitence, and penitence is preparation for God's healing grace. Adversity is thus the means by which God molds us to his holy will. We should not avoid it; on the contrary, we should be open to it. It is no wonder that Luther said of adversity in another essay:

> God overwhelms us with these things which move us to anger, with many sufferings which rouse us to impatience, and last of all, even with death and the abuse of the world. By means of these he seeks nothing else but to drive out of us anger, impatience, and unrest, and to perfect his own work in us, that is, his peace. (vol. 44, p. 77)

Werner Elert, one of the great Lutheran theologians of the first half of the twentieth century, declares that Luther's exposition of Psalm 90 is the entrance way to Luther's thought because it discloses "with unparal-leled gloom" the "primal experience" *(Urerlebnis)* of the human condition that leads to faith (Elert, 1962, p. 18). We live under the wrath of God. Recognition of this fact is the portal to salvation.

Luther believed that the cultural Christianity of his day obscured this primal experience. The church may baptize people but this is not enough: "for the world and the masses are and always will be un-Christian, even if they are all baptized and Christian in name. Christians are few and far between . . ." (*Luther's Works*, vol. 45, p. 91). Most often the church misleads people in matters of fundamental importance because it is ruled by a hierarchy dedicated to the aggrandizement of worldly power. These rulers believe they can control the gates to heaven by ritual, indulgences, and canon law. This is false. Only when the individual believer, under the power of the Holy Spirit, explicitly faces the truth of the Scriptures can regeneration begin as an act of the entirety of one's life. According to the opening of the "Ninety-five Theses":

> 1. When our Lord and Master Jesus Christ said, "Repent" [Matt. 4:17], he willed the entire life of believers to be one of repentance.
> 2. This word cannot be understood as referring to the sacrament of penance, that is, confession and satisfaction, as administered by the clergy. (vol. 21, p. 35)

What does it mean that the "entire life of believers" is "one of repentance"? It means that we must change our lives. "If you have not believed," exhorts Luther, "believe now."

Among the many ways in which Luther investigated this matter, none was more important for the Catholic culture of his time than the theology of the sacraments. In Baptism and Holy Communion, along with their preparatory and attendant rituals, the life of every Christian believer is marked and sealed.

Luther asserts that Baptism must be linked to the "amendment of life." We are called to plunge into the waters of Baptism daily. This means "that the longer we live the more gentle, patient, and meek we become, and the more free from greed, hatred, envy, and pride." The "external sign" of Baptism is tied to faith and its "fruits." "Where faith is present with its fruits, there Baptism is no empty symbol but the effect accompanies it; but where faith is lacking, it remains a mere unfruitful sign" (Tappert, 1959, p. 445).

Luther's seriousness with regard to sacramental practice is evident in the liturgical language he was willing to adopt. In March, 1525, a pastor from Zwickau by the name of Nicholas Hausmann sent Luther a number of proposed "German Masses" for review. The only revision Luther made was the addition of "An Exhortation to the Communicants," the text of which is as follows:

> Dearest friends in Christ: You know that our Lord Jesus Christ, out of unspeakable love, instituted at the last this his Supper as a memorial and proclamation of his death suffered for our sins. This commemora-

tion requires a firm faith to make the heart and conscience of everyone who wants to use and partake of this Supper sure and certain that Christ has suffered death for all his sins. But whoever doubts and does not in some manner feel such faith should know that the Supper is of no avail to him, but will rather be to his hurt, and he should stay away from it. And since we cannot see such faith and it is known only to God, we leave it to the conscience of him who comes and admit him who requests and desires it. But those who cling to open sins, such as greed, hatred, anger, envy, profiteering, unchastity, and the like and are not minded to renounce them, shall herewith be barred [from the Supper] and be warned faithfully not to come lest they incur judgment and damnation for their own souls, as St. Paul says [1 Cor. 11:29]. If however someone has fallen because of weakness and proves by his acts that he earnestly desires to better himself, this grace and communion of the body and blood of Christ shall not be denied to him. In this fashion each must judge himself and look out for himself. For God is not mocked [Gal. 6:7], nor will he give that which is holy unto dogs or cast pearls before swine [Matt. 7:6]. (*Luther's Works*, vol. 53, pp. 104-5)

This remarkable exercise in worship is meant to confront the believer existentially with the truth of the human predicament. Unfortunately, it has been rarely replicated in contemporary liturgical practice among Lutherans. Popular worship today in Lutheran churches usually revolves around assurances of salvation spoken in the indicative mood accompanied increasingly by contemporary hymns in a pop style with upbeat lyrics and peppy tunes. Sober, therapeutically penitential worship is out; celebration is in.

This is not to say that Luther's application of adversity to sacramental theology and worship had no effect. Historically at least, the opposition of true Christianity and ritual or sacerdotal Christianity that marks Luther's thought comes up again and again in the Lutheran tradition, even to the point of becoming a subversive polemic in regional Lutheran churches. In 1855, for example, Søren Kierkegaard treated the issue in his typically provocative manner as he wrote about the Danish state church's baptismal practice:

The interest of Christianity, what it wants, is — true Christians. The egoism of the priesthood, both for pecuniary advantage and for the sake of power, stands in relation to — many Christians. "And that's very easily done, it's nothing at all: let's get hold of the children, then each child is given a drop of water on the head — then he is a Christian. If a portion of them don't even get their drop, it comes to the same thing, if only they imagine they got it, and imagine consequently that they are Christians. So in a very short time we have more Christians than there are herring in the herring season." (Kierkegaard, 1968, p. 147)

Perhaps in our day there will arise another Kierkegaard to point the way.

Calvin and Loyola

Whatever differences Luther and Calvin may have had, the honest appraisal of the individual's predicament before God is a basic insight they shared. "[T]rue and sound wisdom," wrote Calvin at the very beginning of *The Institutes of the Christian Religion,* "consists of two parts: the knowledge of God and of ourselves" (Calvin, 1960, vol. 1, p. 35). The link between these two sources of knowledge is forged when a human being faces up to his utter sinfulness and the desperation of his circumstances. Adversity leads to consciousness of sin, which leads to faith. It is from "our own ignorance, vanity, poverty, infirmity, and — what is more — depravity and corruption, we recognize that the true light of wisdom, sound virtue, full abundance of every good, and purity of righteousness rest in the Lord alone." This "clear knowledge" is never man's "unless he has first looked upon God's face, and then descends from contemplating him to scrutinize himself" (pp. 36, 37). The chief resource to measure ourselves is the Bible, opened to us by the power of the Holy Spirit who brings the gift of regeneration. The harsh self-examination that we are called to exercise includes the candid appraisal of the governing structures of the church and society as well as inherited practices.

If our angle of vision on the sixteenth century is the issue of regeneration through adversity and penitence, then the Protestant reformers were not the only ones engaged in this task. I agree with H. Outram Evennett that, "the Reformation on its religious side and the Counter Reformation on its religious side can reasonably be regarded as two different outcomes of the general aspiration towards religious regeneration which pervaded late fifteenth- and early sixteenth-century Europe" (Evennett, 1970, p. 9). In Roman Catholicism, this aspiration issued in a spirituality which, according to Evennett, "reflected the bustle and energy and determination of sixteenth-century man . . ." (p. 32).

There is no better example of this than Ignatius Loyola. *The Spiritual Exercises* may be fairly described as an invitation to the individual to confront the experience of adversity and embrace it in order "to conquer himself" and attain his proper end: obedience to the First Commandment

(Loyola, 1964, p. 47). Since the human soul commonly has "inordinate inclinations or attachments," one must "work as forcefully as possible to attain the contrary of that to which the present attachment tends" (p. 41). This means engaging in "activity of all kinds" and "striving after self-control and the acquisition of virtues" (Evennett, p. 31). A simple example is the practice of beating one's breast. "Each time one falls into the particular sin or defect," says Loyola, "he should place his hand on his breast, repenting that he has fallen. This can be done even in the presence of many people without their noticing it" (1964, p. 49). By such an exercise we begin to take the measure of sin and reverse its power over us. The spiritual exercises Loyola describes are only for "the persons who wish to make them" (p. 41). They may be practiced in a concentrated fashion if one is willing to retreat from the affairs of the world or they may be undertaken slowly over time if one has responsibilities in social life that remain pressing. In either case, they require a person to undergo the agony of change as he or she bends the will to the purpose of God.

Loyola's approach to character formation has neither the optimism about man that characterizes Renaissance humanism nor the pessimism regarding human capability that marks the theologies of Luther and Calvin. Evennett describes it, accurately and sympathetically, in these terms:

> The counter-reformation doctrine of Christian struggle and effort, laborious, long, chequered, perilous, but aided, fostered and eased by systematic precepts and counsels representing accumulated wisdom and experience, announced that Man — even in face of his Almighty Creator — carried, to some extent, his own fate in his own hands. (p. 36)

Struggle, effort, peril; the recognition of one's fate: is this not the basic acknowledgment that truth and the meaning of life are won through adversity? Does this not bear a significant and not merely superficial similarity to the standard descriptions of the "Protestant ethic"? Luther, Calvin, and Loyola each called the individual Christian to the arduous journey of explicit faith. Only in this way could the individual and the church be renewed.

The Christian imperative to face up to the truth about ourselves is the essence of the critical spirit of the Age of Reform. All things must be brought into conformity with God's word. Perhaps Calvin speaks for Protestant and Catholic alike when he asserts: "For our wisdom ought to be nothing else than to embrace with humble teachableness, and at least without finding fault, whatever is taught in Sacred Scripture" (Calvin, 1960, p. 237).

Toward a Christian Psychology

While I do not presume to speak to the matter of Roman Catholic appropriation of its sixteenth-century heritage, I do wish to say something about the Protestant use of its Reformation tradition. The problem with the "Protestant ethic" since the sixteenth century is that it has been too easy for Christian intellectuals to separate its critical spirit from the "humble teachableness" that its doctrine of man originally demanded. Two centuries after Luther, Gotthold Ephraim Lessing spoke for an entire generation when he said that "The true Lutheran does not wish to be defended by Luther's writings but by Luther's spirit; and Luther's spirit absolutely requires that no man may be prevented from advancing in the knowledge of the truth according to his own judgment" (Lessing, 1957, p. 23). The encounter with adversity which motivated the reformers was replaced with a confidence in the privatized self that is the hallmark of Enlightened reason. Protestants continued to be rebellious, but this rebelliousness got detached from the "primal experience" of human corruptibility, at least among influential intellectuals who claimed to carry on the Protestant heritage. This is the tradition of "liberal Protestantism" which has spawned a "Protestant ethic" defiant of the tradition out of which it comes.

In his recent book, *Protestants: The Birth of a Revolution*, Steven Ozment of Harvard gives an especially provocative description of this modern Protestant ethic, shorn of its sixteenth-century roots:

> Protestantism was born, after all, in reaction to failing spiritual leadership and church piety. In their place the reformers attempted to create a simple and effective alternative. Now, as then, Protestants are society's most spiritually defiant and venturesome citizens. When it comes to making their spiritual and moral lives whole, they have not hesitated to sacrifice institutions to conscience, unity to efficiency, and obedience to results. . . . In a quest for a religious life that works, they unhesitatingly change churches and denominations, shedding the spiritual truths of yesterday as if they were just another bad investment or failed love-affair. No other modern religious communion is marked by such variety and mobility. (Ozment, 1992, p. xiii)

We have already seen in Witten's study how the "shedding of the spiritual truths of yesterday" can lead to a new, accommodating theology that "works" by appealing to its audience's desires.

The teaching of the sixteenth century remains a beacon to which we can constantly return to gain a critical perspective on what we have become. From time to time in the history of modern theology — as, for example, following the First World War at the birth of the neoorthodox movement — the Age of Reform has been reclaimed to notable effect. In the most famous line he ever penned, H. Richard Niebuhr drew upon the inspiration of the Reformation to charge a generation of cultural liberalism with failure. He characterized this failed theology thus: "A God without wrath brought men without sin into a kingdom without judgment through the ministrations of a Christ without a cross" (Niebuhr, 1937, p. 193). This accusation was published over fifty years ago; it is just as relevant today to "our nation of victims" for which adversity is the undeserved depriva- tion of happiness and self-fulfillment.

The sixteenth century is still able to exert enormous authority in Christian communities. What more urgent context could there be for the application of such an authoritative theology than the threat posed by the dominance of the therapeutic culture in contemporary life? Christians should take their stand in opposition to this culture by proclaiming the insight of the Age of Reform that the formation of character begins in the honest recognition of adversity as the means by which God leads us to the truth of our sin and opens the path to regeneration. I would submit that this insight could be the crux of a distinctive Christian psychology.

Ascetic Theology and Psychology

Diogenes Allen

T HE MORAL AND spiritual dynamics of justification in the classical Reformers are well worked out. Luther above all magnificently described the hopeless despair he experienced in trying to make himself acceptable to a holy God, and the immense, transforming experience of the discovery that God in Christ has made us acceptable by sheer grace. God's justification gives great peace and joy, confidence before God, and freedom from the burden of the Law and its social counterpart, social prestige. God's gracious justification also redirects our energies toward the service of others.

There are clear connections between the experience of guilt, the hopelessness of ever making things right before a just and wrathful God, and the multiple effects that follow in the wake of the experience of forgiveness. But these connections only come into operation if a person loves righteousness, that is, believes in justice and in a God who rewards the just and punishes the unjust. If you do not love justice and hold these beliefs, you will not have the experiences. The gracious love of God matters only to people who, like the prodigal son, recognize their lives as the betrayal of trust. Without such a concern for righteousness in one's own life, an assurance of God's gracious love falls on deaf ears.

Thus in a society that does not promote a concern to become a moral or virtuous person, much less a concern to be righteous before God, the sequence Luther and others describe cannot even begin to occur. The fuse is so damp as to forestall the explosive relief and birth of newly directed energy that follows on the genuine experience of God's grace. Clergy who adhere to the classic Reformers' teaching on justification expend a great deal of labor to get their parishioners to rejoice in God's love and forgiveness, to experience the release of guilt, and to be free from anxiety and vain works. A large part of that effort is directed to eliciting

297

from the congregation sufficient moral seriousness to create a background against which God's grace can be appreciated. But all too often, in both pulpit and pew the concept of divine love degenerates into an abstract, amoral sentimentality.

The dynamics of justification are fundamental to a Christian ac-count of character-change. But there are many psychological/spiritual roads leading up to this essential dynamic; not every spiritually develop-ing person needs to *start* with the yearning for righteousness. For example, some people find in the practice of Christianity a power that helps them to deal with their broken and ensnarled lives. Others are initially attracted through a loss of something they love, and find their grief assuaged through the practice of Christianity. Still others start with a desire to understand, and find in Christianity not only a powerful world view that casts light on so many things that baffle us, but also a meaning to life that anchors our otherwise wayward lives and thus brings healing. These diversities of approach do not represent alternative forms of Christianity, but alternative paths to the acknowledgment of sin and acceptance of grace that is offered in the gospel of atonement. The classic Reformers and the powerful American revivalist tradition are right about the decisive and central place of justification in the Christian life.

But they give us less guidance on sanctification or *growth* in the Christian life. If the first letter of the alphabet, "a," indicates conversion, what are the "b, c, d, and so forth" of the Christian spiritual journey? The actual but gradual process of regeneration has been seriously neglected. With a few exceptions, like Søren Kierkegaard, Protestantism has been less rich in psychology, in exploring the details of Christian personality devel-opment, than other parts of the Church and its history. The present day interest in spirituality, as well as the nearly promiscuous enthusiasm in Christian circles for contemporary psychology, suggests that not enough guidance has been provided by Christian ethics, pastoral theology, or present-day academic theology. The need to consider other starting points than a love of righteousness and the need for guidance on growth after conversion have led me to study the classics of spirituality and, in partic-ular, various accounts of the Christian journey.

Seven Questions about the Spiritual Life

Kierkegaard's writings are more or less equally concerned with what it is to become a *Christian* and what it is to become a *person*. We can show the similarity as well as the difference between these two issues by a simple comparison. We have to *become* persons and Christians; we are not born in either condition. Of course our bodies have to develop too, but physical maturity comes more or less automatically, independent of our choice. We can certainly choose more or less healthy regimens of diet and exercise, but we cannot very well choose to have a heavy beard or be six feet tall if it wasn't in the genes. By contrast, we have a rather large range of choices concerning the kind of character we develop, choices that will affect our integrity, our self-control, our truthfulness, etc. In education we face a large range of questions concerning what we may become and what we ought to become as persons. But the range of questions is qualified and extended in a special way when we consider Christian spirituality. Christian spirituality is concerned with what we *may* become because of God and what we *ought* to become because of God. Our horizon concerning what we may and ought to become as human beings is greatly extended because of what God makes possible and what God desires.

There is a large body of literature that describes the Christian spiritual journey. A few of the great guides are John Bunyan, St. John of the Cross, George Herbert, William Law, and Simone Weil. There are easily more than a hundred significant spiritual writers. Each gives a map, so to speak, of the spiritual development of Christians. In all their richness and diversity, they all treat at least seven questions.

Any account of the spiritual life answers the question, What is its goal? The goal of the spiritual life has been described as the vision of God, the vision of the trinity, union with God, participation in God's life and being, and the pure love of God. Calvin put it nicely as "to know God and to enjoy him forever." All these expressions of the goal are in terms of the object of our attention. Other accounts concentrate on what we may become. It is frequently said that we actualize the image of God so that we come to resemble God; or that we become like Jesus; or become holy; or become perfect. Several of these may be found in the same writer, suggesting that more than one concept is needed to express the different aspects of the goal. A writer may stress one aspect more than others, or even neglect some aspects. Besides the ultimate goal, there are proximate or subordinate goals, such as the control of our emotions or the love of neighbor. A task of spiritual theology is to discuss the relation and even compatibility of the different accounts of the goal of the spiritual life, and the relation between its proximate and ultimate goals.

A second question answered by any account of the spiritual life is, What is the path to the goal? A classic path that developed during the early Christian centuries is called the threefold way. It consists of ascetic theology, and then two forms of the contemplation of God, indirect and direct. Ascetic theology, which is a chief concern of this paper, is concerned with exercise or practice. Ἀσκέω is a Greek verb meaning "to engage in," "to practice"; ἄσκησις is a noun meaning "practice" in the sense of what an athlete does to prepare for competition. Ascetic theology is the practice of spiritual disciplines like prayer and fasting, and a special kind of disciplined reading called *lectio divina* that I will discuss later. Paul describes the Christian life as a race to be run, requiring training or discipline (1 Corinthians 9:24-27); he points out that, like a boxer who must acquire skill to fight well, the Christian must submit to rigorous discipline, subduing a human nature that, though forgiven, is still rebellious and weak and subject to temptations which arise for those who seek to follow Christ's commandments.

(The threefold path has been described in a variety of ways across the centuries. The variety in the description of this path should not disturb us. On the contrary, the variety is wonderful, because people differ in intellectual interests, emotional temperaments, gifts, and roles in life; they also live in different periods of history and in different kinds of societies. These factors affect which path or part of a path is most relevant to a person. All accounts of the path stress the need for preparation or purgation, and the lists of vices to be purged overlap significantly in the various accounts; but they are not identical because they are directed to different audiences. George Herbert, the seventeenth-century poet and clergyman, stressed the need to purge lust, gluttony, gambling, and idleness because his account of the Christian pilgrimage in *The Temple* was directed primarily to courtiers, and these vices were rampant at royal courts. Likewise he wrote in verse because in his day people at the court prized poetry and wit and, as Herbert put it, "A verse may find him, who a sermon flies" [1981, p. 121].)

Third, we may ask, What motivates us to begin the spiritual life? Here again we find a long list: fear, remorse, guilt, confusion, loneliness, a desire for justice, for truth, for understanding, and a sense of awe and mystery. Once again, variety is valuable because not everyone begins to seek God for the same reasons. A knowledge of the range of motives may enable the Christian spiritual guide to find those reasons to which some particular individual or group of persons is especially sensitive, so as better to be able to lead them on the spiritual path.

The fourth and fifth questions form a pair. What helps us make progress? and What hinders us? Prayer, meditation on Scripture, and retreats are frequently recommended as aids; and lack of faith, flagrant sins, and, paradoxically, pride in our progress are commonly cited hindrances to progress. The sixth question is closely related to this pair. How do we measure progress? That is, by what standards are we to assess our spiritual condition? In their distrust of works, the classical Reformers spoke of Christian maturity rather than progress, but it comes to much the same thing, since there are criteria of maturity.

Finally, we may ask of any spiritual guide, What are the fruits of the Spirit? Among those usually treated are love, joy, peace, friendship, discernment, victory over death. The letters of Paul and John are particularly rich on this topic. Among theologians, one of the most comprehensive treatments is given in Bonaventure's *The Tree of Life*. It is based on a study of the birth, life, death, and resurrection of Christ. Jesus is described as the tree of life, in an allusion to the tree of life that was in the Garden of Eden. If we are joined to Jesus, the tree of life, our lives will be rooted where his life is rooted and bear the kind of fruit his life bore.

These seven do not by any means exhaust the questions that may be asked of a spiritual psychology. But they can guide a beginner through the maze of accounts of the spiritual life. In addition, they distinguish spiritual theology *precisely* from doctrinal theology. These are distinct fields of theology inasmuch as they are defined by different questions. Spirituality, as the name implies, is focused on the Holy Spirit who brings to fullness in the lives of individual and community the work that God has achieved in Christ. Now let us contrast the seven questions that are asked about the work of the Holy Spirit in spiritual theology with the kind of questions that are asked about the Holy Spirit in doctrinal theology.

According to the Christian doctrine of the trinity, God is one God in three persons. A doctrinal theologian is concerned with the relation between the three persons in the trinity and the nature of their unity. He or she might ask, Is the Holy Spirit a person *in the same sense* of "person" as are the Father and the Son? This question is of special interest in western theology because the west, in contrast to the east, tends to regard the Holy Spirit as little more than the bond between the Father and the Son. In what sense then is the personhood of the Holy Spirit to be understood?

In recent times some academic theologians have spoken of the person of the Holy Spirit as the corporate identity of the Christian community, following the lead of nineteenth-century German Idealism and Romanticism, and twentieth-century social theory. This would mean that the Holy Spirit is not a person in the same sense as are the Father and the Son.

We do not have to agree with this type of answer to recognize that these and other questions asked by doctrinal theologians are perfectly legitimate questions. We can also see that they differ from the questions asked in spiritual theology. Both sets of questions are *theological*. The great theologians of the past treated both the questions of spiritual theology and those of doctrinal theology. Their reflections on the two sets of questions were not kept apart; they richly interacted. Indeed, for most of the history of theology it was believed that one makes progress in doctrinal theology only as one's spiritual state improves, and that one moves spiritually closer to God because one's intellectual condition has improved; understanding and spiritual progress or ascent toward God work hand in hand (see Griffiths, this volume, and Talbot, this volume); spiritual progress without increased knowledge of God or doctrinal inquiry without spiritual effects was inconceivable.

Few things indicate more poignantly how we have lost touch with our heritage than the way academic theology today is pursued independently of spiritual improvement. The study of theology is increasingly influenced by the "objective" and "scientific" way religion is studied in universities. Spiritual improvement is no more sought or expected in the study of religion than it is sought or expected in the study of geology. Theology may be pursued without any religious commitment, and if one happens to have a religious commitment, that commitment must be set aside and not allowed to "intrude" in one's pursuit of theological inquiry.

A renewal of acquaintance with ascetic theology is one way that this abstraction of intellect and heart may possibly be mitigated. A pivotal figure in the history of ascetic theology is Evagrius of Pontus (345-399 C.E.), and one aspect of his thought will be the chief object of my attention.

Eight Deadly Thoughts

Evagrius's influence in the church of the Middle Ages and right down to the present day is chiefly in his legacy of "the eight deadly thoughts," later reformulated as the seven deadly sins. He did not originate the idea, but his formulations became classical. Notable in this basic spiritual/psychological schema are two emphases. On the one hand, spiritual degeneracy or immaturity is conceived as a disposition to certain "passions" (πάθη). As Evagrius's list indicates, his word "passions" encompasses a psychologically diverse set of phenomena. Some of the passions are what we would call appetites (lust and gluttony); others are desires (greed, vainglory, and pride); some are emotions (sadness, anger, acedia, and pride). Uniting them, however, seems to be their having one relation or another to what we might broadly call "concerns," appetites and desires being concerns for their objects, and emotions being based on some concern or other. On the other hand, these passions are all closely connected, again in diverse ways, with thoughts. Certain thoughts *trigger* disordered appetites and can also *color* them, and other thoughts are *constitutive of* disordered desires and emotions. Thus Evagrius views spiritual degeneracy as a fundamentally passional disorder (as we might expect from his belonging to a tradition in which the ideal of psycho-spiritual health is a proper love for God and neighbor; cf. Howsepian, this volume), and he seems to have a highly "cognitive" understanding of what order and disorder in the passions amounts to, and/or of what causes it (as we might expect in a tradition that stresses doctrinal teaching as much as Christianity does). It is Evagrius's careful attention to the ways in which passions become and stay disordered, and the ways in which they can be corrected, that makes his writings a useful supplement to the Reformation's psychology of justification.

My comments so far already suggest that his goal of *apatheia* (literally, lack of passion) is not an eradication of passion (that is, a lack of concern for anything), since the love of God and love of neighbor are passional (involving emotions and desires) in a broad sense of the word. Instead, apatheia must be the eradication only of a certain *kind* of passion, *disordered* passions or perhaps what the Apostle Paul calls "the desires of the flesh" (ἐπιθυμία σαρκός; not to be confused with bodily desires, since Paul mentions envy as one of the desires of the flesh).

Let us now take a look at the eight deadly thoughts and their corresponding passions. We will see that as Evagrius expounds them, they are tightly tied to the monastic context, and thus may seem difficult to generalize. Nevertheless, I shall attempt to generalize them, since I want to apply Evagrius's psychological insights to Christians generally, and not just to monks. The next few paragraphs are based on §§6-14 of Evagrius's *Praktikos* (1981), entitled "The Eight Kinds of Evil Thoughts."

The thought that triggers gluttony in the monk is something like "All this fasting is ruining my health." Thoughts of other monks who have got sick, and of the effect that his deprivations are having on various of his organs, impel him to give up or mitigate his fasts. We can well imagine that these considerations make the food appear more "good" to him, and the fasting repugnant. Thus his hunger (the sensation in the belly) actually feels different under the influence of these thoughts — more urgent and more innocent. Since lay people fast only occasionally and probably not enough to affect their health, perhaps these particular thoughts are not the triggers of gluttony in most Christians. But some analogous rationalization for eating is likely to be involved in gluttony. For example, the glutton may say to himself, "It's not every day you can get fresh corn on the cob," or "It wouldn't be good stewardship to let my wife's dessert go to waste."

Sexual urges are encouraged in the monk who is practicing continence when he is attacked by the thought, "I am gaining nothing by resisting my urges." He can keep the urges in check as long as he keeps before his mind the reasons for doing so (e.g., that the discipline promotes in him the love of God and neighbor); the evil thought undermines those reasons. Again the thoughts, whether good or evil, actually color the monk's perception of the object: Under the influence of the monastic reasons for continence the fantasized woman appears threatening, but under the influence of the evil thought she does not look threatening and so looks all the more enticing. The married Christian practices continence in a different context than the monk, but the basic psychology of lust and temperance is the same. As long as I keep before my mind the reasons for mental faithfulness to my wife (e.g., that my identity and hers in the Lord are spoiled by adultery in the heart), I remain effectively vigilant against exciting sexual fantasies about other women. But if, through the intervention of other thoughts, I become momentarily unable to see the point of the Christian reasons for mental faithfulness, my sexual instincts take over my mind. Examples of such intervening thoughts would be, "A little fantasizing never hurt anybody," or "God gave me gonads, after all."

Avarice is the desire to accumulate things, that is, to have *possessions;* as such it is an attitudinal or spiritual contrary of monastic poverty. The thought characteristic of this desire is "I will be in need of this." Various reasons can form it, and so the monk's mind turns to "a lengthy old age, inability to perform manual labor (at some future date), famines that are sure to come, sickness that will visit us, the pinch of poverty, the great shame that comes from accepting the necessities of life from others" (§9). Thus the object is desired, not just as a good, a blessing, but as something to be owned and held onto. The concept of ownership or possession resides in, shapes, and determines the nature of the desire. Secular Christians are not committed, as the monk is, to not owning anything in the conventional sense of "own," but we are called to think of what we "own" as belonging to God and our neighbor, and so, insofar as we desire and take pleasure in such goods, we are to desire and take pleasure in them under the dominion of the thought that they are from God by grace and are for his kingdom. If instead our desire for and pleasure in goods is shaped by the thought, "This is [will be] my possession," then the desire is what Evagrius calls a "passion," and is not healthy. The deadly thought proper to avarice undermines the impulse of generosity. But generosity is a mark of the regenerative work of the Holy Spirit (since God is generous). This is one of the reasons avarice is harmful, even "deadly" — killing the spirit of generosity.

An emotion that is both contrary to the monastic character and often found in immature monks is a sort of grieving nostalgia ("sadness") for the life on which they have turned their backs — their families, the pleasures and work of bygone times. The thought constitutive of this emotion is "Those were the good old days." In this thought the memories of pre-monastic life are gilded, and the actualities of present life are sooted by the comparison. This sadness is contrary to the monastic life because monastic maturity is characterized by a peaceful joy in and gratitude for the monk's spiritual growth and activities of service. We can think of a couple of secular Christian counterparts of this sadness. One would be regrets about how one's life has gone — say, about missed opportunities for advancement or one's choice of career. This kind of regret corrupts the Christian life. The disciplined ("ascetic") Christian will fight the emotion by turning her mind away from what might have been and by focusing on present opportunities for action and reasons for gratitude. A perhaps closer counterpart would be nostalgia for the pleasures of sin. Perhaps you remember the intense pleasure of taking unrestrained vengeance on an enemy, or of urbane but unmistakably corrupt sexual activity. And you remember these pleasures, not with the regret of repentance, but with the regretting thought, "Those were the good old days."

Anger has the form of the thought, "So-and-so has done me injury, is an offensive person and deserves to suffer evil." In discussing what is evil about anger, Evagrius stresses the inconvenience and pain to the angry person — the distraction he suffers in his prayers, alarming experiences at night, destruction of the faculty of memory (§93), and various bodily ailments that result. But it should be clear that anger also (and perhaps more importantly from a Christian point of view) directly disrupts a person's relationship with his neighbor and God; in most cases it is contrary to the love commanded in the gospel. Evagrius's treatment of anger makes it clear that when he speaks of apatheia and getting rid of the "passions," he does not have in mind a general flattening or eradication of emotional life. Even anger, of a certain kind, may be seen as holy. He says that the angels "encourage us to turn our anger against the demons" (§24), and he advises the monks, when they are tempted, not to fall immediately to prayer, but instead to "utter some angry words against the one [that is, the demon] who afflicts you" (§42). It seems that the chief difference between holy and unholy anger lies in the object toward which it is directed; anger at demons may be holy, but anger at fellow humans is usually not (§93). We are probably less interested in demons than Evagrius was, but his principle is sound: anger is sometimes bad and sometimes good, but anger at our fellow humans should generally be suspect. That anger at other humans is not always wrong is evident from Jesus' anger (Mark 3:1-6; 10:13-14; John 2:14-17), and from Paul's command regarding anger (Ephesians 4:26).

"Acedia" is Evagrius's term for the monk's discouragement, a perception of the monastic life as tedious, constricting, and unfulfilling. It assaults the monk especially between 10:00 a.m. and 3:00 p.m. (the latter being the dinner hour). Perhaps he is hungry and hot and would like to move about more than his cell allows. He watches the sun obsessively and wishes it would move faster towards dinnertime; he paces in front of his cell. If we followed the model of sadness and anger, we might suppose that the deadly thought in this case is "My monastic life is tedious, constricting, and unfulfilling." No doubt the perception has the form of this thought, but Evagrius stresses some thoughts that are *consequences* of this perception, rather than the one that is *constitutive* of it. It makes him think thoughts such as, "that charity has departed from the brethren, that there is no one to give encouragement"; and "after all, it is not the place that is the basis of pleasing the Lord. God is to be adored everywhere." The thoughts all have the character of reasons for leaving the monastic life. Most of us do not pursue the Christian life in a small cell on one meal a day, but we may very well get discouraged. Perhaps our congregation is dwindling and we do not know what to do about it. We are burdened with church work that is unexciting and appears to be bearing no fruit. We pray regularly and read Scripture, but God seems to be absent. All of this sometimes coalesces into an impression of our religious life as a burden from which it would be wonderful to escape.

Vainglory is a desire that arises after a certain progress in the spiritual life, namely the desire to be admired by others for one's spiritual virtues. It is a desire for an irrelevant reward, and an especially nasty evil, inasmuch as it vitiates a positive good that has been achieved. The thought connected with it would seem to be, "It would be a good thing for my excellences to be recognized and admired by somebody." Vainglory leads to vain imaginings of glory, of people coming eager for advice and blessing, of attainment to the priesthood. We should have no trouble transferring these insights from the monastic life to ours. Every time we drop subtle references to our good deeds in conversation with our Christian friends, we should be on the lookout for vainglory: Why did I do that? Was the reference really necessary for information's sake? Did I really do that to edify the young people? Or did I want my virtues lighted up, the better to be admired?

The thought that goes with pride is "I alone am to be credited for my virtues and good actions, and this fact should be recognized by all" (the last part of the thought actually belongs to vainglory, which is closely related to pride). As an emotion, pride is a kind of joy in one's supposed hyperagency; as a desire it is a repugnance for acknowledging God's agency in one's character and actions, a desire to take all the credit oneself. (For a discussion of co-agency, the heartfelt recognition of which is the opposite of pride as Evagrius analyzes it, see Johnson, this volume.) Pride is the "most damaging" of the passions because it is a denial of God's help, and thus rejects the spiritual relationship with him and blots out gratitude. Monks have no corner on pride. Contemporary American culture, with its individualism, promotes it perhaps more strongly than most cultures in history.

I must comment on the place of demons in Evagrius's thought and practice. For him the deadly thoughts are planted in us by various demons, so in resisting the thoughts we are in fact in an interpersonal combat. This seems rather dated and naïve to many today. But we need to understand what it signifies. It was believed that demons seek to injure us by working through people and social institutions; but their effectiveness is blunted by the degree of goodness found in the media used. Just as some electricity is lost in the form of heat because of the resistance of conductors, so too some of the power of temptation that a demon can bring to bear on someone is lost because of the goodness of people and institutions. Many who deeply desired to exhibit the power of Christ to redeem us, went to solitary places to force demons to attack them directly, in their full power, rather than have their power diluted by its conductors. These people realized that they were unable to stand up to demons by their own power, but were willing to endure the terrible force of evil as it tempted them, to witness to the power of Christ who had united himself with all Christians. By having God the Holy Spirit overcome all within themselves that was not yet wholly obedient to Christ, they would be witnesses in their own person to the victory Christ had wrought over evil. To use another analogy, we desire to adorn those we love with gifts. The monks sought to adorn God with the beauty of their lives, lives made possible by God's generosity.

As Evagrius discusses them, most of the eight deadly thoughts and their corresponding passions are problems that arise in the monastic life. I have suggested that these problems are in fact general for Christians, that is, for people who have repented, accepted God's justification in the cross of Christ, and are seeking to follow Christ. The deadly thoughts are the spiritual/psychological obstacle course over which the Christian-in-training must make her way as she "works out" (Philippians 2:12) her already-won salvation — as she becomes in psychological fact the new creation (Galatians 6:15) that God in Christ has made her in relation to himself.

Christian *Apatheia*

The overcoming of these obstacles to the love of God and neighbor is *apatheia*, a state of the mind/heart in which one is free from the turbulence of the eight deadly thoughts and their corresponding passions. "Apatheia" is a term made famous by Stoicism, but the apatheia of the desert fathers is not to be confused with the apatheia of Stoicism. Anger is not acceptable to Stoics; but as we have seen, it is sometimes a holy state of mind according to Evagrius. Even for the Stoics, apatheia is not best thought of as a state of complete non-feeling. The Stoics rejected the "passions" (πάθη), but they allowed a class of "good affects" (εὐπάθειαι): "wish" (βούλησις) is an appetite for virtue, "joy" (χαρά) is a pleasure in virtue, and "caution" (εὐλάβεια) is an aversion to vice (see Diogenes Laertius, 1931, Life of Zeno §116). In any case, Jerome completely misunderstood the desert fathers when he accused them of seeking to become like a stone. They sometimes construe the "passion" of acedia as a state of non-feeling, since a person in this state is unmoved by love of Christian teachings and worship. For the desert fathers apatheia is a purity of heart that enables one to love one's neighbor as oneself, and also to be able to contemplate and pray without undue distraction. "Agape is the progeny of apatheia. Apatheia is the very flower of ascesis. Ascesis consists in keeping the commandments" (Evagrius, 1981, §81). The Stoic aims at perfect self-sufficiency, at being emotionally independent of everyone and everything. The Christian, by contrast, seeks to be free from those things that impede love for others and love for God. Rather than seeking independence, the Christian seeks to become wholly dependent on God's gracious love and to be more deeply involved with the well-being of others.

The Greek word _monachos_ (monk) used to describe the desert fathers and mothers suggests the notion of "single" or "undivided," for the monachos has interior unity or purity of heart. The monachos can bring the whole self to focus on God and to desire God as the sole treasure. "Blessed are the pure in heart, for they will see God" (Matthew 5:8). Unless one can dispel distractions and bring one's scattered thoughts and feelings to focus, one cannot see or understand oneself, one's neighbor, or the created universe aright, and from this indirect knowledge of God through creatures, proceed to a knowledge of God face to face.

Perhaps the following analogy will help. The eye condition known as astigmatism prevents the light rays the eye admits from all being focused. As a result the sufferer cannot see properly. However, a corrective lens can focus the light correctly, insuring proper vision. Likewise, various ascetic practices, such as prayer, fasting, reading, and almsgiving are intended to enable us to gain sufficient mastery over ourselves so that we can bring our entire self into focus, and thus see God and neighbor as the beautiful things they in fact are. As long as our attention is distracted because we ourselves are divided in our wishes, wants, desires, and hopes, we cannot attend to the word of God, and without such contact, we cannot be progressively purified and made whole. Purity of heart is the acquired disposition to gather more and more of the scattered rays into focus because we have come more and more to desire the good that God seeks to give us: holiness, love, peace, and joy; and indeed to desire finally to be united with God, that is, to receive in its fullness God's uncreated life.

Another way to see that the detachment spoken of in ascetic theology is not a detachment from *everything*, but only from the turbulence caused by the eight deadly thoughts, is to consider the "wounds of knowledge." In her *Showings*, Julian of Norwich (1978) describes three wounds that are required in the Christian life: the wound of contrition or repentance, the wound of compassion or love of neighbor, and the wound of longing or the love of God. These wounds are not to be avoided, because there is no knowledge of ourselves and others or of God which is detached and unmoved. The Stoic aims to be independent because the Stoic wants to stay in control of the situation. The Christian seeks to relinquish control of him- or herself in order to yield to God's way, and as long as he or she is subject to the eight deadly thoughts and the corresponding passions, the Christian is unable to yield to God.

Psychology and Christian Spirituality

I am uncomfortable with the expression "Christian psychology." It might be better to speak of the Christian *in* psychology, on the analogy of the Christian in philosophy or political science, or the Christian in science. A Christian in philosophy can point out such things as the fact that the universe is not self-explanatory, as our intellectual culture often assumes. A Christian in political science can show the political significance of Christianity. A Christian in natural science can point out that science does not explain everything, as reductionists frequently claim it can. Similarly, a Christian in psychology will guard against interpreting such things as a desire for God as nothing but a mid-life crisis. (For an example of the danger of misreading a spiritual condition in terms of common human development, see T. S. Eliot [1971], *The Cocktail Party*.)

More positively, a Christian in psychology can draw upon developmental psychology to give us some light on what helps and what hinders us in our spiritual journey, and also on how we may measure progress — the fourth, fifth, and sixth questions addressed in spiritual theology. The formation we have received from our upbringing may make it easier or more difficult for us to respond to Christian teaching. For example, as Cynthia Jones Neal (this volume) has shown, our upbringing may affect the degree of our independence in thought and action. Without a sufficiently developed sense of personal agency, young people may accept their parents' way of life, including their Christianity, but hold to it rigidly rather than with a deep spiritual intelligence. They adopt certain practices and hold to various beliefs, but without understanding or accepting their purpose. The Scribes and Pharisees exhibited a similar rigidity in their objections to some of Jesus' teachings and actions. Ascetic practices, too, run the constant danger of a rigidity in which austerities become an end in themselves, rather than a means to a spiritual goal. One measure of progress in the spiritual life is a flexibility based on an understanding of the intentions or goals of the Christian life, a flexibility that enables us to adapt practices to circumstances. (This trait has traditionally been called "wisdom" or "discernment.") Becoming a responsible person is not identical with becoming a Christian, but it is a necessary ingredient in the development of a mature Christian.

A third connection between spirituality and psychology is that the dynamics of the passions and their control as described in ascetic theology can be connected to a branch of experimental psychology. Psychologists study such things as the emotional effects of life aboard a submarine in the U.S. Navy. They look for connections between the stresses encountered in this unusual kind of living situation and various emotions, attitudes, and actions. Sometimes they seek to correlate patterns of reaction to various kinds of stress with different personality types. Because we are limited in what we may do to human beings in scientific investigation, and because human beings have a degree of independence from the forces being studied, one does not expect all or perhaps even most of the connections found to be laws, in the sense of the laws that are found in macrophysics and chemistry. The connections in psychology are law-like or similar to laws, rather than laws. Nonetheless, psychologists can discover connections between various circumstances and emotions, and between various emotions and actions that frequently occur.

I am influenced here by the long essay on twentieth-century psychology with which R. S. Peters concludes his abridgement of Brett's *History of Psychology* (1965). Peters argues that psychologists should not begin with an all-inclusive theory of human behavior, as did E. Tolman and C. Hull, but instead look for law-like connections between variables and, in particular, search for functional relations between variables that can be tested. Peters stresses that it is the testing of alleged connections, which includes the attempt to falsify them, that makes any investigation a scientific one.

One need not accept all that Peters claims about psychology as a science to conclude that ascetic theology's description of the passions, their connections with one another and with the love of neighbor and of God, and of the effects of the ascetic disciplines upon them, is not scientific psychology in Peters's sense. But the connections ascetic theology describes for those who seek to grow in the Christian life provide *material* for psychologists to test. For example, do all Christian people experience Evagrius's eight deadly thoughts, the connections between them that he describes, and success with the remedies that he prescribes? If only some Christian people do, can we find correlations between certain variables in the cases of those who do and those who do not? I am particularly concerned with the possibility of falsification, as some of the remedies may be ineffective. They are only to be used as a means to an end, and should they be ineffective, they should be abandoned rather than slavishly followed as part of a hallowed tradition. These and similar questions, it seems to me, are legitimate for a psychologist to investigate. The results would be significant to a person who seeks to lead a Christian life and to those who are responsible for guiding others in the Christian life. (For reflection on the relation of psychological investigation of eating disorders to ascetic theology's claims about gluttony, see Okholm, this volume.)

A psychologist's status as a good scientist, like that of any good experimental scientist, is largely a function of an ability to shape claims into a form in which they can be tested. To understand the connections ascetic theology describes or asserts, and to find ways to test them, presents a very great challenge to the ingenuity of psychologists. But this is true of other areas of human life as well. The difficulties suggest that perhaps psychology as a science is rather limited in scope. For example, it is not possible to test whether God is an agent in the relief people find from a particular sin, even though people who find relief in a religious practice think so. Nonetheless, it should be possible to see whether a religious *practice* gives relief from the various passions that Evagrius and other ascetic theologians, such as John Cassian (1955) and Maximus the Confessor (1985), claim. At any rate, it is the branch of psychology that is concerned with the search for and testing of law-like connections in human beings that influenced my selection of ascetic theology as a topic for this essay. Even though my own study of ascetic theology is practical — I want to find some help in living and guiding others to a spiritual life — I believe that the connections ascetic theologians claim to have found provide legitimate materials for psychologists to test. If they are suitable for testing, such tests could contribute significantly to an advance in the psychology of the Christian life.

Autobiographical: The Effect of *Lectio Divina* on Anger

I now want to consider at some length the destructive passion of anger and a remedy for it. This is particularly important to me because for years I have suffered from a short fuse and inordinate anger, rather than feeling and acting out of love of neighbor. I have been able to recognize that some of this anger is the result of frustration. I believe that frequently I know

the best way to get things done or to organize things, and that my colleagues willfully prevent what is really best from happening. All too
frequently as we at the seminary go through the procedures of new appointments or promotions, discuss curricular reforms and the like, I find
myself increasingly agitated by the predictably obstructive tactics trooped
out again and again by people who have become my enemies.

I am reminded of Dante's picture of Satan at the bottom of the
inferno. Satan is frozen in a lake. The water remains frozen, locking him
in impotence, because he keeps flapping his wings in rage and generating
icy gusts. He is angry with the way God orders things because he does
not realize that he is upside down. He thinks he sees how things ought
to be arranged, and is furious with God's arrangement. Understanding
this dynamic of anger helped me some. So too do other psychological
dynamics that I have read. But it was not understanding that relieved me
of the burden of intemperate anger. To my surprise I found immense relief
from the evil thoughts and the agitation of anger they produce by the
ancient practice of *lectio divina*.

Most simply, the *lectio divina* consists of four interlocking aspects:
reading a passage of Scripture to yourself aloud; meditating or thinking
about what you have read; praying about what rises up in your mind and
heart in meditation; and then contemplation, which is simply resting
silently in God for a time after you have prayed. It is vitally important to
read the Scriptures aloud. We have become so skillful at reading rapidly,
that our eyes just race along the page. Not only does reading aloud help
us slow down, but hearing the words uttered aloud helps us take in what
we read much better.

When I was introduced to the *lectio*, I was given Psalm 139 to read.
I was struck by the passage that reads, "They talk blasphemously about
you, regard your thoughts as nothing. Yahweh, do I not hate those who
hate you, and loathe those who defy you? I hate them with a total hatred,
I regard them as my own enemies" (vss. 20-22). I began to think about my
workplace, a theological seminary, and the things said about God in
courses and books by my colleagues. All too often they blaspheme and
regard God's thoughts as revealed in Scripture as nothing. I did hate them
and believed that my anger and hatred were well founded. If only I could
shut them up! If only I could keep others from listening to their poison!
Then it suddenly occurred to me that perhaps God did not regard them
as his enemies, even though they did blaspheme. My mind and heart
began to be stretched by this possibility. I then thought, if God does not
regard them as his enemies, then I cannot align myself with God by saying,
I regard them as my enemies, too. If he does not regard them as his
enemies, then they cannot be my enemies either.

This meditation led immediately into prayer, as it is supposed to do in the *lectio*. In prayer I confessed that I had acted presumptuously in condemning others as God's enemies, and had become self-righteous in scorning them, desiring their elimination from my place of work, and the like. I asked to be forgiven this presumption and to be helped no longer to regard them as my enemies.

A few hours later I found myself with a deep sense of peace, and not long after that a joyful spirit kept bubbling up unbidden. I had not yet been taught that the practice of *lectio divina* often leads to the experience of deep peace and joy. I am glad I had not been told this ahead of time, as I might have suspected psychological suggestion had led to these feelings.

I now find that when irritated or angry with others, I can quite often calm the agitation with the reminder, "They are not my enemies." Also I tend to hum or sing to myself, not a Psalm as Evagrius recommends, but a hymn about loving one another. The results astound me. I think I am finally becoming free of the tyranny of inordinate and senseless anger. Such a condition should not be confused with indifference. I am still deeply concerned with what is taught and written by my colleagues, but when I criticize their work, I no longer do it with as much bitterness and with a tone of scorn as I once did. My impression is that they now take what I say more seriously than they did before.

Some people who have been reared in Christian circles tend to suppress their expression of anger, and when they experience angry feelings feel guilty. For such people, it can be a relief to realize that there is a legitimate expression of anger. I do not know of a single criterion that enables us to distinguish all instances of legitimate from illegitimate anger. Clearly, when a person is treated with disrespect, an angry response is a mark of healthy self-regard. If the anger, however, is connected to jealousy or a desire to dominate, it also shows a lack of proper respect for others. But if the anger is connected with the desire to be reconciled with the person who treats you improperly, the anger need not be destructive to oneself or to others.

Evagrius writes of the peace and joy that arise from the practice of the *lectio divina* as aspects of apatheia. The tranquility can be compared to the harmonizing notes of the bass clef that are sounded more or less continuously beneath a melody in the treble clef. God's peace and joy (bass clef) can thus co-exist with many other thoughts and feelings (treble clef), and they can be brought to awareness by a simple shift of attention. This is one way we may have an habitual presence or awareness of God.

The experience of finding relief from destructive anger brought to mind a year-long course I took in pastoral counseling during my seminary days. I remember our teacher pointing out that church people are constantly told to love each other. Sermons to this effect are preached week after week and year after year. Everyone agrees that they should love one another; but no matter what gets taught, people continue to deal with each other in much the same way. He explained that this was because there are all sorts of psychological barriers that have not been dealt with, and that preaching at people will not remove these barriers. We did not return to this matter directly, but we learned a lot about personality theory, defense mechanisms, and therapeutic practices, and received some training in counseling. We were taught a completely new, non-scriptural and non-theological vocabulary with which to understand ourselves and others. I vividly recall being introduced to hospital calling. We were told that some patients would want to talk about their illnesses in terms of religious beliefs, but that this would probably be a cover story. We were told to dismiss this theological talk and get down to what was really bothering them, which of course was described in the psychological language of counseling.

I am quite sure that psychological barriers greatly inhibit our ability to love our neighbors and to love God. For example, some people transfer their relations with one or the other of their parents onto their relation with God (see Roberts, this volume, b), and this may often be inappropriate. Helping people deal with their projection may be necessary for their spiritual development, but I do not believe that such psychological help is all that is needed. My knowledge of Dante's description of anger, and of anger's psychological mechanisms, did not enable me to get much release from its crippling grip. What was effective, rather, was my reading and meditating on the Scriptures, asking for forgiveness and continued strength, and, finally, just resting in God. A regular practice of the *lectio divina* enabled me, by giving me just a bit of apatheia, to love my neighbor and to love God better.

My guess is that in the pastoral counseling courses I took the professor was suffering from the overspecialization that afflicts almost all education today. His job was to deal with what psychology has to say about human personality. He assumed that other professors told us about the Bible, theology, and prayer, and that we were active in parish life. I expect he also assumed that if psychological barriers are dealt with, then the practices of parish life will mediate God's grace and guidance and create fellowship between us. But none of this was his direct responsibility, nor his speciality. Unfortunately, what we learned in Bible study and theology and the like told us very little about how parish life actually helps us love as we should. In addition, what we were told in pastoral theology often caused us to set aside the vocabulary of God the Word incarnate as our Redeemer and to ignore the power of God the Holy Spirit to regenerate us. I learned much in seminary that I found extremely valuable, and I wish that all clergy could have the same kind of privilege. But there were shortcomings, and the most serious was not being taught how to use the Scriptures in prayer, and not being introduced to such marvelous practices as the *lectio divina*.

Using the Desert Fathers and Mothers

My digression into personal matters is actually appropriate to ascetic theology. Writers on the subject are not theorists, but present their experiences of seeking to become holy as witnesses. In telling my story I have, like the desert fathers and mothers, spoken psychologically in some sense, but have done so in the vocabulary of Christian faith. I believe that it is important to do so, for the experiences and the psychological changes involved are formed by, and require, this particular vocabulary. A pastoral theology that does not take seriously the Christian vocabulary can hardly develop a psychology of Christian sanctification. Still, I have argued that the psychological claims of the desert ascetics can to some extent be checked by psychologists who do not use the vocabulary of faith in their investigations. These scientists can examine people who are actually seeking to become holy — that is, to become free of the burden of evil and to be lovers of God and neighbor — to see which, if any, of their practices are effective and how effective they are. My account of the effectiveness of the practice of the *lectio divina* could be checked out in the same way.

Evagrius's account is but one work in which connections are described between various kinds of thoughts, emotions, and actions. Such writings have not only guided Christians, but also can provide raw material for psychological investigation. John Cassian, who is responsible for taking the teachings of the desert fathers and mothers to the western Church, is another important author, and St. Benedict's monastic Rule is a classic document of ascetic theology.

I have mentioned that falsification of ascetic psychological claims is just as important as confirmation of them, because the practices of the desert fathers and mothers are not necessarily to be followed just as they stand. Evagrius himself points out that the practices he recommends "are to be engaged in according to due measure and at the appropriate time" (1981, §15). He also alludes to the need for a spiritual director or guide, because people may overdo the remedies, such as fasting or reading or prayer, or do them at inappropriate times in light of their responsibilities. He also points out that we can overreach ourselves, and when we are unable to sustain what we have undertaken we can suffer a terrible and destructive reaction. This reminds me of Jesus' parable about the casting out of one demon, and because the Holy Spirit has not occupied its place, seven demons rush into the vacancy and the person is worse off than before. As Evagrius cautions, "What is untimely done, or done without measure, endures but a short time. And what is short lived is more harmful than profitable" (§15).

John Cassian did not hesitate to modify Evagrius's claims and prescriptions where he found them unhelpful or extreme. Likewise, it is a byword that Benedict's Rule, by far the most widespread and influential rule in western Christianity, is a model of moderation and good sense. Ascetic theology is a pool of experience to draw upon and develop, rather than a single tradition to be rigidly followed, and the pool of experience continues to accumulate new contributions even today.

Being Stuffed and Being Fulfilled

Dennis Okholm

Why Gluttony?

When you mention you are writing a paper on gluttony, the reactions can be surprising. Monks at one of my favorite abbeys seemed a bit threatened and teased me playfully, perhaps feeling self-conscious about the twenty-odd varieties of cold cereal in their refectory. A graduate-school librarian giggled; it probably *was* an unusual topic of research at a Protestant school. A bank employee asked for a copy of the paper — a heartening response, but one that makes me suspicious given all of the others.

Why *would* a person want to research gluttony? Initially I was curious why it was considered a *deadly* sin. I teach at a college that proscribes alcoholic beverages, but does not forbid overeating in the dining commons. And when one turns to Scripture, there is not much to be found on the topic of gluttony, unless one relies on the allegorical exegesis of medieval hermeneutics. The word "gluttony" is scarcely mentioned, though Paul implores us to exercise restraint in the use of our bodies. (On "gluttony" see Deuteronomy 21:20; Proverbs 23:20-21; 28:7; Matthew 11:9 and parallels; Titus 1:12. Typical Pauline exhortations include Romans 6:12-13; 12:1; 1 Corinthians 6:15-20; 1 Thessalonians 4:4.) In fact, the biblical writers encourage us to enjoy food as much, if not more, than they warn against it. Food itself is not shunned in the Christian Scriptures (as it sometimes is in other religions, such as Judaism, Islam, and Hinduism), but it is not supremely important, either. One is not to make a god of one's belly, but neither is one to be overly concerned about what one eats. (See Matthew 4:4; 6:25; Philippians 3:19; Matthew 7:18-19; Romans 14:3; 1 Corinthians 8:8; Colossians 2:23; 1 Timothy 4:2-4.) Suspicions about food seem to intensify after the New Testament period — in patristic sources, ascetic theology, and monastic practice. Perhaps this is to be expected in a church contending against encroaching worldliness and the influence of Cynic, Stoic, and Neo-Platonic philosophies.

So, one might ask, "What's so bad about gluttony?" Maybe a person who takes the topic seriously deserves giggles. Maybe contemporary Christian theologians' near neglect of the topic is the right stance. However, Mary Louise Bringle, in *The God of Thinness: Gluttony and Other Weighty Matters*, the only book on gluttony written by a contemporary theologian, disagrees. She comments (p. 16) on the disparity between the topic's importance and the attention it has had from theologians. For one thing, eating is not only a physical necessity for us, it is also centrally important in our lives. Between ages 20 and 50 the average person spends about 20,000 hours eating — over 800 days (Bringle, 1992, p. 29). Our daily schedules are often planned around mealtimes. Business deals are cut among people who "do" lunch together. Foods have adapted to every aspect of our popular culture: we have TV dinners, car drive-up windows, and ballgame tailgate parties. Of course, eating is crucial in biblical narratives as well. Our first parents plunged the human race into sin by violating a prohibition against eating. The Hebrews were given a sense of identity in a meal that signifies the defining moment in their history. The second Adam was victorious over a temptation involving the production and consumption of bread. Christians celebrate their life together in Christ around a family meal initiated by Jesus — one which anticipates an eschatological banquet that will mark the consummation of salvation history. Add to these all the stories many of us learned from the time we were toddlers: Abraham and his three visitors; Esau and his soup; Joseph and the famine; the prodigal son and his father's banquet; the feeding of the 5,000; Mary and Martha; the couple on the road to Emmaus; and breakfast on the beach with the risen Lord.

Another reason theologians should not neglect gluttony is that it's a focal point of alarming social trends today. If a theologian is to have a Bible in one hand and a newspaper in the other, as Karl Barth insists, then we cannot afford to neglect sin, vice, and virtue in the matter of food consumption. One percent of all American girls and women are anorexic. Partly because of cultural expectations and images portrayed by the media and the food-and-diet industries, about 90 percent of anorexics are female (Boskind-White, 1985; Orbach, 1985). About the same percentage of those who suffer from eating disorders get them by age 20, according to the National Association of Anorexia Nervosa and Associated Disorders (ANAD). Early in the 1980s more money was spent on worthless cures for obesity than for all medical research combined. Each day approximately 65 million Americans are dieting. The dietary industry earned $33 billion in 1989; in fact, diet books outsell all books but the Bible. Finally, in one poll, 40 percent of respondents said that "getting fat" was what they fear most in the world (see Bringle, 1992, pp. 24-27). Of course, one must be careful with statistics about eating disorders. For example, Bringle states that 150,000 women die of anorexia each year in the U.S. This wildly inflated and oft-cited figure (three times the annual number of U.S. traffic fatalities) has been traced to a misquotation that made its way even into textbooks (see Sommers, 1994, pp. 11-12).

Given that one of the purposes of the present book is to explore the intersection of ascetic theology with psychology, gluttony is a natural topic. Ascetic theology derives its name from the word *askesis,* which was used, among other things, for the disciplined preparation undertaken by athletes and soldiers. An "ascetic theologian" is so named because he or she reflects on and practices disciplines that build up the muscles of the soul. Exercises such as fasting and abstinence are properly associated with ascetic theology. Furthermore, the ascetic theologians used the concept of the seven deadly sins (or seven deadly thoughts) as a kind of diagnostic schema for articulating and explaining psycho-social dysfunction. Finally, the claims made about gluttony by ascetic theologians, monastics, and Aquinas (who draws heavily on the ascetic theologians) provide a case study for Diogenes Allen's notion (Allen, this volume) that the claims of ascetic theology can be tested by psychologists. As we will see, some dimensions of the ascetic theologians' claims about gluttony are borne out by the empirical observations of contemporary psychology, while other dimensions — in particular the ones closely linked with Christian theology and a norm of mental health inseparable from that theology — are, while consistent with the observations, "underdetermined" by them.

Can the ascetic and monastic theologians help us understand what it means to be a healthy human being with regard to the consumption of food? How do their insights square with modern thinking about food? We will find that our predecessors were quite perceptive about human dysfunction and how to repair it; consequently, their observations should be heeded by a modern church that has ignored them. But inattention to ancient Christian psychology is not confined to thought about food. Thomas Oden has documented recent clinical pastoral counseling's lamentable neglect of centuries of Christian wisdom (Oden, 1984). A Jewish psychologist has a similar reaction to psychotherapy in general, admonishing his colleagues to learn from classical, Jewish, and Christian theologians and moralists: "Modern psychology's disdain for the teachings of the great moral traditions is an example of intellectual hubris" (Schimmel, 1992, p. 5).

Classical theological thought about gluttony has not only been ignored, but also misunderstood. For instance, as we shall see, labelling gluttony a "*deadly* sin" can be something of a misnomer. So, if we are to raid the banquet table laden with the ancient wisdom about this central issue of human life, we need first to understand what gluttony is.

The Recipe for Gluttony

Obviously, gluttony has something to do with the consumption of food, countered as it is by the practice of fasting or abstinence and the virtue of temperance. But gluttony is not simply *over*consumption. Since the goal is a *proper* consumption of food and proper attitude toward it, gluttony may sometimes take the form of *under*consumption. Nor is it to be equated with the modern "sin" of being fat. Some fat people are temperate and some thin people are gluttons. This may be difficult for us to understand because of our cultural and media-induced bias that often depicts fat people as less healthy and virtuous than thin ones. This attitude is not unlike that of some of my students who insist that the first thing we must do with the homeless on the streets of Chicago is to evangelize them. Such a recommendation betrays a bias that poor people are unconverted sinners (or they would not be poor) and overlooks the fact that Jesus himself was homeless. So we must tread carefully through a minefield of biases to understand what gluttony is in the context of our culture.

Gluttony was on Evagrius's (1981) original list of eight evil thoughts *(logismoi)* — thoughts with which demons tempt us. In Cassian's works these became the eight principal thoughts — universal human tendencies from which sins result (Cassian, 1985). Cassian stood as the link between the Eastern theologian Evagrius and Western Benedictine monasticism; thus Gregory, the first Benedictine monk to become a pope, modified Cassian's list and enumerated the "seven principal vices" by placing pride in a category by itself as the root of all sins, adding envy, and merging spiritual lethargy *(accidia)* with sadness *(tristitia)*. These became our present-day list of the "seven deadly sins" (see Gregory, 1850, 39.25; and Schimmel, 1992, p. 25).

The relative importance of the various sins depends in part on the context in which one lives. Given the architectonic structure of a mature medieval society, pride's individualism might come to prominence as undermining the authority of God, the church, and the entitled. There is evidence that in the twelfth and thirteenth centuries — in artistic depictions, for instance — avarice was the worst of the seven (see Schimmel, 1992, p. 25). Gluttony and lust were especially threatening for ascetics in monastic environments.

It is not entirely accurate to call all of these sins *deadly*. As Aquinas makes clear in the *Summa Theologiae* (2a2ae, 148.2), Gregory's seven are capital or chief or cardinal sins, but they are not necessarily always mortal. Each is a cardinal sin in part because it is the parent of "daughter" sins. For instance, Gregory teaches that gluttony propagates foolish mirth, scurrility, uncleanness, babbling, and dullness of mind with reference to the understanding (Gregory, 1850, 39.25; see Aquinas, 2a2ae, 148.6). But whether a particular exemplification of a cardinal sin is mortal or venial depends on whether it is opposed to the love of God. In the case of gluttony, a person who merely eats more than is appropriate has committed only a venial sin; but he commits a mortal sin when he is so taken by the pleasure of eating that the delights of the palate turn him away from God and his commandments. Note the overlap between the concept of a mortal sin and Howsepian's (this volume) concept of psychosis. In effect, gluttony is deadly when a person makes a god of his belly (Aquinas, 2a2ae, 148.2).

Of the seven, gluttony seems to Cassian the least culpable sin for a very important reason that will color much of our subsequent discussion and to which we will explicitly return at the end. Gluttony arises from the constitution of our nature. In *Conferences*, V.3, Cassian classifies gluttony as a principal fault that is natural to us (unlike covetousness, which arises outside our nature), cannot be completed without a bodily act (unlike pride, which needs no bodily act), and is aroused by something external to us (unlike *accidia*, which is aroused only by internal feelings). We will always require food, and food usually brings pleasurable sensations to the palate. For this reason, says Cassian, one can never be fully rid of gluttonous thoughts or temptations. In the wilderness Christ could be tempted through the same passions as Adam because such passions were part of his constitution as designed by God (see *Conferences*, V.6). This is why it is important to distinguish faults which arise outside our nature (after the image is marred) from those temptations which, being natural to us, "do not cease from troubling even the best of monks and those who dwell in solitude. . . . [A]ll their life long they have to fight against gluttony, and cannot be safe from it without striving with the utmost watchfulness of heart and bodily abstinence" (*Conferences*, V.8). Christ was subject to the temptation of gluttony because he was a physical human being. Gluttony is not merely a perversion of something good in human nature, as is true of every other sin; it is a perversion of something necessary to life. In a similar vein, Aquinas comments that temperance is particularly needed because "nature has introduced pleasure into the operations that are necessary for man's life" (2a2ae, 142.1). There may be an inverse proportion of guilt for sins that are due in part to physical givens (see Schimmel, 1992,

p. 247, n. 9). While Aquinas gives the same reason that gluttony is not the greatest sin (though certain grave sins are connected with it), he argues that intemperance is the most disgraceful of sins since it refers to pleasures common to us and lower animals, dimming reason's light and clarity (2a2ae, 148.3, 142.4).

Cassian compares our battle with the eight principal thoughts to Olympic and Pythian games with their qualifying heats. In the "rules and laws of conflict" gluttony, though often the least culpable sin, is the first to be defeated in the battle schema of ascetic theology (see *Institutes*, V.12-13, and *Conferences*, V.3, 6, 10; Aquinas notes the same kind of talk in Gregory; cf. Aquinas, 148.1, and Gregory, 1850, 39.7). At one point Cassian compares gluttony to Egypt: the Hebrews must forsake it and go forth to take possession of the seven nations in Canaan (*Conferences*. V.18). If one cannot conquer a deadly thought that has to do with the body, how can one proceed to more insidious enemies that attack us only in the spiritual arena? Cassian observes that Satan could not defeat Christ through gluttony, so he leapt to the fundamental sins of covetousness and pride. Overcome the earlier sins and the rest die down without difficulty (*Conferences*, V.10). Conversely, gluttony is harmful because it opens the door to all other passions, such as lust, covetousness, anger, dejection, and pride (*Conferences*, V.26). There is wisdom in the observation of this order, though one might question it today given what we know about the genesis of eating disorders.

The order in which these thoughts are discussed is important because they are interconnected: "they are, each of them, so closely connected with each other, that they spring only the one from the other" (Gregory, 1850, 39:25). For example, Cassian groups the vices in pairs; the deadly thoughts form alliances against us (*Conferences*, V.10). So the first two on the list — gluttony and lust — belong together. One who gives in to gluttony is a goner for lust, and, conversely, one who conquers the former should have less trouble with the latter. Gregory's explanation of this connection may sound laughable to us: a full belly puts pressure on the genitals and excites them (Gregory, 1850, 29.25). But A. A. Howsepian, M.D. (personal communication), suggests what may be the physiological explanation behind Gregory's observation of the connection between eating and male lust. The mechanism is the gastro-colic response, by virtue of which eating stimulates the passage of fecal material into the colon, where the resulting pressure on the prostate gland tends to excite sexual interest. The alliance of eating and sex is also not lost on our modern culture, where it is exploited in our television commercials, for instance. Consider a sampling as recent as 1995: A mutual seduction centers around *Taster's Choice* instant coffee. The unusual qualities of *Special K* cereal are linked to a Hawaii-bound woman's preoccupation with her self-flattering figure in a bikini. Red Baron pizza gives one woman an apparition of *the* Red Baron in her apartment kitchen; whereupon she seems to ditch her current boyfriend for the pizza mogul.

We have noted the early Christian awareness that capital sins like gluttony have offspring, are related to other capital sins, and lead to a host of other "thoughts" and grave sins. This claim of the interconnectedness of spiritual pathology is verifiable in our own observation of the debilitating effects of bad habits related to food consumption. For example, to ensure a constant supply of food to satisfy our appetites beyond the body's needs, we might do other things that bring harm to ourselves (such as bulimic episodes) or to others (such as contributing to world hunger). Another way we may experience a gluttony-begotten greed is in overworking to support our expensive appetites. We may envy others who can afford more food or dine more exotically. We may be disoriented from the important things of life by our searching for the ever new taste sensation (something to which the food companies appeal in perennially "new and improved" products, and the cookbook publishers in ever new variations and discoveries of ethnic traditions). Food can become a status symbol and occasion of pride as we try anxiously to top the last dinner party, or treat acquaintances to the most exclusive restaurants. For food we sacrifice the psychological serenity that comes with moderation and simplicity. And to ice the cake, it seems that the more we eat, the less we enjoy (see Schimmel, 1992, p. 151).

To see the connections between these vices and sins in everyday life is the genius of ascetic theologians like Evagrius, whom one translator calls "the anatomist of the passions of the psyche both in their manifestations in behavior and in their intrapsychic activity" (Bamberger, 1970, p. lxxxii). Evagrius calls for careful observation, description, and analysis of our thoughts as a background to mastering them or even the memories of them (Allen, this volume). Some passages in the *Praktikos* even contain insights that it has taken our contemporaries decades to rediscover and record in psychoanalytic literature (see, for example, *Praktikos,* §§43, 50; for examples of how Gregory's *Pastoral Care* anticipates modern psychotherapy, see Oden, 1984, chapter 2). Following in Evagrius's footsteps, Gregory sounds like one of us when he analyzes the connection between melancholy and avarice: "When the disturbed heart has lost the satisfaction of joy within, it seeks for sources of consolation without, and is more anxious to possess external goods, the more it has no joy in which to fall back with it" (Gregory, 1850, 39.25).

These observed connections among thoughts become increasingly clear when we explore the features of gluttony. As we said, the sin of gluttony is neither obesity nor overeating. Nor is gluttony our desire for food, our consumption of it, or our pleasure in eating it. Gluttony is a range of *ways* in which we consume food, involving *inordinate* desire and *immoderate* pleasure (Gregory, 1850, 39.7; Aquinas, 2a2ae, 148.1). To be more specific, Evagrius, Cassian, Gregory, and Aquinas all delineate several aspects of gluttony that we can reduce to six (see Cassian, *Institutes*, V.23 and *Conferences*, V.11; Gregory, 1850, 39.7; Aquinas, 2a2ae, 148.4). They are aspects of acts and of thoughts or attitudes. The first is what we usually associate with gluttony: *eating too much food*. The second is timing: *to eat at any other than the appointed hour* is to be gluttonous. The temperate person eats only at the appointed hours. For the eremite (solitary monk) this usually means eating the one meal at none (the ninth hour after sunrise — afternoon) or later. For the cenobite (communal monk) this means eating with the community at the prescribed times. The third aspect is *anticipating eating with preoccupied, eager longing*. The temperate person is not distracted, between meals, with the thought of food. The hermit who has his desires under control will not be checking the angle of the sun every fifteen minutes. A fourth aspect is expense — it is gluttonous *to consume expensive foods*. A fifth aspect of gluttony is *seeking delicacies*. Since nutritional values of foods were unknown, variety in one's diet was considered unnecessary and distracting. But the point is not historically idiosyncratic: one way to be a glutton is to be a "fussy eater," insisting on interesting, tasty foods or a wide variety. The sixth aspect is attention — gluttony can consist in *paying too much attention to food*. While this last is not a mark of what *we* call gluttony, it certainly applies to our contemporary situation, perhaps even more so than gorging ourselves, for it points to the unhealthiness and sinfulness of being overscrupulous about the food we eat (and how our body looks). Such overconcern can become idolatry of the creation. One can see, then, that the evil of gluttony lies not in food itself, nor in our need to eat it, nor in the accompanying sensations of the palate, but in *how* we go about our eating and in the thought (or lack of thought) we give to our eating. Gluttony is a form of *spiritual* dysfunction.

In her thoughts and activities, the glutton's relationships to others are also undermined. This is especially significant in a culture that preaches entitlement to self-centered indulgence. Increasingly important as we move from Evagrius to Benedictine monasticism is the communal dimension of gluttony. It can foster dislike of the monastic community, manifested in unwillingness to eat at the times appointed for common meals, in a selfish dissatisfaction with the food that is served to all, or a lack of concern for others by seeking more or better for oneself. Eating is to be ruled by concern for the community rather than for one's individual gustatory desires: one is to eat what is offered as it has been prepared, so as not to offend, shame, or annoy other members of the community (see Cassian, *Conferences*, V.11). While I was working on this paper at Blue Cloud Abbey in South Dakota, one of the brothers told me that though he does not eat breakfast, he comes to breakfast because the abbot has insisted that all the monks should be together at every meal. If a monk is voluntarily fasting and guests arrive who need refreshment, he is to eat charitably with the guests (see Cassian, *Institutes*, V.23). This relational emphasis is crucial in our contemporary situation, for we have come to realize that disordered eating often promotes and is promoted by disordered relationships (with ourselves, others, the earth, God). Bringle points out that eating disorders fester in private:

> When I cannot, or do not, or will not eat with my fellow creatures — or, when conversely, I cannot or do not seem to be able to stop eating — I am bodying forth the brokenness of a fallen world and of a distorted will. . . . Not only am I refusing and defying companionship; I am also refusing the carnal medium through which these gifts of grace appear. (Bringle, 1992, pp. 143, 138)

No doubt, some gluttons are compassionate, loving members of communities. But, as Schimmel notes, "there is some correlation between a preoccupation with food and neglect of other responsibilities" — to significant others, to society, and to God (Schimmel, 1992, pp. 152-55).

Ultimately, gluttony is a distorted and misplaced form of a deeper longing. As Gerald May points out, if we were looking at the *deadly* sin of gluttony from a psychodynamic perspective, we could speak of displacing our longing for God upon other things like food; it provides a way of trying to satisfy our longing for God that seems to protect our sense of personal power and demand the least sacrifice, though, in the end, gluttony does neither for us (May, 1988, p. 93). It can begin as a venial sin, disguised as enjoying God's good gifts, and rationalized by our contemporary ideology of self-indulgence. Commenting on this, Gregory seems to describe the contemporary experience of some who are gradually led into dysfunctional eating habits: "Gluttony is also wont to exhort the conquered heart, as if with reason, when it says, God has created all things clean, in order to be eaten, and he who refuses to fill himself with food, what else does he do but gainsay the gift that has been granted him." What follows is a "howling army": "[W]hen the hapless soul, once captured by the principal vices, is turned to madness by multiple iniquities, it is now laid waste with brutal cruelty" (Gregory, 1850, 39.25).

Nonetheless, the temptation to gluttonous acts (what May might call a God-given propensity to addiction) can teach us about ourselves and what it will require to maintain our health. The question now is how best to take what Bringle calls "the gift of hunger" (Bringle, 1992, pp. 148-49) — the desire for necessary nourishment — and make it serve us in our relationships with others and God, rather than be enslaved to it. That is to say, what cures gluttony? What restores and maintains healthy behavior and attitudes toward food?

Curing Gluttony

To pose the question this way — in a medical metaphor — is not to assume that all gluttonous eating habits and contemporary eating disorders are merely physical dysfunctions and thus beyond a victim's spiritual control. Actually, no one understands exactly what causes anorexia, for instance, and approaches to treatment vary with etiological theories. Experts do not even agree on the definitions of anorexia nervosa and bulimia. I shall assume that eating problems have medical *and* moral dimensions, as do most addictions (I am indebted to Schimmel, 1992, Bringle, 1992, and Plantinga, this volume; for a discussion of biological causes and treatments of anorexia nervosa and bulimia, see Pope and Hudson, 1985).

    Ascetic theologians use the medical metaphor (e.g., see Evagrius, 1981, §§56 and 79), but they differ from some of our contemporaries who use the language of disease to encourage the belief that people are not responsible for their vices and the disastrous consequences of their actions. Such misuse of the medical metaphor lessens the feelings of guilt (proper *and* improper) and discourages the development of self-control (see the discussion of agency in relation to other causes of behavior in Jones, this volume). The contemporary view is attractive because most of us would rather be sick than guilty or duty bound to take control of our appetites. But the ascetic theologian talks of sickness, not to excuse us from responsibility, but to motivate attention to spiritual advice: we must change our habits before it is too late. In fact, if gluttony is a bad *habit* — a deadly sin — it is so because the medical model does not tell the whole story.

    The ascetic theologians describe the health of the soul as *apatheia*. Early monastics were influenced by Stoic and Neo-Platonic psychologies, but they adapted, rather than adopted, the Stoic concept of *apatheia*. "Apatheia," which means literally "a state of being without passion," is not really a very good word for the concept they have in mind. It is not at all "apathy" in our sense of a "dull, lethargic absence of caring and interest" (see May, 1988, p. 192, n. 1). Nor is it the leveling out of human emotions or the extirpation of the passions that the Stoics sometimes claim to aim at (see Nussbaum, 1994, chapter 10). The ascetic theologians were really *enthusiasts* of a sort, whose aim was to love God with their whole heart — a state of the soul that is certainly not without disposition to emotions, and is quite different from either apathy, in our sense, or what the Stoics called *apatheia* (see Bamberger, 1970, pp. lxxxiii-lxxxiv, and Cassian, *Institutes*, 4.43). *Apatheia*, for the ascetic theologians, is really not a state of being without passions, but a state of being without *those passions that are contrary to the love of God* — passions such as pride, greed, lust, worldly anger, and gluttony. Ascetics like Evagrius and Cassian took this concept from the Stoics, Clement of Alexandria, and Egyptian sources like Anthony, and put their own stamp on it (see Bamberger, 1970, pp. lxxii-lxxiii). For them *apatheia* is an abiding sense of peace and joy that comes from the full harmony of the passions — an *habitual* state developed through discipline *(askesis)*, which is why we call it a virtue. As such it is perfectly contrary to the misguided or inordinate desire called gluttony. Through various exercises a person trains herself to be in full possession of her affective faculties so that disordered cravings for foods are held in check and rightly ordered, and she experiences a state of deep calm — a "repose" or "purity of heart" as Cassian calls it (*Conferences*, I.4). It is a state of undistracted prayer. According to Evagrius, one of the marks of *apatheia* is the ability to remain calm and peaceful even when one has memories of situations or events that tend to stimulate and disorder the passions (Evagrius, 1981, §§34, 64-67, 69).

This harmonious integration of the emotional life always remains exposed to the attacks of demons, particularly attacks of gluttony, which, as we have said, trades on the need for nourishment and its concomitant pleasure from which we will never be free (see Bamberger, 1970, pp. lxxxv-lxxxvi; and Evagrius, 1981, §§60, 77). So emotional health — *apatheia* — must be maintained with ongoing vigilance. Of course, this is to be expected: good health is never a given; one must work at it with care. *Apatheia*, like other aspects of health, can be had (or lost) by degrees; one continually grows in (or out) of it. Furthermore, it is subject to the limitations of one's individual constitution. This last point should not be overlooked when it comes to the medical side of eating disorders; in fact, we will recall it when we discuss discernment below.

We should mention that *apatheia* is the aim of the first phase of spiritual development — the active ascetic life, which begins in faith, diminishes the force of the inordinate passions "until they are destroyed," and results in charity. This leads to the second phase — the contemplative, which begins with the contemplation of nature, diminishes ignorance, and results, finally, in the union with God that is called "theology" (see

Evagrius, 1981, §84). The disciplines in ascetic theology have to do with the first step (viz., purgation) of the threefold ascent that ends in union with God. This paper examines only the dynamics of *apatheia* and *agape*.

Evagrius teaches that *agape* is the offspring of *apatheia*. Harmony in one's passions prepares a person to love others and God fully, because *apatheia* stamps out anger, sulking, lust, resentment, envy, and all other impediments to self-giving love. Without love, *apatheia* alone is of little value. The mere absence of distracting interests and thoughts, as Evagrius reminds us, is not true prayer (Evagrius, 1981, §55). Gregory points out in practical terms how the disciplines aiming at *apatheia* need to be practiced with *agape* in view.

> . . . [W]e must consider how little the virtue of abstinence is regarded, unless it deserve commendation by reason of other virtues. . . . A man fasts not to God but to himself, if he does not give to the poor what he denies his belly for a time, but reserves it to be given to his belly later. (Gregory, 1950, III.19)

The discipline of fasting to which Gregory refers helps one get a handle on gluttonous thoughts and reform the appetite. Let us see how this discipline, as understood by the ascetic theologians, might be applied to a contemporary imagined case of an eating disorder.

An Illustration

Frieda, a college professor, stashes food in her office, takes advantage of every free all-you-can-eat meal and reception at the college, and frequently visits the vending machines and campus coffee shop. Eating relieves her stress, comforts her, picks up her spirits. But when she comforts herself "too much" she feels depressed. (Recall Gregory's observations about the "howling army.") She does not consider herself anorexic or bulimic . . . yet; she is smart enough to know about the symptoms and rational enough to want to avoid developing bad (and potentially fatal) habits. But she is beginning to notice disturbing patterns. And she feels guilty. She has been known to cancel appointments with students so as not to miss a spread of delicacies at a reception for retiring faculty, the brownies and cookies a half-hour before faculty meetings, or the unlimited food at free luncheons. She can rationalize attending these functions; after all, she is associating with colleagues and not bingeing in private at these times. Still, all this seems to her a bad sign. Then there is her poor self-image when she gorges on food loaded with calories and fat; she has become obsessed with reading food labels and calculating the caloric and fat content of her foods, even though this preoccupation does not stop her from bingeing. The food that sometimes gives comfort and a sense of control now more often causes anxiety, shame, guilt, and feelings of failure.

Frieda is becoming a glutton. She exhibits four features of gluttony that our ascetic theologians have identified. She gorges herself. She anticipates eating and eats far more often than at the "appointed" times. And she pays so much attention to her eating that it preoccupies her mind (and time) inordinately, keeping her from pursuing her gifts and calling, and from spending time with others. Furthermore, she has experienced some of gluttony's offspring. She knows she has a problem — that she is in danger of "making a god of her belly." So she decides to explore the disciplines of fasting and abstinence.

She discovers that fasting is not what Jenny Craig and SlimFast call "dieting," despite some similarities, such as controlling what you eat or don't eat and substituting alternative activities for eating. But her motivation and goal make this discipline different. Simply put, she wants to become a healthy Christian person who is able to love God and others (and herself) as she is commanded. Dieting always tended to put the focus on herself (especially on her appearance) and cultural idols (see Bringle's comment about "caloric Pelagianism": "I cannot heal an obsession with food by replacing it with a counter obsession with dieting" [Bringle, 1992, p. 147]). While a Christian concern for the body will include a moderate concern for fat and calories, for weight and appearance, it will be driven chiefly by the spiritual concern to develop attitudes of contentment, gratitude, trust, and patience. These are the aims that radically distinguish the discipline the church has called "fasting" from what our culture calls "dieting." Let us now look at the features of this *Christian* therapeutic discipline.

First, as Frieda fasts — abstaining from eating between meals (though she does not neglect associating with colleagues) and occasionally even skipping lunch — she *meditates on certain portions of Scripture* such as Psalm 119:57-72 and Matthew 6:25-34, as well as on the creation through which God manifests himself. She is wise to do this, according to ascetic theologians, for the principal thoughts of gluttony and lust require both bodily abstinence and a "fast of the soul" or exercise in alternative and contrary thoughts such as are available in Scripture — a double remedy. Meditating on Scripture will help Frieda to fast from thoughts such as anxiety over not fitting cultural expectations and the distrust that she will not find peace of mind without something to munch on. This will make her bodily fast useful and profitable, according to Cassian (see *Conferences*, V.4, and *Institutes*, V.14, 21).

During these times she gains several insights about herself and God. Through fasting she understands even better what has been controlling her life; and she finds that the small incremental steps she takes toward controlling her eating passions have given her some mastery over other areas of her life. Furthermore, she discovers that underlying her anxiety about food is a distrust of God: a fear of living according to God's commandments, a fear of being satisfied with the way that God has made her, and especially a fear that there may not be adequate food (a common fear among bulimics) — fears with which her meditations on Psalm 119 and Matthew 6 help her, for they teach her about a God whose earth is filled with the steadfast love of a Caretaker who watches over even flowers and sparrows (see Evagrius, 1981, §7). The bonus in all of this is that her love for God grows, since she is learning in various areas of her life what it means to trust God as one trusts a good parent; *and* she displays loving behavior toward her students in a way that she had not been able to because her bad eating habits had interfered. She now keeps her appointments, is not rushed to get through interviews to get to her stash or a reception, and is even more intent on what students are communicating because her mind and body are not filled with food. She has entered the arena of spiritual contest and is beginning to experience victory over the first opponent. Other victories will come in time, such as the defeat of envy of the trim female colleague down the hall. As Cassian puts it, the soul is invigorated by the course of triumphs (*Institutes*, V.19; *Conferences*, V.14).

A second aspect of the ascetic theologian's therapy is a *reliance on community* — an emphasis that gains momentum as the monasticism of the hermits develops into monastic communities such as the Benedictine. A communal dimension is inherent in ascetic and monastic wisdom, for one characteristically learns about the dangers in eating habits, the way to combat them, and the connections such behaviors bear to other sins, through the collective wisdom of those who have experienced the same faults and overcome them. The first therapists are the *abba*s in the desert to whom one goes for advice. Later this role is occupied by the abbot who directs his monks with the wisdom that has been passed down in the community. Reminiscent of the wisdom literature of the Jewish scriptures, the Rule of St. Benedict opens with the sentence, "Listen carefully, my son, to the master's instructions, and attend to them with the ear of your heart." Furthermore, in the monastic community virtues are modeled; as Cassian puts it, we find Christ "bit by bit in all" (*Institutes*, V.4). Evagrius insists that from self-knowledge, observation, tradition, and the wisdom of our forebears come the insights that give us power to deal with our deadly thoughts (*Praktikos*, §§43, 50; *Chapters on Prayer*, §133). Frieda will need to depend on the wisdom of those who have gone before her, whether through a spiritual director (like the *abba* in the desert or the abbot of the monastery) or the modeling and support of the community (or, indeed, both). She has already done this to some extent by meditating on Scripture, which is the property and expression of a religious community. But she might also confide in a trusted and wise friend, a counselor, or a pastor. If her problem has progressed to the point of true bulimia, she will need a support group related to eating disorders. The monastic experience that eating can be ordered in and through community seems to be confirmed both by contemporary psychology's observation that eating disorders feed on privacy, and by the success of the twelve-step groups. The wisdom of the "masters" (those who have successfully dealt with their problem) and communal accountability and support are crucial.

Third, ascetic therapy *aims at moderation and temperance*. Contrary to our stereotype of ascetic and monastic theology, Cassian, Benedict, and Gregory denounce the monk's attempt to become a spiritual superhero. With different degrees of emphasis, from the desert to the Rule of Benedict the focus is on moderation and balance in life. A monk is to take what the body needs, while avoiding satiety. Gregory's observations on moderation are worth citing:

> [S]ometimes, while we endeavour to oppose our desires too immoderately, we increase the miseries of necessity. For it is necessary for a man so to maintain the citadel of continence, as to destroy, not the flesh, but the vices of the flesh. For frequently, when the flesh is restrained more than is just, it is weakened even for the exercises of good works, so as to be unequal to prayer also or preaching, whilst it hastens to put out entirely the incentives of vices within itself. For this very man, whom we bear outwardly, we have as the assistant of our inward intention, and both the motions of wantonness are within it, and there also abound in it the appliances of good works. But often, whilst we attack an enemy therein, we kill a citizen also whom we love; and after which we spare, as it were, a fellow citizen, we nurture an enemy for battle. For our vices become proud upon the same food, on which our virtues are nourished and live. And when a virtue is nourished, the strength of our vices is frequently increased. But when unbounded abstinence weakens the power of vices, our virtue also faints and pants. (1850, 39:7)

In *Pastoral Care* Gregory offers advice on counseling *both* the gluttonous *and* the abstemious, reminding us that "vices commonly masquerade as virtues" (1950, II.9). Anticipating Gregory, Cassian voices a similar insight that corresponds to contemporary treatment of bulimia. Cassian warns us against too severe fasting because it too easily leads to unnecessary relaxation regarding eating after the fast is over: "A reasonable supply of food partaken of daily with moderation, is better than a severe and long fast at intervals. Excessive fasting has been known not only to undermine the constancy of the mind, but also to weaken the power of prayers through sheer weariness of body" (*Institutes,* V.9). Ascetic theologians like Cassian notice that gluttony is often worsened by severe fasting. In contemporary observation of the pattern of bingeing and purging often seen in eating disorders, obsessive dieting and self-restraint often result in compulsive eating, not in response to physical hunger, but in response to stress and anxiety. Those who are overly scrupulous (recall one of the ascetic theologians' six aspects of gluttony) about calories and fat and weight loss are more often those who compensate (in private) by overindulging. "Present evidence suggests that it is simplistic to regard dieting as necessary and sufficient in itself to cause anorexia. However the mindsets, attitudes, and behaviors associated with dieting may predispose individuals to develop these disorders" (Dwyer, 1985, p. 29; see also Bringle, 1992, pp. 45, 129-30, 147).

A fourth dimension of ascetical gluttony-therapy is the principle that *the regimen must be tailored to the individual.* At one point in his Rule, Benedict insists that monks are not to fast severely, because it may damage their spiritual life (e.g., unusually rigorous fasting can lead to pride). If a monk wants to fast in this way, he may do so only with the abbot's permission. Why? Because discernment is needed in *each individual* case. Benedict never intended that souls be mass-produced. Each has different needs, and in the monastic community the abbot is qualified, by his wisdom and by knowledge of the current condition of each of his sheep, to prescribe for them just what they need to remain well and grow spiritually (Fry, 1982, chapters 2, 27, 64). Since Benedict insists that only those who have made spiritual progress within the community (the "*schola* for the Lord's service") can go alone into the desert to fight the demons as hermits, we must assume that after a period of time the discerning qualities of the abbot will have been internalized by the monk, so that he can make his *own* judgments about how to pursue spiritual combat. Cassian calls this discernment the "judgment of conscience" and insists that it does not follow hard and fast rules (*Institutes,* V.9). We are all attacked by these faults, but in significantly different ways. Gregory instructs the counselor to adapt the principles of spiritual development to the individual constitution and needs of each monk, as a skillful harpist plays with a variety of strokes to produce a harmonious melody (1950, III [prologue]). This communal conception of human development, this graduated leading of the less mature by the more mature, this sensitivity of the guide to the abilities and needs of the learner, all remind us of the style of nurture that Cynthia Jones Neal (this volume) finds implied in the Bible and confirmed by some strands of contemporary developmental psychology.

Cassian finds that the need for wise flexibility is especially pertinent to gluttony and fasting because, unlike some of the other vices and virtues, gluttony and temperance have to do with the body; so the time, manner, and quality of refreshment depend on the condition, age, and sex of the person's body (*Institutes,* V.5). Our culture tends to ignore individual differences in matters of nutrition. It imposes a cookie-cutter standard regarding eating requirements and weight-to-height ratios. "RDA" lists on cans and boxes become gospel for people watching their fats and calories; insurance companies determine who is "overweight" based on charts that have not always taken into account ethnic and gender differences. One standard chart was based on white males, but applied to all insurance applicants (see Bringle, 1992, chapter 3). Even the term "overweight" is presumptuous if it neglects the consideration that each person has a *set-point* for his or her weight, namely, the weight that is right for him or her (given peculiarities of bodily make up), which the body works to maintain against extremes at either end (see Bringle, 1992, pp. 123-24). Roller-coaster dieting can actually increase one's set-point. Presently our conception of proper eating is guided too much by the media, the diet industry, and the modeling and entertainment businesses. Their ideal is what a healthy person *looks* like, but we need a more refined and spiritual discernment in order to know our own bodies well enough to feed them what they *need* and apply the remedy that fits our particular compulsions. If we achieve this much, then we make room for the ultimate goal of fasting, which is to learn the love of God and neighbor.

If Frieda compares herself to a trim colleague whose set-point weight is lower than hers or if she buys into the culture's definition of what spiritually and physically healthy people *look* like, her guilt and shame may be irrational by Christian standards, however rational they are by the standards of our society. And the preoccupation with looks is a very close cousin to what the ascetic theologians call gluttony, even if it is accompanied by moderate eating and good control of the appetite for food. Frieda must come to know herself as God has fashioned her and learn to accept herself in a way that may well be countercultural.

A fifth principle of appetite therapy, that follows from the fact that the seven deadly sins are interdependent, is that *progress occurs one step at a time.* This principle reminds us of twelve-step programs, but it is as old as Cassian and Gregory. Both theologians suggest that the deadly thoughts are connected in such a way that vainglory might be used to deal with gluttony as a first step. For example, a monk may keep his fasts out of fear of the embarrassment of having the other monks observe his laxity, or out of the desire to gain their praise. Once gluttonous thoughts are under control, vainglory can be dealt with in turn (Cassian, *Conferences*, V.12). Frieda might be moved to get an initial handle on her gluttonous thoughts by her embarrassment over teaching evaluations like "Professor is not available." "She missed three appointments." Once her eating habits and her relationship with students improve, she may find she no longer needs to be motivated by how others view her, since she finds her improved performance intrinsically rewarding. In fact, her victory over gluttony may encourage and steel her for the later battle against vainglory.

The sixth and last principle of gluttony management that I derive from the ascetic theologians is *attend to your body; honor, but do not worship it.* Cassian is adamant that while we must cut out the roots of the other principal faults, we cannot possibly cut off occasions of gluttony (*Conferences*, V.19). Dallas Willard argues throughout *The Spirit of the Disciplines* that we are created as embodied beings, and can do nothing spiritually that does not involve our body. God deals with us through and in our bodily existence; to ignore that fact would be to join what Bringle calls a "new gnosticism." The ascetic theologians were sometimes suspicious of the body, but they did not disparage it or adopt a gnostic dualism that ignores the body's needs to serve the soul. Martha is needed so that Mary can serve:

> A brother went to see Abba Silvanus on the mountain of Sinai. When he saw the brothers working hard he said to the old man, "Do not labor for the food which perishes (John 6:27). Mary has chosen the good portion" (Luke 10:42). The old man said to his disciple, "Zacharias, give the brother a book and put him in a cell without anything else." So when the ninth hour came the visitor watched the door expecting someone would be sent to call him to the meal. When no-one called him he got up, went to find the old man and said to him, "Have the brothers not eaten today?" The old man replied that they had. Then he said, "Why did you not call me?" The old man said to him, "Because you are a spiritual man and do not need that kind of food. We, being carnal, want to eat, and that is why we work. But you have chosen the good portion and read the whole day long and you do not want to eat carnal food." When he heard these words the brother made a prostration saying, "Forgive me, abba." The old man said to him, "Mary needs Martha. It is really thanks to Martha that Mary is praised." (Willard, 1988, p. 223; cf. Cassian, *Conferences*, XI.14, 15)

Accordingly, Aquinas argues that reason is not operative in one who abstains from *all* pleasures, since one cannot use reason unless the body is sustained, and the body is sustained through operations (like eating) that afford pleasure (Aquinas, 1948, 2a2ae, 142.1). Thus Schimmel's constant refrain (Schimmel, 1992) that we are to choose happiness in place of pleasure is simplistic.

A Christian psychology of eating must neither oversacralize nor desecrate the body (Bringle, 1992, p. 34). It is not wrong to attend to the needs of the body nor to enjoy sensations from what touches the body. But it is unhealthy to worship bodily pleasure, as our culture sometimes encourages us to do. We moderns tend not to believe there can *be* such a thing as improper pleasure. There may, of course, be disastrous *consequences* of pleasurable indulgences, but as long as these can be forestalled, the modern principle is, "The more pleasure the better." But a Christian psychology requires a distinction between healthy and unhealthy pleasures. And insofar as the pleasures in question have food as their object, and no food is in itself "unclean" (Acts 10:15), the distinction must lie in the attitude with which the pleasure is experienced. Gluttony is a "bad attitude." It is an attitude in which God is not given the honor due him, an attitude in which the neighbor becomes spiritually invisible. This attitude is interlaced with bad behavioral habits, and that is why gluttony must be attacked not only with cognitive, but also with behavioral changes. When people like Frieda eat only at regular intervals, slowly, and without being overscrupulous, they tend to savor even ordinary food, and the pleasure they receive from eating has a lasting and healthful effect and finds its proper place in the order of good things that God has created.

Does Modern Psychology Confirm Ascetic Theology?

Diogenes Allen (this volume) has proposed that the claims of ascetic theology might be tested by contemporary psychology. We now have before us some of those claims, and I have remarked, from time to time, about parallels with these claims that can be found in our contemporary psychological thought and practice concerning eating disorders. Of course I cannot here undertake an experimental testing of anything that Evagrius, Cassian, Benedict, or Gregory have to say about the psychology of gluttony. But I would like to consider a couple of the claims that we have noted, with the philosophical question of what it would be for these to be confirmed or disconfirmed by modern psychology.

Consider first the claim that gluttony is causally linked to other sins. Psychologists might very well establish, through careful observation, that overeating (by some appropriate measure) has a higher incidence among people who regularly buy soft-core pornography than among the rest of the population. Of course, this is not itself a causal claim, but perhaps we can imagine observations that are controlled enough to suggest a causal connection. (The connection might go both ways: slovenliness about one's gustatory appetite might "encourage" one to slovenliness about one's sexual appetite, as well as the other way around.) So perhaps psychology could establish a causal link between one kind of appetitive behavior and another kind. But this would be far from confirming that _gluttony is causally linked to other sins_ because, as we have shown, gluttony as the ascetic theologians understand it is not simply or only overeating, but an attitude toward food that disables a person from loving God and neighbor. The reference to God and neighbor is essential to the definition of gluttony. If so, then modern non-Christian psychology has no place for a discussion of gluttony; insofar as modern psychology is skeptical about the existence of God, it must be equally skeptical about the existence of gluttony. If it is to confirm or disconfirm the claim that gluttony is causally linked to other sins, it must impose a different sense on "gluttony" and "sins" than the ascetic theologians give these words, and so must talk of something other than what the ascetic theologians are making their claim about.

But consider the claim that a supporting and disciplining community, with experience of managing disordered appetites, can contribute significantly to the reordering of a person's appetites. The ascetic theologians will, in their own discussions, not make exactly the above claim. They will speak not of a supporting and disciplining community, but of the monastery or the _abba_; and they will more often use the theologically loaded terms "gluttony" and "lust" and "pride" than the more neutral, theoretically noncommital "disordered appetites." But we can imagine them wanting to speak to people in a different community of discourse, perhaps even modern psychologists, and thus using the more generic vocabulary of the claim as I have formulated it. The reader will have been uncomfortable with my discussion of the first claim, and my observation that psychologists who don't believe in God don't believe in gluttony either, and therefore wouldn't confirm its causal connection to something else. The reason for the reader's discomfort is the insight that there is common ground between the ascetic theologian and the modern psychologist. Like the concepts of addiction and sin that Plantinga (this volume) discusses, bulimia is a different concept from gluttony, but the two overlap in significant ways; for example, a mark of each of them is overeating. Furthermore, it is clear that a twelve-step group and a monastery may both count, generically, as "a supporting and disciplining community." So it would seem that observations made within the vocabulary and belief system of some modern psychological outlook could confirm, in a somewhat informal and unrigorous but nevertheless real way, a claim made within the language and belief system of Christian psychology. We seem to have a case of this in the parallel between the involvement of the monastery in the Benedictine ascesis of gluttony and the involvement of twelve-step and other support groups in the control of eating disorders as identified in *DSM IV*.

I conclude, somewhat tentatively, that modern psychology can in principle confirm, and seems actually to confirm, certain *generic* features of the ascetic theologians' claims about the nature and therapy of disordered appetites; but that it does not, and in principle could not, confirm those features of the ascetic theologians' psychological claims that derive from the distinctively Christian theology of these ancient psychologists. To the extent that contemporary Christian psychology is committed to the same theology as these ancient psychologists, the same pattern of possibilities of confirmation by contemporary non-Christian observations exists for it. (For a different view of the possibility of interaction between Christian psychology and modern psychology, see Griffiths, this volume.)

Conclusion

We may all be psychotics (Howsepian, this volume), but the majority of us do not suffer from what the *DSM IV* calls eating disorders. That does not, however, put us beyond the ascetic theologians' advice about gluttony. In some ways the goal of *apatheia* seems a second cousin to one of the three vows that a Benedictine monk takes: stability. Specifically, the vow of stability commits a monastic to the same community for the rest of his or her life. As the desert fathers put it, "Stay in your cell, and your cell will teach you everything." One who stays in her community is open to the transforming effects of God's grace, because, as in a long and good marriage, one eventually cuts through the superficiality, the guile, and the confusion in such a way that a deep and quiet love can flow. This is what the *askesis* — the exercise of the disciplines — is meant to do. The disciplines are an angioplasty for the channels of God's life-transforming grace so that it can eventually flow into love of God and neighbor. In our culture the idea of spiritual discipline is as revolutionary as adolescent virginity and lifetime monogamy. Stability calls us to regulate our desires and impulses, to be satisfied with the food that is set before us, to avoid inordinate preoccupation with what is in the package or how it is going to make us look, to refuse to succumb to the constant titillation of "new and improved" taste sensations, and to reject making food a status symbol. We need to hunger between meals and instead of meals so as to be empty long enough to realize we are dependent and vulnerable, biodegradable creatures who need God's sustaining grace and the loving support of others. Bingeing on pleasure and voraciously seeking new stimulations can keep us from savoring God's faithful presence in the daily bread that can satisfy the needs of our bodily existence. In these and other ways we learn freedom from our appetites for the creature, so as to keep fresh the appetite to taste the faithfulness of God.

Collated References

Adams, R. M. (1985). Involuntary sins. *The Philosophical Review, 94*, 3-31.

Adams, R. M. (1987). The virtue of faith. In R. M. Adams, *The virtue of faith and other essays in philosophical theology.* New York: Oxford University Press.

Ainsworth, M. (1979). Infant-mother attachment. *American Psychologist, 34*, 932-937.

Ainsworth, M. (1985). Attachments across the life span. *Bulletin of the New York Academy of Medicine, 61*, 792-812.

Ainsworth, M., & Bell, S. (1974). Mother-infant interaction and the development of competence. In K. J. Connoly & J. S. Bruner (Eds.), *The growth of competence.* New York: Academic Press.

Ainsworth, M., Blehar, M., Waters, E., & Wall, S. (1978). *Patterns of attachment: A psychological study of the strange situation.* Hillsdale, NJ: Erlbaum.

Allen, D. (1986). *Temptation.* Cambridge, MA: Cowley.

Allen, D. (this volume). Ascetic theology and psychology.

Alston, W. P. (1988). Divine and human action. In T. V. Morris (Ed.), *Divine and human action.* Ithaca, NY: Cornell University Press.

Alston, W. P. (1989a). *Divine nature and human language: Essays in philosophical theology.* Ithaca, NY: Cornell University Press.

Alston, W. P. (1989b). *Epistemic justification.* Ithaca, NY: Cornell University Press.

American Psychiatric Association. (1987). *Diagnostic and statistical manual of mental disorder: DSM III-R.* (3rd ed., revised). Washington, D.C.: American Psychiatric Association.

American Psychiatric Association. (1994). *Diagnostic and statistical manual of mental disorder: DSM IV.* (4th ed.). Washington, D.C.: American Psychiatric Association.

Aquinas. (1948). *Summa theologiae.* (Fathers of the English Dominican Province, Trans.). Westminster, MD: Christian Classics.

Arend, R., Gove, F., & Sroufe, L. A. (1979). Continuity of individual adaptation from infancy to kindergarten: A predictive study of ego-resiliency and curiosity in preschoolers. *Child Development, 50*, 950-959.

Aristotle. (1985). *Nicomachean ethics.* (T. Irwin, Trans.). Indianapolis: Hackett Publishing Company.

Ashcroft, J. J. (1989). *Get slim and stay slim: the psychology of weight control.* Oxford & New York: Oxford University Press.

Atkinson, J. W. (1964). *An introduction to motivation.* Princeton, NJ: Van Nostrand.

Augsburger, D. (1970). *Seventy times seven: The freedom of forgiveness.* Chicago: Moody.

Augsburger, D. (1981). *Caring enough to forgive.* Ventura, CA: Regal.

Augustine. (1961). *Confessions.* (R. S. Pine-Coffin, Trans.). Harmondsworth, Middlesex: Penguin Books.

Baillie, J. (1942). *Invitation to pilgrimage.* New York: Charles Scribner's Sons.

Bamberger, J. E. (1970). Introduction. In Evagrius Ponticus, *Pratikos and chapters on prayer.* (J. E. Bamberger, OCSO, Trans.). Kalamazoo, MI: Cistercian Publications.

Bandura, A. (1978). The self system in reciprocal determinism. *American Psychologist, 33,* 344-358.

Bandura, A. (1983). Temporal dynamics and decomposition of reciprocal determinism: A reply to Phillips and Orton. *Psychological Review, 90,* 166-170.

Bandura, A. (1986). *Social foundations of thought and action: A social cognitive theory.* Englewood Cliffs, NJ: Prentice-Hall.

Bandura, A. (1989). Human agency in social cognitive theory. *American Psychologist, 44,* 1175-1184.

Barnard, G. W. (1992). Explaining the unexplainable: Wayne Proudfoot's *Religious Experience. Journal of the American Academy of Religion, 40/2,* 231-256.

Barth, K. (1960). *Church dogmatics: The doctrine of creation.* (Vol. 3, Part 2. H. Knight, G. W. Bromiley, J. Reid, & R. Fuller, Trans.). Edinburgh: T. & T. Clark. (Originally published in 1948).

Barth, K. (1962). *Epistle to the Philippians.* London: S.C.M.

Basinger, D. (1985). What Christian philosophers may do. *Reformed Journal, 35,* Issue 2, 17-19.

Basinger, D. (1988). Hick's religious pluralism and "Reformed Epistemology": A middle ground. *Faith and Philosophy, 5,* 421-432.

Baumrind, D. (1973). The development of instrumental competence through *socialization.* In A. D. Pick (Ed.), *Minnesota symposia on child psychology.* Minneapolis: The University of Minnesota Press.

Baumrind, D. (1977). Socialization and instrumental competence in young children. *Young Children, 26,* 104-119.

Beach, S., Sandeen, E., & O'Leary, D. (1990). *Depression in marriage.* New York: Guilford Press.

Beattie, M. (1987). *Codependent no more.* San Francisco: HarperSanFrancisco.

Beck, A. (1976). *Cognitive therapy and the emotional disorders.* New York: International Universities Press.

Beckmann, J. (1986). Metaprocesses and the regulation of behavior. In F. Halisch & J. Kuhl (Eds.), *Motivation, intention, and volition.* Berlin: Springer-Verlag.

Beckwith, L., & Cohen, S. E. (1984). Home environment and cognitive competence in preterm children during the first 5 years. In A. W. Gottfried (Ed.), *Home environment and early cognitive development: Longitudinal research.* Orlando: Academic Press.

Beker, J. C. (1982). *Paul the Apostle: The triumph of God in life and thought*. Philadelphia: Fortress.

Bell, S. M. (1970). The development of the concept of object as related to infant-mother attachment. *Child Development, 41,* 291-311.

Bellah, R., Madsen, R., Sullivan, W., Swidler, A., & Tipton, S. (1985). *Habits of the heart: Individualism and commitment in American life*. New York: Harper & Row.

Belsky, J. (1981). Early human experience: A family perspective. *Developmental Psychology, 17,* 3-23.

Belsky, J. (1984). The determinants of parenting: A process model. *Child Development, 55,* 83-96.

Belsky, J., Taylor, D., & Rovine, M. (1984a). The Pennsylvania Infant and Family Development Project II: The development of reciprocal interaction in the mother-infant dyad. *Child Development, 55,* 706-717.

Belsky, J., Taylor, D., & Rovine, M. (1984b). The Pennsylvania Infant and Family Development Project III: The origins of individual differences in infant-mother attachment: Maternal and infant contributions. *Child Development, 55,* 718-728.

Benson, C. K. (1992). Forgiveness and the psychotherapeutic process. *Journal of Psychology and Christianity, 11,* 76-81.

Berger, L. S. (1991). *Substance abuse as symptom*. Hillsdale, NJ: The Analytic Press.

Berkhof, H. (1979). *Christian faith*. (S. Woudstra, Trans.). Grand Rapids: Wm. B. Eerdmans Publishing Company.

Berkhof, L. (1939-1941). *Systematic theology* (4th ed.). Grand Rapids: Wm. B. Eerdmans Publishing Company.

Berkouwer, G. C. (1971). *Sin*. (P. C. Holtrop, Trans.). Grand Rapids: Wm. B. Eerdmans Publishing Company.

Berlin, B., & Kay, P. (1969). *Basic color terms: Their universality and evolution*. Berkeley: University of California Press.

Berns, W. (1994). Getting away with murder. *Commentary, 97* (4), 25-29.

Block, J. H., & Block, J. (1980). The role of ego-control and ego-resiliency in the organization of behavior. In W. A. Collins (Ed.), *Minnesota symposium on child psychology*. (Vol. 13). Hillsdale, NJ: Lawrence Erlbaum.

Bloom, A. (1987). *The closing of the American mind*. New York: Simon and Schuster.

Bonar, C. A. (1989). Personality theories and asking for forgiveness. *Journal of Psychology and Christianity, 8,* 45-51.

Bonaventure (1978). *The tree of life*. In *Bonaventure*. (E. Cousins, Trans.). Mahwah, NJ: Paulist Press.

Bonhoeffer, D. (1960). *The communion of saints*. (E. Bethge, Trans.). New York: Harper & Row. (Originally published in 1930).

Book of common prayer. (1945). New York: The Church Pension Fund.

Boskind-White, M. (1985). Bulimarexia: A sociocultural perspective. In S. W. Emmett (Ed.), *Theory and treatment of anorexia nervosa and bulimia: Biomedical, sociocultural, and psychological perspectives* (pp. 113-126). New York: Brunner/Mazel.

Boszormenyi-Nagy, I. (1987). *Foundations of contextual therapy*. New York: Brunner/Mazel.

Boszormenyi-Nagy, I., & Krasner, B. (1986). *Between give and take: A clinical guide to contextual therapy*. New York: Brunner/Mazel.

Bowen, M. (1978). *Family therapy in clinical practice*. Northvale, NJ: Jason Aronson.

Bowen, M., & Kerr, M. (1988). *Family evaluation*. New York: W. W. Norton and Company.

Bowlby, J. (1959). Separation anxiety. *International Journal of Psycho-Analysis, XLI*, 1-25.

Bowlby, J. (1973). *Separation: Anxiety and anger*. New York: Basic Books.

Bowlby, J. (1980). *Loss: Sadness and depression*. New York: Basic Books.

Bowlby, J. (1982). *Attachment*. (2nd ed.). New York: Basic Books. (1st ed., 1969).

Bowlby, J. (1988). *A secure base: Parent-child attachment and healthy human development*. New York: Basic Books.

Brandsma, J. M. (1982). Forgiveness: A dynamic, theological and therapeutic analysis. *Pastoral Psychology, 31*, 40-50.

Braybrooke, D. (1987). *Philosophy of social science*. Englewood Cliffs, NJ: Prentice-Hall.

Bretherton, I. (1992). The origins of attachment theory: John Bowlby and Mary Ainsworth. *Developmental Psychology, 28*, 759-775.

Bretherton, I., & Waters, E. (1985). Growing points of attachment theory and research. *Monographs of the Society for Research in Child Development, 50* (1, 2, Serial No. 209).

Brickman, B. (1988). Psychoanalysis and substance abuse: Toward a more effective approach. *Journal of the American Academy of Psychoanalysis, 16*, 359-379.

Bringle, M. L. (1992). *The God of thinness: Gluttony and other weighty matters*. Nashville: Abingdon Press.

Bromiley, G. W. (1988). Sin. In G. W. Bromiley (Ed.), *The international standard Bible encyclopedia*. (Vol. 4, pp. 518-525). Grand Rapids: Wm. B. Eerdmans Publishing Company.

Bronfenbrenner, U. (1975). Is early intervention effective? In M. Guttenlag & E. L. Struenig (Eds.), *Handbook of evaluation research*. (Vol. 2). Beverly Hills, CA: Sage.

Bronfenbrenner, U. (1979). *The ecology of human development*. Cambridge, MA: Harvard University Press.

Bronfenbrenner, U. (1989). Ecological systems theory. In R. Vasta (Ed.), *Annals of child development*. (Vol. 6: *Six theories of child development*). Greenwich, CT: JAI Press.

Brown, A. L., Bransford, J. D., Ferrara, R. A., & Campione, J. C. (1983). Learning, remembering, and understanding. In P. H. Mussen (Ed.), *Handbook of child psychology: Cognitive development*. (Vol. III). New York: Wiley.

Browning, D. S. (1987). *Religious thought and the modern psychologies*. Philadelphia: Fortress.

Bruce, F. F. (1982). *The epistle to the Galatians: A commentary on the Greek text*. Grand Rapids: Wm. B. Eerdmans Publishing Company.

Bruner, J. (1982). The organization of action and the nature of adult-infant transaction. In M. von Cranach & R. Harré (Eds.), *The analysis of action*. Cambridge: Cambridge University Press.

Bruner, J. S. (1983). *Child's talk: Learning to use language*. New York: Norton.

Brunner, E. (1939). *Man in revolt.* (O. Wyon, Trans.). Philadelphia: Westminster.

Buber, M. (1953). *Good and evil.* New York: Charles Scribner's Sons.

Buber, M. (1937). *I and thou.* (R. G. Smith, Trans.). New York: Charles Scribner's Sons. (Originally published in German in 1923).

Byne, W., & Parsons, B. (1993). Human sexual orientation: The biologic theories reappraised. *Archives of General Psychiatry, 50,* 228-239.

Calvin, J. (1960). *The institutes of the Christian religion.* (J. T. McNeill, Ed.; F. L. Battles, Trans.). Philadelphia: Westminster.

Calvin, J. (1970). *Institutes of the Christian religion.* (Henry Beveridge, Trans.). Grand Rapids: Wm. B. Eerdmans Publishing Company.

Carnes, P. (1983). *Out of the shadows: Understanding sexual addiction.* Minneapolis: Compcare.

Carnevale, P., & Pruitt, D. (1992). Negotiation and mediation. *Annual Review of Psychology, 43,* 531-582.

Carver, C. S., & Scheier, M. J. (1981). *Attention and self-regulation: A control theory approach to human behavior.* New York: Springer-Verlag.

Cassian, J. (1955). *The Conferences* and *The Twelve Books of the Institutes of the Coenobium.* (E. C. S. Gibson, Trans.). In P. Schaff & H. Wace (Eds.), *The Nicene and post-Nicene fathers.* (2nd series, Vol. XI, pp. 201-545). Grand Rapids: Wm. B. Eerdmans Publishing Company.

Cassian, J. (1985). *Conferences.* New York: Paulist Press.

Chisholm, R. (1966). Freedom and action. In K. Lehrer (Ed.), *Freedom and determinism.* New York: Random House.

Clarke, W. N. (1993). *Person and being. (The Aquinas lecture, 1993).* Milwaukee: Marquette University Press.

Clarke-Stewart, K. A. (1973). Interactions between mothers and their young children: Characteristics and consequences. *Monographs of the Society for Research in Child Development, 38* (6-7, Serial No. 153).

Coates, D. L., & Lewis, M. (1984). Early mother-infant interaction and infant cognitive status as predictors of school performance and cognitive behavior in six-year-olds. *Child Development, 55,* 1219-1230.

Cochran, M. M., & Brassard, J. A. (1979). Child development and personal social networks. *Child Development, 50,* 601-616.

Cochrane, C. (1940). *Christianity and classical culture.* New York: Oxford University Press.

Connor, R. (1990). Relation, the Thomistic *esse,* and American culture: Toward a metaphysic of sanctity. *Communio, 17,* 455-464.

Connor, R. (1992). The person as resonating existential. *American Catholic Philosophical Quarterly, 66,* 39-56.

Crockenberg, S., & Litman, C. (1987). Autonomy as competence in two-year-olds: Maternal correlates of child compliance, non-compliance, and self-assertion. Paper presented at the biennial meeting of the Society for Research in Child Development, Baltimore.

Cunningham, B. B. (1985). The will to forgive: A pastoral theological view of forgiving. *Journal of Pastoral Care, 39,* 141-149.

Damasio, A. R. (1994). *Descartes' error: Emotion, reason, and the human brain.* New York: G. P. Putnam's Sons.

Davidson, D. (1980). *Essays on actions and events.* Oxford: Clarendon Press.

Davies, D. L. (1963). Normal drinking in recovered alcoholic addicts. *Quarterly Journal of Studies on Alcohol, 23,* 94-104.

DeJong, C. A. J., Van den Brink, W., Harteveld, F. M., & Van der Wielen, E. G. (1993). Personality disorders in alcoholics and drug addicts. *Comprehensive Psychiatry, 34,* 87-94.

de Rivera, J. (1989). Love, fear and justice: Transforming selves for the new world. *Social Justice Research, 3,* 387-426.

Derrida, J. (1982). *Margins of philosophy.* (A. Bass, Trans.). Chicago: University of Chicago Press.

Derrida, J. (1988). *Limited inc.* (S. Weber & J. Mehlmann, Trans.). Evanston, IL: Northwestern University Press.

de Sousa, R. (1987). *The rationality of emotion.* Cambridge & London: The MIT Press.

Diaz, R. M., Neal, C. J., & Amaya-Williams, M. (1990). The social origins of self-regulation. In L. C. Moll (Ed.), *Vygotsky and education: Instructional implications and applications of sociohistorical psychology.* Cambridge: Cambridge University Press.

DiBlasio, F. A. (1992). Forgiveness in psychotherapy: Comparison of older and younger therapists. *Journal of Psychology and Christianity, 11,* 181-187.

Diogenes Laertius. (1931). *Lives of eminent philosophers.* (R. D. Hicks, Trans.). New York: G. P. Putnam's Sons.

Dretske, F. (1992). The metaphysics of freedom. *Canadian Journal of Philosophy, 22,* 1-13.

Duffy, S. (1988). Our hearts of darkness: Original sin revisited. *Theological Studies, 49,* 597-622.

Durbin, M. (1972). Basic terms — off-color? *Semiotica, 6,* 257-278.

Dwyer, J. (1985). Nutritional aspects of anorexia nervosa and bulimia. In S. W. Emmett (Ed.), *Theory and treatment of anorexia nervosa and bulimia: Biomedical, sociocultural, and psychological perspectives* (pp. 20-50). New York: Brunner/Mazel.

Edwards, J. (1969). *Charity and its fruits.* Edinburgh: Banner of Truth Trust. (Originally published in 1852).

Egeland, B., & Farber, E. A. (1984). Infant-mother attachment: Factors related to its development and changes over time. *Child Development, 55,* 753-771.

Egeland, B., & Sroufe, L. A. (1981). Developmental sequelae of maltreatment in infancy. *New Directions for Child Development, 11,* 77-92.

Elert, W. (1962). *The structure of Lutheranism.* (W. R. Hansen, Trans.). St. Louis: Concordia.

Eliot, T. S. (1971). *The cocktail party.* In *The complete poems and plays 1909-1950.* New York: Harcourt, Brace, & World.

Ellis, A., & Grieger, R. (1977). *Handbook of rational emotive therapy.* New York: Springer.

Ellis, S., & Rogoff, B. (1982). The strategies and efficacy of child versus adult teachers. *Child Development, 53,* 730-735.

Ellul, J. (1976). *The ethics of freedom.* (G. W. Bromiley, Trans.). Grand Rapids: Wm. B. Eerdmans Publishing Company.

Ellul, J. (1980). *The technological system.* (J. Neugrochel, Trans.). New York: Continuum.

Emmett, S. W. (Ed.). (1985). *Theory and treatment of anorexia nervosa and bulimia: Biomedical, sociocultural, and psychological perspectives.* New York: Brunner/Mazel.

Engler, B. (1991). *Personality theories: An introduction.* (3rd ed.). Boston: Houghton Mifflin Company.

Enright, R. D., & Zell, R. L. (1989). Problems encountered when we forgive one another. *Journal of Psychology and Christianity, 8,* 52-60.

Epictetus (1948). *The enchiridion.* (T. Higginson, Trans.; with an introduction by A. Salomon). Indianapolis: Bobbs-Merrill.

Erickson, M. J. (1983-1985). *Christian theology.* Grand Rapids: Baker Book House.

Erikson, E. H. (1963). *Childhood and society.* (2nd ed.). New York: W. W. Norton.

Erwin, E. (1978). *Behavior therapy: Scientific, philosophical, and moral foundations.* Cambridge: Cambridge University Press.

Evagrius Ponticus. (1970). *Praktikos and chapters on prayer.* (J. E. Bamberger, OCSO, Trans.). Kalamazoo, MI: Cistercian Publications.

Evans, C. S. (1982). *Preserving the person: A look at the human sciences.* Grand Rapids: Baker. (Originally published in 1977).

Evans, C. S. (1989). *Wisdom and humanness in psychology: Prospects for a Christian approach.* Grand Rapids: Baker.

Evans, C. S. (1990). *Søren Kierkegaard's Christian psychology: Insight for counseling and pastoral care.* Grand Rapids: Zondervan.

Evennett, H. O. (1970). *The spirituality of the counter-reformation.* (J. Bossy, Ed.). Notre Dame: University of Notre Dame Press.

Fingarette, H. (1965). *The self in transformation: Psychoanalysis, philosophy, and the life of the spirit.* New York: Harper and Row.

Fingarette, H. (1988). *Heavy drinking: The myth of alcoholism as a disease.* Berkeley: University of California Press.

Fish, S. (1996, February). Why we can't all just get along. *First Things,* (60), 18-26.

Fisher, R., & Ury, W. (1991). *Getting to yes.* (2nd ed.). New York: Penguin Books.

Fitzgibbons, R. P. (1986). The cognitive and emotive uses of forgiveness in the treatment of anger. *Psychotherapy, 23,* 629-633.

Foster, M. (1935 & 1936). Christian theology and modern science of nature. *Mind, 44, 45,* 439-466 & 1-27.

Foster, R. J. (1992). *Prayer: Finding the heart's true home.* San Francisco: Harper.

Foucault, M. (1973). *Madness and civilization.* (R. Howard, Trans.). New York: Vintage Books.

Frankel, K. A., & Bates, J. E. (1980). Mother-toddler problem solving: Antecedents in attachment, home behavior, and temperament. *Child Development, 61,* 810-819.

Frankfurt, H. (1971). Freedom of the will and the concept of a person. *Journal of Philosophy, 58,* 5-21. Reprinted in Frankfurt, H. (1988).

Frankfurt, H. (1988). *The importance of what we care about.* Cambridge: Cambridge University Press.

Frankl, V. (1960). *The doctor and the soul.* New York: Knopf.

Frankl, V. (1963). *Man's search for meaning.* New York: Simon and Schuster.

Frese, M., & Sabini, J. (1985). Action theory: An introduction. In M. Frese & J. Sabini (Eds.), *Goal-directed behavior: The concept of action in psychology.* Hillsdale, NJ: Lawrence Erlbaum.

Freud, S. (1950). A religious experience. In *Collected papers.* (Vol. 5, pp. 243-246). London: Hogarth Press. (Originally published in 1928).

Freud, S. (1959). Inhibitions, symptoms, and anxiety. (A. Strachey, Trans.). In *The standard edition of the complete psychological works of Sigmund Freud.* (Vol. 20). London: Hogarth Press. (Originally published in 1926).

Freud, S. (1961). *Neurosis and psychosis.* In *The standard edition of the complete psychological works of Sigmund Freud.* (Vol. 19, pp. 149-153). London: Hogarth Press.

Fry, T., OSB (Ed.). (1982). *The rule of Saint Benedict in English.* Collegeville, MN: The Liturgical Press.

Fulford, K. W. M. (1989). *Moral theory and medical practice.* Cambridge: Cambridge University Press.

Fulford, K. W. M. (1991). Evaluative delusions: Their significance for philosophy and psychiatry. *British Journal of Psychiatry, 159,* Supp. 14, 108-112.

Gartner, J. (1988). The capacity to forgive: An object relations perspective. *Journal of Religion and Health, 27,* 313-320.

Gauvain, M., & Rogoff, B. (1989). Collaborative problem solving and children's planning skills. *Developmental Psychology, 25,* 139-151.

Gerez, T. de (1984). *My song is a piece of jade: Poems of ancient Mexico in English and Spanish.* Boston: Little, Brown.

Gibson, E. J. (1969). *Principles of perceptual learning and development.* New York: Appleton-Century-Crofts.

Gibson, J. J. (1979). *The ecological approach to visual perception.* Hillsdale, NJ, & London: Lawrence Erlbaum Associates, Publishers.

Gilson, E. (1936). *The spirit of mediaeval philosophy.* New York: Charles Scribner's Sons.

Gilson, E. (1941). *God and philosophy.* Indianapolis: Indiana University Press.

Goldfried, J., Castonguay, L., & Safran, J. (1992). Core issues and future directions in psychotherapy integration. In J. Norcross & M. Goldfried (Eds.), *Handbook of psychotherapy integration* (pp. 593-616). New York: Basic Books.

Goldingay, J. (1977). Expounding the New Testament. In I. H. Marshall (Ed.), *New Testament interpretation: Essays on principles and methods* (pp. 351-365). Grand Rapids: Wm. B. Eerdmans Publishing Company.

Goldman, A. (1970). *A theory of human action.* Englewood Cliffs, NJ: Prentice-Hall.

Gollwitzer, P. M. (1987). Implementation of identity intentions: A motivational-volitional perspective on symbolic self-completion. In F. Halisch & J. Kuhl (Eds.), *Motivation, intention, and volition.* Berlin: Springer-Verlag.

Gordon, D., Nowicki, Jr., S., & Wichern, F. (1981). Observed maternal and child behaviors in a dependency producing task as a function of children's locus of control orientation. *Merrill-Palmer Quarterly, 27,* 43-51.

Gregory the Great. (1850). *Morals on the Book of Job.* (J. Bliss, Trans.). Oxford: John Henry Parker.

Gregory the Great. (1950). *Pastoral care.* (H. Davis, S.J., Trans.). New York: Newman Press.

Griffiths, P. (1991). *An apology for apologetics: A study in the logic of interreligious dialogue.* Maryknoll, NY: Orbis Books.

Griffiths, P. (this volume). Metaphysics and personality theory.

Groeschel, B. J. (1983). *Spiritual passages: The psychology of spiritual development.* New York: Crossroad.

Grünbaum, A. (1984). *The foundations of psychoanalysis.* Berkeley, CA: University of California Press.

Grusec, J. E., & Lytton, H. (1988). *Social development.* New York: Springer-Verlag.

Guidano, V. F. (1991). *The self in process: Toward a post-rationalist cognitive therapy.* New York: Guilford Press.

Guntrip, H. (1973). *Psychoanalytic theory, therapy, and the self.* New York: Basic Books. (Originally published in 1971).

Halisch, F., & Kuhl, J. (Eds.). (1987). *Motivation, intention, and volition.* Berlin & New York: Springer-Verlag.

Hall, C. S., & Lindsey, G. (1985). *Introduction to theories of personality.* New York: Wiley.

Harré, R. (1984). *Personal being: A theory for individual psychology.* Cambridge, MA: Harvard University Press.

Harré, R., Clarke, D., De Carlo, N. (1985). *Motives and mechanisms: An introduction to the psychology of action.* London: Methuen.

Harré, R., & Lamb, R. (Eds.). (1986). *The dictionary of physiological and clinical psychology.* Oxford: Basil Blackwell.

Hart, A. (1988, December 9). Addicted to pleasure. *Christianity Today, 32,* 39-40.

Hartmann, H. (1959). *Ego psychology and the problem of adaptation.* (D. Rapaport, Trans.). London: The Hogarth Press.

Hartup, W. W. (1989). Social relationships and their developmental significance. *American Psychologist, 44,* 120-126.

Heckhausen, H. (1991). *Motivation and action.* (P. K. Lappmann, Trans.). New York: Springer-Verlag.

Heckhausen, H., & Kuhl, J. (1985). From wishes to action: The dead ends and short cuts on the long way to action. In M. Frese & J. Sabini (Eds.), *Goal-directed behavior: The concept of action in psychology.* Hillsdale, NJ: Lawrence Erlbaum.

Heider, F. (1958). *The psychology of interpersonal relations.* New York: Wiley.

Heitler, S. (1990). *From conflict to resolution.* New York: W. W. Norton.

Herbert, G. (1981). *George Herbert: The country parson and the temple.* (J. N. Wall, Jr., Ed.). Mahwah, NJ: Paulist Press.

Hermans, H. J. M., Kempen, H. J. G., & van Loon, R. J. P. (1992). The dialogical self: Beyond individualism and rationalism. *American Psychologist, 47,* 23-33.

Hickerson, N. P. (1975). Two studies of color: Implications for cross-cultural comparability of semantic categories. In M. Dale Kinkade et al. (Eds.), *Linguistics and Anthropology* (pp. 317-330). Lisse: de Ridder.

Hodges, R. (1986). Perception, relativity, and knowing and doing the truth. In Jones, S. (Ed.), *Psychology and the Christian faith: An introductory reader* (pp. 51-77). Grand Rapids: Baker Book House.

Hoffman, I. Z. (1991). Toward a social-constructivist view of the psychoanalytic tradition. *Psychoanalytic Dialogues, 1,* 74-105.

Hoffman, M. L. (1970). Moral development. In P. H. Mussen (Ed.), *Carmichael's handbook of child psychology.* (Vol. 2). New York: Wiley.

Holl, K. (1977). *What did Luther understand by religion?* (J. L. Adams & W. F. Bense, Eds.; F. W. Meuser & W. R. Wietzke, Trans.). Philadelphia: Fortress Press.

Homosexuality debate strains campus harmony: Homosexuals at Christian colleges press for acceptance. (1993, November 22). *Christianity Today, 38*, 39.

Hooker, R. (1865). *The laws of ecclesiastical polity.* Oxford: At the Clarendon Press.

Hooley, J. M., & Teasdale, J. D. (1989). Predictors of relapse in unipolar depressives: Expressed emotion, marital distress, and perceived criticism. *Journal of Abnormal Psychology, 98*, 229-235.

Howard, G., & Conway, C. (1986). Can there be an empirical science of volitional action? *American Psychologist, 41*, 1241-1251.

Howard, R. J. (1982). *Three faces of hermeneutics: An introduction to current theories of understanding.* Berkeley, CA: University of California Press.

Howsepian, A. A. (this volume). Sin and psychosis.

Hull, C. (1943). *Principles of behavior.* New York: Appleton-Century-Crofts.

Hume, D. (1957). *The natural history of religion.* (H. E. Root, Ed.). Stanford, CA: Stanford University Press.

Hume, D. (1960). *A treatise of human nature.* (L. A. Selby-Bigge, Ed.). Oxford: Oxford University Press.

Isabella, R. A., Belsky, J., & von Eye, A. (1989). Origins of mother-infant attachment: An examination of interactional synchrony during the infant's first year. *Developmental Psychology, 25*, 12-21.

Jacobson, E. (1967). *Psychotic conflict and reality.* New York: International Universities Press, Inc.

Jaki, S. L. (1978). *The road of science and the ways to God.* Chicago: University of Chicago Press.

James, W. (1950). *The principles of psychology.* (Vol. I). New York: Dover Publications. (Originally published in 1890).

Johnson, E. (this volume). Human agency and its social formation.

Johnson, K. (1982). *Maternal behavior and self-control in young children.* Ann Arbor, MI: Dissertation Abstracts International.

Jones, S. (1986). *Psychology and the Christian faith: An introductory reader.* Grand Rapids: Baker Book House.

Jones, S. (1988). A religious critique of behavior therapy. In W. Miller & J. Martin (Eds.), *Behavior therapy and religion* (pp. 139-170). Newbury Park, CA: Sage.

Jones, S. (1994). A constructive relationship for religion with the science and profession of psychology: Perhaps the boldest model yet. *American Psychologist, 49*, 184-199.

Jones, S. (this volume). The meaning of agency and responsibility in light of social science research.

Jones, S., & Butman, R. (1991). *Modern psychotherapies: A comprehensive Christian appraisal.* Downers Grove, IL: InterVarsity.

Julian of Norwich. (1978). *Showings.* (E. Colledge and J. Walsh, Trans.). Mahwah, NJ: Paulist Press.

Jung, C. (1933). *Modern man in search of a soul.* (W. S. Dell & C. F. Baynes, Trans.). London: Routledge and Kegan Paul.

Jung, C. (1961). *Memories, dreams, reflections.* (Aniela Jaffé, Ed.; R. & C. Winston, Trans.). New York: Random House.

Jung, C. (1968). *Analytical psychology: Its theory and practice.* New York: Random House.

Justin (Martyr). (1948). *Writings of St. Justin Martyr.* Washington, D.C.: Catholic University of America Press.

Kasl, C. D. (1990, November-December). The twelve-step controversy. *Ms.,* 30-31.

Kaufman, G. (1981). *The theological imagination: Constructing the concept of God.* Philadelphia: Westminster.

Kelly, J. N. D. (1978). *Early Christian doctrines.* New York: Harper & Row.

Kenny, A. (1986). *A path from Rome: An autobiography.* Oxford: Oxford University Press.

Kierkegaard, S. (1938). *Purity of heart is to will one thing.* (D. V. Steere, Trans.). New York: Harper. (Originally published in 1847).

Kierkegaard, S. (1968). *Attack upon "Christendom."* (W. Lowrie, Trans.; new introduction by H. A. Johnson). Princeton: Princeton University Press.

Kierkegaard, S. (1980a). *The concept of anxiety.* (R. Thomte, Trans.). Princeton: Princeton University Press. (Originally published in 1844).

Kierkegaard, S. (1980b). *The sickness unto death.* (H. Hong & E. Hong, Trans.). Princeton: Princeton University Press. (Originally published in 1849).

Kierkegaard, S. (1987). *Either/or.* (Vols. I and II; H. Hong & E. Hong, Trans.). Princeton: Princeton University Press. (Originally published in 1843).

Kierkegaard, S. (1992). *Concluding unscientific postscript.* (H. Hong & E. Hong, Trans.). Princeton: Princeton University Press. (Originally published in 1846).

Kilpatrick, K. W. (1992). *Why Johnny can't tell right from wrong.* New York: Simon and Schuster.

Kindermann, T., & Skinner, E. A. (1988). Developmental tasks as organizers of children's ecologies: Mothers' contingencies as children learn to walk, eat, and dress. In J. Valsiner (Ed.), *Child development within culturally structured environments: Social co-construction and environmental guidance in development.* (Vol. 2). Norwood, NJ: Ablex.

Kirkpatrick, L. (1992). An attachment-theory approach to the psychology of religion. *The International Journal for the Psychology of Religion, 2,* 3-28.

Kirkpatrick, L., & Shaver, P. (1990). Attachment theory and religion: Childhood attachments, religious beliefs, and conversion. *Journal for the Scientific Study of Religion, 29,* 315-324.

Klinger, E. (1987). Current concerns and disengagement from incentives. In F. Halisch & J. Kuhl (Eds.), *Motivation, intention, and volition.* Berlin: Springer-Verlag.

Kohut, H. (1977). *The restoration of the self.* New York: International Universities Press.

Kohut, H., & Wolf, E. S. (1978). The disorders of the self and their treatment: An outline. *International Journal of Psycho-Analysis, 59,* 413-425.

Kopp, C. B. (1982). Antecedents of self-regulation: A developmental perspective. *Developmental Psychology, 18,* 199-214.

Kopp, C. B. (1991). Young children's progression to self-regulation. In M. Bullock (Ed.), *The development of intentional action* (pp. 38-54). Basel: Karger.

Kuhl, J. (1985). Volitional mediators of cognition-behavior consistency: Self-regulatory processes and action versus state orientation. In J. Kuhl & J. Beckmann (Eds.), *Action control: From cognition to behavior.* Berlin: Springer-Verlag.

Kuhl, J., & Beckmann, J. (1985). Historical perspectives in the study of action control. In J. Kuhl & J. Beckmann (Eds.), *Action control: From cognition to behavior.* Berlin: Springer-Verlag.

Lacugna, C. (1991). *God for us: The trinity and Christian life.* New York: Harper Collins.

Laing, R. D. (1965). *The divided self.* Harmondsworth: Penguin Books.

Lamb, M. E., & Bornstein, M. H. (1987). *Development in infancy: An introduction* (2nd ed.). New York: Random House.

Langford, G. (1971). *Human action.* Garden City, NY: Doubleday.

Laporte, J.-M. (1974). Kenosis old and new. *The Ecumenist, 12,* 17-21.

Laporte, J.-M. (1988). *Patience and power: Grace for the first world.* New York & Mahwah, NJ: Paulist Press.

Laporte, J.-M. (this volume). Kenosis as a key to maturity of personality.

Lasch, C. (1979). *The culture of narcissism.* New York: W. W. Norton.

Lear, J. (1988). *Aristotle: The desire to understand.* Cambridge: Cambridge University Press.

Lenters, W. (1985). *The freedom we crave — Addiction: The human condition.* Grand Rapids: Wm. B. Eerdmans Publishing Company.

Lessing, G. E. (1957). *Lessing's theological writings.* (H. Chadwick, Ed.). Stanford, CA: Stanford University Press.

Levitin, K. (1982). *One is not born a personality: Profiles of Soviet education psychologists.* (Y. Filippov, Trans.). Moscow: Progress Publishing.

Lewin, K. (1936). *Principles of topological psychology.* New York: McGraw-Hill.

Lewis, C. S. (1940). *The problem of pain.* New York: Macmillan.

Lewis, C. S. (1947). *The abolition of man.* New York: Macmillan.

Lewis, C. S. (1955). *Surprised by joy: The shape of my early life.* New York: Harcourt, Brace, and World.

Lickona, T. (1991). *Educating for character.* New York: Bantam.

Linn, D., & Linn, M. (1988). *Healing life's hurts: Healing memories through the five stages of forgiveness.* New York: Paulist Press.

Livezey, L. G. (1989). Women, power, and politics: Feminist theology in process perspective. *Process Studies, 17,* 67-77.

Locke, J. (1975). *An essay concerning human understanding.* (P. H. Nidditch, Ed.). Oxford: Oxford University Press.

Loevinger, J. (1976). *Ego development.* San Francisco: Jossey-Bass.

Londerville, S., & Main, M. (1981). Security of attachment, compliance and maternal training methods in the second year of life. *Developmental Psychology, 20,* 1061-1073.

Loomer, B. (1976). Two conceptions of power. *Process Studies, 6,* 5-32.

Lovejoy, A. (1936). *The great chain of being.* Cambridge, MA: Harvard University Press.

Loyola, St. Ignatius. (1964). *The spiritual exercises of St. Ignatius.* (A. Mottola, Trans.; R. W. Gleason, S.J., Intro.). Garden City, NY: Image Books.

Lundin, R. (1993). *The culture of interpretation: Christian faith and the postmodern world*. Grand Rapids: Wm. B. Eerdmans Publishing Company.

Luria, A. R. (1973). *The working brain: An introduction to neuropsychology*. New York: Basic Books.

Luther, M. (1955-1986). *Luther's works*. (J. Pelikan & H. T. Lehmann, Eds., 55 vols.). St. Louis and Philadelphia: Concordia and Fortress.

Lutz, Catherine. (1988). *Unnatural emotions: Everyday sentiments on a Micronesian atoll & their challenge to western theory*. Chicago: University of Chicago Press.

Maccoby, E. (1980). *Social development*. New York: Harcourt Brace Jovanovich.

Maccoby, E. E., & Martin, J. A. (1983). Socialization in the context of the family: Parent-child interaction. In P. H. Mussen (Ed.), *Handbook of child psychology*. (Vol. 4: *Socialization, personality, and social behavior*). New York: Wiley.

MacIntyre, A. (1981). *After virtue*. Notre Dame: University of Notre Dame Press.

MacIntyre, A. (1988). *Whose justice? Which rationality?* Notre Dame: University of Notre Dame Press.

MacIntyre, A. (1990). *Three rival versions of moral enquiry: Encyclopaedia, genealogy, and tradition*. Notre Dame: University of Notre Dame Press.

Macmurray, J. (1957). *The self as agent*. London: Faber & Faber.

MacPhee, D., Ramey, C. T., & Yeates, K. O. (1984). Home environments and early cognitive development: Implications for intervention. In A. W. Gottfried (Ed.), *Home environment and early cognitive development: Longitudinal research*. Orlando: Academic Press.

Maddi, S. (1980). *Personality theories: A comparative analysis*. Homewood, IL: Dorsey Press.

Mahler, M., Pine, F., & Bergman, A. (1975). *The psychological birth of the human infant*. New York: Basic Books.

Mahoney, M. J. (1988). Constructive metatheory: I. Basic features and historical foundations. *International Journal of Personal Construct Psychology, 1*, 1-35.

Mahoney, M. J. (1993). Introduction to special section: Theoretical developments in the cognitive psychotherapies. *Journal of Consulting and Clinical Psychology, 61*, 187-193.

Marcus, E. R. (1992). *Psychosis and near-psychosis*. New York: Springer-Verlag.

Maritain, J. (1947). *The person and the common good*. New York: Scribners.

Marlatt, G. (1982). Relapse prevention: A self-control program for the treatment of addictive behaviors. In R. Stuart (Ed.), *Adherence, compliance and generalization in behavioral medicine* (pp. 329-378). New York: Brunner/Mazel.

Martin, J. E. (1987). Toward an epistemology of revelation. In H. Heie & D. Wolfe (Eds.), *The reality of Christian learning* (pp. 140-152). Grand Rapids: Wm. B. Eerdmans Publishing Company/Christian University Press.

Martin, J. E. (this volume). Human nature vs. the hermeneutics of love.

Martin, M. (1986). *Self-deception and morality*. Lawrence, KS: University of Kansas Press.

Maslow, A. (1968). *Towards a psychology of being*. New York: D. Van Nostrand.

Maslow, A. (1970). *Motivation and personality*. (2nd ed.). New York: Harper & Row.

Masters, W. H., & Johnson, V. A. (1966). *Human sexual response*. Boston: Little, Brown.

Masters, W. H., & Johnson, V. A. (1975). *The pleasure bond*. Boston: Little, Brown.

Matas, L., Arend, R. A., & Sroufe, L. (1978). Continuity of adaptation in the second year: The relationship between quality attachment and later competence. *Child Development, 49,* 547-556.

Maximus the Confessor. (1985). *Maximus the Confessor.* (G. C. Berthold, Trans.). Mahwah, NJ: Paulist Press.

May, G. (1988). *Addiction and grace: Love and spirituality in the healing of addictions.* San Francisco: Harper Collins.

May, R. (1969). *Love and will.* New York: W. W. Norton.

McAdams, D. P. (1990). *The person: An introduction to personality psychology.* Orlando: Harcourt Brace Jovanovich.

McCall, R. B., Appelbaum, M. I., & Hogarty, P. S. (1973). Developmental changes in mental performance. *Monographs of the Society for Research in Child Development, 38* (3, Serial No. 150).

McClelland, D. C., Atkinson, J. W., Clark, R. W., & Lowell, E. L. (1953). *The achievement motive.* New York: Appleton-Century-Crofts.

McCormick, P. (1989). *Sin as addiction.* New York: Paulist Press.

McFall, R. (1982). A review and reformulation of the concept of social skills. *Behavioral Assessment, 4,* 1-33.

McKenzie, S. (1991). Addiction as an unauthentic form of spiritual presence. *Studies in Formative Spirituality, 12,* 325-331.

Meichenbaum, D. (1993). Changing conceptions of cognitive behavior modification. *Journal of Consulting and Clinical Psychology, 61,* 202-204.

Migliore, D. (1991). *Faith seeking understanding.* Grand Rapids: Wm. B. Eerdmans Publishing Company.

Mill, J. S. (1912). *On liberty; Representative government; The subjection of women.* London: Oxford University Press.

Miller, G. A., Galanter, E., & Pribram, K. (1960). *Plans and the structure of behavior.* New York: Holt, Rinehart & Winston.

Miller, N. E. (1951). Learnable drives and rewards. In S. S. Stevens (Ed.), *Handbook of experimental psychology.* New York: John Wiley & Sons.

Minuchin, S., & Fishman, C. (1981). *Family therapy techniques.* Cambridge, MA: Harvard University Press.

Mischel, W. (1973). Toward a cognitive social learning reconceptualization of personality. *Psychological Review, 80,* 252-285.

Mischel, W. (1974). Processes in delay of gratification. In L. Berkowitz (Ed.), *Advances in experimental social psychology.* (Vol. 7, pp. 249-292). New York: Academic Press.

Mischel, W., & Patterson, C. J. (1976). Substantive and structural elements of effective plans for self-control. *Journal of Personality and Social Psychology, 34,* 942-950.

Moll, L. (1990). *Vygotsky and education.* Cambridge: Cambridge University Press.

Mouw, R. (1988, December). The life of bondage in the light of grace: An interview with David Neff. *Christianity Today,* 41-44.

Mowrer, O. H. (1989). Psychopathology and the problem of guilt, confession, and expiation. In L. Aden & D. G. Benner (Eds.), *Counseling and the human predicament: A study of sin, guilt, and forgiveness* (pp. 76-84). Grand Rapids: Baker.

Müller, M., & Halder, A. (1969). Person: Concept. *Sacramentum mundi, 4.* New York: Herder & Herder.

Murray, H. A. (1938). *Explorations in personality.* New York: Oxford University Press.

Neal, C. (1990). Training high-risk parents to be teachers of their own children. Paper presented at the biennial meeting of the Society for Research in Child Development, Seattle.

Neal, C. (1991). Within the zone of proximal development: High-risk parents' scaffolding and their children's performance. Paper presented at the biennial meeting of the Society for Research in Child Development, Seattle.

Neal, C. (this volume). A parental style for nurturing Christian wisdom.

Neal, C., & Diaz, R. (1989). Teaching for self-regulation: A comparison of low and high risk mothers. Paper presented at the biennial meeting of the Society for Research in Child Development, Kansas City, MO.

Neimeyer, R. A. (1993). An appraisal of constructivist psychotherapies. *Journal of Consulting and Clinical Psychology, 61,* 221-234.

New American standard Bible (1970). New York: P. J. Kennedy.

Niebuhr, H. R. (1937). *The kingdom of God in America.* New York: Harper & Row.

Norcross, J., & Goldfried, M. (1992). *Handbook of psychotherapy integration.* New York: Basic Books.

Nozick, R. (1981). *Philosophical explanations.* Cambridge, MA: The Belknap Press of Harvard University Press.

Nussbaum, M. (1994). *The therapy of desire.* New York: Cambridge University Press.

Nuttin, J. (1983). *Motivation, planning, and action: a relational theory of behavior dynamics.* Hillsdale, NJ: Erlbaum Associates.

Obeyesekere, G. (1981). *Medusa's hair: An essay on personal symbols and religious experience.* Chicago: University of Chicago Press.

Oddie, G. (1993). Addiction and the value of freedom. *Bioethics, 7,* 373-401.

Oden, T. (1984). *Care of souls in the classic tradition.* Philadelphia: Fortress Press.

Okholm, D. (this volume). Being stuffed and being fulfilled.

O'Leary, K. D., & Wilson, G. T. (1987). *Behavior therapy: Application and outcome.* Englewood Cliffs, NJ: Prentice-Hall.

Olson, S. L., Bates, J. E., & Bayles, K. (1984). Mother-infant interaction and the development of individual differences in children's cognitive competence. *Developmental Psychology, 20,* 166-179.

Orbach, S. (1985). Visibility/invisibility: Social considerations in anorexia nervosa — A feminist perspective. In S. Emmett (Ed.), *Theory and treatment of anorexia nervosa and bulimia: Biomedical, sociocultural, and psychological perpsectives* (pp. 127-138). New York: Brunner/Mazel.

Ozment, S. (1992). *Protestants: The birth of a revolution.* New York: Doubleday.

Parfit, D. (1984). *Reasons and persons.* Oxford: Oxford University Press.

Parpal, M., & Maccoby, E. (1985). Maternal responsiveness and subsequent child compliance. *Child Development, 56,* 1326-1334.

Passler, M. A., Issac, W., & Hind, G. W. (1985). Neuropsychological development of behavior attributed to frontal lobe functioning in children. *Developmental Neuropsychology, 1,* 349-370.

Pattison, E. M. (1965). On the failure to forgive or to be forgiven. *American Journal of Psychotherapy, 31,* 106-115.

Pattison, E. M. (1989). Punitive and reconciliation models of forgiveness. In L. Aden & D. G. Benner (Eds.), *Counseling and the human predicament: A study of sin, guilt, and forgiveness* (pp. 162-176). Grand Rapids: Baker.

Payne, J. W., Bettman, J. R., & Johnson, E. J. (1992). Behavioral decision research: A constructive processing perspective. *Annual Review of Psychology, 43,* 87-131.

Peck, M. S. (1984). *People of the lie: The hope for healing human evil.* New York: Simon and Schuster.

Peck, M. S. (1993). *A world waiting to be born: Civility rediscovered.* New York: Bantam.

Peele, S. (1985). *The meaning of addiction: Compulsive experience and its interpretation.* Lexington, MA: Lexington Books.

Pelikan, J. (1965). *The Christian intellectual.* London: Collins.

Pelikan, J. (1971). *The Christian tradition.* (Vol. I: *The emergence of the Catholic tradition [100-600].*). Chicago & London: University of Chicago Press.

Peters, R. S. (1965). Twentieth century theories. In *Brett's history of psychology* (revised ed., pp. 691-762; R. S. Peters, Ed.). Cambridge, MA: M.I.T. Press.

Pfeffer, J. (1981). *Power in organizations.* San Francisco: Harper.

Piaget, J. (1954). *The construction of reality in the child.* (M. Cook, Trans.). New York: Basic Books. (Originally published in 1937).

Pines, M. (1987). Mirroring and child development: Psychodynamic and psychological interpretations. In T. Honess & K. Yardly (Eds.), *Self and identity: Perspectives across the lifespan.* London: Routledge & Kegan Paul.

Pingleton, J. P. (1989). The role and function of forgiveness in the psychotherapeutic process. *Journal of Psychology and Theology, 17,* 27-35.

Plantinga, A. (1990). Prologue: Advice to Christian philosophers. In M. Beaty (Ed.), *Christian theism and the problems of philosophy* (pp. 14-37). Notre Dame: University of Notre Dame Press.

Plantinga, A. (1991). An evolutionary argument against naturalism. *Logos, 12,* 27-49.

Plantinga, A. (1993a). *Warrant and proper function.* New York: Oxford University Press.

Plantinga, A. (1993b). *Warrant: The current debate.* New York: Oxford University Press.

Plantinga, C., Jr. (1995). *Not the way it's supposed to be: A breviary of sin.* Grand Rapids: Wm. B. Eerdmans Publishing Company.

Plantinga, C., Jr. (this volume). Sin and addiction.

Plato (1956). *Great dialogues of Plato.* (W. H. D. Rouse, Trans.). New York: New American Library.

Plomin, R., Corley, R., DeFries, J. C., & Fulker, D. W. (1990). Individual differences in television viewing in early childhood: Nature as well as nurture. *Psychological Science, 1,* 371-377.

Pope, H., & Hudson, J. (1985). Biological treatments of eating disorders. In S. W. Emmett (Ed.), *Theory and treatment of anorexia nervosa and bulimia: Biomedical, sociocultural, and psychological perspectives* (pp. 73-92). New York: Brunner/Mazel.

Prestige, G. L. (1940). *Fathers and heretics: Six studies in dogmatic faith with prologue and epilogue.* London: S.P.C.K.

Propst, L. R. (1988). *Psychotherapy in a religious framework: Spirituality in the emotional healing process.* New York: Human Sciences Press.

Propst, L. R. (1992). Spirituality and the avoidant personality. *Theology Today, 49,* 165-172.

Propst, L. R. (this volume). Therapeutic conflict resolution and the holy Trinity.

Proudfoot, W. (1985). *Religious experience.* Berkeley: University of California Press.

Proudfoot, W. (1993). Response to Barnard. *Journal of the American Academy of Religion, 41,* 793-803.

Rapaport, D. (1967). *The collected papers of David Rapaport.* (M. M. Gill, Ed.). New York: Basic Books.

Ratner, C. (1991). *Vygotsky's sociohistorical psychology and its contemporary applications.* New York: Plenum Press.

Ratzinger, J. (1970). *Introduction to Christianity.* New York: Herder & Herder.

Ratzinger, J. (1990). Concerning the notion of person in theology. *Communio, 17,* 439-454. (Originally published in German in 1973).

Reeve, R. A. (1987). The functional significance of parental scaffolding as a moderator of social influence on children's cognition. Paper presented at the biennial meeting of the Society for Research in Child Development. Baltimore.

Richardson, C., Ed. (1953). *Early Christian Fathers.* Philadelphia: Westminster Press.

Ricoeur, P. (1966). *Freedom and nature: The voluntary and the involuntary.* (E. V. Kohak, Trans.). Evanston, IL: Northwestern University Press.

Rieff, P. (1966). *The triumph of the therapeutic.* New York: Harper and Row.

Roberts, R. (1983). *Spirituality and human emotion.* Grand Rapids: Wm. B. Eerdmans Publishing Company.

Roberts, R. (1984a). *The strengths of a Christian.* Philadelphia: Westminster.

Roberts, R. (1984b). Will power and the virtues. *The Philosophical Review, 93,* 227-247.

Roberts, R. (1988a). Therapies and the grammar of a virtue. In R. H. Bell (Ed.), *The grammar of the heart: New essays in moral philosophy and theology.* San Francisco: Harper and Row.

Roberts, R. (1988b). What an emotion is. *The Philosophical Review, 97,* 183-209.

Roberts, R. (1991). Virtues and rules. *Philosophy and Phenomenological Research, 51,* 325-343.

Roberts, R. (1992a). Emotions among the virtues of the Christian life. *Journal of Religious Ethics, 20,* 201-232.

Roberts, R. (1992b). Thomas Aquinas on the morality of emotions. *History of Philosophy Quarterly, 9,* 287-305.

Roberts, R. (1993). *Taking the word to heart: Self and other in an age of therapies.* Grand Rapids: Wm. B. Eerdmans Publishing Company.

Roberts, R. (1995). Forgivingness. *American Philosophical Quarterly, 32,* 289-306.

Roberts, R. (this volume a). Parameters of a Christian psychology.

Roberts, R. (this volume b). Attachment: Bowlby and the Bible.

Rogers, C. (1959). A theory of therapy, personality, and interpersonal relationships, as developed in the client-centered framework. In *Psychology: A study of a science.* (Vol. 2: *Formulations of the person and the social context,* Sigmund Koch, Ed.). New York: McGraw-Hill.

Rogers, C. R. (1961). *On becoming a person.* Boston: Houghton Mifflin.

Rogers, C. R. (1980). *A way of being.* Boston: Houghton Mifflin.

Rogoff, B. (1990). *Apprenticeship in thinking: Cognitive development in social context.* New York: Oxford University Press.

Rogoff, B., & Wertsch, J. V. (1984). *Children's learning in the "zone of proximal development."* San Francisco: Jossey-Bass.

Rogoff, B., Mistry J., Goncu, A., & Mosier, C. (1993). Guided participation in cultural activity by toddlers and caregivers. *Monographs of the Society for Research in Child Development, 58,* Serial No. 236.

Rolston, H. (1987). *Science and religion: A critical survey.* Philadelphia: Temple University Press.

Rorty, R. (1989). *Contingency, irony, and solidarity.* Cambridge: Cambridge University Press.

Rorty, R. (1991). *Objectivity, relativism, and truth.* Cambridge: Cambridge University Press.

Rorty, R. (1992). Trotsky and the wild orchids. *Common Knowledge, I,* (3), 140-153.

Rorty, R. (1996, June 20). Something to steer by. *London Review of Books, 7,* 8.

Rosa, A., & Montero, I. (1990). The historical context of Vygotsky's work: A sociohistorical approach. In L. Moll (Ed.), *Vygotsky and education.* Cambridge University Press.

Rudner, R. (1953). The scientist qua scientist makes value judgments. *Philosophy of Science, XX,* 1-6.

Rule of St. Benedict in English. (1982). (Timothy Fry, OSB, Ed.). Collegeville, MN: The Liturgical Press.

Runner, E. (1981). *The relation of the Bible to learning.* Jordan Station, ON: Paideia Press.

Rychlak, J. (1979). *Discovering free will and personal responsibility.* New York: Oxford University Press.

Rychlak, J. F. (1988). *The psychology of rigorous humanism.* (2nd ed.). New York: New York University Press.

Ryckman, R. M. (1993). *Theories of personality.* (5th ed.). Pacific Grove, CA: Brooks/Cole.

Safran, J. D., & Segal, Z. V. (1990). *Interpersonal process in cognitive therapy.* New York: Basic Books.

Sahlins, Marshall. (1976). Colors and cultures. *Semiotica, 16,* 1-22.

Sarbin, T. R. (1967). On the futility of the proposition that some people be labeled "mentally ill." *Journal of Consulting Psychology, 31,* 447-453.

Sarbin, T. R., & Juhasz, J. B. (1978). The social context of hallucinations. *Journal of Mental Imagery, 2,* 117-144.

Sartre, J.-P. (1956). *Being and nothingness.* New York: Philosophical Library.

Satinover, J. B. (1994). Psychology and the abolition of meaning. *First Things, (40),* 14-18.

Saunders, B. A. C. (1992). *The invention of basic colour terms.* Utrecht: ISOR.

Sayings of the Desert Fathers. (1975). (B. Ward, Trans.). Kalamazoo, MI: Cistercian Publications.

Schaef, A. W. (1989). *Escape from intimacy: The pseudo relationship addictions.* San Francisco: Harper & Row.

Scheler, M. (1973). Ordo amoris. In D. H. Lachterman (Ed.), *Selected philosophical essays* (pp. 98-135). Evanston, IL: Northwestern University Press.

Schimmel, S. (1992). *The seven deadly sins: Jewish, Christian, and classical reflections on human nature.* New York: The Free Press.

Schlesinger, G. (1984). The availability of evidence in support of religious belief. *Faith and Philosophy, 1,* 421-436.

Schmitz, K. (1986). The geography of the human person. *Communio, 13,* 27-48.

Schoeman, F. (Ed.). (1987). *Responsibility, character, and the emotions: New essays in moral psychology.* Cambridge: Cambridge University Press.

Schuller, R. (1982). *Self-esteem: The new reformation.* Waco: Word.

Schutz, A. (1962). *Collected papers.* (Vol. I: *The problem of social reality*). Amsterdam: Nijhoff.

Scott, J. P. (1987). The emotional basis of attachment and separation. In James L. Sacksteder, Daniel P. Schwartz, and Yoshiharu Akabane (Eds.), *Attachment and the therapeutic process: Essays in honor of Otto Allen Will, Jr., M.D.* Madison, WI: International Universities Press.

Seneca. (1958). *The stoic philosophy of Seneca.* (M. Hadas, Ed. & Trans.). New York: W. W. Norton

Shastri, Dwarikadas (Ed.). (1981). *Abhidharmakośa & Bhāṣya of Ācārya Vasubandhu with Sphūṭārthā commentary of Ācārya Yaśomitra.* Varanasi: Bauddha Bharati.

Shedler, J., & Block, J. (1990). Adolescent drug use and psychological health. *American Psychologist, 45,* 612-630.

Sigel, I. E. (1982). The relationship between parental distancing strategies and the child's cognitive behavior. In L. M. Laosa & I. E. Sigel (Eds.), *Families as learning environments for children.* New York: Plenum Press.

Skinner, B. F. (1953). *Science and human behavior.* New York: Macmillan.

Skinner, B. F. (1971). *Beyond freedom and dignity.* New York: Knopf.

Skinner, B. F. (1976). *About behaviorism.* New York: Vintage Books.

Skinner, E. (1986). The origins of young children's perceived control: Mother contingent and sensitive behavior. *International Journal of Behavioral Development, 9,* 359-382.

Smedes, L. B. (1984). *Forgive and forget: Healing the hurts we don't deserve.* San Francisco: Harper & Row.

Sommers, C. H. (1994). *Who stole feminism? How women have betrayed women.* New York: Simon and Schuster.

Sorg, T. (1976). Heart. In C. Brown (Ed.), *The new international dictionary of New Testament theology.* (Vol. II, pp. 180-184). Grand Rapids: Zondervan Publishing House.

Spero, M. H. (1992). *Religious objects as psychological structures: A critical investigation of object-relations theory, psychotherapy and Judaism.* Chicago: University of Chicago Press.

Sperry, R. W. (1988). Psychology's mentalist paradigm and the religion/science tension. *American Psychologist, 43,* 607-613.

Sperry, R. W. (1993). The impact and promise of the cognitive revolution. *American Psychologist, 48,* 878-885.

Sroufe, L. A. (1983). Infant-caregiver attachment and patterns of adaption in preschool: The roots of maladaption In M. Perlmutter (Ed.), *Minnesota symposia on child psychology* (Vol. 16, pp. 41-83). Hillsdale, NJ: Erlbaum.

Stayton, D. J., Hagan, R., & Ainsworth, M. (1971). Infant obedience and maternal behavior: The origins of socialization reconsidered. *Child Development, 42,* 1057-1069.

Stern, D. N. (1985). *Interpersonal world of the infant.* New York: Basic Books.

Sternberg, R. J. (1984). Toward a triarchic theory of human intelligence. *Behavioral and Brain Sciences, 7,* 269-315.

Strawson, P. (1968). Freedom and resentment. In P. F. Strawson (1974), *Freedom and resentment and other essays* (pp. 1-25). London & New York: Methuen.

Strong, S. (1976). Christian counseling. *Counseling and Values, 20,* 151-160.

Strong, S. (1977). Christian counseling in action. *Counseling and Values, 21,* 89-128.

Stump, E. (1988). Sanctification, hardening of the heart, and Frankfurt's concept of free will. *The Journal of Philosophy, 85,* 395-420.

Stuss, D. T., & Benson, D. F. (1984). Neuropsychological studies of the frontal lobes. *Psychological Bulletin, 95,* 3-28.

Sundberg, W. (this volume). The therapy of adversity and penitence.

Sutker, P. B., & Allain, A. N. (1988). Issues in personality conceptualizations of addictive behaviors. *Journal of Consulting and Clinical Psychology, 56,* 172-182.

Sykes, C. J. (1992). *A nation of victims: The decay of American character.* New York: St. Martin's Press.

Szasz, T. (1961). *The myth of mental illness.* New York: Harper and Row.

Talbot, M. R. (1984). On Christian philosophy. *Reformed Journal, 34,* Issue 9, 18-22.

Talbot, M. R. (1985). Reply by Mark R. Talbot (to Basinger [1985]). *Reformed Journal, 35,* Issue 2, 19-20.

Talbot, M. R. (1989). Is it natural to believe in God? *Faith and Philosophy, 6,* 155-171.

Talbot, M. R. (1996a, December). God talk. *First Things, (68),* 42-44.

Talbot, M. R. (1996b). The morality of everlasting punishment. *Reformation and Revival Journal, 5,* Number 4, 117-134.

Talbot, M. R. (this volume). Starting from Scripture.

Tanquerey, A. (n.d., but probably the 1930s). *The spiritual life: A treatise on ascetical and mystical theology.* (Hermann Branderis, Trans.). Westminster, MD: Newman Press.

Tappert, T. G. (Ed.). (1959). *The book of concord.* Philadelphia: Fortress.

Taylor, C. (1985). *Human agency and language.* Cambridge: Cambridge University Press.

Taylor, C. (1989). *Sources of the self: The making of the modern identity.* Cambridge, MA: Harvard University Press.

Torrance, T. F. (1983). *The mediation of Christ.* Grand Rapids: Wm. B. Eerdmans Publishing Company.

Torrance, T. F. (1985). *Reality and scientific theology.* Edinburgh: Scottish Academic Press.

Tronick, E. Z. (1989). Emotions and emotional communication in infants. *American Psychologist, 44,* 112-119.

Tronick, E. Z., & Gianino, A. F. (1986). The transmission of maternal disturbance to the infant. *New Directions for Child Development, 34,* 5-11.

Tversky, A., & Kahneman, D. (1981). The framing of decisions and the psychology of choice. *Science, 211*, 453-458.

Tyrell, T. J. (1994a). *The adventure of intimacy: A journey through broken circles.* Mystic, CT: Twenty-Third Publications.

Tyrell, T. J. (1994b). *Urgent longings: Reflections on infatuation, intimacy, and sublime love.* Mystic, CT: Twenty-Third Publications.

Ury, W. (1993) *Getting past no: Negotiating your way from confrontation to cooperation.* (Revised ed.). New York: Bantam Books.

Valsiner, J. (1987). *Culture and the development of children's action.* Chichester: Wiley.

Van Kaam, A. (1987). Addiction: Counterfeit of religious presence. *Studies in Formative Spirituality, 8*, 243-256.

Van Leeuwen, M. (1985). *The person in psychology: A contemporary Christian appraisal.* Grand Rapids: Wm. B. Eerdmans Publishing Company.

Van Leeuwen, M. S. (1987). Personality theorizing within a Christian worldview. In T. J. Burke (Ed.), *Man and mind: A Christian theory of personality* (pp. 171-198). Hillsdale, MI: Hillsdale College Press.

Van Leeuwen, M. S. (1990). *Gender and grace: Love, work, and parenting in a changing world.* Downers Grove, IL: InterVarsity.

Vaughn, B. E., Kopp, C. B., & Krakow, J. B. (1984). The emergence and consolidation of self-control from eighteen to thirty months of age: Normative trends and individual differences. *Child Development, 55*, 990-1004.

Veenstra, G. (1992). Psychological concepts of forgiveness. *Journal of Psychology and Christianity, 11*, 160-169.

Veenstra, G. (1993). Forgiveness: A critique of adult child approaches. *Journal of Psychology and Christianity, 12*, 58-68.

Vitz, P. C. (1984). A covenant theory of personality: A theoretical introduction. In L. Morris (Ed.), *The Christian vision: Man in society* (pp. 75-99). Hillsdale, MI: Hillsdale College Press.

Vitz, P. C. (1987a). A Christian theory of personality: Covenant theory. In T. J. Burke (Ed.), *Man and mind: A Christian theory of personality* (pp. 199-222). Hillsdale, MI: Hillsdale College Press.

Vitz, P. C. (1987b). Secular personality theory: A critical analysis. In T. J. Burke (Ed.), *Man and mind: A Christian theory of personality* (pp. 65-94). Hillsdale, MI: Hillsdale College Press.

Vitz, P. (1988). *Sigmund Freud's Christian subconscious.* New York: Gilford Press.

Vitz, P. C. (1994). *Psychology as religion: The cult of self-worship.* (2nd ed.). Grand Rapids: Wm. B. Eerdmans Publishing Company.

Vitz, P. C. (this volume). A Christian theory of personality.

Vitz, P. C., & Gartner, J. (1984a). Christianity and psychoanalysis, Part 1: Jesus as the anti-Oedipus. *Journal of Psychology and Theology, 12*, 4-14.

Vitz, P. C., & Gartner, J. (1984b). Christianity and psychoanalysis, Part 2: Jesus as the transformer of the super ego. *Journal of Psychology and Theology, 12*, 82-90.

von Cranach, M. (1982). The psychological study of goal-directed action: Basic issues. In M. von Cranach & R. Harré (Eds.), *The analysis of action.* Cambridge: Cambridge University Press.

Vygotsky, L. S. (1962). *Thought and language.* Cambridge, MA: M.I.T. Press.

Vygotsky, L. S. (1978). *Mind in society: The development of higher psychology processes.* Cambridge, MA: Harvard University Press.

Wachs, T. D. (1984). Proximal experience and early cognitive-intellectual development: The social environment. In A. W. Gottfried (Ed.), *Home environment and early cognitive development: Longitudinal research.* Orlando: Academic Press.

Wakefield, D. (1988). *Returning.* New York: Doubleday.

Wallach, M., & Wallach, L. (1983). *Psychology's sanction for selfishness: The error of egoism in theory and therapy.* San Francisco: Freeman.

Wapnick, K. (1985). Forgiveness: A spiritual psychotherapy. In E. M. Stern (Ed.), *Psychotherapy and the religiously committed patient* (pp. 47-54). New York: Haworth.

Watson, J. B. (1924). *Behaviorism.* New York: Norton.

Weinberg, M. K., & Tronick, E. Z. (1991, April). Stability of infant social and coping behaviors and affective displays between 6 and 15 months: Age-appropriate tasks and stress bring out stability. Paper presented at the biennial meeting of the Society for Research in Child Development, Seattle.

Weiner, B. (1972). *Theories of motivation: From mechanism to cognition.* Chicago: Rand McNally.

Weiss, R. D., Mirin, S. M., Griffin, M. L., Gunderson, J. G., & Hufford, C. (1993). Personality disorders in cocaine dependence. *Comprehensive Psychiatry, 34,* 145-149.

Weissman, M. M. (1987). Advances in psychiatric epidemiology: Rates and risks for major depression. *American Journal of Public Health, 77,* 445-451.

Wertsch, J. V. (1984). The zone of proximal development: Some conceptual issues. In B. Rogoff & J. V. Wertsch (Eds.), *Children's learning in the "zone of proximal development."* San Francisco: Jossey-Bass.

Wertsch, J. V. (1985). *Vygotsky and the social formation of mind.* Cambridge, MA: Harvard University Press.

Westerholm, S. (1988). *Christian faith and the law of Israel: Paul and his recent interpreters.* Grand Rapids: Wm. B. Eerdmans Publishing Company.

Westermeyer, J. F., & Harlow, M. (1988). Cause and outcome in schizophrenia. In M. T. Tsuang & J. C. Simpson (Eds.), *Nosology, epidemiology and genetics of schizophrenia* (pp. 205-244). Amsterdam: Elsevier.

Wheeler, G. (1991). *Gestalt reconsidered: A new approach to contact and resistance.* New York: Gardner.

White, R. W. (1959). Motivation reconsidered: The concept of competence. *Psychological Review, 66,* 297-333.

Willard, D. (1988). *The spirit of the disciplines: Understanding how God changes lives.* San Francisco: Harper and Row.

Witten, M. G. (1993). *All is forgiven: The secular message of American Protestantism.* Princeton: Princeton University Press.

Wojtyla, K. (1979). *The acting person.* Dordrecht, Holland: D. Reidel. (Original in Polish, 1969, *Osoba I Czyn,* Cracow: Polskie Topwarzystwo Teologiizne).

Wolpe, J. (1978). Cognition and causation in human behavior. *American Psychologist, 33,* 437-446.

Wolterstorff, N. (1983). *Until justice and peace embrace.* Grand Rapids: Wm. B. Eerdmans Publishing Company.

Wolterstorff, N. (1987). Why animals don't speak. *Faith and Philosophy, 4,* 463-485.

Wolterstorff, N. (1996). *Divine discourse: Philosophical reflections on the claim that God speaks.* Cambridge and New York: Cambridge University Press.

Wong, D. (1993). Relativism. In P. Singer (Ed.), *A companion to ethics* (pp. 442-449). Oxford: Blackwell Publishers.

Wood, D., & Middleton, D. (1975). A study of assisted problem-solving. *British Journal of Psychology, 66,* 181-191.

Wood, D., Bruner, J., & Ross, S. (1976). The role of tutoring in problem solving. *Journal of Child Psychology and Psychiatry, 17,* 89-100.

Worthington, E. L., & DiBlasio, F. A. (1990). Promoting mutual forgiveness within the fractured relationship. *Psychotherapy, 27,* 219-223.

Wurmser, L. (1978). *The hidden dimension.* New York: J. Aronson.

Wurmser, L. (1985). Denial and split identity: Timely issues in the psychoanalytic psychotherapy of compulsive drug users. *Journal of Substance Abuse Treatment, 2,* 89-96.

Wurmser, L. (1989). Blinding the eye of the mind: Denial, impulsive action, and split identity. In E. L. Edelstein, D. Nathanson, & A. Stone (Eds.), *Denial: A clarification of concepts and research* (pp. 175-201). New York: Plenum Press.

Zeanah, C., & Anders, T. (1987). Subjectivity in parent-infant relationships: A discussion of internal working models. *Infant Mental Health Journal, 8,* 237-250.

Zilbergeld, B. (1983). *The shrinking of America: Myths of psychological change.* Boston: Little, Brown.

Index

Acedia (discouragement or spiritual lethargy): and gluttony, 321; one of the "eight deadly thoughts," 320

Action: analysis of, 155-59, 270; defined, 103; and effort, 157; evaluation of, 271; good or evil, 142-43; relation to self, 270; superficially similar may differ profoundly in meaning, 155; theories of, 270

Addiction: and alienation, 274; characterized, 249-51; defined, 249, 265; as disease, 253-57; as disordered desiring, 265, 272; dynamics of, 260; Graham Oddie on, 265; and human freedom and responsibility, 187-88; as idolatry, 250, 262; and longing, 250, 260-63; and psychosis, 265-78 *passim*; resists precise analysis, 265; and sexual addiction, 251-53, 272-75; and sin, 245-63 *passim* (especially 254-57, 259), 277-78; as symptomatic, 276-77; and the tolerance effect, 251; women addicts, 257-59

Addressability: a central feature of personhood, 108; and God, 121; and the new Christian self, 87

Adversity: and the Bible, 284-85; "the blessing of the New Testament" (Bacon), 285; Charles Sykes on, 283; contemporary reaction against, 286-88; Luther, Calvin, and Loyola on, 289-94; a means to penitence and faith, 284-85; and the modern secular political tradition, 283-84; molds character and deepens religious faith, 283-86

Agape, 308, 328

Agency, 82-84; and Arminianism, 197; and being human, 203; in the Bible, 82, 139-44, 198-99; capacities needed for, 105-6; characterized, 103, 138-39; co-agency, 140-41, 143, 306; and contemporary cognitive-constructivism, 191-93; covers character and behavior, 82; and early upbringing and environment, 106; in ego-psychology, 149; "gifts" that promote, 161-64; heretical and orthodox positions on, 197-98; heteronomous, 182-83; in humanistic psychology, 150; intelligent, 183-85; Jonathan Edwards on, 198; and mature Christian faith, 309-10; more or less mature varieties of, 166-71; natural-science approaches to, 144-49; and parental beliefs, 185; and Pelagianism, 197; personal contexts of, 151-55; promoted but not caused in others, 164; psychology's acknowledgment of, 108; and redemption, 164; and the Reformation, 196-97, 198; requires an evaluative framework, 103; and retrospective evaluation, 158-59; and "scaffolding," 172-85; and self-experience, 192; and sin, 198-99, 247; and social constructivists, 150; its social formation, 159-64; social science's challenge